QUEER EPISODES

IN MUSIC AND MODERN IDENTITY

O Rumors and Visions!
Departing to new affection and new noise!

—Arthur Rimbaud, *Les Illuminations* (1872)

QUEER EPISODES

IN MUSIC AND MODERN IDENTITY

EDITED BY SOPHIE FULLER

AND LLOYD WHITESELL

University of Illinois Press

Urbana and Chicago

Library of Congress Cataloging-in-Publication Data
Queer episodes in music and modern identity / edited by
Sophie Fuller and Lloyd Whitesell.
p.   cm.
Includes bibliographical references and index.
ISBN 0-252-02740-x (alk. paper)
1. Homosexuality and music. 2. Gay musicians. 3. Music—
19th century—History and criticism. 4. Music—20th century—
History and criticism. I. Fuller, Sophie. II. Whitesell, Lloyd.
ML63.Q44   2002
780'.86'64—dc21   2001005639

CONTENTS

Acknowledgments   ix

Introduction: Secret Passages   1
Sophie Fuller and Lloyd Whitesell

PART 1: PRIVATE PERFORMANCE

1. "Desire Is Consuming Me": The Life Partnership between
    Eugenie Schumann and Marie Fillunger   25
    Eva Rieger

2. Ravel's Way   49
    Lloyd Whitesell

3. "Devoted Attention": Looking for Lesbian Musicians in
    Fin-de-Siècle Britain   79
    Sophie Fuller

PART 2: PUBLIC APPEARANCES

4. "He Isn't a Marrying Man": Gender and Sexuality in the Repertoire of
    Male Impersonators, 1870–1930   105
    Gillian Rodger

5. Tchaikovsky and His Music in Anglo-American Criticism,
    1890s–1950s   134
    Malcolm Hamrick Brown

6. Transcription, Transgression, and the (Pro)creative Urge   150
   Ivan Raykoff

7. Musicology and Sexuality: The Example of Edward J. Dent   177
   Philip Brett

PART 3: DOUBLE MEANINGS

8. Cross-Dressing in Saint-Saëns's *Le Rouet d'Omphale:*
   Ambiguities of Gender and Politics   191
   Jann Pasler

9. The "Dark Saying" of the Enigma: Homoeroticism and
   the Elgarian Paradox   216
   Byron Adams

10. "An Anthology of Friendship": The Letters from John Ireland
    to Father Kenneth Thompson   245
    Fiona Richards

PART 4: QUEER LISTENING

11. Tristan's Wounds: On Homosexual Wagnerians at
    the Fin de Siècle   271
    Mitchell Morris

12. When Subjects Don't Come Out   293
    Sherrie Tucker

Contributors   311
Index   315

ACKNOWLEDGMENTS

The original idea for this book came from the 1995 annual meeting of the American Musicological Society in New York, where Chip (Lloyd) participated in a panel entitled "(Homo)erotic Enigmas," in which he and Byron Adams presented versions of research included here. Chip then came up with the idea for a historically focused collection of essays examining queer identity and music at the fin de siècle. After a series of transatlantic e-mails, Sophie came on board and *Queer Episodes* was born. Whole-hearted thanks to Martha Mockus for bringing the two of us together; it has been a dream collaboration.

We are especially indebted to Philip Brett for his untiring advocacy of our project in its early stages, offering advice and encouragement and steering us in the right direction. We would also like to thank Sue-Ellen Case and Susan Foster, who together with Philip took the time for an exacting and authoritative critical reading of the manuscript when it was most needed. Further thanks to Lawrence Kramer and an anonymous press reader for their extremely helpful comments at the polishing stage.

It has truly been a pleasure at every step working with the people at the University of Illinois Press. Thanks go to Joan Catapano, Judith McCulloh, Margo Chaney, David Perkins, and Bruce Bethell for their enthusiasm, hard work, and generosity. We are grateful to the many scholars and friends who contributed their ideas and research as the book made its way to its final incarnation and to the Lloyd Hibberd Publication Endowment Fund of the American Musicological Society for financial support.

Lloyd Whitesell would like to thank the various colleagues who encouraged his research during a vulnerable and peripatetic period of professional life. He is especially grateful to Judith Lochhead, Joseph Auner, and Sarah Fuller for their steadfast support of all sorts. Sanna Pederson has lightened his load with her friendship and inspired him with her brilliance and scholarly integrity.

Sophie Fuller expresses heartfelt thanks to Liz Wood and Nicky Losseff for conversations, support, and inspiration over the years.

Finally, to our partners, a few words will have to do: Udayan Sen, through thick and thin; Elaine, as ever, thank you.

QUEER EPISODES

IN MUSIC AND MODERN IDENTITY

INTRODUCTION

SECRET PASSAGES

SOPHIE FULLER AND LLOYD WHITESELL

> Doubtless the notes which we hear at such moments tend, according to their pitch and volume, to spread out before our eyes over surfaces of varying dimensions, to trace arabesques, to give us the sensation of breadth or tenuity, stability or caprice. But the notes themselves have vanished before these sensations have developed sufficiently to escape submersion under those which the succeeding or even simultaneous notes have already begun to awaken in us. And this impression would continue to envelop in its liquidity, its ceaseless overlapping, the motifs which from time to time emerge, barely discernible, to plunge again and disappear and drown, recognized only by the particular kind of pleasure which they instil, impossible to describe, to recollect, to name, ineffable—did not our memory, like a laborer who toils at the laying down of firm foundations beneath the tumult of the waves, by fashioning for us facsimiles of those fugitive phrases, enable us to compare and to contrast them with those that follow.
> —Marcel Proust, *Swann in Love*

At certain points in Marcel Proust's famous novel, characters treat the idea of listening to or making music as code for gay sex. When Baron de Charlus first meets the soldier Morel in a railway station, he uses the following pick-up line: "I should like to listen to a little music this evening. . . . I pay five hundred francs for the evening, which may perhaps be of interest to one of your friends, if you have any in the band." Later in their relationship, to maintain the illusion of the secrecy that the baron believes he has achieved, one of his friends uses the code as well: "Mme. Verdurin would then give them adjoining rooms and, to put them at their ease, would say: 'If you want to have a little music, don't worry about us. The walls are as thick as a fortress, you have nobody else on your floor, and my husband sleeps like a log.'"[1] Musical pleasure is a ready figure for the delights of the flesh, a euphemistic figure whose innocent appearance conceals the knowledge of forbidden practices. For Proust, as for many of his contemporaries, musical expression and the expression of queer sexuality were sympathetically linked. Both depend on mysterious ontogenies of personal preference and innate faculty: "[the inverts'] special taste [is] unconsciously inherited like predispositions for drawing, for music, towards blindness." As the latter passage implies, both attributes can carry the undertones of an imperfection of character.[2]

Thus urbanely double-edged references to music making appear alongside passages such as the following, in which musicality serves as a metaphor for the anomalies of one's inner being.

> When I was at school, I was terrified of my musical gift; I hated it, and did my utmost to suppress it, because I thought that it was that which made me different from the other boys. I loathed being "different"; it made me feel so alone, so I played hard games with the others, and tried to make friends with the others, and tried to forget that there was something inside my brain that turned everything I felt and experienced into music, which clamoured to be released, and which I refused to release, because I knew that if I did so, it would widen still more the gulf between me and the others.[3]

This is from the English novel *Despised and Rejected,* first published in 1918, an illuminating story of pacifism and homosexuality during World War I. It was written, under the pseudonym A. T. Fitzroy, by Rose Allatini, a lesbian author who was married for several years to the composer Cyril Scott.[4] In this passage her gay composer hero, Dennis, describes his childhood in a letter to the lesbian heroine, Antoinette. The letter goes on to tell how Dennis rejects Eric, another "musical" boy at the school, and then gradually accepts his musicality and, by implication, his homosexuality: "After that, I didn't make any attempt to crawl back behind my barriers; they weren't strong enough anyway to stand against the floodtide that had broken out. Everything that I felt about Eric would set itself to weird horrible music that drummed unceasingly in my ears, and demanded expression, and I was dead tired of choking it back. So I had to let myself become a musician. But I put up an awfully hard fight against it. It's queer to think of it now." Dennis is a thoroughly modern composer, writing what his younger brother Reggie describes as "mouldy sort of stuff . . . [;] there's no tune in it, however hard you listen for one."[5] By the end of World War I the crisis throughout Western Europe and the United States in both musical style (leading for some to the "creation" of modernism) and sexuality (leading for some to the "creation" of a homosexual identity) was causing profound cultural repercussions, although Allatini's novel remains a rare example of a text in which the two themes are unequivocally melded together. In particular, the hero's modernist inspiration (that "weird horrible music") is linked to queer, hidden paths of desire.

The essays in *Queer Episodes* explore some of the points of intersection between music and queerness in Europe and the United States during the period that surrounds the turn of the century and the upheavals of two world wars, the years 1870 to 1950. Dennis's personal metaphor of a flood tide, with its overtones of overwhelming inevitability, is useful as well for this period, when dramatic changes in both musical expression and in the expression of individual sexual identity played a similarly relentless part in sweeping away the certainties of the past.

In 1870 Wagner's *Tristan und Isolde*—the work that has become a symbol for the breakdown in the common-practice tonal system of the preceding two centuries—was five years old, and various European writers, including Karoly Maria Benkert, who coined the term *homosexuality* in 1869,[6] had begun to formulate the modern concept of sexuality itself, thus giving birth to identities newly conceived in terms of psychosexual orientation.[7] As the nineteenth century drew to a close, increasing numbers of composers began to create works that challenged the old patterns of harmony, rhythm, and form, fashioning what two recent commentators have called "the unprecedented flux of the post-Wagnerian musical climate—the Pandora's Box of experiment opened by *Tristan*."[8] Another newly opened Pandora's box had unleashed a series of medical discourses on sexuality, including works by sexologists such as Richard von Krafft-Ebing and Havelock Ellis, which sought to explain or understand the condition of the "invert," the "Uranian," the homosexual man and woman. The period 1870–1950 also saw a parallel crisis in gender identity. The "New Woman" of the late nineteenth century brought with her a series of challenges to the established order of gender roles. Women increasingly refused the traditional attributes of femininity, taking on characteristics and life choices that had previously been seen as both masculine and appropriate only to men. Women's gradual entry into the public musical world, for example, further problematized the position of men within a profession already seen by many as troublingly feminine.[9]

It will be useful to survey some of those queer theorists working outside musicology who have helped to lay the groundwork for our focus on the turn of the twentieth century as a watershed in the formation of sexual identities.

Most often cited is Michel Foucault, who argued that "the homosexual" is a properly modern identity type formed in relation to specific structures of social power and knowledge and christened in 1870 in the medical literature.[10] Admittedly not all agree with his premises. Some see the birth of the modern type in earlier centuries; some (such as Terry Castle) are skeptical of attempts to bracket off recent identities from previous sexual roles and labels.[11] But Foucault's argument has proven highly influential on three counts: the notion of a paradigm shift in modern times, the conception of sexual identity as a social construct in line with relations of power, and the recourse to nineteenth-century sexologists for evidence of new ways of thinking. Elaine Showalter has explored how the fin-de-siècle paradigm shift manifested itself as a full-blown crisis in conceptions of gender and sexuality.[12]

Although the medical-scientific literature has provided a valuable fund of evidence concerning sexual history, it largely reflects an outsider perspective, placing descriptive authority in the hands of experts and detached observers, often with a disciplinary agenda. For the queer folk under its aegis, its power of identification has cut both ways.[13] Other scholars have highlighted the dramatic legal battles faced by prominent individuals whose well-publicized scandals helped put a face to the figure of the homosexual in the general imagination. These include the trials of Oscar Wilde in England (1895), the Eulenburg affair on the Continent (1907–9), and the obscenity trials in England and the United States over Radclyffe Hall's book *The Well of Loneliness* (1928–29).[14] As Alan Sinfield puts it, many of the elements of the modern (male) homosexual image were already there but amorphous until galvanized by the trials: "At that point, the entire, vaguely disconcerting nexus of effeminacy, leisure, idleness, immorality, luxury, insouciance, decadence and aestheticism, which Wilde was perceived, variously, as instantiating, was transformed into a brilliantly precise image. . . . A distinctive possibility cohered, far more clearly, and for far more people, than hitherto."[15]

Of course this set of images, as filtered through the court system and marketed for a media audience, also represents an outsider discourse. Its outlines were annealed under the glare of the spotlight and shaken by the aftershocks of punitive damage. Some recent scholars have aimed to counter such distortions by attempting to reconstruct the living subcultures themselves. Despite the difficulties inherent in such a project, the research has produced fascinating and valuable topographies of queer life. Among these can be counted Shari Benstock's portrayal of the lesbian intellectual coteries of avant-garde Paris and George Chauncey's glimpse into the haunts and rituals of gay New York a century ago.[16] Implicit in these accounts is the idea that such lifestyles and milieus were made possible only by the conditions of modern, postindustrial urban society. Henning Bech makes this point in a provocative way: he claims that the (male) homosexual has a "special proximity to the particular conditions of modern life"—not only to "gender problematization, the self-analysis apparatus, the uncertainty of identity," and such matters, but to the life-space of the city itself. Bech pursues a phenomenological investigation of this space, with its unique social possibilities. "Here, the homosexual['s] peculiarity can vanish in the blanket anonymity; . . . here, he can make contact: either in the common urban space or in the special areas that, so to speak, concentrate the social space of the city: railway stations, urinals, parks and bath houses." In the railway station, for instance (the setting for the previously cited Proustian encounter), "all the elements are there, compacted and condensed within a delimited space: the crowd, the constant flux of new people, the mutual strangeness and indifference; the feeling of motion, options, sexual excitement, potential danger and surveillance."[17] For Bech, the conditions of modern life make up the essential background to the "homosexual form of existence."

Finally, some scholars perform what could be called a sexual hermeneutics, probing modernist styles and works to discover how they are implicated in the changing discourse of sexuality. Sandra Gilbert and Susan Gubar have considered how lesbian writers used their work as a proving ground for new ways of understanding their own bodies and identities, as well as the converse—how their innovations in style and grammar were partly a response to the circulation of "new words about lesbian eroticism."[18] In her book *Epistemology of the Closet,* Eve Sedgwick generalized a similar insight about male writers into a theoretical axiom of sweeping significance, claiming that "many of the major nodes of thought and knowledge in twentieth-century Western culture as a whole are structured . . . by a chronic . . . crisis of homo/heterosexual definition . . . dating from the end of the nineteenth century."[19] Thus patterns of sexual knowledge are inextricable from the aesthetic and interpretive categories we bring to bear on modern artistic practice, a point Sedgwick explores in readings of Wilde, Proust, and Henry James. Thomas Yingling has focused on the poetry of Hart Crane to pursue his own investigation into the epistemological burden of homosexuality, but one that constitutes an oppositional, minority discourse with its own semiotic economy.[20]

The visible rise of queer studies in the field of musicology has occurred within our own fin de siècle. The first annual meeting of the American Musicological Society to incorporate an entire session devoted to sexuality took place in 1990. The year 1994 saw the publication of the trailblazing essay collection *Queering the Pitch: The New Gay and Lesbian Musicology,* edited by Philip Brett, Elizabeth Wood, and Gary C. Thomas, following hot on the heels of *Musicology and Difference: Gender and Sexuality in Music Scholarship* (1993), a wide-ranging collection, edited by Ruth Solie, that includes important queer work by Brett, Mitchell Morris, and Wood.[21] In the preface to *Queering the Pitch,* the editors noted the context of their work: "Like feminist studies twenty years ago, ours is a field seeking to define itself."[22] *Queering the Pitch* has done much to shape the diversity of the field by presenting a broad collection of work that focuses on a variety of genres, places, and times as well as a range of theoretical approaches. Several of the essays have already reached classic status, including Wood's important exploration of the "Sapphonic" voice, particularly in its relationship to the work of the lesbian composer Ethel Smyth, and Suzanne Cusick's moving meditation on her own queer relationship with music.[23] The editors of *Queering the Pitch* were concerned to move away from establishing the sexual preferences of composers and musicians and to focus instead on "representations, performances and roles."[24] As was inevitable, however, some of these essays do explore the issue of queer identity; recognizing queer communities and individuals has, in the stark reality of the late twentieth and early twenty-first century, continued to be a necessary and engaging aspect of queer musicology.

In her 1991 collection of essays entitled *Feminine Endings,* the feminist musicologist Susan McClary called for gay studies in music to out composers "not for the sake of sensationalism" but to engender pride in "gay individuals" and to "permit much more interesting and human readings of the music."[25] Perhaps the most notorious recent outing of a canonic composer took place at an American Musicological Society meeting in 1988, when the biographer Maynard Solomon presented evidence suggesting that Schubert might have played a part in male homosexual circles in early nineteenth-century Vienna.[26] This provoked a predictable uproar, and the debate has continued. In 1993 the journal *19th-Century Music* addressed the topic in a special issue edited by Lawrence Kramer. Entitled *Schubert: Music, Sexuality, Culture,* it included a further essay by Solomon and a contribution by McClary in which she examined possible ways in which Schubert's sexuality might be read into his music, a question she revisited in her contribution to *Queering the Pitch.* The editors to that collection pointedly claimed that "it is . . . less interesting to assert that Handel or Schubert was 'gay' than to reveal the homophobia, as well as the pathetically limited terms, of a scholarly inquiry terrified that either might have been."[27] More recently, in "Piano Four-Hands: Schubert and the Performance of Gay Male Desire," Philip Brett has provided a useful overview of the debate, moving the discussion on to examine possible queer readings of Schubert through the medium of performance.[28]

Outside musicology proper, books such as Boze Hadleigh's *Vinyl Closet* (with, according to the author, "enough dirt to break a vacuum-cleaner") or John Gill's *Queer Noises* continue to ask (and sometimes answer) questions about individuals' sexual identities.[29] But the anecdotal and undocumented nature of the former book underlines the need for a considered and rigorous approach to biographical research into sexual identity. This area is as yet little explored in music, despite the illuminating work that continues to appear. Among several notable contributions are Anthony Tommasini's impressive life of Virgil Thomson and David Hajdu's sensitive and revealing biography of the songwriter Billy Strayhorn.[30]

As for more theoretically based work, the world of opera and musical theater has provoked a particularly rich variety of queer responses. The gay male diva worshiper, or "opera queen," has become a central figure of queer musicology in works such as Wayne Koestenbaum's book *The Queen's Throat: Opera, Homosexuality, and the Mystery of Desire,* a lyrical essay exploring the overriding queerness of music theater and the queer spectators that delight in it.[31] The queer female fan finds a voice in Corinne E. Blackmer and Patricia Juliana Smith's invigorating collection *En Travesti: Women, Gender Subversion, Opera,* which also explores all women—singers, composers, and producers— who "wear the trousers" in the world of opera.[32] *En Travesti* includes work by literary critics such as Terry Castle and Margaret Reynolds, and the inclusion of queer work on music by scholars from other disciplines has become a notable feature of queer musicology. In fact queer musicology owes a significant debt to the exciting criticism undertaken by these scholars, exemplified, for instance, by Richard Dyer's nuanced analysis of the iconic status Judy Garland enjoys among gay men.[33]

Studies of queer performativity and of the relationship between sexuality and performance have ranged from the elite world of opera and high cultural criticism to the myriad arenas of popular culture. Kevin Kopelson's *Beethoven's Kiss,* for example, contemplates the relationship between queer sexuality and a range of pianists from Roland Barthes to Liberace.[34] Scholars such as Brian Currid and Barbara Bradby have explored the ways in which certain popular musics work to create queer communities and identities.[35] And work such as that by Cusick, on the queer listener's relationship with music, has led to a variety of investigations into ways of hearing and understanding all sorts of music, such as Jennifer Rycenga's article on the possibilities for "lesbian-ic hearing" of songs by Kate Bush, P J Harvey and Tori Amos.[36]

Despite being scarcely a decade old, queer musicology has already considerably enriched and enlivened our understanding of music, sexuality, and the relationship between the two.[37] *Queer Episodes* aims to add to that understanding by reconsidering the culture of the modernist period from a specifically queer perspective. It approaches modern sexuality by way of music. From this idiosyncratic angle we hope to avoid or at least bump against many of the assumptions that otherwise might guide historical thought into familiar channels. Both male and female subjects are represented; our contributors focus variously on composers, scholars, patrons, performers, audiences, repertoires, venues, and specific works. Interpretation is grounded in discussion of particular social and artistic environments; by including a range of national and cultural contexts, we aim to evoke a polyphony of responses to the shifting ideological terrain while avoiding generalization from a privileged set of circumstances.

Our individual contributors each wield their own brands of talent and bravery. Some, by ingenuity and persistence, have delved into archives to recover hidden or forgotten stories of lives, loves, and gathering places. Historical "evidence" is extremely fragile in many cases; interpretation, highly speculative. Thus some are led to a rigorous examination of their own motives and methodologies in the interests of mapping out the risky theoretical territory. Finally, several essays explore the connections between dissident identity and concrete aspects of musical style, gestures, or personae. Uncovering the intersection of personal and aesthetic strategies requires an analysis that is psychologically acute, attuned to musical semiotics, and highly context dependent.

The link between musicality and queerness as related forms of suspect subjectivity was forged in modern times. Philip Brett has most directly confronted this formation and its implications for those in the music world.[38] In his contribution to this volume, Brett traces the institutionalization of the equation in the new field of sexology. The identification of music with deviant knowledge and experience has often worked against musicians, queer and nonqueer alike, but we would like to turn it to a positive use. It is the very instability in its nature and effects that lends music a special power as a conceptual model. Anyone seeking to reflect on music's charm will need to come to grips with an experience at once transitory, intangible, famously elusive, and yet intensely visceral. What better analogue for the more troublesomely personal, wayward, and inscrutable aspects of past lives? Musical concepts, we feel, can serve as models for understanding queer history or for pursuing a queer approach to history in general. In this tenor, we propose an analytical repertory, a series of motifs that guide the chapters to follow. Our aim, however, is not (à la Proust) to cover for any artistic or biographical deviations but to tune our awareness to them more finely.

LOST CHORDS

Before the advent of sound-recording technologies, the preservation of music was an inexact affair. The polyphonic achievements of aural tradition could be captured only in an oblique way, through a hodgepodge of verbal, numeric, and graphic symbols. The realm of musical experience still typifies Western culture's honored concept of that which cannot be expressed. Our terms for the written representation of music betray this underlying sense of inadequacy: *notation* sounds like peripheral jottings or at best a system of shorthand—which in fact it is; many scholarly struggles have centered on the reconstruction of crucial musical qualities that needed no notation when current. *Transcription* implies the repackaging of a living discourse in terms not belonging to the original, a necessary convenience but no real substitute for the music itself.

The evidence collected by those in search of sexual history exhibits the same incompletion and fragility. In the case of such private discourse—within individual minds, between partners, or within a subculture—many crucial qualities from the experiential realm may not have made it into the written records. Such clues as have been preserved are likely to use a shorthand whose key may elude us. This situation is intensified by the fact that the personal matters involved, already resistant to transcription, are unspeakable in a social sense as well. The scholar must be alert to the most delicate intimations, dexterous in the art of speculation, and untiringly creative in imagining the impassioned words that once filled the silences left to us.

Only one of our contributors (Sherrie Tucker) was able to engage in oral histories. Many of the rest are faced with the inadequacy of the biographical notation. Sophie Fuller uncovers the richly interconnected musical careers of various British women at the turn of the century. Some of her bolder, more privileged subjects moved in known lesbian circles. For others, it is more difficult to discern the character of their creative and passionate relationships. Fuller deftly explores the nuances of their personal, professional, and compositional choices that together betoken a "queerable history."

Eva Rieger shares her discovery of a romantic correspondence between Eugenie Schumann (daughter of Clara and Robert) and the singer Marie Fillunger. Their tender letters open a rare window onto a shared life in which the demands of international concertizing were balanced by the comforts of a humble home. In their very intimacy and domesticity, however, these documents ramble past fundamental questions (about the couple's sexual self-concepts, the public understanding of their relationship, and their awareness of a larger subculture) we long to pose.

IMPROVISATION

In trying to detect one's queer forebears, it seems logical to consider the degree to which certain likely individuals conformed to standard models of queer identification and socialization. Many of these individuals, however, proved to be fundamentally ill-suited to conformity. In any case, we have little reason to suppose standard models of queerness operated in the period of Western history with which we are concerned, or indeed at any time. Certainly there were widely recognizable areas of personal and social taboo, newly hatched medical theories, and the beginnings of mass-mediated imagery showcasing urban curiosities, but none of this adds up to the recipe for a lifestyle. Certainly one might stumble on thriving pockets of queer street culture or elitist culture, but the epistemological repercussions of such groups were highly localized. The available coming-of-age narratives seem unified only by perplexity. And this perplexity often extended well into adulthood: the Victorian intellectual John Addington Symonds, for instance, though intimately acquainted in his schooling, travels, and scholarship with the knowledge and practice of homosexuality, struggled for much of his life to forge a sexual identity suitable to his personal values and orientation.[39]

Queer identities were thus partly cobbled together from archetype, rumor, and compared notes, but the rest was improvised from varying measures of eccentricity, perverse pleasure, self-assertion, and camouflage. As E. M. Forster has written somewhere, life is a performance on a violin that one has to learn to play as one goes along. Indeed, makeshift identity categories and living arrangements proliferated in the modernist period. One might arrange a marriage of convenience, treasure one's bachelorhood, carve out a comfortable space within a larger household, or carry out a same-gender wedding by subterfuge (as Gillian Rodger has discovered in the case of one of her more rakish vaudevillians). The sexual quotient was not necessarily primary to one's self-definition and was in fact indivisibly welded in particular cases to one's dress, artistic taste, economic independence, support group, or religion. Some individuals apparently had no name or concept for their difference. Others identified as dandy or male impersonator; as Wagnerian or Decadent; as salonnière or New Woman; or as solitary aesthete, health-cult *Eigene,* or Uranian Catholic.

The challenge for the scholar is to retain a sense of fluidity in his or her analytical approach, to recognize improvisation at work and to cultivate spontaneity and creativity in response. Exemplary in this regard is Elizabeth Wood's invention of the term *Sapphonic* to christen an unnamed but historically notable bond of musical seductiveness between women.[40] In the present collection Mitchell Morris reveals how groups of German men fashioned homosexual identities by way of the cult of Wagner. In his dramatic exploration of illicit love, homosocial bonding, and male suffering, not to mention his flamboyant personal tastes, Wagner provided an exuberance of material for the nurturance of queer sensibilities.

PERFORMANCE PRACTICE

Musicologists have shown the importance of historical and geographical specificity for crucial decisions in the modern performance of past musical repertoires. Likewise, in reconstructing the performance of sexual identities within a subculture, local customs and traditions are likely to have a deciding impact. One way to read this book is to regroup the essays by their national settings—English, American, French, and German. This arrangement would highlight certain implicit connections between chapters, such as a common cast of characters, common cultural and political backgrounds, and a horizon of shared mores.

Nonetheless, geography is not the only frame for local customs, which are further determined by other factors, such as class, profession, and performing genre. Gillian Rodger's purview is the American vaudeville stage and the phenomenal vogue for male impersonation from 1870 to 1930. At first these popular performers were working-class women poking fun at the middle class through their realistic portrayal of masculine characters. Rodger shows how the style and repertoire of male impersonators changed after the turn of the century to reflect changing constructs of gender, largely due to anxiety in the face of newly visible sexual minorities.

Ivan Raykoff examines the Romantic practice of showcasing other composer's works in showy arrangements for the piano. This practice fell into disfavor in the twentieth century, with its reigning ideal of faithful reproduction. Yet transcriptions played an important role in the repertoire of gay pianists such as Vladimir Horowitz and Liberace. This leads Raykoff to discuss the politics of musical appropriation as a perverse mode of artistic expression.

Both these arguments are meaningful only within the framework of a particular set of performance customs. Nevertheless, another tendency worked against the gravitational pull of local circles. This follows on the ideal inherent in Western culture of music as a lingua franca, a conduit of cosmopolitanism with the potential to bridge cultural differences. Cross-national commerce is evident in many of the essays that follow. The established international networks of patronage, journalism, and touring circuits meant that musical culture was actively involved in the far-reaching transmission of personal performance customs. Music provided the accompaniment for confrontations between disparate conventions of social propriety in general and, in particular, for encounters between diverse idiolects of sexual identity.

MODULATION

In the eighteenth century, modulation—the transition between tonal centers—occurred at moments of structural stress. Formal divisions in music were joined and articulated by these circumscribed passages of instability. By the late nineteenth century, in the wake of Wagner and Liszt, the situation was practically reversed. Composers infiltrated their harmonic procedures with a continuous instability; it was now the momentary points of arrival that provided formal articulation. Such procedures are understood to reflect shifting epistemological foundations during the period in question. The representational crisis led in the early twentieth century to the deliberate and at times existentialist formulation of new systems of understanding, as well as a veritable explosion of self-designed musical premises and styles.

The wandering tonalities and pervasive modulation found in the music of post-Wagnerians, impressionists, and neoclassicists alike are symbolic of epistemic changes overtaking all areas of cultural expression. The decades surrounding the turn of the century saw an apparent "anarchy" in the embodiment of gender and sexuality, with traditional definitions dissolving or under attack and new terms of possibility emerging. Sexual historians from Foucault on have made much of this period's invention of the term *homosexuality* and the idea of the homosexual type. But many other terms were in use, and in any case, *homosexuality* by itself tells us very little. Other than carrying very palpable connotations of a cultural bugbear, the term resists attempts to affix a stable, widely applicable identity concept to it, especially in the early years of its use.

It is our postulate that during this time, categories of sexual identity were still in transition, caught up in the larger cultural modulation. In analogy with hyperchromatic or pandiatonic music, a suitable analytical approach to such categories would avoid dependence on a stable center and instead seek a sense of inbetweenness, passage, diversion. Jann Pasler, for instance, highlights a dramatic transitivity of gender in the self-image of French composer Camille

Saint-Saëns. She explores how such gender crossing is thematically embodied in the mythological program for his symphonic tone poem *Le Rouet d'Omphale*. The exchange of raiment and power between Hercules and the Lydian queen provides a pretext for a rich field of interpretation, in terms of both gender psychology and France's place in the European political arena. As Pasler shows, Saint-Saëns's masterful use of musical transition conveys the allegory with charm and cunning.

Malcolm Hamrick Brown's theme is the modulation of a composer's reputation. As information concerning Tchaikovsky's sexual character filtered into the awareness of Anglo-American critics, early outpourings of esteem were gradually overtaken by prejudice and contempt. The literature presents graphic evidence of the insidious spread of a closet epistemology, as the achievements of an expressive symphonic aesthetic are folded into an overarching discourse of mental illness and secret depravity. One could add here that Tchaikovsky stands in the musical world in a position analogous to that of Oscar Wilde in the literary, as the first well-known modern homosexual. Wilde's sexual notoriety coincided with a drama of public humiliation, however, a situation that differed from the composer's. Thus on one level the phobic criticism of Tchaikovsky's music that flourished in the twentieth century rehearses the cultural need to cast the homosexual as a scapegoat. The same need is evident behind the sensational myths, still circulating, of Tchaikovsky's suicide as a result of a secret "court of honor" set up by his former schoolfellows.[41]

VIBRATING BODIES

As everybody knows, music is the food of love. Our subjects testify to music's power to set hearts aflame and feed the fires of passion, whether within the confines of a shared piano bench or projected across an aching distance, as Marie Fillunger confesses in one of her letters: "I love you and often feel an indescribable desire for you, especially when I am singing in public." But, perhaps less obviously, the sympathetic vibration works in both directions. That is, just as music impels and incarnates love, so do the vicissitudes of love subtly but forcefully shape musical creation. Not all music scholars will subscribe to this premise, and there is little hope for a systematic, encompassing theory of such influence. Nevertheless, though this connection be contingent and lawless, the myriad discoveries of fervent expressions, submerged narratives, and stylistic preoccupations traceable to the experience of love convince us that this is a fruitful path to pursue. We chime in with those scholars who consider music a form of thought with its own ways—whether airy, hypnotic, or intense—of posing and untangling problems. Thus, aside from the acknowledged emotional discourse of music, there is a kind of musical knowledge, a knowledge in the form of music, in which the personal, experiential knowledge of one's life can be invested.

To date the most extensive scholarship along these lines in the field of queer musicology has focused on the music of Benjamin Britten. Scholars such as Philip Brett, Christopher Palmer, Humphrey Carpenter, and Clifford Hindley have sought to trace Britten's development, over the course of a long career, of rhetorical strategies, ethical quandaries, and psychological textures referable to his experience of sexual identity. The scope of such an approach has barely begun to be realized. In the present collection, Fiona Richards examines the rarefied sexuality of the English composer John Ireland, who was smitten by young choristers. The most valuable evidence to hand is a collection of confessional letters to a close friend. Richards considers how the love of youth may be sensed in Ireland's lyrical, intense, and introspective music; through homoerotic references, both classical and personal; and through the delicate symbolic interplay of sensuality and innocence.

Philip Brett takes as his subject not a body of musical work but a body of music criticism as he ponders the generous and unorthodox vision of the musicologist Edward J. Dent. Brett establishes a provocative correlation between the modern crisis in the understanding of sexuality and the development of the study of musical activity. He argues that Dent's homosexuality led to the possibility of a counterdiscourse within the approved paradigms of musicology.

CHAMBER MUSIC

The modern rethinking of gender, family, and sexuality was part of a struggle to redraw the boundaries between public and private domains. Thus an inescapable element in the new queer anatomies is an overarching injunction to silence and secrecy. Even if individuals strove to resist it or find ways around it, every subject in this book was palpably affected by that injunction in one way or another. First, it restricted the flow of information about other queer lives, past and contemporary, creating a culture of willful ignorance and keeping even the knowledge of alternative sexual traditions from those who might benefit. Second, the taboo against exposure or indiscretion hung like a blade over all interpersonal relations. To unlock the resulting protective contrivances, today's historian must practice what amounts to a modernist hermeneutics of identity.[42]

Lloyd Whitesell, for instance, discusses the highly secretive Maurice Ravel, whose identity as dandy, aesthete, and solitary can be interpreted as self-protective strategies of disguise. Even to his closest friends his sexual nature remained a riddle. Whitesell sorts through fiction, police records, and memoirs to reconstruct Parisian gay subcultures and taxonomies. Particularly telling are the elaborate subterfuges many men used to hide disreputable liaisons.

But perversely, and even more to our purposes, the restrictions on disclosure also extended to a composer's musical persona. The musical realm, with its legends of unmediated expression and yet uncapturable meanings, could indeed be seen as constituting a special pressure point for issues of private envoicing. One needed to be on guard perhaps nowhere more than in one's music, that medium of interiority, that subjective display that so readily invites flamboyance. Thus in many instances, the shaping influence of sexuality on musical creation is evident only in closet formations. This may be given concrete form in the thematization of solitude, stopped mouths, closed rooms, or ominous secrets. Ravel's piano piece *Gaspard de la nuit* (based on poems by Aloysius Bertrand) provides an example, with its importunate water nymph tapping at the window, its maleficent sprite sneaking into the bedroom.

Closet formations may be felt more elusively in rhetorical positions of detachment, indirection, or obscurity.[43] Byron Adams discusses the music of Edward Elgar from such an angle, exploring the role of the deliberately enigmatic personae appearing in certain key works. Adams speculates that an imaginative projection into such ambiguous perspectives freed Elgar from inhibitions against the expression of homoerotic devotion.

Roger Shattuck, in his book *The Banquet Years,* has identified an intriguing rhetorical stance in the music of Erik Satie. For those oddly annotated miniatures that demand the tiniest audience, Shattuck invents his own designation: "*Musique de placard* (*placard* means both closet and poster), in the double sense of extreme intimacy and deliberate publicity. . . . Closet music is one degree more private than chamber music. Yet [when Satie] threw his little closet pieces in the face of traditional concert music, they assumed the proportions of manifestos: poster music."[44] Although Shattuck does not relate this concept to the composer's sexual identity, our own theorizing invites the connection. Satie was an eccentric, celibate recluse who preferred homosocial artistic circles and published a passionate statement about his friendship with Debussy yet who vehemently disapproved of open homosexuals such as Cocteau.[45] Even without the key to Satie's enigmatic identity, one can argue that, at some level, his detached and paradoxical authorial stance represented a response to the new injunctions surrounding privacy and sexuality. The underlying knowledge—

that even music intended to shelter one's inner life may be as revealing as a public announcement—forms the crux of the matter.

BLOW IN MY EAR

We have discussed composers and performers; our final leitmotif has to do with music's intended destination: its audiences. The social, cohesive power of music is well attested. Shared performance is of course a timeworn source of conviviality, but shared audition also brings people together in what we might call listening communities. Common musical tastes can affirm and resonate with other common bonds. We can see this dual role of the music lover at work in the queer Wagner cults and the queer-friendly Parisian musical salon of the princesse de Polignac. Or the bonds can be bonds of denial, as in the case of the increasingly homophobic reception of Tchaikovsky in the early twentieth century.

But music's destination stretches beyond the time of its origin. Can there be a "community" between the musical statements of a century ago and the listeners of today? Especially given the continuing changes in the meaning and expression of queer identity over the intervening years, we must wonder about our own acts of listening queerly. Are our musical longings for queer meaning too aggressive? Clueless? Do they deviate in all the right places?

Pursuing issues along these lines, Sherrie Tucker ponders an ethnographic dilemma arising from her research interviewing women jazz musicians active in the 1940s. These women faced suspect or deviant status merely for being jazz instrumentalists, and the researcher wishing to uncover unconventional personal histories must negotiate their hard-won sense of privacy. Brought up short by these narrative gaps, Tucker reflects on the potential for misrecognition haunting her project. By framing our questions according to late twentieth-century values, do we sometimes miss the unique virtues of earlier adaptations?

The notion of queer listening implies an element of perversity, an orientation somehow at cross-purposes with that of music's creators. This notion may appear disrespectful, especially in the light of the current craze for musical "authenticity" (in the sense of historical accuracy, pedigree, and faithfulness). But we prefer to see it as taking advantage of a loophole built into the musical contract. Perhaps because of its lack of conceptual specificity, or its medium of bodily engulfment, music can offer no real guarantees of a faithful passage of meaning from the composing to the listening mind. In fact, the composer depends on the liveliness of the listener's sensibilities and imagination. Listening is a collaboration, with no way for the composer to object when we turn "everyone to her own way." The queer possibilities are inherent in the poly-morphous nature of music's bodily engagement: "The underlying, uncon-scious fantasy was of a collaborative ear. It was both hard and soft, encompass-ing outer space and inner space, capable of being awesome and shameful and of engendering creativity, even life itself. . . . It was, in fantasy, a truly bisexual organ, and therein lay its power and its threat."[46]

Thus all music is open to deviant forms of reception that need not have anything to do with the conditions of the music's origin. But there is another kind of queer listening, one whose goal is the recovery of an original mean-ing or the reinstatement of a hypothetical meaning, originative but once un-publishable. Those who practice this mode of interpretation imagine an im-plicit address from historical subjects to an audience unconstrained by the ignorance and bad faith their creative expression originally met. They look for hidden meanings to become audible when received outside their former con-ditions of censorship and oppression. They pursue a tactic of identification and projection from a homoerotic or queer perspective, as if to establish com-munity with their forebears, answering back to them in a renewed voice.[47] Such a stance may be controversial, but it is the only way to recognize elisions and ciphers for what they are and to counter the ideologies channeling expression into silence. In an oblique but familiar way, such projection receives support from the many composers who have appealed to posterity for whatever rea-sons: "On the initial performance of a new musical composition, the first impression of the public is generally one of reaction to the more superficial elements of its music, that is to say, to its external manifestations rather than to its inner content. The listener is impressed by some unimportant peculiar-ity in the medium of expression, and . . . often it is not until years after, when the means of expression have finally surrendered all their secrets, that the real inner emotion of the music becomes apparent to the listener."[48]

Even with the passage of time, these compositions have not yet surrendered all their secrets. Nor have the secret passages within these musical lives lost their magical allure. And so we invite you to join us in "a little music."

NOTES

1. Marcel Proust, *In Search of Lost Time*, 6 vols., trans. C. K. Scott Moncrieff and Terence Kilmartin, rev. D. J. Enright (New York: Modern Library, 1993), 4:352, 602.

2. Ibid., 4:24–25, trans. modified. Elsewhere: "They form in every land an oriental colony, cultured, musical, malicious, which has charming qualities and intolerable defects" (4:43).

3. A. T. Fitzroy, *Despised and Rejected* (London: GMP, 1988), 79.

4. On Allatini, see Jonathan Cutbill, intro. to *Despised and Rejected*.

5. Fitzroy, *Despised and Rejected*, 84, 14.

6. Jeffrey Weeks, *Sex, Politics, and Society: The Regulation of Sexuality since 1800* (London: Longmans, 1981), 21.

7. See, for example, Eve Kosofsky Sedgwick, *Epistemology of the Closet* (Berkeley: University of California Press, 1990), 157–59; or Vernon A. Rosario, "Novelising Fin-de-siècle Homosexuality," in *Science and the Homosexualities,* ed. Rosario (London: Routledge, 1997), 89–107. It should be noted that alternative (homo-)sexual subcultures and identities have existed throughout the world and throughout recorded history. See, for example, Louise Fradenburg and Carla Freccero, eds., *Premodern Sexualities* (London: Routledge, 1996); David M. Halperin, "Forgetting Foucault: Acts, Identities, and the History of Sexuality," *Representations* 63 (1998): 93–120.

8. Robert Stradling and Meirion Hughes, *The English Musical Renaissance 1860–1940: Construction and Deconstruction* (London: Routledge, 1993), 45.

9. Catherine Parsons Smith has argued, following the work of Sandra Gilbert and Susan Gubar in the field of literary studies, that antifeminism, a reaction to the numbers of women working as composers in the late nineteenth century, was a "fundamental, motivating factor" in twentieth-century modernism (Smith, "'A Distinguishing Virility': Feminism and Modernism in American Art Music," in *Cecilia Reclaimed: Feminist Perspectives on Gender and Music,* ed. Susan Cook and Judy Tsou [Urbana: University of Illinois Press, 1994], 90–106).

10. Michel Foucault, *The History of Sexuality,* vol. 1: *An Introduction,* trans. Robert Hurley (New York: Random House, 1978), 43. Foucault's social constructionist argument was anticipated by Mary McIntosh in her article "The Homosexual Role," *Social Problems* 16, no. 2 (1968); rpt. in *The Making of the Modern Homosexual,* ed. Kenneth Plummer (London: Hutchinson, 1981), 30–44.

11. Alan Bray follows McIntosh in placing the birth of the modern "homosexual" type at the end of the seventeenth century; see Bray, *Homosexuality in Renaissance England* (London: GMP, 1982). See also Terry Castle, *The Apparitional Lesbian: Female Homosexuality and Modern Culture* (New York: Columbia University Press, 1993), 8–10.

12. Elaine Showalter, *Sexual Anarchy: Gender and Culture at the Fin de Siècle* (New York: Penguin, 1990).

13. E.g., see Carroll Smith-Rosenberg, "Discourses of Sexuality and Subjectivity: The New Woman, 1870–1936," in *Hidden from History: Reclaiming the Gay and Lesbian Past,* ed. Martin Duberman, Martha Vicinus, and George Chauncey Jr. (New York: New American Library, 1989), 264–80.

14. Ed Cohen, *Talk on the Wilde Side: Toward a Genealogy of a Discourse on Male Sexualities* (New York: Routledge, 1993); Alan Sinfield, *The Wilde Century: Effeminacy, Oscar Wilde, and the Queer Moment* (New York: Columbia University Press, 1994); James D. Steakley, "Iconography of a Scandal: Political Cartoons and the Eulenburg Affair in Wilhelmin Germany," in *Hidden from History,* ed. Duberman, Vicinus, and

Chauncey, 233–63; Esther Newton, "The Mythic Mannish Lesbian: Radclyffe Hall and the New Woman," in *Hidden from History,* 281–93.

15. Sinfield, *The Wilde Century,* 3.

16. Shari Benstock, *Women of the Left Bank: Paris, 1900–1940* (Austin: University of Texas Press, 1986); George Chauncey, *Gay New York: Gender, Urban Culture, and the Making of the Gay Male World, 1890–1940* (New York: Basic Books, 1994).

17. Henning Bech, *When Men Meet: Homosexuality and Modernity,* trans. Teresa Mesquit and Tim Davies (Chicago: University of Chicago Press, 1997), 188, 98, 159. It remains to be seen how useful Bech's theory is for modern lesbian experience.

18. Sandra M. Gilbert and Susan Gubar, "'She Meant What I Said': Lesbian Double Talk," *No Man's Land: The Place of the Woman Writer in the Twentieth Century,* vol. 2: *Sexchanges* (New Haven, Conn.: Yale University Press, 1989), 217.

19. Sedgwick, *Epistemology,* 1.

20. Thomas E. Yingling, *Hart Crane and the Homosexual Text: New Thresholds, New Anatomies* (Chicago: University of Chicago Press, 1990).

21. Philip Brett, Elizabeth Wood, and Gary C. Thomas, eds., *Queering the Pitch: The New Gay and Lesbian Musicology* (London: Routledge, 1994); Ruth Solie, ed., *Musicology and Difference: Gender and Sexuality in Music Scholarship* (Berkeley: University of California Press, 1993).

22. Brett, Wood, and Thomas, eds., *Queering the Pitch,* x.

23. Elizabeth Wood, "Sapphonics," in *Queering the Pitch,* ed. Brett, Wood, and Thomas, 27–66; and Suzanne G. Cusick, "On a Lesbian Relation with Music: A Serious Effort Not to Think Straight," in *Queering the Pitch,* 67–83.

24. Brett, Wood, and Thomas, eds., *Queering the Pitch,* x.

25. Susan McClary, *Feminine Endings: Music, Gender, and Sexuality* (Minnesota: University of Minnesota Press, 1991), 78.

26. Later published as Maynard Solomon, "Franz Schubert and the Peacocks of Benvenuto Cellini," *19th-Century Music* 12 (Spring 1989): 193–206.

27. Brett, Wood, and Thomas, eds., *Queering the Pitch,* x.

28. Philip Brett, "Piano Four-Hands: Schubert and the Performance of Gay Male Desire," *19th-Century Music* 21 (Fall 1997): 149–76. Another important voice on this issue is Lawrence Kramer; see his *Franz Schubert: Sexuality, Subjectivity, Song* (Cambridge: Cambridge University Press, 1998).

29. Boze Hadleigh, *The Vinyl Closet: Gays in the Music World* (San Diego: Los Hombres, 1991); John Gill, *Queer Noises: Male and Female Homosexuality in Twentieth-Century Music* (London: Cassell, 1995).

30. Anthony Tommasini, *Virgil Thomson: Composer on the Aisle* (New York: Norton, 1997); David Hajdu, *Lush Life: A Biography of Billy Strayhorn* (New York: Farrar, Straus, and Giroux, 1998).

31. Wayne Koestenbaum, *The Queen's Throat: Opera, Homosexuality, and the Mystery of Desire* (New York: Poseidon, 1993). See also Mitchell Morris, "Reading as an Opera Queen," in *Musicology and Difference,* ed. Solie, 184–200; and Paul Robinson,

"The Opera Queen: A Voice from the Closet," *Cambridge Opera Journal* 6 (Nov. 1994): 283–91. The musical is explored in D. A. Miller, *Place for Us: Essay on the Broadway Musical* (Cambridge, Mass.: Harvard University Press, 1998).

32. Corinne E. Blackmer and Patricia Juliana Smith, eds., *En Travesti: Women, Gender Subversion, Opera* (New York: Columbia University Press, 1995). The lesbian experience of the musical is examined in Stacy Wolf, "The Queer Pleasures of Mary Martin and Broadway: *The Sound of Music* as a Lesbian Musical," *Modern Drama* 39 (Spring 1996): 51–63.

33. Richard Dyer, "Judy Garland and Gay Men," *Heavenly Bodies: Film Stars and Society* (New York: St. Martin's, 1986), 141–94.

34. Kevin Kopelson, *Beethoven's Kiss: Pianism, Perversion, and the Mastery of Desire* (Stanford, Calif.: Stanford University Press, 1996).

35. Brian Currid, "'We are Family': House Music and Queer Performativity," in *Cruising the Performative: Interventions into the Representation of Ethnicity, Nationality, and Sexuality*, ed. Sue-Ellen Case, Philip Brett, and Susan Leigh Foster (Bloomington: Indiana University Press, 1995), 165–96; Barbara Bradby, "Lesbians and Popular Music: Does It Matter Who Is Singing?" in *Popular Music—Style and Identity*, ed. Will Straw, Stacey Johnson, Rebecca Suhram, and Paul Friedlander (Montréal: Centre for Research on Canadian Cultural Industries and Institutions, 1993), 33–44.

36. Jennifer Rycenga, "Sisterhood: A Loving Lesbian Ear Listens to Progressive Heterosexual Women's Rock Music," in *Keeping Score: Music, Disciplinarity, Culture*, ed. David Schwarz, Anahid Kassabian, and Lawrence Siegel (Charlottesville: University of Virginia Press, 1997), 204–28.

37. See Philip Brett and Elizabeth Wood, "Gay and Lesbian Music," *The New Grove Dictionary of Music and Musicians*, 29 vols., 2d ed., ed. Stanley Sadie (London: Macmillan, 2001), 9:597–608.

38. Philip Brett, "Musicality, Essentialism, and the Closet," in *Queering the Pitch*, ed. Brett, Wood, and Thomas, 9–26.

39. *The Memoirs of John Addington Symonds*, ed. Phyllis Grosskurth (London: Hutchinson, 1984).

40. Elizabeth Wood, "Sapphonics."

41. The scholarly controversy is summarized in Alexander Poznansky, "Tchaikovsky's Suicide: Myth and Reality," *19th-Century Music* 11 (1988): 199–220. See also his contributions to *Tchaikovsky and His World*, ed. Leslie Kearney (Princeton, N.J.: Princeton University Press, 1998), 3–96.

42. Allon White, in *The Uses of Obscurity: The Fiction of Early Modernism* (London: Routledge and Kegan Paul, 1981), relates the obscure languages of modernism to cultural discourse over privacy.

43. A direct parallel between sexual secrecy and obscure artistic language is subtly implied by the gay composer Virgil Thomson in recalling his friend and collaborator Gertrude Stein: "The two things you never asked Gertrude about, ever, were about her being a lesbian and what her writing meant" (in Tommasini, *Virgil Thomson*, 163).

44. Roger Shattuck, *The Banquet Years: The Origins of the Avant-garde in France, 1885 to World War I,* rev. ed. (New York: Vintage, 1968), 176.

45. Robert Orledge, *Satie the Composer* (Cambridge: Cambridge University Press, 1990), 39–40.

46. Stuart Feder, *Charles Ives, "My Father's Song": A Psychoanalytic Biography* (New Haven, Conn.: Yale University Press, 1992), 335.

47. For a valiant and affirmative confrontation with the theoretical risks involved in such interpretation, see James Creech, *Closet Writing/Gay Reading: The Case of Melville's "Pierre"* (Chicago: University of Chicago Press, 1993).

48. Maurice Ravel, "Contemporary Music," in *A Ravel Reader: Correspondence, Articles, Interviews,* ed. Arbie Orenstein (New York: Columbia University Press, 1990), 42.

PART 1

PRIVATE PERFORMANCE

1 "DESIRE IS CONSUMING ME"

THE LIFE PARTNERSHIP BETWEEN EUGENIE SCHUMANN AND MARIE FILLUNGER

EVA RIEGER

The epilogue of the 1995 German edition of Eugenie Schumann's *Erinnerungen* (Remembrances) states that "Eugenie Schumann's urn was buried next to Marie's in the Gsteig cemetery near Interlaken."[1] Marie is Eugenie's sister—both were the daughters of Clara and Robert Schumann. So far, so good. But why is there no reference to another Marie who was also buried next to Eugenie? Under Marie Schumann's name on the tombstone is written: "Eugenie Schumann 1851–1938 rests here between her sister and her friend." At the bottom of the large tombstone a smaller one is set upright, containing only two words: "Marie Fillunger."

Encyclopedias and other sources contain little information on Marie Fillunger. This is odd. After all, she studied with the famous singer Mathilde Marchesi in Vienna, was a good friend of Johannes Brahms and the Herzogenbergs, and lived in Clara Schumann's home for several years. She sang under renowned conductors such as Hans Richter, August Manns, Sir Charles Villiers Stanford, and Arthur Sullivan and performed in Australia and South Africa with Sir Charles Hallé and his wife, the celebrated violinist Wilma Norman-Neruda, as well as singing throughout Germany, England, Switzerland, and other European countries. She was especially successful in England, singing at various Crystal Palace and Popular concerts in London, as well as in many other cities, and worked as a professor at the Manchester Royal College of Music from 1904 until her resignation in 1912. She excelled in interpretations of lieder, oratorios, and sacred works but also in concert performances of operas. The beauty of her soprano and her diversity of expression were praised equally. One of the few dictionary entries devoted to her reads: "Early in 1889 she made her first appearance in London at a Popular Concert, where her singing of Schubert's songs stamped her at once as a great interpretative artist, while the exquisitely beautiful quality of her soprano voice gave peculiar charm to all she sang."[2] The reason for her departure from Germany is not given, for who now knows that she quarreled bitterly with Clara and Marie Schumann and fled in an emotional turmoil, leaving behind her lover, Eugenie Schumann?

Marie Fillunger would probably have remained an almost forgotten singer if her letters to Eugenie Schumann, one of Robert and Clara Schumann's daughters, had not been preserved.[3] I was electrified to hear that love letters existed between these two artists (for artists they both were, even though Eugenie hardly ever performed in public). How could it be possible, I asked myself, for two women to conduct a love affair at a time when homosexuality was often condemned as a perversion? Did they admit to their relationship? Did they hide all traces of it? Were there other couples with whom they could identify? And how did Clara Schumann cope with the fact that her daughter was involved with another woman? All these questions prompted me to pay the Vienna Library a visit and take a close look at the letters.

Marie Fillunger was born on 27 January 1850 in Vienna. Her father, Johann Fillunger, was a train builder and director of the Viennese North Train Line. She came from a large family of five boys and three girls and, unlike Eugenie, was never sent to boarding school. She studied with Mathilde Marchesi de Castrone from 1869 to 1873, just after the opera class at the Vienna Conservatory had been instituted.[4] No mention of Fillunger is made in Marchesi's autobiography,[5] possibly because she concentrated on a concert hall career (opera singers usually achieved more fame). Franz Liszt visited Vienna in 1870 and promoted music by Wagner in a series of concerts, including one in which a pupil of Marchesi's, Caroline Smeroshi, sang Elisabeth's prayer from *Tannhäuser*. Fillunger no doubt attended this concert, and it probably sparked her fascination with Wagner, a fascination that contrasts to the attitude of Clara Schumann, who could not come to terms with his music. Besides, Fillunger's singing teacher was Ottilie Ebner (1836–1920), a good friend of Brahms.[6] The famous composer, who lived in Vienna, probably heard Fillunger sing there, for she performed publicly while still studying. He recognized her extraordinary voice and musical talent and engaged her to sing in concerts of his works—for instance, the first performance of his *Lieder und Gesänge* for voice and piano, op. 63, which she sang on 27 November 1872 in Vienna, although she was still a student.[7] Brahms advised her to continue her studies in Berlin at the Berlin Royal Musikhochschule, which had been founded in 1868 with Joseph Joachim, Brahms's and Clara's close friend, as the first director.

Eugenie's childhood was less protected than Fillunger's. After Robert's death, Clara had to earn money by performing, so she sent her children to boarding schools. Eugenie went to a very strict institution that she later compared to Mr. Brocklehurst's inhuman school in Charlotte Brontë's *Jane Eyre*. From there she moved to a more liberal establishment. In 1869 she began piano studies with Ernst Rudorff at the Berlin Royal Musikhochschule; Clara and Johannes Brahms gave her lessons as well. She helped her mother by teaching piano pupils until they were fit to be instructed by Clara and assisted her in other ways as well, although her elder sister Marie had more responsibility.

When Fillunger came to Berlin, the Schumann family was already living there. In early 1874 Clara traveled to Kiel, where she took a cure for a few months. Eugenie stayed in Berlin, and it was there that she first met Fillunger (figure 1.1):

> During those months of separation my life experienced an enrichment through a close acquaintance with a young concert singer. She was a Viennese by birth and had been trained at the Vienna conservatory by Mathilde Marchesi. Brahms advised her to move to Germany, in order to make more progress and to smooth her way to public success. She arrived with a number of letters of recommendation in her handbag. She had already knocked on the door of the Herzogenbergs in Leipzig, where those remarkable people welcomed her with their usual cordiality, first as a visitor, then as a family friend. She then traveled to Berlin and visited my mother, who also welcomed her with great sincerity.
>
> We became intimate with one another in no time, and she got to be my lifelong beloved friend. She differed entirely from those people I had hitherto met. Possessing a healthy sense of humor, a mother wit that always infected others around her with cheerfulness, a typically Austrian goodnaturedness, and a dose of rashness, she always stood solidly with both feet on the ground of life, could quickly come to terms with others, was always true to herself, not bothering in the least about the world's opinion, declining to let herself be influenced by others, and energetically opposing everything that had to do with North German culture—that was Marie Fillunger. I soon called her Fillu in order to avoid clashes between the two Maries—and Fillu she remained for the rest of the world.
>
> Fillu was small, brown haired and owned a pair of intelligent, good brown eyes. She possessed painfully defiant lips and tiny little hands and feet, spoke with the deepest alto ever, but possessed the most wonderful soprano I ever heard. Joachim once said she had one of those rare voices that have a sensual attraction. I have never since heard such a beautiful voice. Even when she had not sung

FIGURE 1.1. Marie Fillunger, date unknown (Archiv des Robert-Schumann Hauses, D-08056 Zwickau, Archiv No. 11953-B2).

for weeks it sounded soft and sonorous. Nevertheless her life was not easy, and we experienced many periods of anxiety together. But she would not let anything drag her down and preserved such a happy vein that she could even pull me out of depressive moods, which attacked me now and again.[8]

The fact that Eugenie's mother, Clara, was absent for a long stretch of time obviously gave the two young women the chance to get intimately acquainted. They enjoyed the physical and erotic aspect of their love, as Fillu's letters reveal: "Your kisses satisfied my thirst, they also make me thirsty and this thirst is now burning within my deepest soul. The fire will not be extinguished until your lips touch me once more."[9]

Space limitations preclude quoting the many letters that continue in this vein, some of which are written in code. Those written in the late 1870s are especially full of love and desire and overflow with fondness:

My dear Genchen,[10] you write so seldom and I am impatient to get news, so completely consumed with desire, that I feel utterly powerless. You barbarian, your last letter was dated the 5th of April, so that you have not thought of me for ten days. Genchen, I shall come to Merano and see what the matter with you is. I didn't write much and jotted it down hastily during the last few days, my mother's presence disturbs me and I cannot write to my Genchen while someone who would never understand my love for you sits opposite me. . . . Do you understand me, Kitten? With a thousand kisses, your Fillu.

My dear Genchen, I didn't want my plea for you to remain faithful to sound ironic, it is just that I keep worrying in order to be contradicted by you. You are my second thought, everything I come across I put before you in my mind's eye. . . . It would be my greatest wish to live with you in some fine place and to wander about the woods and meadows by day and night. . . . my thoughts always end up with my craving to be with you . . . and all the time desire is consuming me. . . . You write that you don't feel well, what is wrong? Can't you sleep? If only I could lull you to sleep, my sweet Genchen, I would not tire. Black thoughts don't suit you, not at all, please engage only in rosy thoughts. If you should have dark thoughts again just jot them down for me, that would be a help in itself and when I help in fighting them, we will both manage to conquer them. . . . My Genchen, I feel physical pain when I contemplate the many miles that separate us . . . my dear sweet golden angelic Genchen! Good night!

My dearest Genchen! My serenity has vanished since we separated. . . . I am perpetually counting the hours that separate me from you, all the more as the complete turbulence which melts all days into one and does not allow me to come back to my senses serves to concentrate my desire on your corner-room.[11]

Eugenie must have been fascinated by her new friend's temperament and daring—something she herself had been taught to bridle. Fillu stayed in Berlin until 1879 and then moved with the Schumanns to Frankfurt. Clara had been offered an attractive post as a piano teacher at the Hoch Conservatory, and Eugenie and Marie were accepted as assistants to their mother. Fillu lived in a room on the second floor next to Eugenie's. In 1884 Clara wrote to Johannes Brahms: "Hearty greetings from us all (including the second floor) from your old Clara," indicating that she regarded the inhabitants of the second floor as one entity.[12]

Eugenie did not often mention Fillu in her memoirs, but when she did, we can guess how happy the two were:

> In July [1878] I accepted an invitation together with my second and better half, my friend Marie Fillunger, to visit Mr. and Mrs. Gomperz in Habrowan Palace near Brünn. We spent unforgettable weeks there and established the friendliest relations with our hostess, the famous former opera singer Caroline Bettelheim.[13] It was a delightful, sociable life; visitors were free to do as they wished, and we met only during meals and in the music hours, when the dark and powerful alto of the housewife resounded together with the clear, high soprano of my friend. Then we all united in the large, bright rooms of the palace. My favorite pastime was walking pleasantly in the open countryside. I saw cornfields for the first time in my life, real cornfields. As far as I could look I saw ears of corn billowing in the wind.[14]

One can imagine Eugenie roaming for hours side by side with Fillu, enjoying the physical exhaustion and the beauty of the countryside, reveling in her love and companionship and tingling with the thrill of hearing her lover's voice mingle with that of a famous opera singer.[15]

These years were probably the happiest for the two young women, both then in their twenties. A year later, back in Frankfurt, Eugenie wrote to Mary Levi: "Fillu is spoiling me; just like your husband she writes daily, which is unusual for her"[16]—a sign that the two were still very much involved with each other. Fillu continued performing in public and was often away traveling, but she always returned to Frankfurt and lived with Eugenie and Marie in Clara's house on Myliusstrasse for ten years. She called Clara "Mama" and assisted her in writing letters, establishing contacts, and running the household. In a letter to Brahms Clara Schumann refers to her as "my secretary."[17]

Fillu could be vivacious and full of mischief, and she infected Eugenie with her sense of humor. "We are expecting some piano pupils tomorrow, and Fillu and Eugenie are just practicing a joke with a Punch and Judy show. Elise's children received a puppet theater as a present and lent it to us," wrote Clara.[18] However, a serious rupture occurred in the family around the end of 1888, when Marie apparently committed an aggressive act toward Fillu and was backed by Clara in doing so. There are signs that the conflict had begun about two years previously. In early 1887 Fillu wrote to Eugenie: "I will not let myself be punished. I am finished with Marie, who was deliberately spiteful. Whatever you say in her defense, it won't change my opinion, so don't bother to. The urgent necessity to have a scapegoat will guarantee my staying in Myliusstrasse 32, but I will entrench myself and not let myself be defeated."[19] This sounds as if a war was raging, and indeed it might have been a psychological battle. Marie, who was Eugenie's eldest sister, had devoted her whole life to her mother and was her closest companion. Whether Clara and Marie realized the nature of the relationship between Fillu and Eugenie is unclear, but Marie obviously regarded Fillu as an intruder and perhaps even as a rival, especially as Fillu was helpful with household jobs and also assisted Clara wherever possible. Clara, who was dependent on Marie to manage her career, sided with her eldest daughter. Eugenie was caught in a trap. She did not have the energy or courage to fight with her mother and sister and thus isolated Fillu, who suffered the loss not only of a home but also of a partner.

Clara dismissed Fillu from the house, which upset Fillu because she had wanted to dissociate herself from the "unhealthy state of things" beforehand and thus forestall Clara's decision.[20] In January 1889 Fillu left Frankfurt for good and traveled to England. The fact that Clara gave Fillu permission to see Eugenie now and again was especially humiliating for Fillu: "Even today I am not allowed to have any emotions of any sort or any sense of honor—this made me swear never to visit Mama's house ever again."[21] This noteworthy remark contains the whole conflict in a nutshell. Clara was unable to accept Eugenie or Fillu as independent human beings and considered Eugenie to be her child and property. Fillu was an intruder who could visit Eugenie now and again but should otherwise go her own way. This means that she either had no idea what was going on or she strove to use her authority to terminate the relationship. A letter to her old friend Emilie List demonstrates this:

> Here at home things have changed somewhat, as Fillunger has gone to England to settle down there. . . . Her departure was difficult for Eugenie and some grievous hours were the result for Marie and me. Eugenie demanded that we should regard her as someone belonging to us, and that was out of the question, is impossible with a stranger, especially when she is so disagreeable. Having had her in the house for five years, surely that was no small proof of my love for

Eugenie. . . . She seems to be very fortunate in England; all reviewers praise her high pitch and her high-spirited performances. Thank God, say I, for who knows what would happen if she were not successful.[22]

Fillu was firmly resolved to earn her own living in England. "I was so unhappy during the last days, now I feel free and have not cried any more or been sad. This is not due to heartlessness, my dear Genchen, it is a feeling of release from oppressive conditions that you will surely understand. I am planning to work and earn money wherever and whenever I can and as soon as I have enough money and a job I will return to you. If only I knew you were satisfied; I hope that my release will be good for you and spare you much unpleasantness."[23]

Soon after her debut early in the year, Fillu performed a program of Schubert's lieder in London.[24] This successful performance marked the beginning of a series of concerts that made her well known in England. Eugenie could not bring herself to follow and stayed in Frankfurt. Although Fillu often suffered from loneliness in the evenings, she never tried to persuade Eugenie to join her. But bitterness prevailed: "The breakup is a fact and cannot be repaired. Surely when Marie realizes that I have left for ever, she will stop tormenting you. If she doesn't give in, do assure her that she need not fear any renewed advances from my side. I have drawn a line for good and my feelings of gratitude for Mama are not yet very virulent."[25]

In October the conflict was still raging. Fillu received "a long and unpleasant letter" from Eugenie and replied: "I have the impression that Mama still does not believe that I am gone for good, although I told her so in my last letter. You must find methods and ways to calm down Mama and to get on with her as well as possible. . . . Marie is a hopeless case—she is a lonely person and will surely remain so, but Mama is the exact opposite and cannot shut herself off from you forever."[26] Later she wrote: "Mama is in many respects as naive as a child, and she is only dimly conscious of having done you a wrong, she simply cannot admit it."[27]

In her letters Fillu repeatedly returns to the subject of Clara, who must have hurt her considerably. On 21 November 1889 she wrote: "I know nothing more except that I love you and often feel an indescribable desire for you, especially when I am singing in public. Does that have something to do with my success here?"[28] Shortly before Christmas she told Eugenie that she would not send her a present, for unpleasant scenes might follow, and she feared that Clara would forbid Eugenie to write to her. Wishing Eugenie Happy Christmas, she added: "How glad I am that this year is coming to an end and a new life will begin in 1890. I am drawing a line under the past and beginning anew as if I were newborn, despite my 40 years. One needs courage for that, but I never lacked courage since I got to know my strength. My voice sounds fresh and young and I feel so healthy and strong that nothing exhausts me. . . . I experienced 15 Christmas trees in the house of the Schumanns and I helped to decorate the last 10, and now — — —."[29]

Brahms appears to have been oblivious of the upheaval, for he innocently suggested that Fillu and Eugenie buy the Herzogenbergs' house in Berchtesgaden and live there together.[30] Fillu trod in Clara's steps in London, for Clara had often performed at the Crystal Palace and more than a hundred times at the Popular concerts in the 2,000-seat St. James's Hall. For over forty years the director Arthur Chappell was able to offer moderate admission prices while engaging prominent British and international musicians, which helped to increase the popularity of the music and the musicians. Fillu frequently sang at these concerts, and she was often engaged to perform at choral festivals and concerts in many cities, including Bath, Bristol, Liverpool, Torquay, Leeds, Manchester, Halifax, Oxford, Cambridge, Glasgow, and Edinburgh,[31] often returning to the Continent to sing in Holland and Switzerland. She was a regular guest at Cumberland Lodge, the home of Prince and Princess Christian (daughter of Queen Victoria), where she was invited by the lady-in-waiting, Emily Loch, and she was often asked to perform at drawing-room concerts.[32] No doubt her acquaintance with Clara Schumann and her network of friends helped her, but it was unquestionably her own performances that ultimately made her successful.

In 1891 Sir Charles Hallé and his wife invited Fillu to accompany them on their tour to Australia, where the couple had performed violin sonatas the previous year. Hallé, who was a German by birth, must have taken a liking to Fillu, in addition to appreciating her accomplishments, since she performed with them in forty-eight concerts. Eugenie traveled to England to see her off and joined her and another of Fillu's friends (probably Mary Hope) on a holiday trip to Malta and Sicily a week beforehand. Brahms could not resist making an ironic remark to Clara in a letter: "I involuntarily imagined that Eugenie's letters from Palermo and Syracuse were faked and she was on the way to India with her friend, who would not let her return."[33] He is careful not to mention Fillu's name, as Clara would not have approved. He obviously hit the mark, for Eugenie had indeed considered joining Fillu. A newspaper cutting informs us: "Had it not been for the delicate state of her mother's health Miss Schumann would have proceeded to Melbourne."[34] It seems that the rivalry between Clara and Fillu continued and that Clara gave Eugenie the impression that she needed her youngest daughter, although Marie was able to nurse her. Eugenie was at sea for a week and sent letters to Clara describing her experiences.[35]

The Hallés had been enthusiastically received during their previous year's tour of Australia.[36] We can assume that the triumph in 1891 was similar. Fillu was announced in Adelaide as "Marie Fillunger, an Austrian prima donna of great repute" who "at once became a great favourite on her appearance in Melbourne and Sydney."[37] One review describes her entrancing her audience "with the lovely tones of her rich and pure soprano, and the finished excellence of her vocalism, stamping her as an artist of the first calibre," adding that "her recalls were enthusiastic from all parts of the house and she obligingly responded to the imperative encores."[38] What an unforgettable experience this must have been, to be cheered by huge audiences, honored, and admired—and how she would have loved Eugenie, her life partner, to share her happiness.

A diary page reveals that Fillu performed seventy-one concerts in 1891 and earned £700, which was quite a sum of money at the time. She sang regularly at the famous Hallé concerts in Manchester (including Brahms's Requiem, arias by Gluck and Mozart, and the third acts of *Tannhäuser* and *Lohengrin*). The more Fillu was in demand, the more the strain of living apart increased for Eugenie. Eugenie realized that it was possible to earn a living from art and that—with her famous name to assist her—she would find sufficient pupils to teach in England, if only she could dare to leave her mother and sister. In December 1891 she confided to Mary Levi:

> I am actually quite well and so busy that I have no time to think about my situation. That is fortunate, because—notwithstanding all the satisfaction which I derive from Mama's love and Marie's sisterly affection and from fulfilling my duties—in my heart of hearts I miss Fillu awfully. I am certain you can sympathize with me in this matter, as you were always full of understanding and sympathy for my relationship with her. Since our separation her career has developed so happily that this is a slight compensation for me, at least I know that she is fully satisfied.[39]

The conflict weighed too heavily on her, and shortly after writing this letter Eugenie fell seriously ill. She was no longer able to divide herself between her mother, her sister, and Fillu. "I suffered terribly, although I was only ill with anemia and a weak heart," she wrote to Mary Levi in May 1892, unsuspecting that the diagnosis was probably put forward as a pretext by the doctor, who could find no physical ailment. In a letter to Marie Schumann an alarmed Clara described her illness as "a serious attack of depression."[40] Eugenie lay in bed for three weeks. Realizing that her condition was critical, Fillu arranged for a friend to look after her, because she herself was engaged in concerts in Switzerland, and then met Eugenie in Basel in the home of her good friends, the Zur Muhlls. There she nursed her for a fortnight. "For many weeks, I gave up all hope of ever recovering and am now overjoyed because my vitality is returning," wrote Eugenie.[41] We can imagine that the two lovers exchanged many tender words in Basel, and Eugenie finally decided to move to England and live with Fillu. She probably told her mother that her desire to earn her own living by giving piano lessons was the main reason for leaving, since in November 1892 Clara confided to her diary: "Knowing that Eugenie feels satisfied in her full independence is a comfort for me."[42] Nevertheless, Clara felt she had to make amends with Fillu, for she gave Eugenie a letter for her when Eugenie left for England. Six days later she wrote to Eugenie: "I hope my letter to Fillu will have appeased you both, for her heart cannot harbor resentment eternally, if one is willing to lean toward her. As to me, I am willing to forget what has happened."[43] As Fillu had foreseen, Clara was not able to admit any fault of her own. In 1894 the two met in Frankfurt, and Clara joined in the discussion about their new flat in London, advising them to rent an additional two rooms that they could sublet.[44] In the following years the couple separated only for summer holidays and for Christmas, when Eugenie visited her mother, sister, and the rest of the family.[45]

In 1895 Fillu once again joined the Hallés on a tour, this time to South Africa, where she sang in twenty-four concerts. It was probably Sir Charles Hallé who persuaded Fillu to accept a post at the newly founded Royal College of Music in Manchester. Hallé had successfully campaigned to raise funds; a new concert hall and a college were built and the teaching staff was chosen in 1893. In 1904 Fillu succeeded Cecilia Hutchinson, who had held the chief professorship of singing for seven years,[46] and taught for twelve hours per week, receiving fifteen shillings per hour, or four hundred pounds annually. This was a high salary, for other colleagues received only half that, while the librarian received merely twenty pounds per annum. In 1911 Fillu's salary was for some reason reduced to three hundred pounds per annum for the next two years. She found this unacceptable, and her letter of resignation runs as follows:

February 7, 1912
Dear Sir,

Will you kindly bring before the council of the "Royal Manchester College of Music" my request to be released of my duties at the end of July 1912. My agreement binds me till July 1913 but I trust there will be no difficulty in finding a substitute.

It is with intense regret that I am taking this step for I have been very happy in my work but the conditions at the college have become so untolerable [*sic*] for me that I cannot endure it any longer.

I will not trouble you with any details but I am ready to give them should the council wish so.[47]

After Clara's death in 1897, her eldest daughter, Marie, bought a plot of land in Interlaken and had a large chalet built on it, where she lived for the rest of her life, putting the estate in order and helping Berthold Litzmann and others with their research on Robert and Clara Schumann. At some point a friend named Maria Maassen moved into the chalet with her. In 1918 Eugenie, disappointed with the political situation after World War I, decided to move from England to Switzerland and to live near Marie. Fillu initially moved to her family in Austria, joining Eugenie later. The fact that Eugenie took separate lodgings shows that she had planned for Fillu to join her soon, for Fillu would have refused to live in the same house as Marie (and vice versa). In Matten (which now belongs to Interlaken) Eugenie rented a simple flat that she furnished artistically. Some time later Fillu joined her. Eugenie's German savings were destroyed by inflation, which must have shocked her deeply. In 1923 a pound of meat cost over 4 trillion marks. Her mother had often warned her of the dangers of being without an independent income; she and Fillu had worked hard in England, and now they saw their money melting before their eyes. Fillu gave singing lessons; Eugenie taught piano and English. Eugenie also received financial support from a Swiss woman who preferred to remain anonymous.[48]

Not much is to be heard about Fillu during this time. In a 1927 letter to her friend Gertrud Aebi, Eugenie wrote: "Miss Fillunger is well; we played bridge and she had nothing but nonsense in her head."[49] In 1920 Eugenie decided to write her memoirs, in which she commemorated her mother. She tended to idealize both Clara and Marie and ignored the difficult conflict back in 1888. In a letter to a friend in Interlaken she spoke of her "double life," obviously referring to her walks to and from Marie, to whom she read chapters of her memoirs. This first book was enormously successful, so much so that she started work on a book on Robert Schumann soon afterward.

The simple flat in Matten that Eugenie rented stood in Hauptstrasse. Marie died in 1929, and instead of moving into her chalet, Eugenie sold it. A year later Fillu also died. Thus a fifty-six-year love relationship came to an end. Eugenie remained alone—living at first in a clinic in Bern in 1931 and 1932 and then back in Interlaken. In the preface to her book on Robert Schumann she wrote: "The two beloved people, my sister and the friend and companion of my life Marie Fillunger, who both made the completion of this book possible—the one by perfect agreement, which made me happy, the other by sacrificing participation—are not living any more to experience the publishing of this work. Both are gone, and I can only call after them my indelible thanks."[50] On 5 February 1932 she wrote to her friend Gertrud Aebi: "I receive many friendly letters on account of my book. How happy I would be if my sister and my Fillu could read them."[51] In an atmosphere of privacy, she spoke of "my" Fillu; in the more public preface she mentioned "the" friend and life companion. A slight difference, but what a difference.

o   o   o

Fillu and Eugenie lived in a time when the outcast status of the homosexual man and the lesbian was virulent. They would hardly have been able to ignore the various medical, religious, and pedagogic accounts of homosexuality that were published in large numbers during the second half of the nineteenth century. Whether the arguments stated that homosexuality was inborn or acquired, they all agreed that same-sex erotic relationships were pathological and morbid. Some historians of lesbianism have tended to divide lesbian identity into two categories: women who passed as men and used dildos to give their partners the impression that they were men and "women who entered into long-term romantic friendships [and] were presumed to be in relationships that involved no sex acts."[52] Fillu and Eugenie would certainly have regarded their relationship as emotional. They clearly did not identify with the cross-dressed masculine-appearing woman, and yet there can be no doubt that their relationship was based on an erotic attachment.

Did they have any friends, literature, or social movements on which to lean, with which to identify? Was there a cultural space for lesbian couples that established an atmosphere of sympathy at the turn of the century? What information can we draw from Eugenie herself? She gave only fragmentary evidence. She boldly called Fillu her "second and better half" and made some remarks that could be interpreted as indicating an awareness of her desire for women. Pauline Viardot's performance of Gluck's aria "J'ai perdu mon Eurydice," for example, impressed her so deeply that she could not forget it for months.[53] Was it only the beautiful performance of Viardot, or was she enchanted by listening to a woman expressing her desire for another woman? Eugenie also wrote of the "splendid women's movement"[54] that she witnessed when in England, although one would not expect the daughter of a woman as conservative as Clara to praise the suffragettes. Most likely Fillu, who depended on earning her own living and was far more open-minded, helped her to accept their cause. "My mother's way of thinking and feeling was so straightforward, simple and clear that she could not sympathize with entangled pro-

cesses of the human soul," Eugenie once remarked.[55] She probably did not dare
talk to her mother about the intensity of her relationship, fearing Clara could
not understand, and therefore preferred to keep the intricate complexity of the
relationship to herself.

Were there literary traditions to which they could turn? In a letter to Mary
Levi, Eugenie mentioned that Fillu was reading Balzac, adding: "What a devil
of a fellow!"[56] Balzac often discussed same-sex relationships in his novels.
Eugenie also mentioned reading novels by Paul Heyse (1830–1914). This is
significant, since Heyse published one of the few contemporary novels to deal
with lesbian desire. In *Die Schwarze Jakobe* he describes an intimate friendship
between two women. A certain Frau von F. meets Jakobe, a lower-class girl, and
remarks: "And suddenly she took my head between her large strong hands and
kissed me twice on the mouth. A feeling of delight thrilled me intensely, such
as I had never experienced before. Then she let go and laughed again, but I
saw her blushing. She bent towards the meadow flowers and picked me a small
bunch. We hardly spoke any more on that day. I felt quite solemn, as if I had
formed a life tie, and she was also engaged in all kinds of serious thoughts."
The two women separate, and Frau von F. marries but later acknowledges: "I
don't think I can ever experience a similar passionate feeling for a man as I
still feel for this girl. I was even less capable of ever conquering a man as I had
conquered my blackhaired love." The novel ends with a plea for the acceptance
of homosexual love: "Are you still going to defend your philosophers who are
oblivious of the fact that friendship is an elementary drive of nature, irrespon-
sible and unfathomable, just like the force which attracts man and woman in
blind passion?"[57]

Apart from novels, there were other female couples in the German music
world who lived at the same time as Fillu and Eugenie and may well have been
acquainted with them. The music educator and author Lina Ramann (1833–
1912; see figure 1.2) was the author of various books, including the first large
biography of Franz Liszt, a hefty three-volume work written in collaboration
with Liszt and his lover, Sayn-Wittgenstein.[58] In 1858 she founded a music
school in Glückstadt together with her life partner, the pianist Ida Volckmann.
Later they moved to Nuremberg and continued the music school there. Ramann called Volckmann "my companion, my ally . . . with whom I am connected in profession and life."[59] Marie Lipsius (1837–1927; see figure 1.3) used
the pseudonym "La Mara" and wrote a number of books on music. One of
her collections of biographies of women musicians includes a chapter on Clara
Schumann.[60] There is no evidence that La Mara met Eugenie, yet she wrote an
autobiography that the latter could have read. It contains various allusions to

FIGURE 1.2. The pianist, writer on music, and pedagogue Lina Ramann (right) with her life partner, Ida Volckmann (from Marie Ille-Beeg, *Lina Ramann: Lebensbild einer bedeutenden Frau auf dem Gebiete der Musik;* photograph in possession of the Bavarian State Library, no. 4 Mus.th. 1848 n).

FIGURE 1.3. The writer on music Marie Lipsius ("La Mara") (photograph taken from La Mara, *Durch Musik und Leben im Dienste des Ideals*).

her relationship with Similde Gerhard, "my lifelong partner who called me her 'second me.'" They met in 1865 while helping out in a military hospital in Leipzig after the war between Prussia and Austria had broken out: "I could not have a better lifelong friend than her. We were compatible in our inclinations, our characters differed but we complemented one another perfectly, so that no boredom could ever arise."[61] At the age of forty La Mara moved into Similde's house, where she stayed till her death. And finally there was a group of women in the 1920s who pushed the solfège method forward in Germany. The leader of this movement, Agnes Hundoegger (1858–1927; see figure 1.4), lived in relationships with women, and the group had strong bonds with the women's movement.[62]

Some similar points are valid for all these women: their relationships provided the freedom to work as long as they liked—no husband gave orders, and they supported and strengthened one another; they enjoyed sexual self-determination while simultaneously striving for acceptance in the bourgeois world; and they were conservative, as if they wished to apologize for their role as outsiders. This is no wonder, considering that independent and therefore sexually uncontrollable women were feared by many men at the end of the nineteenth century; they consequently accused male-identified women of being lesbians. These three couples therefore tried to avoid anything that could stamp them as degenerate or immoral.

The British composer Ethel Smyth was close to many of Eugenie's acquaintances, including Brahms, Kirchner, Elisabeth and Heinrich von Herzogenberg, and the conductor Hermann Levi and his wife, Mary. With her bold and outspoken personality, Smyth stood in contrast to the aforementioned couples and obviously intrigued Eugenie, who suffered from inferiority complexes. In 1880 Eugenie wrote to Mary Levi: "I saw Miss Smythe [sic] in Leipzig, but did not speak to her. I always found her very handsome and special, and had heard a lot about her through Fillu. I hope I will make her acquaintance." And some months later: "How is Ethel Smyth? You promised to send us some of her music!"[63]

In February 1881 they met at last. Eugenie and her mother met the Herzogenbergs and spent two full evenings with them and Ethel: "I had not yet made the acquaintance of Ethel and was pleased that I had the good fortune to get more familiar with her. I like her quite a bit and believe she is someone who improves the more one knows her. One notices right away how talented she is, she played the cello sonata with Lisl on two pianos, and Mama also found her very talented."[64] Two years later Ethel visited Clara Schumann in Frankfurt and reported on the visit in letters to Elisabeth von Herzogenberg:

FIGURE 1.4. The music pedagogue Agnes Hundoegger (right) with a friend (Hochschule der Künste Berlin, Archive).

I get on very well with Marie and Eugenie and find the latter as attractive on further acquaintance as I did at first, but I think both their minds want poking up; they give out so very little of what is in them. . . . They are very funny together and find me more than comic, so we amuse each other well. Our start for the party that evening was very funny. Eugenie nearly pulled Frau S.'s cap off wrapping her up, and then when the cab came it was so small we could hardly get into it, and Marie was in a fury and saying: "Nein, da bleib' ich doch zehn-mal lieber zu Haus" (No! if it comes to that, I'd ten times rather stay at home) as if she had been doing anything but grumble all day at having to go. And then she and Frau S. abused the cab-driver in a tragic tone I cannot describe, but which you, knowing the people, can well imagine, for having so small a cab, and he privately informed me it was not his fault if four such unusually stout people (me stout!!) got in at once. I laughed so at the whole thing, as did Eugenie, that they ended by laughing too and we had a jolly evening. . . . Y.Z. sang weakly and charmingly, and he and I and Eugenie sat at a "Katzen Tisch" [a little side table] and were very jolly, and sending Frau Schumann and Marie home stayed on ourselves and played idiotic games and the fool generally.

And then Smyth adds a cryptic sentence: "I was so sorry F. left before I came; I do like her much, with her clown's pathos and nice eyes and shyness of Frau Schumann."[65] Undoubtedly "F." is Fillu, who probably had an engagement at the time and had to leave before Ethel arrived. Smyth's letters show that Eugenie was at ease with her and enjoyed her presence. Yet we have no evidence that she knew that Ethel Smyth loved women or whether Fillu was anxious for her to meet an open lesbian.[66]

o o o

Eugenie was the daughter of a composer who—along with Franz Schubert—wrote the most compelling and touching songs in Western music history and of a pianist who achieved international acceptance and fame, despite the obstacles faced by female musicians. Both her parents were internationally renowned, and she herself mentions the problems that this posed for her. For one thing, she was placed in a family in which her role as a musician was established without her agency, even though she suffered the inevitable comparisons to her mother. "When I left boarding school, I found a complete world, and it never occurred to me to rebel against it; I was content to love and admire."[67] At the same time, however, she lived with her partner—in Germany, England, and Switzerland—and she defied her mother by deciding to move to her lover in England. She had to overcome the breach between the compulsion to live a traditional life style and her desire to live with Fillu. Eugenie's frank mention of Fillunger as her "second and better half," together with Fillu's erotically tinged letters to Eugenie, which Eugenie saved until her death; the more than fifty-five years' duration of their relationship despite many conflicts; and the fact that Eugenie and Fillu are buried together—all this points to an intense love relationship.

Blanche Wiesen Cook defines lesbians as women who create life situations with women in which they can work independently and creatively. She criticizes tendencies to reduce lesbians to their sexual preferences and regards physical love as only one mode of expression within an endless complexity of human relationships.[68] Yet the sexual question cannot be ignored, and explaining how women who loved women coped with the restrictions of their times, without condemning them for being insufficiently outspoken or idealizing them as courageous heroines, remains a problem for future research.

My partner, Mariann, and I visited Interlaken in August 1998 to find traces of Fillu and the Schumann family. Marie's chalet can still be found in Alpenstrasse 26, just as the Sonnenhof in which Clara Schumann stayed (Alpenstrasse 6) survives along with other holiday lodgings of the Schumanns (Villa May, Alpenstrasse 28, and Chalet Sterchi, in Parkstrasse 14). Eugenie's and Fillu's home in Matten was unfortunately pulled down in 1981 but was rebuilt in the village of Alpligen, where it still stands today.

We managed to contact a former pupil of Fillunger, Liberta Baumann, née Sterchi, a ninety-one-year-old woman living in the Swiss town of Langenthal.[69] She was the daughter of a baker who lived opposite the couple's home and remembered that "Fräulein Fillunger," as she still calls her today, took over the cooking of the household. On our visit she presented me with two precious gifts: a napkin ring with "C.S." engraved on it and a silver cake slicer that her mother had received from Eugenie. We decided to bequeath them to the Robert Schumann archive in Zwickau, but I could not refrain from using both utensils at home beforehand. Thus I felt connected in some odd way with these two women, not as heroines or models for today, but as personalities with their own contradictions, problems, and successes. Whereas Fillu preserved her integrity in every situation, Eugenie was burdened with conflicting forces that we can understand only within the context of her time.

The combined grave of the three women can be found in the Gsteig cemetery of the picturesque Wilderswil village near Interlaken. One walks over the quaint wooden bridge and up the wide staircase next to the Steinbock Gasthof and ascends the steps to the right. Mariann and I decided that the dates of Fillunger's birth and death should be added to her little stone, and this was permitted by the cemetery administration.[70]

When Fillu died in 1930 Eugenie obviously threw away her own letters to Fillu but could not bring herself to destroy Fillu's letters. She probably reread them after Fillu's death. Thus some of the most compelling letters in lesbian music history have been preserved and show us, who live our lesbian relationships in comparative freedom today, what it meant to resist the pressure of society and the family and to remain true to oneself and to one's lover.

NOTES

1. Eugenie Schumann, *Clara's Kinder* (Clara's children) ed. Eva Weissweiler (Cologne: Dittrich, 1995), 365; first published in 1925 as *Erinnerungen*. (Translations, from this and all other works cited herein, are my own.)

2. J. A. Fuller-Maitland, "Marie Fillunger," in *Grove's Dictionary of Music and Musicians*, 5th ed., ed. Eric Blom (London: Macmillan, 1954), 93. Other entries can be found in K. J. Kutsch and Leo Riemens, *Grosses Sängerlexikon* (Large dictionary of singers) (Bern: Saur, 1987); and Oscar Thompson, *The International Cyclopedia of Music and Musicians*, 9th ed. (New York: Dodd, Mead, 1964).

3. The letters were first acknowledged in print by Weissweiler in her concluding remarks on the occasion of the republication of Eugenie Schumann's *Erinnerungen*.

4. Fuller-Maitland, "Marie Fillunger," 93.

5. Mathilde Marchesi, *Marchesi and Music: Passages from the Life of a Famous Singing-Teacher* (New York: Harper and Brothers, 1897).

6. Ottilie von Balassa, *Die Brahmsfreundin Ottilie Ebner und ihr Kreis* (Brahms's friend Ottilie Ebner and her circle) (Vienna: Franz Bondy 1933), 34, 121, 129.

7. Renate Hofmann and Kurt Hofmann, *Johannes Brahms: Zeittafel zu Leben und Werk* (Brahms: chronology of his life and work) (Tutzing: Hans Schneider, 1983), 240.

8. Schumann, *Clara's Kinder*, 213–14. In German the word *filou*, which is of French origin, means a cheeky, daring person and is mostly connected with young men. It seems that Eugenie chose the right nickname.

9. Letter from Marie Fillunger to Eugenie Schumann, 11 July 1875, from the collection in the Österreichische Nationalbibliothek, Handschriften-Sammlung (Austrian National Library, Autograph Dept.), autographs, cassettes 979/1–27 and 980/1–27; reproduced by permission. All further references to these letters indicated as "MF to ES" with the date. Thanks to Rosemary Moravec Hilmar, Vienna, who helped with the transcriptions.

10. *Genchen* is a pet name for Eugenie.

11. Various letters, MF to ES, 1875–76.

12. Letter dated 29 Sept. 1884, in Berthold Litzmann, ed., *Clara Schumann, Johannes Brahms: Briefe* (Schumann, Brahms: letters), 2 vols. (Leipzig: Breitkopf und Härtel, 1927), 2:282.

13. Caroline von Gomperz-Bettelheim (1845–1926) was a famous mezzo-soprano until she married the wealthy manufacturer Julius Ritter von Gomperz in 1867. See

Anton Bettelheim, *Caroline von Gomperz-Bettelheim: Ein biographisches Blatt* (Bettelheim: a biographical pamphlet) (privately published, 1905).

14. Schumann, *Clara's Kinder*, 194.

15. We have become more aware of the erotic quality of same-sex voices since the work of scholars such as Terry Castle (see her article "In Praise of Brigitte Fassbaender: Reflections on Diva-Worship," in *En Travesti: Women, Gender Subversion, Opera*, ed. Corinne E. Blackmer and Patricia Juliana Smith [New York: Columbia University Press, 1995], 20–58) and Sam Abel (see his *Opera in the Flesh* [Boulder: Westview, 1996], 80–81). Castle has described the thrill Brigitte Fassbaender's voice gives her, especially when she is singing with female partners.

16. Letter from Eugenie Schumann to Mary Levi, 1 July 1879, Munich State Library. All further references to these letters indicated as "ES to ML" with the date. Mary Levi was the wife of the conductor Hermann Levi (1839–1900).

17. Letter dated 23 Dec. 1889, in Litzmann, *Schumann, Brahms*, 2:286.

18. Letter dated 30 Dec. 1885, in Litzmann, *Schumann, Brahms*, 1:299. Elise was Eugenie's elder sister, who married and lived in the neighborhood.

19. MF to ES, 20 Feb. 1887.

20. MF to ES, 19 Oct. 1889.

21. MF to ES, 4 Oct. 1889.

22. Letter dated 3 Mar. 1889, in Clara Schumann, *"Das Band der ewigen Liebe": Briefwechsel mit Emilie und Elise List* ("The bond of eternal love": correspondence with Emilie and Elise List), ed. Eugen Wendler (Stuttgart: J.B. Metzler, 1996), 412–13.

23. MF to ES, 16 Jan. 1889.

24. MF to ES, 18 Jan. 1889.

25. MF to ES, 5 Apr 1889.

26. MF to ES, 26 Oct. 1889.

27. MF to ES, 29 Nov. 1889.

28. MF to ES, 21 Nov. 1889.

29. MF to ES, 22 Dec. 1889.

30. Letter dated 23 Dec. 1889, in Litzmann, *Schumann, Brahms*, 2:399.

31. The industrial centers in the Midlands and northern England had a growing appetite for choral festivities, which gave vocalists good job possibilities.

32. All these concerts are discussed at length in Fillunger's letters. An edition of the letters is planned for 2002. For more information on women's participation in the London music world, see Paula Gillett, *Musical Women in England, 1870–1914* (New York: St. Martin's, 2000).

33. Letter, May 1891, in Berthold Litzmann, *Clara Schumann: Ein Künstlerleben nach Tagebüchern und Schriften* (Clara Schumann: an artist's life from diaries and letters), 3 vols., 4th ed. (Leipzig: Breitkopf und Härtel, 1920 [1902–8]), 3:536.

34. Undated newspaper cutting with MF's letters to ES, folder 980/26.

35. See Dietz-Riediger Moser, ed., *Clara Schumann: Mein liebes Julchen. Briefe* (Clara Schumann: my dear Julchen—letters) (Munich: Nymphenburger, 1990), 146.

36. See C. E. Hallé and Marie Hallé, eds., *Life and Letters of Sir Charles Hallé; Being*

an Autobiography (1819–1860) with Correspondence and Diaries (London: Smith, Elder and Co., 1896), 373–7.

37. *The Melbourne Advertiser,* 11 July 1891.

38. Ibid., 20 July 1891.

39. ES to ML, 13 Dec. 1891.

40. Letter, Clara Schumann to Marie Schumann, 22 May 1892, Robert Schumann Archive (RSA), Zwickau.

41. ES to ML, 9 May 1892.

42. In Litzmann, *Ein Künstlerleben,* 3:564.

43. Letter, Clara Schumann to Eugenie Schumann, 13 Oct. 1892, RSA.

44. Letter, Clara Schumann to Eugenie Schumann, 9 Oct. 1892, RSA.

45. No research has yet been done on the whereabouts of their home, the number of concerts in which Fillunger participated, and the teaching careers of both Fillu and Eugenie in England.

46. See Michael Kennedy, *The History of the Royal Manchester College of Music* (Manchester, U.K.: Manchester University Press, 1971).

47. MF, letter of 7 Feb. 1912, RMCM Archive. The salary details were also obtained from the archive. No reason is given for the salary reduction.

48. Walter Bettler, *Robert Schumann, Clara Schumann und ihre Töchter Marie und Eugenie in Interlaken* (Robert Schumann, Clara Schumann, and their daughters Marie and Eugenie in Interlaken) (Interlaken/Spiez: privately published, 1994). If copyright rules had existed in those times Eugenie would have been a millionaire, for as her father's fame spread, his music was played the whole world over.

49. Bettler, *Robert Schumann,* 90.

50. Eugenie Schumann, *Robert Schumann* (Leipzig: Koehler und Amelang, 1931), preface.

51. Bettler, *Robert Schumann,* 92.

52. Martha Vicinus, "'They Wonder to Which Sex I Belong': The Historical Roots of the Modern Lesbian Identity," in *Homosexuality, Which Homosexuality?* ed. Dennis Altman, Carole Vance, Martha Vicinus, et al. (London/Amsterdam: GMP/Uitgeverij An Dekker, 1989), 175.

53. Schumann, *Clara's Kinder,* 137. See also note 15.

54. Ibid., 170.

55. Ibid., 188.

56. ES to ML, 9 Aug. 1882.

57. Paul Heyse, *Gesammelte Werke* (Collected works), vol. 8: *Novellen* (Novellas) (Berlin: Hertz, 1872), 12–132.

58. Lina Ramann, *Franz Liszt als Künstler und Mensch* (Liszt as artist and man), 3 vols. (Leipzig: Breitkopf und Härtel, 1880, 1887, 1994).

59. Marie Ille-Beeg, *Lina Ramann: Lebensbild einer bedeutenden Frau auf dem Gebiete der Musik* (Lina Ramann: life portrait of an influential woman in the music world) (Nuremberg: Verlag der Friedrich Kornschen Buchhandlung, 1914).

60. La Mara [Marie Lipsius], *Musikalische Studienköpfe* (Eminent musicians), vol.

5: *Die Frauen im Tonleben der Gegenwart* (Women in contemporary music culture) (Leipzig: Breitkopf und Härtel, 1882).

61. La Mara [Marie Lipsius], *Durch Musik und Leben im Dienste des Ideals* (Through music and life in the service of ideals) (Leipzig: Breitkopf und Härtel, 1925).

62. See Eva Rieger, "Agnes Hundoegger (1858–1927)," in *Sophie & Co.: Bedeutende Frauen Hannovers* (Sophie and co.: influential women of Hanover), ed. Hiltrud Schroeder (Hannover: Fackelträger, 1990), 139–56.

63. ES to ML, 6 Feb. 1880, 6 Dec. 1880.

64. ES to ML, 23 Feb. 1881.

65. Ethel Smyth, *Impressions That Remained,* 2 vols. (London: Longmans, Green, 1919), 2:87.

66. Eugenie writes in a letter to Mary Levi (17 Apr. 1893, no. 32): "Ich habe jetzt 'Miss Hopper in die Welt' gelesen und mich sehr dabei amüsiert. Ethel kommt aber recht gut dabei weg!" ("I have just read 'Miss Hopper goes out into the world' and found it amusing. Ethel is described quite flatteringly!"). Unfortunately I have not yet traced the essay or book to which Eugenie refers.

67. Schumann, *Clara's Kinder,* 240.

68. Blanche Wiesen Cook, *Women and Support Networks* (New York: Out and Out Books, 1979).

69. Liberta Baumann died in 1999.

70. A photograph in Eugenie's estate, held by the Stadtarchiv (Municipal Archive) Bonn, proves that Eugenie had originally had a tombstone erected for Fillunger with her birth and death dates included. In addition, the word *geliebte* ("beloved") can be discerned on the photo. Someone must have been interested in obliterating all traces of the relationship.

2 RAVEL'S WAY

LLOYD WHITESELL

SUSPICION

Maurice Ravel (1875–1937) was fiercely protective of his privacy. In personal recollections the composer's friends attest repeatedly to his aloofness, modesty, or reserve.[1] He never married or, as far as we know, engaged in any long-term sexual relationship. For much of his adult life he lived with his beloved mother, staying with her until her death in 1916. After World War I he moved outside Paris to "Le Belvédère," a house in Montfort-l'Amaury, where he lived alone to the end of his life.

Ravel's first biographer, Roland-Manuel, tells us: "At a first meeting Ravel was courteous and reserved. His best friends could not help feeling secretly disappointed by the feeling that they were not able to become more fully intimate with him; for the most devoted sympathy and close relationship scarcely altered the manner of his greeting. It took a long time to discover that Ravel was the surest, most faithful and most profoundly affectionate of friends."[2] Straightaway, in the book's preface, Roland-Manuel alerts his readers to his subject's secrecy while trying to reassure them about it: "Although [Ravel] was a man of such fastidious reserve, he had no secret but the secret of his genius. . . . The relations and friends of the master, who have nothing to conceal, have freely given me their help."[3] Marguerite Long, a pianist who toured with Ravel in performances of his Piano Concerto in G, was more curious and less dismissive: "His eyes were brown and deep set. Their expression, open and enquiring, was welcoming, yet often alert to signal imminent danger. His mouth was thin, hinting at reserve, and perhaps uneasiness. When he smiled, it sometimes seemed to suggest mocking but at times it was dark with shadow. What were his fears? What secret grief did he nourish?" (see figure 2.1).[4]

FIGURE 2.1. Ravel, on the banks of the Nivelle, near Saint-Jean-de-Luz, about 1902.

Both friends register the provocative quality of Ravel's remoteness. One says trust me when I tell you it doesn't mean a thing. The other can't resist peering beneath the surface.

Of course, there are many conceivable motives for treasuring privacy. By the end of the nineteenth century, Westerners had come to rely more and more heavily on the private sphere as a means of pursuing individual autonomy and fulfillment. As industrial capitalism advanced, upheavals in social and economic organization, as well as ever more intrusive forms of social control, contributed to a widespread sense of vulnerability.[5] This situation created a populace adept at personal styles of self-masking; signs of similar strategies in others, meanwhile, were the object of an ambivalent fascination. The awareness of the tension between public facades and inner secrets gave rise to a knowing, mistrustful mode of interpretation that Ricoeur has called a "hermeneutics of suspicion."[6] One manifestation of this awareness is the development of the modern language of psychology, with its terrain of hidden struggles and occluded internal narratives. This is the background behind Marguerite Long's probing chiaroscuro reminiscence.

Given Ravel's determined bachelorhood, however, it makes sense to frame the question of his secrecy in sexual terms. We wouldn't be the first to do so. The article in the New Grove states the problem with admirable forthrightness and composure, issuing both a warning and a challenge:

> Ravel felt an intense need for privacy. His sexual life was shrouded in secrecy; and he made a mystery of the creative process, exposing his music only when the final touch had been applied. Undoubtedly Ravel felt vulnerable. There is too little evidence for an adequate picture of his sexual relationships to be formed, although one cannot doubt that their nature would be relatable to . . . the music. However, where an over-zealous commentator has been compelled to eke out the slender direct evidence with assumptions deduced from the works, these deductions . . . fail to be of interest.[7]

The author, G. W. Hopkins, adopts two axioms that the historian of sexuality could well take to heart. On the one hand, Ravel's secrecy means something. His guarded manner was not arbitrary, and we should not rule out connections between his affective and creative lives. On the other hand, we should be prepared to accept the limitations of our knowledge. Although we can discern the effects of his defenses, we might not be able to discover their rationale.

If you're like me, though, you'll want to hear more about those gossips, those "over-zealous commentators." Hopkins doesn't bother to provide references, but such commentators form a tenacious part of the literature. The leftist gay historian Daniel Guérin (1904–88), recalling his youth in Paris in the 1920s, included Ravel in his list of gay royalty: "If initiates knew that Mauriac was homosexual—more or less repressed—people knew that Proust was one, Gide too; one knew that René Crevel, the most talented of the surrealists, was; I knew him at the Terrasse du Flore and we got along well. Maurice Ravel was an obvious homosexual [*un homosexuel affiché*]. One was encouraged by the fact that so many famous people were homosexual."[8] Music historian Michel Faure, meanwhile, has sketched a psychological portrait of a man "crammed with complexes" concerning the composer's diminutive size, emotional life, and sexuality. He hypothesizes that Ravel's "sexual problems" ("homosexual tendencies, even impotence") were due to an almost exclusive attachment to his mother.[9] The author of a recent biography is cautiously speculative about a possible love in Ravel's life:

> If Ravel did have a romantic attachment to anyone—which is not necessarily the same thing as a sexual relationship—it was before Poulenc knew him [about 1917]. Of all the men and women in his circle at that time, the most likely candidate is Léon-Paul Fargue, the talented poet and brilliant conversationalist who in his Apache period combined the looks of Rimbaud with the profile of a "young Roman Emperor." According to Hélène Jourdan-Morhange, Fargue was "united to Ravel by a tender friendship of youth" and he remained an object of his admiration, though not a constant companion, for the rest of his life.[10]

On the other side of the coin are those sources or historians who forestall speculation about Ravel's sexuality by citing the lack of concrete evidence. The discreetly gay composer Francis Poulenc, who entered Parisian musical circles as a teenager in the late 1910s, stated firmly that "he had no love-life to be spoken of; no one knows of any Ravel love affair."[11] Ravel's friend Manuel Rosenthal spoke of the composer's casual relations with female prostitutes:

> At other times he and I used to meet . . . in a large *brasserie* by the Porte Champerret. . . . He said, "That's where I'll be from eleven o'clock and, you'll see, it's very nice, there are ladies there." What he called "ladies" were, in fact, prostitutes and indeed . . . I saw several of these "ladies" making signs at him; they knew him very well and he gave them a very friendly wave, saying "Bonjour, bonjour." I think it was a sort of outlet. Being conscious of his smallness and of his position as a creative artist, he turned to prostitutes. It was very understandable and, for me anyway, completely refutes the suggestion people have made—without any sort of proof, and indeed I have proof to the contrary, as you see—that he was homosexual. Not that it would have mattered in the least: he could have been homosexual without prejudice to his musical genius, but he wasn't.[12]

Note that his interpretation rests on rather dubious assumptions. First is the belief that any sign of heterosexual activity establishes a default heterosexual identity. A binary hetero/homo model is descriptively impoverished, as I will explore later. Moreover, in the process of disclaiming prejudice on his own part, Rosenthal denies homosexuality any meaning—not just the negative, damaging sort but any meaningful impact at all on the composing mind. As for Ravel's "ladies," this is corroborated by other witnesses.[13] The American Ravel scholar Arbie Orenstein has summarized his research as follows: "The facts are quite simple: occasional discreet visits to prostitutes were essentially the whole story." He does not admit the long-standing tradition of "speculation" into the discussion.[14]

So we have two interpretive limits on this issue, the rumormongers and the rumor squashers. Some are convinced that homosexuality is the key to Ravel's secrecy; some insist that his secrecy means nothing.[15] It's true there is no "proof" connecting Ravel sexually with other men. This has not stopped speculation, however, because sexuality encompasses more than just the life of the body. Even without any overt evidence of homosexuality, Ravel's portrait brings together many of its cognates: a mama's boy, he was a shy, tasteful bachelor with an eye for interior decoration, a dandy's impeccable facade, and the lingering aura of childhood. These traits place him in a field of connotation that some have understood in terms of gay identity. Before we reach any such conclusion, however, we might want to recalibrate our instruments according to the identity categories in currency at the time. And as with any definitional system, we should leave room for individual improvisation and evasion, in recognition of those who find it useful to slip between the cracks.

QUEER PEERS

We can begin with a survey of the diverse ways a gay identity was experienced in Paris around the turn of the century. I don't intend to jump to conclusions here. Nonetheless, in an area as intimate, vexed, and socially censored as sexual identity, it is unrealistic to base one's interpretation solely on concrete knowledge of sexual activity. It is perfectly valid for other kinds of evidence, including gossip and connotative knowledge, to come into play.[16] By examining the taxonomies and kinds of social interaction current in the demimonde and the sexual subcultures, we will be in a better position to judge whether Ravel could fit a particular profile. We can test the gay hypothesis by comparing Ravel's self-presentation to what we know of his gay contemporaries. At the same time, we can be on the lookout for more specific or more elusive categories of sexual identity. I will focus on members of Ravel's own station, artists and intellectuals.

First, let's consider the relative openness or guardedness of sexual identity. One can come up with a short list of characters famous for wearing their hearts on their sleeve. This would include the bohemian Paul Verlaine (1844–96), who published lusty, explicit gay lyrics and whose stormy entanglement with Rimbaud in the 1870s was the first in a series of affairs with younger men.[17] The lesser-known symbolist poet and journalist Jean Lorrain (1856–1906) was outrageously flamboyant, signing himself Salterella, Mimosa, or Stendhaletta for his reviews. Something of his spirit is preserved in an anecdotal reminiscence of intimate detail:

> This Byzantine Paris . . . was dominated by a tall, odd person, Jean Lorrain, who amused it by his bad form. . . . In each generation some of those men who share women's tastes cannot resist borrowing their finery. . . . Thus, in 1900, such people made Sarah Bernhardt their model: their torsoes became narrow and prominent, they imagined that their voices were "golden," their waistcoats were fashioned from Theodora's purple stole, and the gems of the Princesse Lointaine were mislaid on their fingers. . . . Jean Lorrain records how [the actor Edouard] de Max played Heliogabalus and Nebuchadnezzar and lived in such a fashion that both his appearance and his scandals became a terrible warning to others.[18]

This same dangerous de Max of the theater set was the man who brought out the young Jean Cocteau (1889–1963) to the gay elite of Paris, which included the equally notorious impresario Sergei Diaghilev.[19] All these powerful personalities attracted circles of younger admirers, as much through their notoriety as through their creative abilities.

But of course not every homosexual was gifted with such sangfroid. Many men who freely participated in the gay subculture took pains to relegate this activity to their private lives while resisting the consequences of a publicly gay identity. Marcel Proust (1871–1922) was anxious to maintain an outward pose of heterosexuality. In 1897 he fought a duel with Jean Lorrain over a review of his first book not only because Lorrain criticized it as effete in tone and subject matter but also because the journalist alluded to an affair Proust was having with Lucien Daudet. Proust spoke of the need to defend his reputation against the stigmas of "effeminacy" and "dangerous morals." He alluded proudly to this duel for the rest of life and "let it be known that he stood ready to revert, at the least suggestion that he was anything other than exclusively heterosexual, to the ancient French [male] code of honor."[20] During the scandal of Oscar Wilde's trial in 1895, Jules Huret, a literary critic at *Le Figaro,* suggestively published the names of certain writers—Jean Lorrain, Catulle Mendès, and Marcel Schwob—whom Wilde had sought out on a visit three years before. All three vigorously repudiated the insinuations; the incident led to another duel, this one between Huret and Mendès.[21] The public protestations of Proust and Lorrain were not wildly successful in dispelling the rumors and unofficial knowledge of the men's exploits. Proust must have been aware at some level of the comic aspects of such transparent masquerade, for he made it an important component in his novel *A la recherche du temps perdu.* In Baron de Charlus, Proust created a character fascinating in his eccentricity but ridiculously self-deluded in his attempts to mislead his society fellows as to his sexual inclinations. The figure of Charlus was based on the real-life poet and aesthete Count Robert de Montesquiou (1855–1921), of whom I will have more to say.

Aside from the threat to reputation and personal honor, there were other powerful reasons to dissemble. Much of our knowledge of the sexual subcultures in the first four decades of Ravel's life comes from records of police arrest and the actions of the vice squads.[22] One story of spectacular ambush from 1904 will have to stand for a multitude of demeaning entrapments.

> Ernest Bulton, a young English painter recently settled in Paris, has planned to celebrate a "white wedding" in his studio, 83 Boulevard Montparnasse. He sends invitations to eighteen homosexuals, French and foreign, of very diverse occupations. This includes an Irish newspaper correspondent, an American caricaturist, a library employee, a designer, an opera singer, a valet, an insurance agent, a Dutch merchant dealer, a Zouave, two men of letters (one of whom was the son of composer Emmanuel Chabrier), three men of independent means, and four teenagers—two students, a nurse, and a telegraph boy. [The police prefect receives an anonymous tip about an orgy involving youths and sends a team to the area.]
>
> Bulton soon appears, draped in a white burnous, crowned with a fez, an ample puffy culotte billowing over green Turkish slippers embroidered with gold. While the painter goes up to his studio, two inspectors climb to the top of the building, where they have a clear view through the glass roof. They are stupefied. Not a single easel, canvas, or box of paints, but red and white draperies completely concealing the walls. Rose petals strew the floor. "In the corners of the room, vessels were filled with burning scents, casting tawny glimmers." In the center, a long table covered with a lace cloth and garnished with rare dishes, Oriental pastries, bottles of wine and champagne. What grips the attention of the two policemen above all is an immense bed at the back of the studio, engulfed in tiger skins and studded with boxes of rice powder, multicolored ribbons, and diverse instruments "the nature of which it would be difficult to dwell on."

The guests arrive. Some in evening dress, the Zouave in uniform, others cos-
tumed as a highlander, as a pasha. . . . One is even dressed as a Japanese woman, hair concealed under a black wig pierced with long pins, ears hidden by
enormous chrysanthemums, feet squeezed into wooden pattens.

[The guests kiss and caress one another and expose their bodies.] "The most
eager care was lavished on those two individuals, one of whom was experienc-
ing the extreme debauchery for the first time. They used so much rice powder
that the police inspectors breathed it from far away."[23]

According to the report, the police took no action until the climactic moment,
when "captivated by the example before them, [the guests] gave themselves
over directly to the act on which Sodom of old prided itself." Somehow the
press was alerted, and for the next few days the daily papers ran detailed accounts of the scandal, down to the names of the participants. Two months later
the matter went to court. The father of the "young bride" received one thousand francs in damages; Bulton and seven of his friends received sentences of
five hundred francs in fines and from eight to twelve months in prison.

Homosexuals of the period had to guard against the threat of humiliating
legal reprisals as best they could. Most arrests targeted public sexual activity
and places of business such as brothels and baths. Rarely would the police have
word of a private party. But thanks to that anonymous tipster (evidently a
vendor of goods for the evening) and that glass roof, we have a glimpse into a
hidden society cutting across age, status, and nationality. Bulton and his friends
were devising a social ritual steeped in excess and perhaps wry mockery of
accepted sacraments. Their festivities seem directed toward furthering a sense
of cohesion among the disparate members of their group; passing on hard-
won social and self-knowledge to the younger generation; and providing a safe,
caring (not to say luxurious) setting for the rite of passage to sexual adulthood.
The safety, however, was fragile.

Because of the need for secrecy, some homosexuals found themselves vulnerable to blackmail.[24] The composer Camille Saint-Saëns (1835–1921) was
harassed by his former valet and several men who had been or claimed to have
been involved with him as youths in North Africa. Remarkably he appealed
to the police for help in restraining these men. The correspondence (1893–94,
1909) detailing his troubles was discovered by Jeanine Huas in the Paris police archives.[25] Faced with threats of imprisonment, blackmail, and public
humiliation, many gay men were no doubt even more secretive and self-con-
strained than the individuals mentioned so far. Some must have been reluctant to seek out the company of the like-minded. The police chief F. Carlier,
writing of his experience on the vice squad in the 1860s, described such an

extreme type. "The least imprudence can provoke troublesome comments, set terrible consequences in motion; so they never enter into amorous attachments with each other. Each one in isolation turns exclusively to [male] prostitutes on the sly. In these conditions, one can easily understand that they avoid each other as much as possible, even in the ordinary relations of life, that they rub shoulders in the world while feigning only the most superficial acquaintance."[26] It was widely recognized in artistic circles that a person could live a hidden life. A well-established heterosexual reputation was not always a firm guarantee against gossip. Proust, for instance, believed that Baudelaire had been homosexual; the Goncourt brothers speculated about the sexuality of Gautier, Maupassant, and Barbey d'Aurevilly in their journal.[27]

We can thus establish a range of openness about sexual identity from the flamboyant to the imperfectly camouflaged to the invisible. In attempting to reconstruct the latter end of the spectrum, we may despair of finding solid evidence. But a picture might take shape from the signs and suspicions of concealment, as one might discover a hidden room by tracing the odd dimensions of the rooms around it.

To that end, the next area to consider involves the opportunities available for socializing or rendezvous. Another continuum emerges, encompassing gatherings of the like-minded, mixed-company locales, and individual pursuits. Gilles Barbedette and Michel Carassou have painted a colorful picture of the many gay establishments that flourished in the 1920s: "shady bars, fashionable bars, dance halls, transvestite balls, nightclubs, music-hall promenades." This period is a little later than the time of Ravel, however, who turned forty-five in 1920, and the authors claim that the situation was markedly different in previous years. "A specifically homosexual culture developed during the Mad Decade, and its diversity offers a striking contrast to the uncertain embryos of the 'Underground' of the Belle Epoque." They quote the German sexologist Paul Näcke, writing in 1905:

There are no homosexual restaurants [in Paris], as Berlin has. In the Grand Café, Boulevard de la Madeleine, numerous homosexuals meet, or at any rate they did a few years ago, but completely mixed with other people. Similarly, there are certain other known cafés or restaurants, situated on major boulevards. But as for homosexual restaurants in the Berlin sense, there are none. On the other hand, there are certain steam baths frequented almost exclusively by homosexuals. In the industrial and business quarter in the neighborhood of the Place de la République, there was a bath frequented by young men from fifteen to twenty-two years old. They all sold themselves to homosexuals, right there in the bath. They were young unemployed workers or others eager for supplementary income.[28]

This probably fails to represent the whole picture, however.[29] Judging from George Chauncey's recent reconstruction of gay life in New York around the turn of the century, there is no doubt more to be uncovered regarding the sexual topography of pre-1920s Paris.[30] For instance, William Peniston, researching the Paris police archives from the 1870s, has discovered case files preserving extensive details about the lives and social network of a male working-class couple. This includes mention of a homosexual ball held at "Gaillard's wine bar" (disrupted by the police), and a favorite meeting place, the Bamboulème restaurant. "Intentionally or not, this restaurant was part of the homosexual subculture, and the proprietor, Mme Bamboulème, either ignored the sexual interests of her clientele or openly tolerated and catered to them."[31] The existence of such specialized establishments in the 1870s makes it likely that similar places continued to exist in pockets of society until the explosion after World War I.

Men and women from the upper classes enjoyed a special privilege regarding sexual pursuits; they had "the time and means to conduct their erotic relationships in private."[32] This would have included not only relations à deux but also private gatherings of the elite. The wealthy American expatriate Natalie Barney was the center of a fashionable lesbian circle that served both as an artistic community and as a protected social space for the cultivation of friendships and romantic adventure.[33] Others, such as the count de Montesquiou, were more delicate in their habits, preferring to enjoy gay society from a distance. Before the count met his lover and secretary, Gabriel Yturri (see figure 2.2),

> Yturri had knocked about a good deal and had become familiar with the intrigues of the homosexual world. Montesquiou wished to know everything and to be involved in nothing. Yturri . . . would bring stories of tea-parties (these gentlemen used to drink enormous quantities of tea under pink shades) at the home of John Audley, a friend of Wilde, who lived in a mezzanine in the Avenue Montaigne where a curious mixture of peers and boxers could be met; . . . of the latest conquests of Monsieur de Schlichting, a collector of eighteenth-century works of art who was famous for his white whiskers. But when Count Robert went to the house of this last in order to admire Watteau's "L'Indifférent," the baron hid the gigolos.[34]

Apparently the classes could mix at these parties, as the motley guest list for Ernest Bulton's soirée confirms.[35]

But the gay world was by no means confined to private parties. One of the most important aspects to recognize about gay life in the Belle Époque is the

FIGURE 2.2. Robert de Montesquiou, Jean Louis Forain, and Gabriel Yturri, in a caricature by Sem (date unknown).

permeable nature of its boundaries and its intermixture with the structures of conventional social life. A major part of gay fraternization occurred in mixed-company settings. One such setting was the salon. Salons were semi-private gatherings of the elite, often with an intellectual or artistic focus.[36] This is the social world Proust took for his novelistic canvas. The ambience of a salon depended on its host; certain salons attracted a large number of gay men or lesbians. One of the most famous of these, of course, was at the home of Gertrude Stein and Alice B. Toklas, where the shared interests were literature and painting.[37] A prominent salon dedicated to new music was led by another wealthy lesbian American expatriate, the princesse de Polignac. Her friends and guests included many homosexual notables—Wilde, Proust, Reynaldo Hahn, Ethel Smyth, Poulenc, and Diaghilev—as well as musicians of a more enigmatic sexual character, including Nadia Boulanger, Manuel de Falla, and Ravel.[38] The nature of the socializing surely varied with each salon, but friendships and matches were made. Consider the baroness "Elsie" Deslandes, who received her guests "lying on a precious carpet beneath her portrait by Burne-Jones, in the company of a bronze toad which she fed each evening with her jewels." Her salon in the 1880s, frequented by Lorrain, Montesquiou, and Wilde, was a center for the aesthetic movement in Paris and a lively social scene as well. "Baroness Deslandes hovered about, twittered, and without seeming to have anything to do with the matter, wafted their boy-friends in the direction of her habitués."[39]

The intermingling of hetero- and homosexual patrons also occurred in many eating and drinking establishments, as Dr. Näcke found, as well as at performance spots such as theater promenades, outdoor concerts, and café concerts. Daniel Guérin recalls "tiny clubs [on the rue de Lappe] where there were accordionists with a little orchestra on a balcony; one drank mint or currant lemonade. . . . there was dancing between boys, between girls, between men and women." He remembers "Jean Cocteau, his musician friends and his darlings [mignons]" spending evenings at Le Boeuf sur le Toit, a club that was also a favorite spot for Ravel in the 1920s. Guérin emphasizes that his youthful sexual experiences in Paris occurred "in surroundings which were not closed-off like homosexual ghettos."[40]

The sexual underground was another milieu where customers and tastes commingled. The actor Jean Weber recalls the Graff, a hot spot in the 1920s: "Homosexuals were lost in the crowd. First there were female prostitutes, then a little farther the male prostitutes, then followed the brasserie itself, and finally the diners at their tables. It wasn't a homosexual club, but rather a mix [brassage]. The whole panoply of Paris was there!"[41] There are a few references to all-male brothels,[42] and there were specific public areas known for male prostitution, notably the city's street urinals. But men who haunted these places were the most vulnerable to arrest and blackmail.[43] To protect against such threats and to maintain a clandestine setting for homosexual encounters, underground entrepreneurs developed a repertoire of ingenious ruses and covers by which male partners were hidden among the female.

One such ruse recorded by Carlier was worked out by pederasts in garrison towns. The proprietors of certain establishments acted as go-betweens for soldiers in the ground-floor café and their male partners, who would await them in furnished rooms upstairs. In case of military investigation, the soldier would remove himself to the room of one of the female prostitutes lodging there for just such a purpose. In another recorded arrangement, older madams would employ young men living in the neighborhood, who came to the premises only when summoned. Their visit might be under the pretext of an errand, or they might be disguised as women. In one case the signs in a shop window referred not to the items displayed there but to the urchins lingering on the street outside.[44] A rendezvous might be effected at a female brothel, two men choosing partners, engaging a room for a foursome, and then sending the women away.[45] Such an assignation occurs in Proust's novel at a certain luxurious house of prostitution: "Morel, during this time, was in fact with the Prince de Guermantes; he had, for form's sake, pretended to go into the wrong room by mistake, and had entered one in which there were two women, who had made haste to leave the two gentlemen undisturbed."[46]

By now it should be obvious that, in the absence of intimate records, there is no telltale public pattern of behavior by which we might recognize a man of this period as homosexual, but neither is it a simple matter to rule out such an identification. A homosexual who tended toward personal secrecy, isolation, and camouflaged sexual encounters would have presented a front very similar to Ravel's. The lack of any connection to the gay subculture could be a protective strategy. Visits to ladies of the night might not be what they seem. Indeed, instead of furnishing the answer to Ravel's secret, such visits pose another nagging question. For someone who was so guarded about his sexual and affective life, why didn't he keep his relations with prostitutes a secret as well? He did not trouble to hide this habit from his friends; in the account given by Rosenthal, he appears perfectly open and casual. Could it be that it had nothing to do with the real reasons for his secrecy—or was he engaging in misdirection to thwart speculation? Whatever the answer may be, we have established in a negative way that Ravel's profile is not inconsistent with a secret homosexual identity. But why homosexual? Given the success of his defenses, how can we know what he was guarding? For a more positive identification, we need to turn our attention to the details of the image he presented to the world.

Before taking up this question, however, one topic remains to be considered in this survey of received homosexual knowledge: the topic of nomenclature. I have been using the medical term *homosexual* as a neutral descriptor, but the usage at the time was by no means so clear-cut. A full investigation into period designations would uncover a veritable zoo of terms. This variety is due partly to the terminology's diverse purposes and communities of origin and partly to the fact that the concept was still up for grabs. Victoria Thompson has claimed that the fluid representation of gender and sexuality during the July Monarchy (1830–48) gave way to increasingly rigid categories of definition in the Second Empire (1852–70)—"pederast or *antiphysique* [unnatural] (for men), tribade or lesbian (for women)"—paving the way for the medicalized and criminalized invert or homosexual of the late nineteenth century.[47] While these years certainly saw an increased tendency to conceptualize sexuality in terms of identity types, the linguistic situation by 1900 was not nearly as stable as Thompson and others have implied. The medical terms were freshly minted, and the doctors were involved in heated squabbles over the new tools and methods of classification. Neologisms such as *invert, homosexual,* and *unisexual* took their place alongside the timeworn (but still useful) *pervert, pederast,* and *sodomite.*[48] Different descriptors were wielded to theorize differences in gender identification (*feminiform invert*), sexual aim (*passive invert*), age of object choice (*pederast*), innate versus acquired tendencies (*born invert*), and so on. Same-sex activity was not reduced to a single type but represented by multiple identity types in the medical literature. Far from trying to disentangle the arguments, I want to emphasize that there was no consensus. Given the monolithic influence sometimes accorded to the medical establishment by historians of sexuality, it's refreshing to hear of individual doctors at odds in their annals and correspondence.

While some terms from medical theory did trickle down to general use, the man on the street found other frameworks for identifying himself. Certain pockets of the subculture developed their own slang. The police records have preserved some of the colorful character designations associated with street hustler culture: *amateurs, honteuses* (bashful girls), *petits jésus.*[49] A rare memoir from the 1860s written by a "male courtesan" supplies a social stratification of the current argot: "These strange personalities the common people in their vulgar language have baptized with the name of *Tantes* [aunts]; well-mannered men call them *Petits* [little ones], or *Filles* [girls]; ladies [*filles*] of pleasure in friendly rapport with them and to distinguish them from their own sex and profession name them *Tapettes* [tongues, chatterboxes]; I myself have decorated them with the more expressive titles of *Complaisants* [obliging ones], and *Mignons* [dainty ones, darlings]."[50]

Numerous authors of the time exploited the various perversions as thematic material; a few courageous writers undertook apologias. André Gide's essay *Corydon* (1911) constitutes a justification of homosexuality in which pederasty, defined as the love of young boys, receives the most attention and empathy.[51] *Sodom and Gomorrah* (1921), the fourth volume of Proust's novel, begins with a lengthy disquisition on the characteristics of the "cursed race" of inverts. His classification of their subvarieties includes a differentiation according to socializing habits most useful in substantiating my own survey. He speaks of the various groups as distinct subtypes within the general identity type of inverts, who live, as a whole, "at least to a great extent, in an affectionate and perilous intimacy with the men of the other race. . . . But certain among them, more practical, busier men . . . [,] have formed two societies of which the second is composed exclusively of persons similar to themselves" (23–24). Such separatist groups, which he wryly compares to "professional organizations," are further subdivided into the discreet and the daring. He offers this description:

> No one in the café where they have their table knows what the gathering is, whether it is that of an angling club, of an editorial staff, or of the "Sons of the Indre," so correct is their attire, so cold and reserved their manner, so modestly do they refrain from any but the most covert glance at the young men of fashion. . . . But these groups are at various stages of evolution; and, just as the "Union of the Left" differs from the "Socialist Federation" or some Mendelssohnian musical club from the Schola Cantorum, on certain evenings, at another table, there are extremists who allow a bracelet to slip down from beneath a cuff, or sometimes a necklace to gleam in the gap of a collar, who by their persistent stares, their cooings, their laughter, their mutual caresses, oblige a band of students to depart in hot haste (25–26).

Finally, there is the "solitary class." "Supposing their vice to be more exceptional than it is, they have retired into solitude from the day on which they discovered it, after having carried it within themselves for a long time without knowing it. . . . they go away to live in the country, shunning the society of their own kind . . . from horror of the monstrosity or fear of the temptation" (32–33).

The gay literary lions themselves were no closer to a consensus on the definition and status of their sexual identity; Gide issued the first public edition of *Corydon* (1924) in part as a challenge to Proust's published views on homosexuality.[52] The terms of identity were still in flux in the early twentieth century, and the medical experts, gay intellectuals, and men on the street all had a hand in forging the concepts bequeathed to us. Each "strange personality" had to find his own way among the available concepts for self-understanding or else make some up to fit. The slang lexicon shows improvisatory minds at work, and Proust's designations of "professional," "extremist," and "solitary" have a wonderfully unassuming, ad hoc quality about them. For some, "the lack of a current, widely accepted definition of a homosexual identity was . . . seen . . . as the space of a considerable liberty" for avoiding stigma or avoiding commitment to a particular sexuality.[53] For others, the lack of ready models was a source of anxiety, a sense of misplacement with its own agonized leitmotif: "Why am I different?"

This is the burden of Gide's schoolboy cry to his mother: "I'm not like other people . . . not like other people!"[54] It appears as well in the aforementioned autobiography of the male courtesan known as La Comtesse: "I have often been told that, morally, I was not made like other men; I alone can add that I differ from them corporally even more, and that this *difference* was the pain, the gnawing canker of all my moments of joy, the poison corrupting my life from the age of manly awareness. This potent pain is the true cause of the attraction I found in veiling my sex under the appearance of a woman's."[55] Each had to find his own path toward self-recognition. La Comtesse resolved her sense of difference by crossing gender identities and achieving celebrity as a fashionable kept woman. Gide eventually found resolution by crossing generational and racial boundaries in his sexual life, but he came to this awareness only with the aid of a more worldly mentor, namely, Oscar Wilde.[56] It becomes clear that the unadorned, undifferentiated concept "homosexual" is insufficient to describe the variables and personal trajectories that go into the experience of a particular sexual identity. For instance, if we read Thomas Mann's *Death in Venice* (1912) as a narrative of self-recognition, it's not enough to speak of homosexuality. Aschenbach, we find, is a slow learner severely hindered by a scarcity of unconventional sexual models, a puritan offended by dandified affectation, a classicist, a boy lover, a solitary.

SOLO

Ravel's public identity clearly registered a sense of personal difference. This at least was no secret. As he confided to his friend Mme Alfredo Casella: "Artists are not made for marriage. We are rarely normal, and our lives are even less so."[57] Ravel's professions of nonconformity cluster around the issue of marriage. He recognized his temperamental unfitness for such a life. "'They're a true pair,' he used to say admiringly [about his friends the Delages], 'they're never apart for a moment. If I had a wife she would have to be like that with me . . .' Then, after a few seconds' thought, he added confidentially, '. . . but I'd never stand it!'"[58] However, he often articulated this sense of his own character in terms of moral principles. When Marguerite Long said to him: "Maurice, you ought to marry. Nobody understands and loves children as you do.

Get rid of your hermit life and have a real home," Ravel replied: "Love never rises above the licentious."[59] In fact, the previously quoted passage about the abnormality of the artist begins: "Morality . . . this is what I practice, and what I am determined to continue."[60]

There were other French intellectuals for whom artistic and moral integrity were dependent on a determined bachelorhood—Flaubert, for instance: "When will I get married? you ask me. . . . Never, I hope. . . . The enormous public contact I have come up against for fourteen months makes me retreat more and more into my shell. . . . As for my moral disposition, I will keep the same one until the new order. . . . I've found my footing, my center of gravity. . . . I'm resigned to live as I have lived, alone, with my crowd of great men who take the place of a circle for me, with my bear-like hide, being a bear myself."[61] Several factors are involved in such a stance: the general turn from public life to the private sphere,[62] a repudiation of bourgeois values of reproduction and domestication, and of course, matters of personal orientation.

For Ravel, the antibourgeois stance took on a more specific form: dandyism. Ravel's dandyism is well documented, not only the delight in the precisions and caprices of fashion, the coiffures, ties, and audacious color schemes, but also the attitude of disdain for worldly pursuits (see figures 2.3, 2.4, and 2.5). "The Ravel we knew," says Roland-Manuel, "corresponded in almost every detail with Baudelaire's definition of the dandy: an elegant coldness, discreet refinement in dress, a horror of triviality, a refusal to grant a government the right to decorate one."[63] Baudelaire and, earlier, Jules Barbey d'Aurevilly had hailed dandyism, reinterpreting the imported fashion tradition as a spiritual attitude of detachment from the values and pressures of bourgeois society. In Barbey's view, the dandy became a kind of artist-priest, "a man who carries in himself something superior to the visible world."[64]

At this time dandyism was by no means generally taken to compromise one's masculinity; it was a semantically diffuse but acceptable social role. However, the hint of ambivalence as to gender or sexual identity seems in varying degrees to have attended the dandy's exaggerated elegance. In late eighteenth-century Paris, the pederasty patrols recognized offenders by their "obstinacy in dressing in an indecent manner"—that is, with an elegance above their station.[65] The *complaisants* of the nineteenth century ("*gantés, frisés, parfumés et fardés* [gloved, coiffed, perfumed, and made up]") expressed gender transitivity partly through refinement of dress.[66] And the Goncourt journal brands Barbey's daring ensemble for one evening a "ridiculous, homosexual outfit," as if the clothes themselves could confer or parody a particular sexual identity.[67] Yet Barbey was not a laughingstock; his writings subtly capitalized on the element of sexual

FIGURE 2.3. Ravel as a student, about 1898 (Bibliothèque Nationale de France, Paris).

FIGURE 2.4. Competitors for the Grand Prix de Rome, 1901. From r. to l.: Maurice Ravel, Albert Bertelin, André Caplet, attendant, Aymé Kunc, Gabriel Dupont, attendant (Lebrecht Collection, London). In contrast to the more or less bohemian style of the other composers, Ravel's dandyism is evident in the impeccable trim of handkerchief and shirtsleeves and the bold details of boater, high collar, white shoes and dynamic socks.

FIGURE 2.5. Portrait by Ouvré, 1909 (Bibliothèque Nationale de France, Paris).

ambivalence by glamorizing androgyny and a resistance to (hetero)sexual involvement.[68] As for Ravel, none of the personal recollections of his dandyism
treat it as suspect—save one, perhaps: Alma Mahler's isolated snapshot from
1920 of Ravel coming to breakfast made up, perfumed, and wearing colorful
satin robes. She treats it as an ironic attraction to "kitsch," a "highly perverted
mask" affected by some of the cultivated musicians of the day.[69] All this suggests the incoherence of the relations between dandyism, personal style, and
underlying gender and sexual conventions.

There is an interpretation that seeks to make sense of the confusing and
contradictory reception of dandyism in correspondence with the changing
paradigms of sexual identity. Alan Sinfield has traced the reputation of the
concept of "effeminacy" and related modes of personal comportment. He
argues that until the highly publicized scandal of the Oscar Wilde trials in 1895,
this constellation of terms (including "insouciance, decadence and aestheticism") did not signify homosexuality in any clear way; after the trials, however, it became increasingly harder to separate them from homosexual signification.[70] This new coalescence seems to be borne out within French culture
by Jean Weber's recollections of the climate in the late 1920s. "The more a man
was groomed, bejeweled, refined, the more he might be thought to be 'that way'
[plus il donnait à 'penser que']. Masculine elegance was extremely equivocal.
I've had the chance to meet men who were so arched, so corseted, so affected,
that they made one think of little Marquis de Molière! So that between an effeminate homosexual and a perfumed ladies' man, there was a very slender
distance. And since these men were very cultivated, they frequented all places
with the same facility."[71] This testimony is still definitionally incoherent: is the
point that elegance "meant" homosexuality or that it established nothing?
Nonetheless, it provides evidence of one paradigm's overtaking another; the
older, aristocratic comportment, which bore no significant connection to sexual behavior, giving way to a new code whereby such comportment translated into, or "betrayed," a suspect sexual identity.

The situation during Ravel's lifetime was indeterminate enough for men
to use dandyism as a cover for unconventional sexual pursuits. Significantly
(and confusingly), this was as true for men who knew exactly what they wanted
and weren't afraid to mix in the subculture (Wilde, the young Cocteau) as it
was for men who didn't quite know what they wanted or were reluctant to
commit to a particular identity (Montesquiou, the novelist J.-K. Huysmans,
and the young Gide).[72] Dandyism stood for a devotion to beauty and sensation, a glorification of artifice and refinement for its own sake, and a detachment from conventional values, all of which could be enjoyed in the compa-

ny of like-minded young male companions. It is to this aristocratic model Ravel was referring when he claimed: "I am a fellow in the style of Ludwig II of Bavaria, but less mad."[73] As for Ludwig's homosexual inclinations, did Ravel know of them? The scattered field of reference evoked by the figure of the dandy leaves us unsure whether a point is being made.

Nor are we much the wiser regarding the young Ravel's path toward self-recognition. There is in fact one intimate document surviving from Ravel's formative years that might shed some light on the situation, if indirectly. This is the diary of his schoolmate Ricardo Viñes, partially published in a French translation in 1980.[74] Viñes, another bachelor-artist, would become a leading interpreter of modern French piano music, giving first performances of many of the works of Ravel and Debussy (see figure 2.6). The young Ricardo and "Mauricio" met in 1888 when they were both thirteen. Their friendship centered on music and literature. By the time they were seventeen, Ricardo wrote of spending afternoons at Ravel's: "We didn't go out all day and we still enjoyed ourselves, almost all the time at the piano, trying out new chords, playing the ideas we had, Maurice and I, etc." They begin to discuss and exchange favorite books, beginning with Poe and Baudelaire, followed a few years later by Rimbaud, de Montesquiou, and Huysmans. In 1896 (when they were twenty-one), Viñes let Ravel borrow a copy of Bertrand's *Gaspard de la Nuit;* the following year Ravel lent him Barbey d'Aurevilly's essays on *dandysme.*[75] It is evident that the two young men were helping each other create their adult identities, through a sophistication of taste, through musical experimentation and the shared experience of modern literature, and through the fashionable stances of decadence and aestheticism.

Viñes records a memorable instance in 1896 when the facade crumpled. At a performance of Wagner's Prelude to *Tristan,* he realized that his friend,

> who appears so cold and cynical, Ravel the super-eccentric decadent, was trembling convulsively and crying like a child. . . . Until now, in spite of the high opinion I had of Ravel's intellectual powers, I thought, because he is so completely secretive about the least details of his existence, that there was perhaps a touch of parti pris and chic in his opinions and literary tastes. But since this afternoon I see that this fellow was born with inclinations, tastes and opinions and that when he expresses them he does so not to put on airs and follow fashion but because he really feels that way; and I take this opportunity of declaring that Ravel is one of the most unlucky and misunderstood people of all because, in the eyes of the crowd, he passes for a failure, whereas in reality he is someone of superior intellect and artistic gifts, at odds with his surroundings and worthy of the greatest success in the future.[76]

Figure 2.6. Ricardo Viñes (left) and Ravel, 1905 (Lebrecht Collection, London).

One senses the intense admiration between the two friends, their intellectual and moral affinity, but also the barricades of privacy Ravel has erected, even at twenty-one.

In 1897, the year the two men read Barbey, Viñes described an ongoing dispute with his family over his refusal to curry favor for the sake of his career. "I argued again with mom and Pepe, . . . [and] they told me that no one will ever get to hear of me. I couldn't care less; anything's better than being a kiss-ass, a ragpicker, a miser; I have my ideal and no one can make me depart from it. . . . Never in my life would I accept a decoration. They told me that with my character, I'll die of hunger; I replied that I didn't care; indeed, why live when you're different from everyone else?"[77] Viñes's statement of artistic integrity perfectly exemplifies a dandy's scorn for material values, yet it resonates into wider personal spaces of difference. The editor of his diary speaks of the "moral solitude" in which Viñes found himself, and such a concept is beautifully suited to Ravel.

This is the character recalled by all his friends. According to Marguerite Long, his habit of dandyism "helped Ravel to create an appearance and to carry the mask he ever used to thwart all invasion of his privacy. . . . One thought one knew him, and then—all of a sudden—by some response, or silence, or unexpected decision he would disconcert one, to escape and retreat into his dungeon."[78] Manuel de Falla, another bachelor-composer whom Viñes introduced to Ravel, shared this profound impression: "The good and quiet soul of Ravel broke out only in . . . circumstances [of special distress], never in his music, forged in some inner world that was a refuge against an intrusive reality. . . . I can see his extremely modest study, and feel how it contrasted with the precious quality of music that Ravel revealed to us on an old piano as modest as the whole room."[79] As this passage implies, Ravel's music was intimately shaped by his protective strategies. An underlying stance of detachment enabled him to create exquisite, impeccable surfaces and inscrutable, evasive aesthetic spaces. This tantalizing insight demands further exploration. What is pertinent here is the recurrent image of escape: escaping into emotional solitude, retreating to his solitary life outside Paris, finding refuge in his music.

By fiercely guarding his privacy, Ravel was able in the end to escape the ascription of a particular sexual identity. Even to his friends and close acquaintances he remained to some degree an emotional and sexual enigma.[80] This elusiveness is conveyed in personal interviews conducted for a documentary film about Ravel made in the late 1980s. The topic of his love life is broached quite frankly by André and Lucienne Asselin.

André: The intimate life—the love life if you like—of Maurice Ravel remains an absolute mystery. He was never known to have had a mistress. He never married. What was surprising was his fascination with childhood. He loved children. In his life, he had loyal friends, many of them. But as for his love life—zero! Nothing was ever known about it.

Lucienne: Nor was there ever any talk about a male lover.

André: No, never, never, never.

This is followed by testimony from the pianist Gaby Casadesus: "We can suppose all sorts of things, but there wasn't anyone who could be considered the love of his life, someone he really shared his life with. No, not at all. He did not want to reveal his feelings. He was a man that kept his feelings hidden and didn't like to share them."[81]

Ravel defined for himself a social persona according to the roles of bachelor-artist, dandy, solitary, and enigma. Although to some extent these roles have traditionally shared discursive space with a vulnerable mode of homosexuality, in themselves they handily avoid the question of sex. Ravel in fact was careful to create his personal identity in aesthetic terms rather than interpersonal ones. His dandyism took the form of a modernist empty sign—obscure, tantalizing, all probing deflected by the burnished surface. If his evasive maneuvers never wholly forestalled speculation, that is because the aesthetic facade has fit so many gay men like a glove. But perhaps it is also because gossips, historians, and even admirers find it hard to believe that Ravel—or anyone else—could have managed to keep his privacy inviolate or to escape the alternatives dictated by his society and his time.

NOTES

1. Roger Nichols, ed., *Ravel Remembered* (New York: Norton, 1988), 19, 25, 32, 56, 161, 189.

2. Roland-Manuel, *Maurice Ravel*, trans. Cynthia Jolly (London: Dobson, 1947; New York: Dover, 1972), 128–29 (French original, *A la gloire de Ravel* [Paris: Nouvelle Revue Critique, 1938]).

3. Ibid., 11.

4. Marguerite Long, *At the Piano with Ravel*, ed. Pierre Laumonier, trans. Olive Senior-Ellis (London: Dent, 1973), 117 (French original, *Au piano avec Ravel* [Paris: Julliard, 1971]).

5. Richard Sennett, *The Fall of Public Man* (New York: Knopf, 1976); D. A. Miller, *The Novel and the Police* (Berkeley: University of California Press, 1988); James Eli Adams, *Dandies and Desert Saints: Styles of Victorian Masculinity* (Ithaca, N.Y.: Cornell Uni-

versity Press, 1995), 13; George Chauncey, *Gay New York: Gender, Urban Culture, and the Making of the Gay Male World, 1890–1940* (New York: Basic Books, 1994), 111.

6. Paul Ricoeur, *Freud and Philosophy: An Essay on Interpretation*, trans. Denis Savage (New Haven, Conn.: Yale University Press, 1970); he is discussing Marx, Nietzsche, and Freud, and thus his concept is grounded in a particular historical period. Allon White discusses the same interpretive mode under the Althusserian term "symptomatic reading" (White, *The Uses of Obscurity: The Fiction of Early Modernism* [London: Routledge and Kegan Paul, 1981], 4–5). Eve Kosofsky Sedgwick theorizes resistance against a too widespread use of a hermeneutic of suspicion in "Paranoid Reading and Reparative Reading: or, You're So Paranoid, You Probably Think This Introduction Is about You," in *Novel Gazing: Queer Readings in Fiction*, ed. Sedgwick (Durham, N.C.: Duke University Press, 1997), 1–37.

7. G. W. Hopkins, "Maurice Ravel," *New Grove Dictionary of Music and Musicians*, 20 vols., ed. Stanley Sadie (1980), 15:613–14.

8. Gilles Barbedette and Michel Carassou, *Paris Gay 1925* (Paris: Presses de la Renaissance, 1981), 51. This and all other translations are my own unless otherwise noted.

9. Michel Faure, *Musique et société du Second Empire aux années vingt* (Music and society from the Second Empire to the 1920s) (1985), quoted in Marcel Marnat, *Maurice Ravel* (Paris: Fayard, 1986), 458–59. This diagnosis is offensive in its pathologization of both homosexuality and maternal bonds. I include it as an example of those commentators who claim to know the answer to Ravel's sexual riddle.

10. Gerald Larner, *Maurice Ravel* (London: Phaidon, 1996), 220. Benjamin Ivry's book *Maurice Ravel: A Life* (New York: Welcome Rain, 2000), which portrays the composer as a "very secretive gay man" (4), is untrustworthy on points of translation and documentation.

11. Francis Poulenc, *My Friends and Myself*, conversations assembled by Stéphane Audel, trans. James Harding (London: Dobson, 1978), 131 (French original, *Moi et mes amis* [Paris: La Palatine, 1963]). Poulenc was not publicly gay, and as this was part of a radio broadcast, perhaps he didn't consider it a comfortable forum for speculation.

12. From an interview with Rémy Stricker broadcast on "France Culture," April 1985, quoted in Marnat, *Ravel*, 464–65; and in Nichols, *Ravel Remembered*, 36. Rosenthal's reliability as a witness has been questioned; see Larner, *Ravel*, 230.

13. Long, *At the Piano*, 119, 121; Désiré-Emile Inghelbrecht, in H. H. Stuckenschmidt, *Maurice Ravel: Variationen über Person und Werk* (Ravel: variations on the man and his work) (Frankfurt: Suhrkamp, 1966), 138.

14. Personal communication, 3 Oct. 1995; Arbie Orenstein, ed., *A Ravel Reader: Correspondence, Articles, Interviews* (New York: Columbia University Press, 1990), 16–17.

15. Marcel Marnat, in his vast, unwieldy biography, has it both ways: after including an almost comprehensive survey of the speculation surrounding Ravel's sexuality, he dismisses all hypotheses as irrelevant "if one simply admits that he hadn't made of his sexuality or even his affective life the axis of his existence" (Marnat, *Ravel*, 458–62; quotation, 462).

16. In fact, connotative knowledge, with its potential for evasion and deniability, is often a structural corollary of taboo sexuality.

17. Gretchen Schultz, "Paul Verlaine," in *The Gay and Lesbian Literary Heritage: A Reader's Companion to the Writers and Their Works, from Antiquity to the Present,* ed. Claude J. Summers (New York: Henry Holt, 1995), 710–13.

18. Philippe Jullian, *Prince of Aesthetes: Count Robert de Montesquiou, 1855–1921,* trans. John Haylock and Francis King (New York: Viking, 1968), 102. "Theodora" and so on were dramatic roles of Bernhardt's.

19. "'Your son knows de Max; he's a goner!' said Cocteau, mimicking the warning given by friends to his mother." See Arthur King Peters, *Jean Cocteau and His World: An Illustrated Biography* (New York: Vendome, 1986), 33; Charley Shively, "Jean Cocteau," in *Gay and Lesbian Literary Heritage,* ed. Summers, 169–71.

20. J. E. Rivers, *Proust and the Art of Love: The Aesthetics of Sexuality in the Life, Times, and Art of Marcel Proust* (New York: Columbia University Press, 1980), 32–38.

21. Robert A. Nye, *Masculinity and Male Codes of Honor in Modern France* (New York: Oxford University Press, 1993), 123.

22. F. Carlier, *Études de pathologie sociale: Les Deux prostitutions* (Studies in social pathology: the two prostitutions) (Paris: Fayard, 1880); Jeanine Huas, *L'Homosexualité au temps de Proust* (Homosexuality in Proust's day) (Dinard: Danclau, 1992).

23. Huas, *Homosexualité,* 20–22 (quotations are from *Le Matin,* 21 March 1904; *L'Eclair,* same week). A cartoon in *Le Journal* provides a touch of urbane sophistication while mocking the voyeuristic method of the police. Two officers are depicted in conversation, one leering through the glass roof: "All right, we've seen enough. We just have to arrest them." "What's the hurry, boss? No one seems to be in any distress."

24. "It is especially in the matter of pederasty that [blackmail] takes on the most odious nature and acquires worrisome proportions" (Carlier, *Deux prostitutions,* 235).

25. Huas, *Homosexualité,* 154–69.

26. Carlier, *Deux prostitutions,* 316.

27. Rivers, *Proust,* 275; Gretchen Schultz, "French Literature: Nineteenth Century," in *Gay and Lesbian Literary Heritage,* ed. Summers, 297.

28. Barbedette and Carassou, *Paris Gay 1925,* 15 (quoting Paul Näcke, "Le Monde homosexuel de Paris," *Archives d'anthropologie criminelle* 20 [1905]).

29. Barbedette and Carassou's research focused on the 1920s, not the earlier period. Näcke himself was a German doctor, not a French homosexual; his knowledge of the underground was secondhand. See Vernon A. Rosario II, "Pointy Penises, Fashion Crimes, and Hysterical Mollies: The Pederasts' Inversions," in *Homosexuality in Modern France,* ed. Jeffrey Merrick and Bryant T. Ragan Jr. (New York: Oxford University Press, 1996), 146–76. Huas, in her discussion of meeting places, accepts Näcke's statement uncritically (Huas, *Homosexualité,* 24).

30. Chauncey reports that in general, the gay subcultures in Berlin and Paris at the time were more highly developed than that in New York (*Gay New York,* 12, 144).

31. William A. Peniston, "Love and Death in Gay Paris: Homosexuality and Crimi-

nality in the 1870s," in *Homosexuality in Modern France,* ed. Merrick and Ragan, 128–45; see 136. The couple's circle of friends and acquaintances, while mostly working class, included some upper-class men as well. See also Francesca Canadé Sautman's article "Invisible Women: Lesbian Working-Class Culture in France, 1880–1930," from the same collection, 177–201.

32. Nye, *Masculinity,* 107.

33. See Shari Benstock, *Women of the Left Bank: Paris, 1900–1940* (Austin: University of Texas Press, 1986); idem, "Paris Lesbianism and the Politics of Reaction, 1900–1940," in *Hidden from History: Reclaiming the Gay and Lesbian Past,* ed. Martin Duberman, Martha Vicinus, and George Chauncey Jr. (New York: Meridian, 1989), 332–46; W. G. Rogers, *Ladies Bountiful* (New York: Harcourt, Brace and World, 1968), 35–60; Catherine van Casselaer, *Lot's Wife: Lesbian Paris, 1890–1914* (Liverpool: Janus, 1986).

34. Jullian, *Prince of Aesthetes,* 114.

35. For further references to private gatherings, see Huas, *Homosexualité,* 25; and, for a memoir of the subculture in the 1860s, Pierre Hahn, ed., *Nos ancêtres les pervers: La vie des homosexuels sous le Second Empire* (Our ancestors, the perverts: homosexual life in the Second Empire) (Paris: Olivier Orban, 1979), 308–9.

36. For a discussion of the artistic salon in relation to the public-private axis, see Marcia J. Citron, *Gender and the Musical Canon* (Cambridge: Cambridge University Press, 1993), 100–108.

37. For a discussion of the different attitudes toward openness among Parisian lesbians, see "Paris-Lesbos," in Benstock, *Women of the Left Bank,* 173–77. Although their salon had a healthy homosexual population, "Stein and Toklas appear to have [been unwilling] to participate in a larger lesbian culture or in a more public display of their attraction to women" (175).

38. Elizabeth Wood, "Sapphonics," in *Queering the Pitch: The New Gay and Lesbian Musicology,* ed. Philip Brett, Elizabeth Wood, and Gary C. Thomas (London: Routledge, 1994), 47.

39. Jullian, *Prince of Aesthetes,* 67, 104.

40. Huas, *Homosexualité,* 24, 102; Guérin, quoted in Barbedette and Carassou, *Paris Gay 1925,* 48, 54, 44. See also Hahn, *Nos ancêtres les pervers,* 306–7.

41. Barbedette and Carassou, *Paris Gay 1925,* 68.

42. A. R. H. Copley, *Sexual Moralities in France, 1780–1980: New Ideas on the Family, Divorce, and Homosexuality* (London: Routledge, 1989), 102; Huas, *Homosexualité,* 29; Rivers, *Proust,* 75; Barbedette and Carassou, *Paris Gay 1925,* 49.

43. Carlier, *Deux prostitutions;* Copley, *Sexual Moralities,* 102–103.

44. Carlier, *Deux prostitutions,* 416–17, 426–27.

45. Huas, *Homosexualité,* 28.

46. Marcel Proust, *In Search of Lost Time,* 6 vols., trans. C. K. Scott Moncrieff and Terence Kilmartin, rev. D. J. Enright (New York: Modern Library, 1993), 4:653. Further references will be given parenthetically in the text.

47. Victoria Thompson, "Creating Boundaries: Homosexuality and the Changing

Social Order in France, 1830–1870," in *Homosexuality in Modern France,* ed. Merrick and Ragan, 102–27; see 104.

48. Rosario, "Pointy Penises."

49. Copley, *Sexual Moralities,* 103.

50. Hahn, *Nos ancêtres les pervers,* 288.

51. Copley, *Sexual Moralities,* 173–75.

52. Ibid., 170.

53. Adrian Rifkin, *Street Noises: Parisian Pleasure, 1900–40* (Manchester, U.K.: Manchester University Press, 1993), 142.

54. André Gide, *If It Die . . .* , trans. Dorothy Bussy (London: Secker and Warburg, 1951), 116–17.

55. Hahn, *Nos ancêtres les pervers,* 285.

56. Copley, *Sexual Moralities,* 161–62.

57. Letter of 19 January 1919, in Orenstein, *Ravel Reader,* 185.

58. Hélène Jourdan-Morhange, quoted in Nichols, *Ravel Remembered,* 148; see also 35.

59. Long, *At the Piano,* 121.

60. This doesn't mean he couldn't joke about it, as when he portrayed his taste in decoration as that of "a provincial old maid" (in Ivry, *Maurice Ravel,* 105) or when he referred to his bachelor friend Ricardo Viñes as a "neuter" (Ravel, *Lettres à Roland Manuel et à sa famille* [Letters to Roland Manuel and to his family], ed. Jean Roy [Quimper: Calligrammes, 1986], 106; Ivry, *Maurice Ravel,* 99).

61. Flaubert, letter to his mother, 15 Dec. 1850, quoted in Jean Borie, *Huysmans: Le Diable, le célibataire et Dieu* (Huysmans: the devil, the bachelor, and God) (Paris: Bernard Grasset, 1991), 31.

62. A passage in the Goncourts' journal speculates on the contrast between the busy social involvement of the eighteenth-century man of letters and the withdrawn "*ourserie*" (bearishness) of their contemporaries: "The man of letters is no longer a part of society, he no longer rules it, he no longer even enters it" (entry for 11 May 1859, in Borie, *Huysmans,* 30).

63. In Nichols, *Ravel Remembered,* 143–44.

64. From *Du dandysme* (1845), in Ellen Moers, *The Dandy: Brummell to Beerbohm* (London: Secker and Warburg, 1960), 265.

65. Michael Rey, "Parisian Homosexuals Create a Lifestyle, 1700–1750: The Police Archives," in *'Tis Nature's Fault: Unauthorized Sexuality during the Enlightenment,* ed. Robert Purks Maccubbin (Cambridge: Cambridge University Press, 1987), 189.

66. Hahn, *Nos ancêtres les pervers,* 307.

67. Edmond and Jules de Goncourt, *Pages from the Goncourt Journal,* ed. Robert Baldick (New York: Penguin Books, 1984), 306 (entry for 12 May 1885).

68. Moers, *The Dandy,* 262–65.

69. She mentions Milhaud and Poulenc; see Alma Mahler-Werfel, *Mein Leben* (My life) (Frankfurt: Fischer, 1963), 120–21.

70. Alan Sinfield, *The Wilde Century: Effeminacy, Oscar Wilde, and the Queer Moment* (New York: Columbia University Press, 1994), 3.

71. Barbedette and Carassou, *Paris Gay 1925*, 65.

72. On Huysmans's ambivalent sex life, see Rosario, "Pointy Penises," 165; Clarence McClanahan, "Joris-Karl Huysmans," *Gay and Lesbian Literary Heritage*, ed. Summers, 380–81.

73. Letter to Geneviève Marnold, 24 August 1921, in Marnat, *Maurice Ravel*, 500.

74. Ricardo Viñes, "Le Journal inédit de Ricardo Viñes" (Unpublished journal of Ricardo Viñes), intro., trans., and ed. Nina Gubisch, *Revue internationale de musique française* 1–2 (June 1980): 154–248.

75. Ibid., 179, 183, 185–89, 192; see also Nichols, *Ravel Remembered*, 3–7.

76. Viñes, "Journal," 190; trans. modified from Nichols, *Ravel Remembered*, 6.

77. Viñes, "Journal," 162–64.

78. Long, *At the Piano*, 118, 120.

79. Nichols, *Ravel Remembered*, 81.

80. On the "sexual enigma," see Émile Vuillermoz's comments in *Ravel par quelques-suns de ses familiers* (Ravel as seen by those who knew him) (1939), in Marnat, *Ravel*, 143.

81. *Ravel*, film, dir. Niv Fichman and Larry Weinstein (Toronto: Rhombus Media, 1987). I am grateful to Sylvia Kahan for introducing me to this film.

3 "DEVOTED ATTENTION"

LOOKING FOR LESBIAN MUSICIANS IN FIN-DE-SIÈCLE BRITAIN

SOPHIE FULLER

> Though Miss Zimmermann's public career was a good deal interrupt-
> ed for eighteen years by her devoted attention to Louisa Lady Gold-
> smid, whose home she shared after the death of Sir Francis Goldsmid,
> she never lost interest in her art, and continued to give her annual
> recitals for several years in succession.
> —Lady Arbuthnot, "In Memoriam Agnes Zimmermann"

I have spent many years immersing myself in the lives and work of various late Victorian and Edwardian women for whom music was a consuming passion. I have been gripped by the energy and power that so
often bursts through their memoirs, letters, and compositions. I have been intrigued by the stories that have been told about these women who, as I have,
found in music a place of refuge, excitement, and desire. In dusty corners of
libraries, chatting over tea with their descendants, staring out my window at
twenty-first-century South London, I have puzzled over the similarities and
differences between their lives and mine and tried to come closer to understanding their worlds and the ways in which they chose to live in them.

When trying to piece together the world of a woman such as the pianist and
composer Agnes Zimmermann (1847–1925), how do I interpret the preceding
statement from her *Musical Times* obituary? What does eighteen years of "devoted attention" suggest to me? What did it mean to Lady Arbuthnot, author
of the obituary? What did it mean to Agnes and Louisa? Were they physically
attracted to each other? Did their shared home include a shared bed? If it did,
what happened in it? In the face of society's disgust and disapproval, sexual

activity between women has usually been kept so hidden and secretive that, without the discovery of explicit personal papers, it is probably impossible for me to discover whether Agnes and Louisa expressed their devotion through sex.

The passionate friendships between women in the eighteenth and nineteenth centuries have been well documented, and the debate as to whether such couples engaged in sexual activity has ranged widely.[1] It is possible that friends such as Agnes and Louisa physically expressed their devotion with no more than sisterly hugs and kisses and that they would have regarded the idea of defining themselves as women who loved women (and therefore different from women who loved men) as unthinkable. It is also quite possible that they eagerly embraced both erotic sexual activity and an identity that set them apart from the heterosexual norm. Both possibilities could be, and have been, called lesbian.[2]

Why is it important to me that there were women musicians such as Agnes Zimmermann who never embarked on marriage or motherhood and who chose to make homes with and express their devotion for other women? What were they turning away from, and what were they turning toward? And what does this mean for their artistry and creativity? For me, all devoted relationships between women, whether explicitly sexual or not, present the possibility of differing queer histories that will challenge those conventional retellings of the past that have simply assumed a heterosexual world. These queer histories tell of late Victorian and Edwardian women who inhabited emotional worlds in which they were not subservient to men and children or to images of wifely and maternal devotion. Their time and energy could turn to wider communities outside an immediate family circle, to themselves, and to artistic creativity. They could express devotion and passion beyond the constricting behavior demanded of respectable wives and mothers and turn instead to the wilder emotions of love for other women and for music.

However I, living and working in a different century, decide to name Agnes Zimmermann and Louisa Goldsmid's relationship, the facts of the devotion, the interrupted career, and the shared home remain a powerful reminder that women's varied relationships with each other have always played a vital, if often neglected, role in their histories. Despite what can seem like overwhelming attempts to show otherwise, not all women can be defined by their relationships with men and male institutions. I am intrigued by the place that women's passionate commitments to each other, whatever kind of physical sexual expressiveness was involved, might have played in enabling them as female musicians to negotiate their lives and careers in the often hostile climate of late nineteenth- and early twentieth-century Britain.

This was a time of ferment and change in many different aspects of people's lives, including relationships between men and women. The work of sexologists such as Havelock Ellis and Richard von Krafft-Ebing meant that sexual identities were being discussed and dissected (and some would argue created) as never before, while women were entering the work force in ever increasing numbers. This was, indeed, the age of the "New Woman," fighting with every weapon at her command for women's right to legal equality, suffrage, education, and access to professional careers as well as struggling to dispel the stereotypical image of the devoted middle- or upper-class woman as wife and mother, quietly content to minister to the needs of husband and children in the private sphere of her home. By the end of the century many women felt that doors were opening, obstacles were being demolished, and almost anything was possible. Women's triumphs in many different spheres were considerable, and the musical world was no exception. While instrumentalists fought their way onto the concert platform and into professional orchestras, composers such as Frances Allitsen, Dora Bright, Rosalind Ellicott, Liza Lehmann, Adela Maddison, Ella Overbeck, Ethel Smyth, Maude Valérie White, and Agnes Zimmermann were receiving high-profile performances and enthusiastic critical reception of their wide-ranging music.

My years of research into these composers and their female contemporaries who worked as instrumentalists and singers have produced various patterns and questions. What was the relationship of these musicians to other creative women and to campaigning feminists? Excluded from much, although by no means all, of the mainstream musical establishment, what other networks and support mechanisms did they embrace? What role did the private or semiprivate concert play in furthering the music and careers of these women? How did they fit into the growing desire to find a distinctive native music and the construction of the so-called British musical renaissance? What did the entry of all these women, as both composers and performers, into the public arena mean for contemporary ideas about professionalism and the place of professional musicians in the musical world? And how did the changing contemporary constructions of both femininity and masculinity relate to ideas about music, especially given music's long association with the feminine?[3]

I am also fascinated by the individual lives of the women whose careers and music I have been slowly uncovering. In the face of a persistent refusal to believe in their capabilities and the widespread belief that, as public figures, they had embarked on a thoroughly unladylike path, how did they see themselves as musicians and composers? As women entering into what was still seen largely as a man's world, how did they view themselves as women and how did they negotiate relationships, whatever the degree of eroticism or devotion, with other women?

Many of the women musicians and composers active in turn-of-the-century British musical circles certainly did not conform to traditional expectations concerning the role of women—in terms of either their creativity and musical expression or their personal relationships. What exactly were these expectations? Much depended, as always in Britain, on questions of class. Since the eighteenth century women from the artist-musician class[4] had been working as professional performers, many writing music as well as playing it. By the late nineteenth century, such women were playing every conceivable instrument in mixed and all-women orchestras and bands in venues ranging from the theater and concert hall to the exhibition hall and the seaside pier.[5] For middle- and upper-class women, with whom my work is largely concerned, the expectation was still that they would dabble at music, playing for family and friends or perhaps for charity, in the half-hearted and thoroughly unprofessional way so cuttingly described by Jane Austen in her early nineteenth-century novels. If they wrote music, it was expected to reflect contemporary ideals of femininity—small-scale, lyrical, undemanding works, especially songs and piano pieces.

For such women, any hint of a public, professional life could still be seen as shockingly unsuitable and potentially disgraceful. They were expected to strive for nothing other than marriage and children. For many, however, reality was strikingly different. Despite opposition from their families, they threw themselves into a life-long commitment to music, which often meant that marriage, with its straitjacket of respectability and stranglehold over female independence, was simply out of the question. A significant number of the female musicians and composers working at the fin de siècle never married, and the problem of combining marriage and creative musical work was widely acknowledged at the time. In 1892 an article entitled "Women and Music," which appeared in the radical magazine *Shafts,* claimed that "the chief cause of woman's inferiority has been—marriage. Artistic duties demand the whole strength and devotion of a lifetime; women have given up these duties for the sake of personal gratification; their genius and talent have been recklessly stifled."[6]

At much the same time, the polemical antimarriage writer Mona Caird was working on her novel *The Daughters of Danaus* (1894), in which one of English literature's rare female composers, Hadria Fullerton, gradually loses her strikingly individual creative voice as she sinks into the suffocating responsibilities of marriage and motherhood.[7]

What were the alternatives to the exclusively monogamous heterosexual relationship demanded of the respectable fin-de-siècle woman? Although some contemporary feminists, such as Christabel Pankhurst, argued that women should embrace celibacy,[8] Victorian woman could and did embark on sexual and emotional relationships outside heterosexual marriage. As historians such as Michael Mason have shown, later generations have consistently misunderstood Victorian attitudes toward sex and sexuality. While there was undoubtedly much general ignorance about female genitalia, the female orgasm and women's sexual pleasure were acknowledged as important in contemporary sexual literature,[9] and to assume that eroticism and sensuality were unknown to our great-grandmothers may say more about our own attitudes to sexuality than about theirs. Heterosexual relationships outside marriage included the idle dalliances of the upper classes or the more considered positions of late nineteenth-century New Women, such as Olive Schreiner or Eleanor Marx, who were prepared to publicly acknowledge relationships with men to whom they were not married.[10] Some women who conducted such liaisons with men also had sexual relationships with women. The clavichord player Violet Gordon Woodhouse (1871–1948) not only lived with her husband and her three male lovers in a notorious *ménage à cinq* for a significant part of her life but also conducted what is likely to have been a sexual relationship with Adelina Ganz, as well as inspiring adoring devotion in several other women who were well known for their lesbian relationships, including the composer Ethel Smyth and the writers Christopher St. John and Radclyffe Hall.[11]

The mask of marriage did not necessarily mean that one or both of the couple were not more interested, sexually and emotionally, in members of the same sex. The most notorious homosexual of the period, Oscar Wilde, was married and had two sons. Some of these marriages were doubtless never intended to be sexual partnerships (apart from the purpose of producing children), but others undoubtedly were. Many people of the time had a variety of relationships with both men and women, just as they do today. One of the most notoriously lesbian musicians of the period, Ethel Smyth, had one relationship with a man that, while not sexually fulfilling, was clearly of extreme emotional significance in her life.[12] The composer Adela Maddison married, had two children, and was obviously close to her husband, but one of her most important (and almost certainly sexual) relationships was with a woman. The fluidity of sexual identities at the turn of the century opened up a world of possibilities for such women, including the possibility of embracing a life devoted to music rather than to home, husband, and children. Those women who never married or who placed their marriages and heterosexual relationships on a back burner while turning to other sexual and emotional relationships were able to engage in alternative networks, often female and often queer, that were of huge importance to their work as musicians. Before suggesting ways in which queer themes can be read into the creative work of certain women musicians, some of their individual stories will demonstrate the different ways in which they embraced relationships with other women.

Several of the women I have investigated, including both Ethel Smyth and Adela Maddison, were connected to the fascinating world of upper-class musicians and musical patrons whose semiprivate concerts and musical evenings have been sadly neglected by scholars of British musical life. The private sphere's widely recognized femininity is doubtless one of the main reasons musicologists have dismissed such an abundantly rich source for understanding the wider function of music in Victorian and Edwardian society. One of the many women central to this world was Mabel Veronica Batten (1856–1916), best remembered today as the first significant lover of the novelist Radclyffe Hall (1880–1943) but thoroughly deserving of study in her own right.[13] Born into an Anglo-Irish army family in Calcutta, Batten studied harmony and composition in Dresden and Brugge before marrying at eighteen. Rumored to have been one of Edward VII's mistresses and known to have had an affair with the poet Wilfred Scawen Blunt, she is also thought to have had relationships with other women before meeting Radclyffe Hall in 1907. Regarded as one of London's leading society singers, Batten also wrote many songs, including several settings of Hall's early poetry.[14]

Radclyffe Hall's own relationship to music is intriguing. Her stepfather was the singing teacher Alberto Visetti, and her first passionate attachment was to one of his pupils, Agnes Nicholls. Visetti's friend, the conductor Arthur Nikisch, on hearing some of the young Hall's compositions, suggested she should study with him in Germany. But Hall's attitude toward the systematic study of harmony and counterpoint was obviously that of her character Sidonia in *A Saturday Life*, whose considerable musical talents dry up once she is in the hands of the music professors Mr. Willowby-Smith and Mr. Lovell.[15] Nevertheless, Hall's musicality was vital to her early literary career as a poet. As she later explained, she was "never able to write verse except at the piano, improvising a musical setting to my words."[16] Her own settings were rarely preserved,[17] but the musical qualities of her lyrics attracted the attention of many other composers, including Liza Lehmann and Robert Coningsby Clarke, the husband of one of Hall's first lovers.

Hall's musical and literary talents were always nurtured by Batten, who provided considerable support and encouragement to a variety of musicians, including Percy Grainger and Mischa Elman. Batten was an important figure in London's semiprivate musical world, as was her close friend Winnaretta Singer, princesse de Polignac (1865–1954). Polignac, once described by Virginia Woolf as someone who had "ravaged half the virgins in Paris,"[18] is best known for her Paris salon and her promotion of composers ranging from Fauré to Stravinsky.[19] But she also owned a house in London, and her role in London musical circles has remained unexplored.

Ethel Smyth was a friend of both Batten and Polignac, although her participation in their musical circles seems to have been at times somewhat grudging.[20] She was determined to be accepted by the professional musical establishment's world of public concerts and festivals and may have felt that, as a general's daughter with an inherited income, too close an association with London upper-class musical circles would have marked her as nothing more than a talented amateur. Smyth's work was promoted by key society figures such as the wealthy gay patron Frank Schuster, but she was not always enthusiastic about such performances.[21]

A more willing participant in these circles was Adela Maddison (1866–1929)—a self-confident and highly talented composer whose career stood almost entirely outside the world of the British musical establishment. Until recently Maddison has found a place in music history only for her supposed affair with Gabriel Fauré, whom she first met in the mid-1890s, after her marriage and the birth of her two children.[22] Mabel Batten was one of her closest friends, and the surviving archive of Batten's letters and diaries has proved to be an essential source of information about Maddison.[23] By the time she and her husband, Fred, first met Fauré, Maddison had already published several of her songs and was beginning to find her own distinctive musical voice. Fred, a lawyer who was also a director of the music publisher Metzler, was probably responsible for Fauré's contract with that firm in 1896, while Maddison herself provided English translations for several of Fauré's vocal works. During the 1890s Fauré stayed at the Maddison villa in Brittany, and his music was performed at concerts held in their London house, while works by both composers were heard together in at least two public London concerts.[24] Fauré appears to have given Maddison composition lessons[25] and had a high opinion of her work, writing to the singer Elsie Swinton in 1898: "Has she never let you hear the five or six most recent songs from Paris and London? They are quite remarkable! but difficult to figure out and take in at first acquaintance. She is extraordinarily gifted and I would like her to be encouraged as much as she deserves."[26]

In 1898 Maddison moved to Paris, where she was to remain for the next six or seven years. Perhaps, as Fauré's biographers believe, she abandoned her husband and children to be with her lover. Nonetheless, the move seems more likely to have been an artistic decision: several of Maddison's works had been published in Paris, and she always found French musical circles especially welcoming. It is perhaps not surprising that such an explanation did not occur to Fauré's biographers, who do not regard Maddison as an independent artist who might have made such a decision for creative reasons. During her years in Paris, Maddison does seem to have been supporting herself financially by taking lodgers, which might suggest a rift from her husband.[27] But there is also evidence that the Maddison marriage was by no means over. In an undated letter to Delius written from Berlin in the first decade of the twentieth century, Maddison refers to looking after her sick husband.[28]

Maddison moved to Berlin in 1906, to the surprise of her French friends. It was a city she disliked and where she found little support as a composer. But a possible reason for the move can be found in her relationship with Marta Gertrud Mundt, whose family lived there. After Fred Maddison's death,[29] Mundt became Maddison's constant companion and almost certainly her lover. In the years immediately before World War I, while Mundt appears to have been working as a secretary to Polignac, Maddison and Mundt often visited Batten and Hall, especially during a summer spent in England in 1913. As well as dining and making music together in London, the four women stayed at Batten and Hall's cottage in Malvern: Batten sang them Spanish songs under a walnut tree, Mundt and Hall went for walks together, and they all visited Tewkesbury Abbey, where they watched the sunset.[30]

When the war broke out, Maddison and Mundt managed to get to England, where they found themselves homeless and almost penniless. In a desperate and revealing letter to Batten, Maddison explained that Polignac, having decided that she could no longer employ someone who was German, had dismissed Mundt:

> The best thing to help us (& we need help indeed) is to try & *find a small flat* which could be lent to me for as long as possible—& Marta would do the work for us both if she did not get any work "outside," which is of course likely to be the case. It is impossible to give employment to foreigners when Englishmen and women are needing it so. . . .
>
> For M. to go into a home for German governesses or something of that sort would break my heart & I need her with me for my heart is very bad & who could look after me?
>
> I know you are yourself worried, poor dear Mabel. I feel a brute writing all this—*I don't want money* & hate anyone thinking I am begging at this terrible moment—but if the roof can be provided somehow I can for a time manage our food etc. on £2 a week. . . .

I am doing the cooking & all here—& am so *sick* of life in general & so tired of "ideals" that only lead to the utmost *abimes* of sordid realities.

But one can't be untrue to one's nature!!![31]

It is tempting to read the last two sentences as an acknowledgment by Maddison of the difficulties into which her relationship with Mundt had led her and a defiant recognition of her lesbianism, the "nature" to which she can not be untrue. A letter Maddison sent to Edward Dent suggests that Mundt eventually had to return to Germany: "The war has separated us, & broken up our dear little home—alas! I am being taken care of by friends for the present. Poor Marta is in Berlin—very 'pro-ally' & heartbroken."[32]

Maddison reestablished herself as a composer in London during the war but seems to have been less involved in society circles, which in any case were never again to have the importance that they had during the prewar period. At some time before 1920 she moved to Glastonbury, in Somerset, where she became involved with Rutland Boughton's festival movement. It is not clear whether Mundt was living with her at this time, but by 1921 the two women were together for at least part of the year in Switzerland. Maddison had been suffering from unspecified ill health since the war and died in 1929 at a nursing home in Ealing. As Fred's wife or Fauré's lover, she was regarded, both by contemporaries and by later scholars, as little more than a decorative appendage or a lovesick nuisance. But as Mundt's lover and friend of women such as Batten and Polignac, she took her place in a circle of independent, creative women, defined by and valued for her art.

Another composer who had at least one acknowledged sexual relationship with a woman was Ella Overbeck (1874–19?), who was born in Russia to Russian parents and brought to England as a young child. After her parents died, she was adopted by an English woman and educated at the Royal College of Music. In 1894 *The Musical Times* praised Overbeck's incidental music for Gordon Craig's adaptation of Alfred de Musset's play *On ne badine pas avec l'amour,* in a performance at Uxbridge Town Hall.[33] Overbeck had probably been introduced to Craig by his sister Edith ("Edy") (1869–1947). Nina Auerbach, a biographer of the Craigs' mother, Ellen Terry, refers to Overbeck as "Edy's cross-dressing friend, the Baroness 'Jimmy' Overbeck."[34]

Overbeck's early works, such as a violin sonata and various songs, were well reviewed in the musical press, but she might have faded into oblivion were it not for her affair with the Russian poet Zinaida Nikolayevna Hippius (1869–1945), one of the most significant Decadent and symbolist writers of her generation.[35] Hippius was married to the writer Merezhkovsky but regarded bisexuality as a divine state and saw herself as androgynous: "In my thoughts, my desires, in my spirit—I am more a man; in my body—I am more a woman. Yet they are so fused together that I know nothing."[36]

According to Hippius's memoirs, the two women met in the late 1890s in the Sicilian town of Taormina, described by Hippius as "Taormina, Taormina, white and blue town of the most humorous of all loves—homosexuality! I am speaking, of course, about its external form. It is equally good and natural for each person to love any other person. Love between men *may be* endlessly beautiful and divine, like any other. I am equally attracted toward all God's creatures—when I am attracted."[37] Hippius and Overbeck also appear to have spent time together in Russia. In the winter of 1902–3 Merezhkovsky's translations of Euripides' *Hippolytus* and Sophocles' *Antigone* were performed with Overbeck's incidental music at the Alexandrinsky Theater in Saint Petersburg.[38] Judging by Hippius's retelling in both diaries and stories, the affair was not without its difficulties, although toward the end of her life she remembered it with affection.[39] By 1904 Overbeck was spending at least part of the year in the South West of England. Her orchestral music became a regular feature of Frank Winterbottom's "Symphony Concerts" in Plymouth, with Overbeck herself conducting on at least one occasion.[40]

As yet Overbeck remains a shadowy figure. She does not seem to have moved in the London musical society circles frequented by lesbian and bisexual women such as Batten, Maddison, and Smyth, although through her friendship with Edy Craig she might well have known Craig's long-term partner, the writer and music journalist Christopher St. John. Overbeck's nickname "Jimmy" and Auerbach's suggestion that she dressed in masculine clothes place her firmly in the tradition of British women such as "John" Radclyffe Hall, Clare "Tony" Atwood, Vera "Jack" Holme, and Naomi "Mickie" Jacob, who signaled their butch lesbian identities through names and clothes. Such women form the most easily recognized lesbian community of the time, flamboyantly acknowledging their own and each others' queer identities.

None of the other women I have studied are as unambiguously lesbian as Batten, Maddison, Overbeck, or Smyth, all of whom came from a privileged class that gave them the financial freedom to ignore the many different pressures to conform. Nevertheless, many other female musicians enjoyed powerful working and emotional relationships with other women that were central to their creative and personal lives. Taking, in the words of Donna Penn, "a queer approach" that "might permit reading lesbianism where, initially, it doesn't seem to be" can provide an illuminating explanation of the ways in which women found practical and emotional support for their creative, musical careers.[41]

One intriguing example is the songwriter Maude Valérie White (1855–1937); having already become the first female recipient of the coveted Mendelssohn Scholarship for composition, White sprang to public attention in the early 1880s when her songs began to be performed throughout Britain. By the 1890s she was at the height of her success and popularity, referred to in *The Musical Times* as "that foremost of English songwriters" and receiving praise such as that offered by a contributor to Grove's *Dictionary of Music and Musicians* who described her song "My Soul Is an Enchanted Boat" (Shelley) as "one of the best in our language."[42] White's songs gradually fell out of fashion, even during her lifetime, despite an increasingly inventive and compelling musical output that sadly remains little known today.

In her memoirs White gives a somewhat evasive and typically light-hearted reason for her avoidance of marriage. Explaining that her grandfather had been married four times and one of her aunts three times, she adds: "And then people ask me why I am a spinster! Of course the reason is obvious. I am a person with some idea of proportion, and an overpowering sense of duty has compelled me to restore the balance of things as far as lies in my power."[43] Her grandnephew Edward Compton, who knew her toward the end of her life, had "a feeling that it [marriage] never crossed her mind."[44] White's memoirs give no hint of sexual relationships with either men or women, although there are numerous references to close friends and to the overriding importance of friendship in her life. A nonspecific concept of love between men and women is given central place in passages such as the following: "the beautiful, unfailing kindness of the man to the woman he loves, and who loves him—what music can equal that?"[45]

But White's earliest close friendships were those with the women, such as Edith Santley and Mary Wakefield, who first sang her songs. White met Wakefield in the mid-1870s, before she started studying at the Royal Academy of Music, and the two musicians became close friends, performing music together throughout the country. Wakefield's biographer, Rosa Newmarch, noted: "The intimacy between the two girls ripened apace, and soon we find Miss White a constant visitor at Sedgwick, where she had her own particular room in the lower story of the tower, and was gently scolded from time to time by Mrs Wakefield, because in moments of inspiration she often left traces of ink on other surfaces than that of her music paper, an infallible, but unappreciated, sign of genius!"[46]

Mary Wakefield (1853–1910), a talented singer and lecturer who played a leading role in the competition festival movement, never married, and her friendships with women were intense. Newmarch writes movingly of her relationship with the writer Valentine Munro Ferguson. The two women lived together, and according to Newmarch, Ferguson's death in 1897 left Wakefield with a sorrow "to which, even ten years later, [she] could hardly endure to allude."[47] She spent the last years of her life with a woman named Stella Hamilton.

White's close female friends in her later life included Margot Tennant (later Asquith), the actor Mary Anderson, and the composer Liza Lehmann, all of whom also played important roles in supporting her composing career. Tennant was a leading member of "The Souls," an unconventional aristocratic group of friends who seem to have taken White under their collective wing in the 1880s. In the early twentieth century Tennant, by then married to the politician Herbert Asquith, was widely rumored to be a lesbian and closely associated with the scandalous bisexual dancer Maud Allan.[48] White's friendships with Anderson and Lehmann, both of whom were married and attracted no hint of sexual impropriety, involved living close to each woman—near Lehmann and her husband in the village of Pinner and next door to Anderson and her husband in Broadway.[49] Lehmann, a singer before her marriage, had included songs by White in her earliest recitals in the mid-1880s. White accompanied Lehmann at numerous concerts, dedicated three songs to her, and called her "one of my best friends."[50] A fourth song, "Soft Lesbian Airs," to words by J. F. Kelly, was published in 1890 and inscribed "To L.L.," doubtless Lehmann. This song was simultaneously issued under the alternative title "Soft Lydian Airs." Was either White or her publisher worried about the implications of the word *lesbian*, despite its apparently geographical sense in this particular lyric? Was the unusually ambiguous dedication also a desire to shield Lehmann from any association with this word?

Many of White's most important friends were women who gave her invaluable support by singing her songs, listening to work in progress, or providing financial help. She was also extremely devoted to her sister Emmie: "I loved her dearly; we have been close friends all our lives, nor has any woman living been so much to me."[51] In the last decades of White's life, the two sisters lived together in Britain and in Italy, where for several years the household also included Emmie's friend (and perhaps lover) Bertha Martindale.

White also had friendships with several gay men, including Frank Schuster and Roger Quilter, but her closest male relationship was with the novelist Robert Hichens, whom she met in the late 1890s. He was her "dear best friend," and he described her as "one of the best friends I ever had."[52] They frequently traveled together (especially to Taormina, in Sicily)[53] and used each other as a sounding board for their work. In her memoirs White mysteriously decides to "decorate dear Robert Hichens with the badge of Silence—the decoration

I know he would prefer."[54] Was she perhaps shielding his homosexuality?[55] White's memoirs are obviously a public record, aimed at creating a particular image to fit her position as a successful and popular songwriter. In a way familiar to lesbian and gay historians, however, they abound with admissions of necessary secrets and things that cannot be told.

In the end we know little about White's emotional or sexual life other than that, like many of her contemporaries, she rejected the conventional path of marriage and had close friendships with several women and men who were lesbian, bisexual, or homosexual. Through Schuster she must have come in contact with the artistic and frequently lesbian London aristocratic musical circles frequented by Maddison, Batten, Polignac, and sometimes Smyth. However, as a merchant's daughter who needed to support herself by working as a professional musician, White was from the wrong class to become an intimate member of such a network. Her closest friendships were with other professional artists. It is almost impossible to imagine White, an avid traveler and effusive lover of beauty in nature, people, and music, tied down to a convention heterosexual relationship or the unadventurous life expected of a conventional turn-of-the-century woman.

Do the various queer aspects of the lives led by women such as Smyth, White, Overbeck, or Maddison simply reflect the experiences of many middle- or upper-class women's negotiations of personal relationships during this time of social change, or is the fact that they were creative musicians in some way relevant? Is the queerness of these women reflected in their public identity as composers or even in their compositions themselves? Elizabeth Wood's pioneering work on Ethel Smyth has shown how Smyth's primary commitment to women and her own particular sexual identity can be read into her music.[56] Links between sexuality and creativity can also be found in the work of other composers of Smyth's generation.

Smyth chose to publish her work using just her initials and surname ("E. M. Smyth"), as did many other composers, including Ella "Jimmy" Overbeck ("E. Overbeck"). Leaving one's gender ambiguous was a sensible move in a world where women's work was so often automatically regarded as second-rate. E. M. Smyth caused notable consternation among reviewers when, on taking the platform at early performances of large-scale orchestral works, she turned out to be a woman.[57] But for women such as Smyth or Overbeck, who dressed in masculine clothes and probably identified with the contemporary concept of the "mannish lesbian," such a choice can also be seen as a form of creative androgyny that mirrors their physical androgyny.[58]

Several of the composers of this generation were primarily songwriters, and even those, like Smyth, who were determined to succeed in larger genres also wrote and published songs. There were many reasons for Victorian and Edwardian women to embrace songwriting, from the fact that composing songs had been an accepted musical outlet for women ever since the successes of composers such as Claribel and Virginia Gabriel in the 1860s to the fact that creating a song does not necessarily require thorough training in orchestration or counterpoint, skills often difficult to acquire in an age when comprehensive education was not always easily accessible to women. Songwriting was also the only compositional activity that might be able to provide financial security to women, who were barred from many musical professions. Finally, women were socialized not only to be gentle and nurturing but also to communicate the emotions that were seen to be a deep-rooted part of their being. The song, with its distilled fusion of music and text, was an exemplary vehicle for conveying a range of ideas, feelings, and emotions as well as aspects of sexuality.

The texts that composers such as White or Maddison chose for their songs deserve deeper exploration than this present study can provide, but even an initial survey throws up some interesting features. Many women had no hesitation in choosing love lyrics that unambiguously expressed desire for a woman. Although this was the accepted tradition of song and lieder writing, in the hands of women composers such songs take on intriguing layers of meaning and express a range of potentially subversive desires. Such meanings took on additional potency when they were performed, as they so often were, by the composer's female friends (frequently accompanied by the composer herself). Whether as composer or performer, a woman taking on a male voice or addressing a female beloved, while to a certain extent acceptable to a general audience at the turn of the century,[59] must have presented a pleasing queerness to those who wanted to hear beneath the surface; it certainly has the power to do so today.

White translated her intense feelings about faith, nature, and love into her songs, choosing an astonishing array of texts in a wide variety of different languages. Many of her most successful songs, such as "So We'll Go No More a'Roving" (Byron, 1888) or "My Soul Is an Enchanted Boat" (Shelley, 1883), use poetry in which the singer's gender is ambiguous, but in several the beloved being addressed is clearly female. One of her most popular songs was "The Devout Lover" (1882), to words by Walter Herries Pollock:

> It is not mine to sing the stately grace,
> The great soul beaming in my lady's face,
> To write no sounding odes to me is given,
> Wherein her eyes outshine the stars in heaven.

Not mine in flowing melodies to tell
The thousand beauties that I know so well,
Not mine to serenade her ev'ry tress
And sit and sigh my love in idleness. . . .

Edith Santley performed the song until her father, Charles Santley, took it over, saying, "That isn't a song for little girls—that is a song for me." Telling the story in her memoirs, White adds, perhaps somewhat grudgingly: "That it was a man's song was, of course, undeniable." Charles's reaction displays his discomfort at hearing his daughter declaring love for another woman in the rich harmonies of White's intense setting. For other listeners such a performance may have provided a thrill of recognition. Edith did remain the performer of "Mary Morison" (Burns, 1883), a love song that was dedicated to Mary Wakefield:

O Mary at thy window be
It is the wished the trysted hour,
Those smiles and glances let me see,
That make the miser's treasure poor. . . .

"Mary Morison" is a fairly jaunty love song, unlike White's heartfelt setting of Shelley's "To Mary," written while she was in Chile for ten months after the death of her mother in 1881.[60] The song was dedicated to her sister Annie, with whom she was staying in Chile, but was Mary Wakefield perhaps in her mind?

O Mary dear, that you were here
With your brown eyes bright and clear
And your sweet voice like a bird
Singing love to its lone mate
In the ivy bower disconsolate.

The songwriter who took on the most persistently male "voice" was Frances Allitsen (pseudonym of Mary Frances Bumpus [1848–1912]). Allitsen was best known for her patriotic and religious songs, but she also composed many impassioned love songs and several larger-scale vocal works, including an opera, *Bindra the Minstrel,* using her own libretto and published in 1912. Her typically dramatic song cycle *Moods and Tenses (Phases in a Love Drama)* (1905) set eight poems by different authors, all from a male perspective, and was dedicated "to my friend Louise Sutherland Morris."[61] The singer is specified as a baritone, a characteristic choice of a low-timbred voice. Allitsen's three large-scale vocal works all use strikingly low-registered voices. *Cleopatra,* a scena for contralto and orchestra with a text by Shakespeare, was first performed at the Royal Albert Hall in 1903. It was written, as several of her shorter vocal pieces had been, for the contralto Clara Butt, who was extremely popular with the British public at the turn of the century and doubtless responsible for countless contralto works by British composers (including Edward Elgar's *Sea Pictures*). Allitsen's dramatic cantata *For the Queen* (1911), with a libretto by Frank Hyde, was written for baritone, mezzo-soprano, and bass soloists, as well as chorus and orchestra. In *Bindra the Minstrel* (which was never performed, although it was published as a vocal score) the two heroes are baritones and the heroine is a mezzo-soprano. Only the villain, sung by a tenor, has a high-register voice.

Since songs were usually published in several keys to attract the widest possible market, it is often hard to establish the voice that the composer originally intended, but in these large-scale works Allitsen's intention is clear. She was herself a mezzo-soprano. Was she simply writing in her own range? Did the singers for whom she liked to write (including the contralto Ada Crossley and the baritone Charles Hayden Coffin, as well as Clara Butt) happen to have low voices? Does her avoidance of the soprano voice, as well as the heroic female characters of her stage works, signal an avoidance of the stereotypical dramatic female role of the time? Or is her use of lower female voices an expression of the "Sapphonic" voice so vividly described by Elizabeth Wood?[62] Allitsen's private life remains deeply veiled. All that is known is that she never married and had close friends who were women, including the novelist Marie Corelli and Louise Sutherland Morris.[63] In her public musical voice, however, this often depressed and sickly woman found a way to create strength and vigor as well as a powerfully ambiguous sexual identity.

Adela Maddison's music was markedly different from that of Frances Allitsen—more subtle and delicately nuanced, as well as more daring in its exploration of harmony, melody, rhythm, and silence. Maddison chose texts, such as French lyrics by the writers Paul Verlaine, Albert Samain, or Edmond Haraucourt, that reflected the cosmopolitanism of her social circles. Strikingly, the love lyrics she set almost never reveal the singer's gender. Her early songs are also notable for her choice of lyrics by the still somewhat risqué Algernon Swinburne. Of the ten songs in her op. 9 collection of 1895, for example, five are settings of Swinburne. None of the poems Maddison chose reflect Swinburne's notorious interest in Sappho and lesbianism, but the lingering emphasis on words such as *pain* and *sting* in her setting of the erotic lyric "Stage Love" shows a willingness to embrace unconventional images of sexuality.

Maddison's choice and interpretation of Swinburne's poetry suggests a bond with fin-de-siècle Decadents, characterized by Martha Vicinus as obsessed with "unrequited love, violence and death."[64] More than one contemporary critic found Maddison's musical language to be reminiscent of Wagner, the composer most admired by the Decadents.[65] A similarly Decadent connection appears in the subject matter of some of Overbeck's compositions, such as her orchestral suite *Salome,* performed at Plymouth in 1906. Salome was one of the most pervasive Decadent icons, used to represent a threatening and dangerous female sexuality by artists from Moreau and Klimt to Huysmans and Wilde. The art historian Shearer West has written of Salome as a late nineteenth-century icon assuming "some qualities normally associated with men," adding that she was "both beautiful and monstrous; sexual and heartless."[66] It is perhaps not surprising that there should be a strong tradition associating Salome with queer women, from Ida Rubinstein, who performed Wilde's play in early twentieth-century Saint Petersburg; through Maud Allan and her infamous "Dance of Salome"; to Alla Nazimova, who produced and starred in the 1922 silent film version of Wilde's play.[67] The painter Edvard Munch made three lithographs of his friend the British lesbian violinist Eva Muddocci (pseudonym of Hope Evangeline Muddock [1883?–1953]), including one with her lover, pianist Bella Edwards, and another entitled "Salome"—a head-and-shoulders portrait of Muddoci with Munch's head in the place of her violin.[68]

While Decadence has been seen by scholars such as Elaine Showalter as an aesthetic opposed to many of the goals and ideals of the New Woman and as a movement that both objectified and feared women,[69] it seems that its embrace of powerful images of female sexuality struck a chord with queer women, not least composers such as Maddison and Overbeck. Such an association suggests the possibility of a lesbian fin-de-siècle aesthetic closely related to a gay male aesthetic and running counter to some of the ideals of contemporary heterosexual feminism.

Should we really be surprised if the history of fin-de-siècle women composers should turn out to be such a queerable history? As can be seen by the vehemence of those arguing that women were incapable of producing "great music,"[70] there is little doubt that of all artistic careers taken up by women at the turn of the century, that of the composer offered the sharpest challenge to male dominance of artistic creativity. For most women, taking up such a challenge involved abandoning traditionally held ideas about female identity, perhaps especially the belief that a woman's central aim in life should be marriage and motherhood. Once that first rejection of societal expectations and stereotypes had been made, taking steps to renounce the heterosexual norm and recognize or act on queer impulses became entirely possible. And queer women, already seen as walking outside the path of true femininity, were placed in a position where acknowledging their musical talents by embracing such a subversive career was probably the lesser of the two perversions. The networks of creative women that surrounded queer figures such as Mabel Batten or the princesse de Polignac and the close female friendships embraced by many fin-de-siècle women gave musicians and composers encouragement and support as they stepped outside the narrow roles prescribed for them by the British musical establishment.

I will probably never know the exact nature of Maude Valérie White's feelings for Mary Wakefield. Nor will I know whether Agnes Zimmermann and Louisa Goldsmid or Adela Maddison and Marta Mundt had sexual relationships as they are defined in the twenty-first century. But I do know that passionate friendships, devoted attention, and immersion into circles of female friends and lovers, all important elements of a queer history, provided an alternative space in which women, excluded as they so often were from the musical mainstream, were able to find a voice.

NOTES

1. See, for example, Lillian Faderman, *Surpassing the Love of Men: Romantic Friendships and Love between Women from the Renaissance to the Present* (London: Women's, 1985); or Emma Donoghue, *Passions between Women: British Lesbian Culture 1668–1801* (London: Scarlet, 1993).

2. The problems of the historical definition of lesbians and lesbian identity has been thoroughly explored by many scholars. Donoghue, for example, shows that the word *lesbian* was used to describe sexual relationships between women as early as 1732 (Donoghue, *Passions,* 3), and Helena Whitbread's decoding of Anne Lister's early nineteenth-century diaries has clearly shown that there was such a thing as a lesbian identity before the fin de siècle (Helena Whitbread, ed., *I Know My Own Heart: The Diaries of Anne Lister 1791–1840* [New York: New York University Press, 1992]). For a recent discussion of differing approaches toward defining lesbian identity, see Martha Vicinus, "'They Wonder to Which Sex I Belong': The Historical Roots of the Modern Lesbian Identity," in *Lesbian Subjects: A Feminist Studies Reader,* ed. Vicinus (Bloomington: Indiana University Press, 1996), 233–59. For the purposes of this essay, I have used the terms *sexual relationship* or *lesbian* when referring to relationships that appear likely to have included physical expressions of desire beyond the sisterly.

3. My exploration of such questions can be found in Sophie Fuller, "Women Composers during the British Musical Renaissance, 1880–1918" (Ph.D. diss., King's College, London, 1998).

4. As defined by Nancy Reich, "Women as Musicians: A Question of Class," in *Musicology and Difference: Gender and Sexuality in Music Scholarship,* ed. Ruth Solie (Berkeley: University of California Press, 1993), 125.

5. See, for example, Greta Kent, *A View from the Bandstand* (London: Sheba Feminist Publishers, 1983); and Paula Gillett, *Musical Women in England, 1870–1914* (London: Macmillan, 2000).

6. Virginie Linders, "Women and Music," *Shafts,* 3 Dec. 1892, p. 68. *Shafts* was subtitled "a paper for women and the working classes."

7. Mona Caird, *The Daughters of Danaus* (London: Bliss, Sands, and Foster, 1894).

8. Sheila Jeffreys, *The Spinster and Her Enemies: Feminism and Sexuality 1880–1930* (London: Pandora, 1985), 89.

9. Michael Mason, *The Making of Victorian Sexuality* (Oxford: Oxford University Press, 1994), 195–205.

10. On Schreiner and Marx, see Ruth Brandon, *The New Women and the Old Men: Love, Sex and the Woman Question* (London: Martin Secker and Warburg, 1990), 1.

11. See Jessica Douglas-Home, *Violet: The Life and Loves of Violet Gordon Woodhouse* (London: Harville, 1996), 23, 33–36, 52, 105–8, 137–38.

12. Elizabeth Wood's forthcoming biography of the composer will doubtless present us with a deeper understanding of Smyth's intriguing relationship with Harry Brewster.

13. On Batten, see Una Troubridge, *The Life and Death of Radclyffe Hall* (London: Hammond and Hammond, 1961), 30–31; Michael Baker, *Our Three Selves: A Life of Radclyffe Hall* (London: Hamish Hamilton, 1985), 31–80; and Cline, *Radclyffe Hall,* 59–106. Batten's diaries and letters are held by the Lancaster family.

14. Her nine published songs include *Two Songs,* which sets words by the earl of Lytton (1885), and a setting of Kipling's poem "The Love Song of Har Dyal" (1892).

15. Radclyffe Hall, *A Saturday Life* (London: J. W. Arrowsmith, 1925), especially chap. 6.

16. In Cline, *Radclyffe Hall,* 28.

17. In 1906 a collection of three Heine lyrics, entitled *Remembrance,* was published by Joseph Williams. A setting of her own "To-day I Heard the Cuckoo Call" was published by Chappell in 1920.

18. In Leonie Rosenstiel, *Nadia Boulanger: A Life in Music* (New York: W. W. Norton, 1982), 80.

19. On Polignac, see Michael de Cossart's rather unsatisfactory study *The Food of Love: Princesse Edmond de Polignac (1865–1943) and Her Salon* (London: Hamish Hamilton, 1978). Sylvia Kahan's forthcoming biography is eagerly awaited.

20. For further discussion of Smyth's place in British musical life and her curious refusal to promote the work of her female contemporaries, see Fuller, "Women Composers," 137–41.

21. See, for example, the disparaging letter Smyth wrote to Percy Pitt after her songs were performed at Frank Schuster's house in March 1908, held at the British Library, Percy Pitt Papers, Egerton 3306, f. 87.

22. See Robert Orledge, *Gabriel Fauré* (London: Eulenburg Books, 1979); and Jean-

Michel Nectoux, *Gabriel Fauré: A Musical Life*, trans. Roger Nichols (Cambridge: Cambridge University Press, 1991). Nectoux adopts every stereotype of a twentieth-century woman composer and gives a particularly scathing portrayal of Maddison as nothing more than a frivolous dilettante. Orledge is rather more generous in his assessment of her talent and achievements.

23. I suspect that I might not have made the connection between Fauré's supposed mistress and Batten's friend had I not been, as are many academically minded British lesbians, obsessed with Radclyffe Hall, thus stumbling across references to Maddison in Baker's biography of Hall. My thanks to Baker for putting me in touch with Cara Lancaster, who holds the Batten archive (hereafter MBA), London.

24. The two composers' works were heard together at a concert given by the baritone David Bispham in St. James's Hall at which both Fauré and Maddison accompanied their own works (see *The Musical Times* 37 [June 1896]: 387) and at a concert organized by the magazine *Melody* (see the concert program for St. James's Hall, 2 May 1896, British Library, d487).

25. When her song "Rien qu'un moment" was published in *Le Figaro* in 1898, Maddison was described as "a remarkable pupil of Fauré" ("Notre Page Musicale" [Our musical page], *Le Figaro*, 1 Oct. 1898, p. 2 [my translation]).

26. Fauré to Swinton, received 11 July 1898, in David Greer, *A Numerous and Fashionable Audience: The Story of Elsie Swinton* (London: Thames, 1997), 144–45.

27. See Maddison to Delius, 29 May [1899], in Lionel Carley, *Delius: A Life in Letters I 1862–1908* (London: Scolar, 1983), 155.

28. Letter held by the Delius Trust, London.

29. He died probably in 1906 but certainly before 1910.

30. Mabel Batten's diary, 9 May, 11 May, 1 June, and 8 June 1911; 11 July, 13 July, and 5–12 Aug., 1913 (MBA).

31. Maddison to Batten, n.d. but ca. 15 Aug. 1914 (MBA).

32. Maddison to Edward Dent, 12 Nov., no year, held at the Cambridge University Library, Add. MS 7973 M/21.

33. *The Musical Times* 35 (Jan. 1894): 45.

34. Nina Auerbach, *Ellen Terry: Player in Her Time* (London: J. M. Dent, 1987), 401. Unfortunately Edith Craig's biographer, Katharine Cockin, does not mention Overbeck; see Cockin, *Edith Craig (1869–1947): Dramatic Lives* (London: Cassell, 1998).

35. I am extremely grateful to Boris Thomson for alerting me to Overbeck's lesbian relationship. On Hippius, see Temira Pachmuss, *Zinaida Hippius: An Intellectual Profile* (Carbondale: Southern Illinois University Press, 1971). Pachmuss transliterates *Overbeck* as *Overbach* and mistakenly claims that she was of German descent, although it is clear from Hippius's own writings as well as from later British reviews of Overbeck's music that she was Russian. Her title "baroness" is widely acknowledged.

36. Zinaida Hippius, *Between Paris and St. Petersburg: Selected Diaries of Zinaida Hippius*, ed. and trans. Temira Pachmuss (Urbana: University of Illinois Press, 1975), 77; see also 14.

37. Ibid., 73.

38. Ibid., 98.

39. In one of her letters to the Swedish artist Greta Gerell from the 1930s, she refers to her "longstanding friendship with a foreign musician," adding that "it lasted for many years" (Zinaida Hippius, *Intellect and Ideas in Action: Selected Correspondence of Zinaida Hippius,* ed. Temira Pachmuss [Munich: Wilhelm Fink Verlag, 1972], 536 [my translation]; see also 548 and 579).

40. Works performed included Introduction and Caprice; the overture *Antigone; Phèdre,* for strings and harp; *Danse Russe;* music from the ballet *La Reine de neige;* and the suite *Salome* (see *The Musical Times* 45 [May 1904]: 306; 47 [June 1906]: 413; and 48 [Jan. 1907]: 48).

41. In Scott Bravmann, *Queer Fictions of the Past: History, Culture and Difference* (Cambridge: Cambridge University Press, 1997), 24.

42. *The Musical Times* 37 (Jan. 1896): 49; Mrs. Edmond Wodehouse, "Maude Valérie White," in *A Dictionary of Music and Musicians,* ed. George Grove (London: Macmillan, 1899), 451.

43. Maude Valérie White, *Friends and Memories* (London: Edward Arnold, 1914), 3.

44. Conversation with Sir Edward Compton, 18 Jan. 1991.

45. White, *Friends and Memories,* 175.

46. Rosa Newmarch, *Mary Wakefield: A Memoir* (Kendal, U.K.: Atkinson and Pollitt, 1912), 22.

47. Ibid., 111.

48. See Philip Hoare, *Wilde's Last Stand: Decadence, Conspiracy and the First World War* (London: Duckworth, 1997); and Felix Cherniavsky, *The Salome Dancer: The Life and Times of Maud Allan* (Toronto: McClelland and Stewart, 1991).

49. Broadway had been colonized by painters from Kensington in the mid-1880s and remained a social center for artists, musicians, and writers for many years. Among the musicians with whom White put on concerts at Broadway's Lygon Arms was Lady Maude Warrender, lover of the singer Marcia van Dresser and friend of Radclyffe Hall. See White, *Friends and Memories,* 367; and Cline, *Radclyffe Hall,* 288.

50. White, *Friends and Memories,* 239.

51. Ibid., 205.

52. Ibid., 371; Hichens, *Yesterday,* 122.

53. Taormina's association with homosexuality for Hippius has already been mentioned. In her biography of Ethel Smyth, Louise Collis makes an undocumented reference to Smyth's associating Sicily with "'lots of painters squatting about,' poets and 'colonies of Oscar-Wilde men'" (Collis, *Impetuous Heart: The Story of Ethel Smyth* [London: William Kimber, 1984], 156).

54. White, *Friends and Memories,* 371. Compton described Hichens as "White's protector" (conversation, 1991).

55. Hichens was a friend of Oscar Wilde and Alfred Douglas, whom he satirized in one his best-known novels, *The Green Carnation* (1894). On his own homosexuality,

which Hichens only hints at in his memoirs, see Richard Ellmann, *Oscar Wilde* (New York: Knopf, 1988), 425.

56. See, for example, Elizabeth Wood, "Lesbian Fugue: Ethel Smyth's Contrapuntal Arts," in *Musicology and Difference,* ed. Solie, 164–83; or Elizabeth Wood, "Sapphonics," in *Queering the Pitch: The New Gay and Lesbian Musicology,* ed. Philip Brett, Elizabeth Wood, and Gary Thomas (London: Routledge, 1994), 27–66.

57. The best-known review to reflect this surprise was that by George Bernard Shaw (republished in *Music In London 1890–94,* 3 vols., rev. ed. [London: Constable, 1932], 2:37) after the premiere of Smyth's Overture to *Antony and Cleopatra* in 1892. Two years earlier the first performance of her Serenade for orchestra had elicited the following: "But surprise rose to absolute wonder when the composer, called to the platform, turned out to be a member of the fair sex" (J.B.K., *Monthly Musical Record,* June 1890, p. 137).

58. Many women chose to identify themselves by initial and surname, but it is notable that the most flamboyantly heterosexual women, such as Liza Lehmann or Hope Temple, never did.

59. References to singers choosing songs "inappropriate" to their gender appear to be few in the media of the time. In 1879 an anonymous writer in *The Musical Times* complained that songs rarely indicated whether they were to be sung by men or women: "It might reasonably be imagined that the nature of the words would, in many cases, sufficiently show whether they were to be sung by a lady or a gentleman; but considering that we now hear singers of the gentler sex warbling the most impassioned serenades, it is evident that we are not to be in the slightest degree guided by the character of the composition." But the writer goes on to concentrate on matters of timbre rather than gender (*The Musical Times* 19 [Aug. 1879]: 423). Over twenty years later, A. Percival, reviewing a recital by Muriel Foster, decided that "to introduce Garnet Cox's 'Because my Love is a Rose,' a man's song, with peculiarly pointless words, were surely an error of judgement" (*The Vocalist* 23 [Feb. 1904]: 342). But here the pointlessness of the words is as much a problem as the gender of the singer.

60. See White, *Friends and Memories,* 220.

61. Louise Sutherland Morris was obviously a close friend. She was left the largest legacy (£300) in Allitsen's will as well as Allitsen's "collection of autograph letters that is marked with her name and the collection of letters marked 'For dark days.'" I have not yet been able to discover anything more about their relationship or about Morris herself.

62. See Wood, "Sapphonics."

63. Corelli's own sexuality is at least ambiguous. Despite instigating the notorious "Cult of the Clitoris" article, which led Maud Allan to sue MP Noel Pemberton Billing for libel, Corelli spent most of her life with her beloved female companion, Bertha Vyver. Corelli's biographers usually insist that the relationship was not sexual, despite recording great physical affection in public between the two women and a "bas-relief above the fire-place in the music-room which represented the initials M.C. and

B.V. in a heart, above the inscription AMOR VINCIT" (Brian Masters, *Now Barabbas Was a Rotter: The Extraordinary Life of Marie Corelli* [London: Hamish Hamilton, 1978], 276).

64. Martha Vicinus, "The Adolescent Boy: Fin-de-Siècle Femme Fatale?" in *Victorian Sexual Dissidence,* ed. Richard Dellamora (Chicago: University of Chicago Press, 1999), 85.

65. See *Athenauem* 3576 (9 May 1896): 627; and Christopher St. John, "Music," *Time and Tide* 1 (18 June 1920): 132.

66. Shearer West, *Fin de Siècle: Art and Society in an Age of Uncertainty* (London: Bloomsbury, 1993), 74. See also Elaine Showalter, *Sexual Anarchy: Gender and Culture at the Fin de Siècle* (London: Bloomsbury, 1991), chap. 8.

67. My thanks to Lloyd Whitesell for alerting me to Alla Nazimova and this film.

68. See Elizabeth Prelinger and Michael Parke-Taylor, *The Symbolist Prints of Edvard Munch: The Vivian and David Campbell Collection* (New Haven, Conn.: Yale University Press, 1996), 202–10. I am grateful to Tamara Bernstein for this reference.

69. See Showalter, *Sexual Anarchy,* 170.

70. See, for example, V.B., "Failures of Women in Art: In Music," *The Sketch* 21 (1898): 468.

PART 2

PUBLIC APPEARANCES

4 "HE ISN'T A MARRYING MAN"

GENDER AND SEXUALITY IN THE REPERTOIRE OF MALE IMPERSONATORS, 1870–1930

GILLIAN RODGER

Male impersonators, women who sang songs in male character and wearing fashionable male clothing, were active on the American variety and vaudeville stage from the late 1860s to around 1930. During this period these performers were among the highest-paid performers, male or female, in variety and vaudeville.[1] The most successful male impersonators consistently drew large audiences to theaters and had a broad appeal that crossed both class and gender lines. Given the great success and popularity of these performers over a sixty-year period, it is curious that after 1900 few American women were active in this genre. Most of the prominent male impersonators appearing in vaudeville after 1900 were based in Britain and performed primarily in music halls. The last British-based impersonator to tour the United States did so in 1929. After that there were no "star" vaudevillians performing in this specialty. It is also curious that the turn of the century saw a radical shift in the performance style and repertoire of male impersonators, as well as in their self-promotion through advertising and interviews. Indeed, the performance styles and repertoires of the first and the last generations of male impersonators active in the United States have little in common beyond the fact that the female singer was dressed in male clothing.

These women were singers of popular songs, whose brief shelf lives explain why their repertoire changed during this period, but the shifts in their performance style and in the kinds of men they portrayed cannot be explained simply by the passing of time, the changing of public taste, or the emergence of vaudeville. This chapter will examine the performance styles and repertoires of the earliest American male impersonators and of male impersonators active in vaudeville after the turn of the century in order to explain why the performance style shifted. I will show that many of the changes in male impersonator acts were self-imposed modifications in anticipation of public criticism, not responses to expressed audience displeasure or distaste. I will also argue that the principal reasons for the demise of male impersonation in the United States, and probably elsewhere also, were changing social constructions of femininity and masculinity and the fact that by the 1920s, if not earlier, the stigmatized social categories "gay man" and "lesbian," had come to be associated with the central feature of this performance style: cross-dressing.

It is important, first, to distinguish male impersonation in variety and vaudeville from the many styles of cross-gender performance present in other theatrical forms of late nineteenth-century America. Women appeared in male roles in almost every form of American theater during this period. Operatic "trouser roles" enjoyed a renewed vogue. In spoken drama actresses such as Charlotte Cushman, Sarah Bernhardt, Maude Adams, and others took male roles such as Romeo and Hamlet to extend their repertoires (see figure 4.1). In burlesque and in British pantomime, "principal" and "second" boy roles were written to be played exclusively by women, and typically these companies also included a "dame" role, which was played by a man. Young women were frequently cast as young men in musical comedy and farce, and the plots often called for the leading female character to provide one of the many inevitable plot twists by assuming male disguise. Cross-dressing, and particularly female-to-male cross-dressing, was hardly an uncommon occurrence on the nineteenth-century stage (figure 4.2).

The fundamental difference between male impersonators in variety and vaudeville and women who took male roles in spoken theater, trouser roles in opera, or principal boy roles in musical theater was that as solo acts, male impersonators were not governed by the needs of a script or a narrative plot. They did not perform scripted material, nor were they expected to portray a single character over a long period of time. In fact, in an act of approximately twenty minutes, a male impersonator could sing three or four songs, each featuring a different character in distinct changes of clothing. Song did not interrupt or suspend the narrative but rather provided it, and unlike actresses in a play, the male impersonator could freely exchange banter with the audience without necessarily slipping out of character. Unlike principal boys, whose brief costumes, corseted waists, and exposed legs left little doubt that they were women, male impersonators dressed in the height of men's fashion, including

"ROTOGRAPH"
SERIES

MAUDE ADAMS
AS "PETER PAN"

B 1444

Oct 3rd

I have fallen in love with her.

Aida

Otto Sarony Co

Figure 4.1. Maude Adams as "Peter Pan," Rotograph Series postcard posted in 1907 (from author's collection). The sender, Aida, noted to her friend Miss Lottie Kyle: "I have fallen in love with her."

FIGURE 4.2. Grace Sherwood as Robinson Crusoe, from the burlesque of the same name (from author's collection). Cabinet cards such as this were extremely popular in the 1880s and were sold through sporting newspapers such as the infamous *National Police Gazette*.

long trousers and a jacket, a hat, and other appropriate accessories, and they wore their hair cut short, in the style of men. Moreover, until the first decades of the twentieth century, male impersonators took on male characters almost exclusively.

THE FIRST GENERATION, 1868–85

Male impersonators during the 1870s and 1880s were women considered to be particularly suited to portraying men through song. They often had masculine facial features and plump or thickset bodies and could have passed as male off the stage if dressed in men's clothing. The first generation of performers active in this style in America tended to be older women who had already had singing or dancing careers in variety or other musical theater.[2] These women rarely if ever appeared before an audience in women's clothing; on the stage they embodied masculinity. They did not just play the role of a man, speaking lines written by somebody else; rather, they used song to transform themselves into the character about whom they sang. These women observed men and male fashion carefully, always acting in a way appropriate to the characters they assumed. Younger, more feminine male impersonators did not begin to gain any substantial success in American variety until the late 1880s and 1890s, and until around 1885 American male impersonation was dominated by a small number of older women.

The first woman to gain significant attention as a male impersonator in American variety was Annie Hindle. Born in the middle to late 1840s, Hindle had been active as a male impersonator in British music halls before her arrival in the United States in 1868. During the 1860s a number of women working in British music hall had begun to parody *lions comiques*, male performers who parodied middle- and upper-class male behavior. Some elements of this double parody were no doubt lost on an American audience, but Hindle proved to be a great success in variety. She billed herself as a "character singer" and a "character change vocalist," titles also used by male singers of character songs, and stressed her British origins in her advertising.

By the mid-1870s Hindle had a number of rivals. The most prominent was Ella Wesner, who was born in 1841 and began her stage career as a dancer in Philadelphia in 1850. Wesner came from a large family of dancers and seems to have played "boy" roles in burlesque or musical comedy companies during the late 1860s, as well as appearing as a dancer in early variety.[3] It is also likely that Wesner worked for one theatrical season as Annie Hindle's dresser and learned the performance style from her. In 1870, at the age of twenty-nine,

Wesner debuted at Tony Pastor's theater as a male impersonator, and her success in this specialty was phenomenal (figure 4.3).

Contemporary reviews of both Hindle and Wesner stressed their realism in performance. They were often praised for their versatility as performers and for their skill in depicting men. A review in the *New York Clipper* noting Hindle's appearance in Galveston, Texas, attests to her realism while in male character: "Annie Hindle has proved a great success. As a male impersonator her sex is so concealed that one is apt to imagine that it is a man who is singing."[4] In 1891 the *New York Sun* described Hindle as "a striking person in every way. Her face was masculine in all its lines; her eyes were gray, but with a kindly expression; her mouth was firmly cut, and . . . one could detect that this . . . was a woman of great mental force and capabilities."[5]

If anything, Wesner was even more masculine in appearance than Hindle. The *Clipper* described Wesner at her debut in the following way: "Nature has liberally endowed her for this specialty with an almost faultless form, a face quite masculine and jet black curling hair, which she wears cut short. She might easily walk Broadway in male attire without her sex being suspected."[6]

Hindle and Wesner had a number of younger rivals during the 1870s and 1880s, but none of these women ever matched their success. It also appears that none of the younger male impersonators approached the realism of Hindle and Wesner, and reviewers criticized them for this. Two of their most successful rivals were Blanche Selwyn and Alecia Jourdan. Selwyn, described as a well-built woman who never managed to hide her feminine curves, was a competent performer but flashy as a dresser.[7] She had some success as a male impersonator during the 1870s and even led her own variety troupe at the end of that decade. Jourdan was less successful than Selwyn and rarely appeared as a solo act in variety. During the 1870s she worked primarily with Sheridan and Mack's company, often appearing in a double act with John Sheridan, a female impersonator. Some of the younger, less realistic male impersonators of this period appeared at theaters noted for the daring entertainment they offered to a primarily male audience, while others were minor performers active in regional variety who rarely, if ever, performed at theaters in large cities.

The realism of the male impersonator's act depended to a great extent on her physique as well as her vocal range and acting skills. Despite the differences in realism, however, these acts were similar in content and performance style. Acts lasted around twenty minutes, during which the performers sang at least three songs. Each song depicted a different male character, and between songs the actress changed her costume in the wings. These changes had to be accomplished as quickly as possible, and reviewers were quick to note sloppy or slow

FIGURE 4.3. Ella Wesner in her stage costume, circa 1872 (photograph by Sarony, New York; photo courtesy of "John Culme's Footlight Notes Collection," <http://footlightnotes.tripod.com>).

changes. Each male character was performed with the appropriate gestures and props. Between verses of songs performers interpolated comic or topical commentary inspired by the song texts or interacted with their audience, generally staying in character as they did so. Reviews of these performances clearly indicate when the performer fell short of the expectations and the ideal for this style. In addition, these reviews make it clear that this ideal had been established by Hindle and Wesner.

Ella Wesner and Annie Hindle were realistically masculine not only in appearance but also in the kinds of claims they made through song. Wesner and Hindle, along with a number of the earliest American male impersonators, shared parts of their repertoire with men and presented a similar range of characters as male singers. Wesner's repertoire included material sung by Charles Vivian and British *lions comiques* such as George Leybourne and Alfred Vance, as well as songs written especially for her. Blanche Selwyn shared repertoire with Tony Pastor, and composers of popular songs advertised them in the *Clipper* boasting that they had been sung by Hindle, Vivian, and William Horace Lingard.[8]

Reviews of Hindle, Wesner, and other male impersonators during the 1870s and 1880s gave no indication that any portion of their acts or their appearance as any particular type of character was seen as transgressing standards of decency. In many ways reviewers treated these women much as they treated the male singers with whom they shared repertoire, and their performance style shared characteristics with male performers. Claims of sexual virility or sexual knowledge made in their songs only reinforced their likeness to men, and this seems to have enhanced their acts. As a result their material often makes claims that might have been seen as shocking if made by a female singer dressed in women's clothing.

Hindle was the only early male impersonator described as singing in an alto range or lower. Wesner's voice was described as mezzo-soprano, although her range may have dropped over time because of throat problems that plagued her throughout her career. Reviews of other performers did not mention their vocal range and commented on their singing only when it did not meet the reviewer's standards.[9] None of the songs sung by these performers called for a particularly wide vocal range; most of them stayed within an octave, only occasionally employing as much as a tenth.

The sheet music of this period offers little evidence to suggest the way in which these songs were performed. Clues about performance style can be gained from later British recordings and from the collection *Music from the New York Stage, 1890–1920,* which includes recordings of songs from some of the most popular musical theater productions of that era.[10] While *Music from the New York Stage* does not include any male impersonators, it does include late nineteenth-century recordings of a number of character and comic songs that were interpolated into musical theater productions. The available recordings show that singers relied as heavily on their acting skills as on singing skills in delivering songs. Singers frequently spoke or used heightened speech to avoid certain pitches.

The existing recordings of the three most successful male impersonators active in Britain after the turn of the century clearly show them avoiding sung pitch, particularly when the melody moves to the upper part of the singer's vocal range, where the fact that she is a woman becomes most obvious. Reviews of the first generation of performers suggest that, unlike those represented in later recordings, these women included interpolated spoken commentary, performed over orchestral vamping, that commented on or expanded on the lyrics. Spoken commentary continued to be used by male comic performers in both Britain and the United States after 1900, but it seems to have disappeared from the acts of American male impersonators during the late 1880s and 1890s. It may never have been present in the acts of British male impersonators— London reviews did not mention this as a feature of their acts. Unfortunately only a small proportion of the surviving sheet music records spoken interpolation by male impersonators, and none of the recordings does so.

The repertoire of male impersonators during the 1870s and early 1880s included a fairly broad variety of male characters, although the "swell," or dandy, was the most common. During the 1870s the swell was depicted as a young (and sometimes not so young) "man about town" who was overly fond of fashion, alcohol, and good times in general.[11] He was often a character so interested in pursuing leisure that he had no interest in pursuing women, although they always worshiped him, and many of the songs implied that he knew all too well the pleasures that women had to offer.

The young man about town was such a fixture of urban life in America that he was featured in at least three of the "City Characters" columns that ran in the *National Police Gazette* during 1879. Described as "an idler with snap, a butterfly with some virility," the man about town was also "a fellow of enterprise, whose whole object is to keep up a perpetual round of excitement while he's awake, and to be considered a regular trump by actresses, ballet girls, and the ladies. . . . This ambition extended to his clothes which were always a little different in cut and texture from other peoples [*sic*], and to his hats. Luminous neckties helped out the idea."[12] The picture painted is one of excess, loud or flashy clothes, and fast behavior—the perfect material for parody. A few of the swell songs sung by male impersonators depicted reformed swells, but most boasted of the swell's exploits. Many of these songs allowed the singer to express affection toward women in general or one woman in particular.

The swell songs of Hindle, Wesner, and others usually begin with the claim that the singer is the most fashionable of swells, go on to describe fashionable behavior and leisure, particularly drinking, and often discuss the singer's relationship with women. One of Blanche Selwyn's swell songs, "I'm No. 1," follows this model.[13] It begins:

> I'm the first on the list of the nobby swells,
> My style it tells, my form excels,
> Of course admiration my dress compels,
> You see I'm the ladies ideal!

In the final verse of this song the swell offers himself as a potential husband, claiming to surpass other members of elite society as a potential mate.

Many of Wesner's swell songs, particularly those that were also performed by British *lions comiques,* extol the virtues of alcohol. These included "Champagne Charlie," "Moet and Chandon for Me," and "Louis Renouf." Wesner's song "Hi Waiter! A Dozen More Bottles" depicts a man who grows progressively drunker in each succeeding verse. The text also leaves no doubt about the virility of the central character; he loves women as well as wine.[14] The first verse of this song is quite explicit in its claims to sexual activity, and it allowed Wesner a moment to tease and taunt the less sexually experienced men in her audience:

> Lovely woman was made to be loved,
> To be fondled and courted and kissed;
> And the fellows who've never made love to a girl,
> Well they don't know what fun they have missed.
> I'm a fellow, who's up to the times,
> Just the boy for a lark or a spree
> There's a chap that's dead struck on the women and Wine,
> You can bet your old boots that it's me.

One can imagine how these lyrics affected an audience when they were delivered with a broad wink and appropriate gestures by a female singer. If read literally, this song allowed Wesner to claim to be sexually active with women. In fact a literal reading of many of these songs allows a female singer to claim to be the equal or superior to men in dress and action as well as sexual exploits.

It is difficult to know exactly how variety audiences read these songs or received the claims made by male impersonators. It can be safely assumed that the performances did not displease the men in the audience, for otherwise these women could not have been successful. So where did the appeal of these performances lie? There is a slight possibility that the principal attraction was a costume that allowed a clear view of the singers' legs. Compared to female performers in burlesque, however, and even to other female performers in variety, there was little overt sexual display in these acts. A portrait of Ella Wesner in male costume in the *Police Gazette* of 1883 showed only her head and shoulders; visually there was little difference between Wesner and the male theatrical manager whose picture appeared next to hers. In sharp contrast to this, portraits of burlesque actresses, displaying the performer's entire body, often in the briefest of costumes, regularly occupied the best part of a page in the *Police Gazette*. Wesner was viewed, and displayed, by the *Police Gazette* as though she were a man, which suggests that her appeal was not overtly sexual.

It is more likely that the appeal of these women lay in the commentary they provided on manhood in this period and in their ability to both celebrate and denigrate different constructions of masculinity. The dominant character type in their repertoire was an upper-class swell, and while many of the songs depicting swells denigrate him and could be seen as casting some doubt on his masculinity, they also unabashedly celebrate his excessive lifestyle. These songs may have been read in a number of ways. On the one hand, performers such as Annie Hindle and Charles Vivian stressed their British origins in their advertising, so that these songs may have functioned to shore up nativist constructions of American masculinity by denigrating British gentlemen. Many of the songs also make a point of identifying the central character as either a genuine upper-class swell or a young man aspiring to be seen as one. These songs could therefore also be seen as criticizing the upper class, whether British or American, and those who aspired to be like them. On the other hand, these songs also celebrate those parts of the swell's lifestyle—particularly loud, flashy clothes, leisure, womanizing, and excessive drinking—that most appealed to working-class men. The song texts often negate the social distinctions drawn between upper-class, middle-class, and working-class men, exposing urban "society" as a fraud, even as they seem to encourage men to strive for the life enjoyed by upper-class socialites.

These readings are clearly contradictory, and yet each separate interpretation is plausible, especially when the songs texts are read against other contemporary sources, such as the *Police Gazette,* which were sympathetic to the causes and concerns of white, native-born workingmen. These songs functioned to articulate an oppositional model of masculinity that did not exclude the values of working-class men, particularly their desire for leisure. The open celebration of the excesses of the swell, which ran counter to the predominant construction of middle-class manhood, served to undercut the then dominant middle-class ideal of the "self-made man."

Although swell songs made up a large part of a male impersonator's repertoire, they were not the only kind of songs sung by these women. Male impersonators presented other characters in their acts, including sailors and soldiers, rural characters, city clerks, and even workingmen. These male characters varied in age from barely adolescent boys to mature men; Wesner included an elderly drunk, Captain Cuff,[15] in her act during the 1880s and became so associated with this character that she was billed as the "Captain." Both Hindle and Wesner also included "seriocomic" or sentimental songs such as "Down by the Old Mill Stream," which laments the passing of a simpler, more rural life, and "motto" songs, which tend to carry a moral and give advice. They both also sang songs that express sympathy with men facing hard times and advise men in the audience to share meager resources with other men in need. It was through these songs, which feature characters not dissimilar to the men in the audience and express concerns and fears that resonated with the audience, that early male impersonators expressed their kinship with and sympathy toward working-class men.

These songs and many of their swell songs let Hindle and Wesner address the men in their audiences as equals. When they offered them advice, it often concerned courtship and marriage—how best to win a girl and, once she was won, how to keep her happy. While they did not directly acknowledge the presence of any women who might have been in the audience, it should be noted that many of their songs were sympathetic to women as well as men. They occasionally took women to task for an excessive interest in fashion and makeup to disguise their physical shortcomings, but they also advised men to take courtship slowly and to be sensitive to women's needs. While the advice they gave may well have been intended to spare their male audience from rejection in courtship, it no doubt benefited both sexes, and even in the 1870s these performers held great appeal for the women in their audience.[16]

Interestingly, there is ample evidence that both Hindle and Wesner had primary emotional and probably sexual relationships with women. In this they were not typical of male impersonators, the majority of whom were married women for whom I can find no evidence of any same-sex attachments.

Hindle married three times after her arrival in the United States, and there is no indication that she was ever divorced. In 1868 she married the character singer Charles Vivian,[17] and in 1878 the *Clipper* noted her second marriage to

W. W. Long.[18] Hindle did not live with either husband for any length of time; indeed, I can find no evidence that she ever lived with Long. Her third marriage took place in 1886 in Grand Rapids, Michigan, while Hindle was touring the Midwest with her own specialty company. This marriage came to the public's notice because it caused a stir not only within the theatrical community but also in the town itself. After her performance on 6 June, Hindle and her dresser, Annie Ryan, returned to Hindle's room at the Barnard House, a hotel in Grand Rapids, where they were married by a Baptist minister. Hindle apparently stayed dressed in her stage costume, while Ryan wore a dress. The marriage record, which was filed by the minister at the local county office, shows that Hindle gave her name as "Charles," while Ryan used her real name. A reporter for a local newspaper found the couple celebrating later in the evening at a local restaurant (Hindle had changed back into female costume, although the newspaper report depicts her smoking a celebratory cigar), and he hounded the couple, following them back to the hotel. At 2 A.M. Hindle relented and gave him an interview, admitting that she was really a man.[19]

While the story of Hindle's wedding was never picked up by more reputable national newspapers, it was reported by the *Clipper* over two consecutive weeks and also by the *Police Gazette*. Both papers stated emphatically that Hindle was a man and also published surprised reactions from various women with whom Hindle had shared theatrical dressing rooms. The *Police Gazette*'s reaction to Hindle's marriage is surprising given its previous denunciation of a number of women active on the American stage for their interest in other women. Three years before Hindle's marriage, the newspaper had loudly decried the affection the Swedish soprano Christine Nilsson lavished on her female friends.[20] This paper was also quick to denounce women, particularly educated and professional women, who sought equality to men. Despite this, Hindle was not seen as usurping male privilege; her skill as a male impersonator combined with her affection for women was seen by the writer as proof that she was a man.

Hindle and Ryan lived together in retirement, both dressing as women, in Hindle's house in Jersey City Heights until Ryan's death in late 1891. Although Hindle's marriage to Ryan was the most public of her relationships with women, it was probably not the first. During the 1870s Hindle had published a number of love poems, almost all of which addressed a female subject, in the pages of the *Clipper*. In addition, she may well have had a relationship with another of her dressers, Augusta Gerschner, during the mid-1870s.[21]

Unlike Hindle, Ella Wesner never married, and the *New York Sun* claimed that "the only romance in her life" was with the notorious ex-mistress of Col.

James Fiske, Helen Josephine Mansfield. Fiske had been assassinated by a rival for Mansfield's affections in January 1872, and Josie Mansfield began to be linked to Wesner by the summer of the same year. Reviews of Tony Pastor's touring company in the *Clipper* noted that Mansfield was traveling as Wesner's companion. In September, at the beginning of the theatrical season, Wesner and Mansfield eloped to Paris together. Wesner was booked solidly for years in advance, and her unexpected and unannounced departure might have ruined her career had it not been for the speedy intervention of Tony Pastor and Wesner's agent, T. Allston Brown. Wesner returned to American variety by the end of the season, in time to join Pastor's 1873 summer tour, presumably when her affair with Mansfield ended.[22]

Although the claims Hindle and Wesner made in their songs may have reflected their own personal experience in courting women, there is no indication that audiences knew anything about their offstage lives or that their realism in performance was seen as being related to their intimate relationships with women. Audiences had little way of knowing anything about any of the performers who were active in variety during the 1870s, and they seem to have shown little interest. The *Clipper* included a certain amount of news about performers, but it was often highly abbreviated and written for performers who knew each other well enough to fill in the missing details. Other papers, such as the *Police Gazette,* included theatrical commentary but focused more on actors and theatrical forms admired by the middle and upper classes. Gossip denigrating these performers served to denigrate the social elite, and the variety performers were only rarely targeted.

The lack of publicity and personal promotion aimed at a general rather than a theatrical audience gave these performers a freedom that later performers did not enjoy. The fact that they played to audiences composed largely of working-class men and women freed the early male impersonators from the obligation to conform to middle-class standards of propriety. Middle-class standards of behavior and middle-class constructions of femininity seem to have been largely irrelevant to these women, and when they were acknowledged, they were frequently the butt of a joke. As the century came to a close, however, and the new century dawned, this situation changed quite dramatically.

THE FINAL GENERATION, 1900–1930

By the 1890s male impersonation in the United States had undergone a number of subtle changes. Performers continued to present three to four songs in their acts, and they continued to perform rapid changes of costume between songs, but the spontaneous interpolation of dialogue into songs disappeared, and the range of male characters they assumed narrowed considerably. Men depicted by male impersonators after the turn of the century tended to be young, sometimes barely adolescent, innocent in the ways of the world and sexually inexperienced. The women who performed these roles also tended to be less realistic in their portrayals of masculinity.

The move away from realism in male impersonator acts began during the late 1870s with the appearance of a number of younger American performers, but it was cemented by the importation of British male impersonators beginning in the middle to late 1880s. These performers, many of whom had been active in British music hall since the 1870s, were considerably younger than Hindle and Wesner and were perceived as being inherently more refined simply because they were British.[23] Bessie Bonehill, who was one of the first big-name stars imported by Pastor, broadened the range of the theatrical reviewers who covered shows at his theater. Presumably her audience appeal was also broader, and she attracted patrons who would not have normally visited a variety theater. Another impersonator imported by Tony Pastor, Vesta Tilley, went on to become the dominant male impersonator in vaudeville and established the new ideal performance style for American male impersonators after the turn of the century.

Vesta Tilley, who was born in 1864, began to perform in the music hall at the age of four and appeared exclusively in male character from around 1870. Tilley's career was astutely managed by her father, Harry Ball, who also wrote most of the material she sang. Ball was determined to protect his daughter from the hardships of the music hall performer's life and to preserve her innocence and respectability. Tilley's early advertising was careful to stress her act's "refinement," and she was a much less spontaneous performer than many of her contemporaries. Tilley did not swear or spit, and she did not interact with her audience through ad-libbed commentary and asides (figure 4.4).

The trend toward a more scripted, less interactive performance style had begun in the early 1880s, most probably in response to stricter standards of decency that managers imposed to attract a wider audience. The popularity of touring British performers seems to have reinforced this change and encouraged the move toward a more feminine performance style. During the 1880s the changes were subtle, and although older performers were obviously less popular, they could still find regular employment performing in the "old" style. Hindle's career came to an abrupt end after her marriage to Annie Ryan in 1886. A number of newspapers, including the *Clipper*, had seen the marriage, as well as her great skill as a performer, as proof that she was actually a man. Wesner

MISS VESTA TILLEY

FIGURE 4.4. Vesta Tilley, dressed as a British soldier (Real Photo postcard, ca. 1915; from author's collection). Note that Tilley's feminine curves were never completely hidden by her costume.

continued to perform until 1902, but she no longer found bookings in the best vaudeville theaters. By the end of her career she performed mostly in casinos, dime museums, and small-time vaudeville.

After 1900 a new style of American male impersonation emerged. The young women who adopted this performance style did so in response to the success of the British performers who had dominated during the 1890s. In addition, after 1900 the most successful Americans tended to be women who had won some level of success in narrative musical theater and were capitalizing on that success with periodic performances in vaudeville. Della Fox, a soubrette active in DeWolf Hopper's productions of the 1890s, appeared as a male impersonator in vaudeville after 1900. She had suffered a breakdown at the end of the 1890s and was sometimes mentally or physically unable to perform. Vaudeville served to extend her career, which would otherwise have been over, for ten years. Other prominent Americans active after 1900 included Kathleen Clifford and Kitty Doner, both of whom had won success in musical theater and revue before appearing as male impersonators in vaudeville. The most successful performers, however, were all active in British music hall: Vesta Tilley, who toured on six occasions between 1894 and 1912; Hetty King, who appeared in vaudeville in 1909 and 1911; and Ella Shields, who toured during the 1920s.

Male impersonators displayed no anxiety regarding the ways audiences read their acts until after the turn of the century. Complaints about women in "pants" roles had begun to appear in American newspapers in the mid-1890s, and these proliferated after the new century began.[24] After 1900 these commentaries usually asserted that a woman cannot realistically portray a man, and if she could, it would be in bad taste. They also assured the reader that the actresses who took these roles were essentially "feminine" women playing roles on the stage for the amusement of their audience. A fairly typical commentary that appeared in 1898 noted:

> The most versatile actress in the world could never really play a man convincingly, and the fact that she cannot do it and wouldn't if she could is the real reason why audiences like to see women in knee breeches and short jackets. That sounds a trifle paradoxical, but it is true. . . . Women play male roles because in this way they are enabled to be more graphically womanly than ever. And audiences go to see them because such is the case. They deceive none but the idiots in the cast, and managers don't propose that they shall ever try to do so.[25]

Vesta Tilley was the first male impersonator to exhibit any defensiveness about "mannish" women. The *Pittsburgh Gazette Home Journal* published her article "The 'Mannish' Woman" in advance of her 1904 performances in vaude-ville in that city. In it she denounces women who wore male clothing exclu-sively, as well as women who adopted "a mannish style apeing in a degree the various characteristics of the sterner sex."[26] She is also careful to distinguish her onstage "business" from her offstage "private" life and invokes late nine-teenth-century middle-class constructions in which women properly belong in the home, or private sphere, while men occupy the public sphere: "There is nothing so charming as the little home woman, whose soft voice and gentle manner have done so much to make the world a better place."[27] She did not, however, apologize for her own transgression of the doctrine of separate spheres or suggest that women should not work as actresses.

This article is interesting because it suggests that a proportion of Tilley's greatest admirers were women who made her extremely uncomfortable. She mentions women who saw her as a role model for mannish women and dis-misses them as silly. Tilley also discusses a number of her avid female fans in her autobiography,[28] showing that she was very aware of the kinds of passionate feelings her performances evoked in some women in her audience. It is likely that many if not all of the male impersonators active in this period attracted the attentions of lesbians, and this may well have increased their antagonism to mannish women and feminists, as well as their resolve not to be identified as such by their wider audience.

Tilley's defensiveness on the subject of mannish women shows that audi-ences and critics were viewing male impersonators in a fundamentally new way. In the 1870s realism had been valued and indicated the performer's great acting skills. After 1900 it was seen as reflecting on the performer's inherent femininity. A comparison of variety reviews from the 1870s and 1880s and vaudeville reviews from after 1900 shows a growing emphasis on personality in the latter. Whereas earlier performers were praised for skills such as acting, singing, dancing, or comedy, later performers were often described as having a singular personality that carried the act regardless of their other talents. Personality in the early twentieth century went hand in hand with celebrity, and audiences came to expect performers, especially stars, to be themselves on the stage. Offstage interviews with such performers, and reporting on events in their private lives, often served to reinforce this impression.

For performers whose acts relied on cross-dressing, there was an inherent danger in this assumption. From the late nineteenth century both male and female homosexuals had been thought by many to have the inner nature of the opposite sex, and this condition at its extreme was most often thought to manifest itself in cross-dressing.[29] Among working-class men, for example, "fairies"—men who sought sex with other men and took the passive, "female" role in these encounters—were identified by their appearance, which included rouged lips, a powdered face, plucked eyebrows, and feminine gait or body language.[30] Feminists had been identified by their no-nonsense, tailored approach to dressing since well before the turn of the century, and "masculine" women in men's formal evening dress had begun to appear dancing with femininely dressed female partners in Bowery clubs and dance halls as early as 1890.[31] Public anxiety over homosexuality, which peaked in the early 1930s, affected all actors and actresses who were also homosexual, but it also affected all performers who performed cross-dressed, regardless of their sexuality.[32]

As a result male impersonators began to feel the need to impose a distance between themselves and the characters they portrayed in their acts. Extreme realism, which had been waning since the 1880s as actresses began to conform more closely to middle-class expectations of gender, all but disappeared. After 1900 the expression of knowledge appropriate to men alone or singing in a believably male range was seen to indicate the performer's essential manliness, not her superior acting skills. This imposition of distance between the performer and the character she portrayed can be seen in the repertoire and performance style of male impersonators after the turn of the century. Tilley acknowledged that she was never too masculine in her impersonations, saying: "I leave just enough of a woman in my impersonations to keep my work clean."[33] The younger American performers, particularly Kathleen Clifford and Kitty Doner, found novel ways to maintain their femininity in performance. Clifford performed her rapid changes of costume behind a "shadow screen," which allowed the audience to see her changing her clothes in silhouette. Doner also performed her changes onstage but dispensed with the screen. She disrobed in a pink spotlight, which had the effect of making her underwear invisible and created the illusion that she was naked.

The singers' voices also became an important means of imposing distance between the singer and the song's central character. Most of the star male impersonators active in vaudeville after 1900 were mezzo-sopranos or sopranos, and the moment they began to sing the illusion of masculinity was shattered. The disappearance of spoken interpolated commentary from the male impersonators act during the 1880s had placed a renewed emphasis on singing and song. This is not to say that these women never spoke in the context of the song, but the speech was not improvised, nor did it interrupt the song. When speech was employed, it was used in brief moments to reinforce the character portrayed, either by allowing the singer to speak lines of the song text in an accent or speech pattern appropriate to the kind of man depicted or to allow the singer to create short, realistic moments in the context of the song as she avoided the highest pitches of the melody. These moments tended to be contained and generally occurred only after the performer's gender had been established.

A third way to impose distance between the singer and the central character of the song was through the lyrics. The first generation of performers had sung in the first person, thereby claiming firsthand experience of the behaviors described in the song. After 1900 singers almost always referred to the character they portrayed in the third person. Moreover, after 1900 male impersonators no longer shared repertoire with male performers. Any shared repertoire was shared with other women, and there was little except their costumes to distinguish male impersonators from other female singers in vaudeville.

Vesta Tilley's popular song "Jolly Good Luck to the Girl Who Loves a Soldier" is a good example of these approaches to performance.[34] In a 1915 recording of Tilley singing this song, the pitch makes it immediately obvious that the singer is female.[35] In addition, the lyrics do not clearly identify the singer as a male character until the chorus. As a result Tilley's style of dress became vital in identifying her character as male. Tilley's style of dress was not entirely masculine. Her costumes were tailored but also clearly revealed her waist and the curve of her thighs, and she never assumed fake facial hair, as a number of earlier performers had. As a purely aural experience, the performance takes on a teasing quality and a campiness that was certainly not intended by the performer.

At the beginning of the song, Tilley sounds as though she is an older, more experienced woman offering advice to younger women. All references to military men are in the third person, and it is not until the third line of the chorus—"You know we military men always do our duty ev'rywhere"—that a male character is positively established (although the pitch of the final word undercuts the characterization). In this recording Tilley often speaks the lines that identify the singer as a male and uses heightened, slurred speech in the final chorus of the song, when she refers to herself as a "military gent," which serves to reinforce the characterization momentarily. Her realism, however, is continuously undermined by the register at which the song is sung. For audience members there could be no question that a woman was singing, despite the short hair and military uniform Tilley wore in performance, and they could safely enjoy her "correct" depiction of a British soldier without having to be at all concerned about Tilley's essential femininity and respectability.

Tilley's younger rival Hetty King specialized in nautical characters, and many of her songs depict sailors on shore leave. She also occasionally played careless young men about town and, in the recorded examples I have found,[36] often offered advice to the men in her audience. The songs that Wesner and Hindle had sung tend to carry the message "learn from my mistakes." They are always in the first person, and the singer became the butt of the joke as "he" told of the ways that women had got the better of him. In sharp contrast to this, both Tilley and King warned men about the dangers of women in a much more general way—the songs do not claim to tell of the singer's own experience in any detail.

Tilley and King tended to portray barely pubescent and sexually inexperienced men; their youthful appearance allowed them to boast of exploits with women without being taken too seriously. The swell continued to be the central figure in male impersonators' repertoires, but by the turn of the century he was a more problematic figure than he had been thirty years earlier. These women constantly trod a fine line between two different perversions. If they appeared to be too realistically masculine, they were open to charges of lesbianism, but if the male characters were portrayed as too effeminate, they could appear to be homosexual and therefore distasteful for an increasingly middle-class audience that included women. Most American male impersonators also portrayed young men; Kitty Doner portrayed prepubescent boys in her act, suggesting that American women felt a greater pressure than their British counterparts to avoid appearing at all masculine.

Given the heterogeneity of the vaudeville audience after the turn of the century, it is difficult to determine the appeal of these performers. British music hall scholars often explain the popularity of performers such as Tilley and King by noting that these women flattered the men in their audience, presenting them with a sympathetic portrayal of themselves through song. This seems a less than satisfactory explanation for their popularity in the United States. Maitland noted that when Tilley toured in American vaudeville in the 1900s, she revived songs depicting high-class swells that she had dropped from her repertoire because they were no longer as popular with a British audience. It is also evident from reviews and advertising that American audiences ignored the parodic intent of these songs, seeing them instead as a guide to high-class living and currently fashionable European behavior and dress.

The American audiences' close identification with the central characters of swell songs reflects early twentieth-century American desires for upward mobility. This desire had been reflected to some extent in the swell songs of the 1870s, but the early male impersonators balanced these swell songs with songs advocating workers' solidarity, expressing a nostalgia for preindustrial or at least rural America, giving men friendly courtship advice, and actively criticizing middle-class hypocrisy. These other kinds of songs had almost completely disappeared from the repertoires of later male impersonators in American vaudeville.

By concentrating on swell characters and portraying very young men, male impersonators in the early twentieth century allowed the audience to revel in the excesses of youthful, moneyed masculinity. It is interesting that the American audience preferred the swell songs to songs that portray ordinary, upwardly mobile young bank and shop clerks, the characters preferred by Tilley's London audience. This suggests that men in American vaudeville audiences had no desire to see themselves portrayed by male impersonators, preferring instead a more abstract, idealized upper-class gent. This aversion to seeing themselves portrayed by women may well have reflected the middle-class American man's fear of feminization on which Anthony Rotundo and George Chauncey, among others, have commented.[37]

Again, male impersonators in the early twentieth century had begun to be concerned that they might be associated with mannish women, both inverts and feminists. They also needed to avoid raising the specter of the effeminate man, or "fairy," in their performances, not only to avoid offending their audience, but also to protect their own respectability. Performers such as Clifford and Doner avoided any suggestion that the male characters they portrayed knew anything about sex while at the same time changing in view of the audience to reassure the viewers of their essential femininity. The increasing youth of characters portrayed by male impersonators enabled both the actress and the character she portrayed to be innocent of any improper sexual knowledge.

Male impersonators' appeal to women in their audiences after the turn of the century is hard to determine. Such performers certainly offered a model of independent working women who could earn as much or more than men. Their repertoire, however, probably did little to endear them to women. Many of the songs in Tilley's and King's repertoires, for example, are quite hostile to women, and King's songs encourage men to keep women in their place. Both King and Tilley poked fun at independent women, such as spinsters and flappers, and it is difficult to understand how they might have appealed to women. Given the increased proportion of women in the audience, it is odd that there should be little reflection of this in these performers' acts and that their songs are more critical of women than are those of the earlier generation.

It is likely that male impersonators in the early twentieth century felt an increased pressure to ally themselves with men on and off the stage to avoid being mistaken for feminist sympathizers. Christine Simmons has shown the emergence of the caricatured figure of the sexually repressed or sexually inverted career woman in the first decades of the twentieth century.[38] As work-

ingwomen whose earning capacity equaled that of many men on the vaudeville stage, and as women who seemed, visually at least, to conform to the most
feared parts of that stereotype, male impersonators may have felt that it was
necessary to avoid expressing any sympathy with women in their songs.

After 1900 relatively few women won success in vaudeville as male impersonators. Vesta Tilley completely dominated this genre in both Britain and the
United States, setting the standards against which all other performers were
measured. Although many young American performers adopted this form,
only a small number managed to find bookings in big-time vaudeville. Audiences and reviewers so strongly associated the genre with British women that
Kathleen Clifford began to claim in interviews that she had been born in Britain and educated in Europe, possibly to strengthen the validity of her male
impersonations.[39]

In 1920 Vesta Tilley retired when her husband was elected to Parliament.
Hetty King continued to be active in Britain into the 1950s and 1960s, but she
did not return to perform in the United States after 1911. The last British-based
star performer to tour vaudeville was Ella Shields, who toured periodically
between 1920 and 1929. Shields was based in Britain, and American audiences
generally considered her to be a British performer, but in fact she was American. Born in Baltimore in 1879, Shields made her vaudeville debut in 1898 as
a "coon" and ballad singer and performed in small-time variety and burlesque
until 1904. She made her British debut at Forester's Music Hall in London in
October 1904 and continued to perform as a "coon" singer in music hall until
her debut as a male impersonator at the end of 1910.[40]

Shields's performance style owed more to the influence of Ella Wesner than
to Vesta Tilley, something Shields acknowledged in an interview published in
the *New York Star* during her 1921 tour. She began the interview by expressing
her gratitude to British music hall, British audiences, and Tilley, suggesting that
Tilley had named Shields as her "successor" in her farewell speech at the Col-
iseum. Shields then compared her performance style to that of Tilley, insisting that they were quite distinct: "Ella Wesner was the original male impersonator. She was of a different type than Miss Tilley. Miss Tilley showed the
Johnny. She was light and dainty, and dandy. Ella Wesner was of a weightier
type. She gave her characters dignity. Each character was a creation and all types
of a more substantial kind than dear Miss Tilley wished to portray. I am proud
to be compared with Miss Wesner. When I was a child I saw her on the stage.
She was a handsome woman with a mass of black curls. She was the darling
of the music halls."[41] In this interview Shields is careful never to be disrespectful
of Tilley, but her admiration for Wesner is clear, as is the fact that she saw her-

self as performing in a style similar to Wesner's. Shields's performance style, which has been captured in sound recordings, is substantially different from that of both King and Tilley, probably because she self-consciously modeled her performances on her memory of Ella Wesner's performances of the 1880s.

Throughout her career Shields was more realistically masculine than either Tilley or King. Of the three performers, Shields was the only alto, and her speaking voice was quite low. Instead of singing, she often spoke the majority of the text to the song over the accompaniment of the orchestra. Shields's style of speaking through songs managed to give the impression that she was improvising text or including interpolated commentary, even though the text itself belies this impression. The characters in Shields's repertoire included young and old men, and she seemed to have specialized in swells of various sorts. Her signature character was an elderly bum called "Burlington Bertie from Bow."

Even though Shields was more realistic than either Tilley or King, and a good proportion of her songs employed the first person, the changes from the earliest performers are still clear. In her songs Shields never claimed to be sexually active, and her material avoided the explicit bawdiness of many of Wesner's songs. Her uneven spoken delivery of song texts gave the impression of improvised text, but she did not interpolate comic commentary into her songs. And even though Shields was one of the few performers who represented older men and working-class characters, they were generally depicted as laughable or as failures. In addition, when Shields sang songs in which the central male character professes love to a woman, she used the third person and a performance style that came closer to those of Tilley and King. There were some claims that even Shields was unwilling to make through song.

o   o   o

Shields's last American tour took place in 1928, and male impersonation had all but disappeared from American vaudeville by 1930. The British tradition did not fare much better, and only two performers, Shields and King, remained active in British music hall into the 1950s, their careers extended by the postwar nostalgia for the "good old days" of the Victorian and Edwardian eras. In both the United States and Britain male impersonation continued to be seen in films, where the cross-dressing was usually justified by the plot. This was most often achieved by including a scene depicting a theatrical performance in which the actress sang dressed in male clothing. The performance was framed within the plot, bounded on both sides with the actress appearing in female clothing, and in most cases having an appropriate male love-interest. Marlene Dietrich, who was notorious for the ambiguity of her sexuality as well as her strength of character, often appeared in such scenes. Other actresses who appeared in male clothing include Eleanor Powell, Judy Garland, and Betty Grable.

The film depiction of male impersonation represented the first major change to the structure of the genre in approximately sixty-five years. Unlike their counterparts in variety and vaudeville, male impersonators in films appeared in a single song rather than in a series of songs that would have allowed the actress to develop several different character types. In film the male impersonator became a novelty inserted into a narrative structure for the amusement of the audience. There was little or no attempt at realism; the song and the costume functioned to highlight the performer's femininity while introducing a suggestion of the thrill of the forbidden—sexual ambiguity.

By the 1930s the performance style of male impersonators had changed radically from that of the first generation of performers. I have shown that these changes were largely self-imposed, resulting from the performer's desire not to be mistaken for a mannish woman. The emergence of socially recognizable sexual minorities had a profound impact on the depiction of gender in all popular culture of the early twentieth century. But the first victims of the social distaste for, and hostility toward, homosexuals were those performers who performed cross-dressed. The discomfort of these performers affected all levels of performance, from the choice of repertoire and the kinds of claims that could be made through song to the vocal register at which songs were sung and the performer's appearance.

Although male impersonation, even in its early days, did no more than poke gentle fun at middle-class constructions of gender, it was dangerous in that it transgressed a number of middle-class ideals. A "good" woman knew her place; she did not seek independence. She did not want to adopt the costume and gestures of men, nor did she interact in a familiar way with men she did not know. The earliest male impersonators, who were working-class women, did all of these things, spitting, smoking, striding, swearing, and joking with men in the audience. As vaudeville emerged and managers sought to attract a more respectable, middle-class audience, male impersonators came under pressure to be more respectable. By the turn of the century the male impersonator was no different from many other female singers, except for the fact that she wore male clothing as she sang. In the end even this transgression became unacceptable, mostly because of its association with another social group that also transgressed middle-class values—homosexuals—and male impersonators ceased to be active in vaudeville before 1930, a decade or more before vaudeville lost its battle with moving pictures. Male impersonation disappeared from vaudeville not because it was banned but because it became a specialty that was distasteful to the performers themselves, the majority of whom shared the same middle-class values or aspirations as their audiences.

NOTES

1. Annie Hindle, the first male impersonator in American variety, was reputed to have earned $150 per week in 1868, and her most serious competitor, Ella Wesner, was paid $200 per week to perform in California during the summer of 1871 (*New York Sun,* 27 Dec. 1891, p. 13; "Advertising," *New York Clipper,* 2 Sept. 1871). Parker Zellers has noted that the average double act was lucky to earn as much as $50 per week week until the 1880s (Zellers, *Tony Pastor: Dean of the Vaudeville Stage* [Ypsilanti, Mich.: Eastern University Press, 1971], 24). Early in the twentieth century Vesta Tilley, probably the best-known male impersonator, was reputed to be earning around $2,000–$3,000 per week (*Variety,* 5 May 1906, p. 6).

2. "Older" in this case meant mature women in their mid- to late twenties rather than young women or girls in their teens. See note 23 for a comparison between the ages of American performers and their British counterparts.

3. "City Summary," *New York Clipper,* 6 Aug. 1870.

4. "Variety Halls," *New York Clipper,* 16 Dec. 1876.

5. *New York Sun,* 27 Dec. 1891, p. 13.

6. "City Summary," *New York Clipper,* 6 Aug. 1870.

7. "Variety Halls," *New York Clipper,* 31 Aug. 1872.

8. William Horace Lingard gained great success in America in the late 1860s and early 1870s, performing both male and female characters. See Sigmund Spaeth, *History of Popular Music* (New York: Random House, 1948), 167–68.

9. The aesthetic for male impersonators at midcentury seems to have preferred a lower vocal range. A number of male impersonators active in British music halls billed themselves as "female tenors." Hindle most likely belonged to this category, although she never used the title tenor in her billing. Of the British performers active in this period, only Vesta Tilley sang in the soprano range. Later in the century soprano male impersonators became more common.

10. *Music from the New York Stage, 1890–1920* (Pearl GEMM CD 9050–9061).

11. For an extended discussion of swell songs on the British music hall stage, see Peter Bailey, "Champagne Charley: Performance and Ideology in the Music-Hall Swell Song," in *Music Hall: Performance and Style,* ed. J. S. Bratton (Milton Keynes, U.K.: Open University Press, 1986), 23–48.

12. *National Police Gazette,* 13 Sep. 1879.

13. George Cooper and William F. Wellman Jr., "I'm No. 1" (New York: C. H. Ditson, 1872). Like many other such songs, it is held in the Lester Levy Sheet Music Collection, Johns Hopkins University, Baltimore, Md.

14. J. F. Mitchell, "Hi Waiter! A Dozen More Bottles" (New York: E. Harding, 1888).

15. "Captain Cuff" was introduced by George Leybourne in London in early 1877. It is likely that Wesner heard the song while touring Britain from 1876 to 1880.

16. The *New York Sun* (27 Dec. 1891, p. 13) noted that Hindle had once "compared ['mash'] notes with H. J. Montague, that handsome actor at whose shrine so many silly women had worshipped; but Hindle's admirers far outnumbered his, and they were all women."

17. The *New York Sun* noted that while Vivian claimed they had spent only one night together (implying that Hindle failed to perform her wifely duties), Hindle offered a very different version of the breakup: "He lived with me . . . several months—long enough to black both my eyes and otherwise mark me; yet I was a good and true wife to him" (27 Dec. 1891, p. 13). Advertising and reviews support Hindle's claims that the marriage lasted longer than a single night.

18. *New York Clipper,* 28 Sept. 1878, p. 214.

19. Details of this marriage can be found in Gillian Roger, "Male Impersonation on the North American Variety and Vaudeville Stage, 1868–1930" (Ph.D. diss., University of Pittsburgh, 1998), chap. 2. I have drawn on a number of newspaper accounts of this event, including *New York Sun,* 27 Dec. 1891, p. 13; *Grand Rapids Telegram-Herald,* 7 June 1886, p. 4; *Grand Rapids Evening Leader,* 7 June 1886, p. 4; *Grand Rapids Daily Democrat,* 8 June 1886, p. 5; *New York Clipper,* 12 June 1886, p. 198, and 19 June 1886, p. 217; *National Police Gazette,* 3 July 1886, p. 2, and 21 Aug. 1886, p. 2.

20. Nilsson toured the United States in 1883. Calling her "the Swedish Sappho" and the "lyric Lesbian," the *National Police Gazette* consistently depicted Nilsson as a woman who overwhelmed other women with her attentions and even dared to compete with men for women's affections. It also suggested that her affection for women was affecting her voice, stating "Christine Nilsson is developing such remarkable traits that no one would be astonished to find her bloom forth as a tenor soon" ("Stage Whispers," *National Police Gazette,* 17 Nov. 1883, p. 3). The *Police Gazette's* use of the terms *Sappho* and *lesbian* suggest that these terms were already becoming associated with what contemporary sexologists referred to as "sexual inversion."

21. In 1879 a theatrical gossip column in the *Clipper* noted: "Miss Augusta Gerschner, or Mrs. Berger, for the past six years valet of the 'male impersonator' Miss Annie Hindle, is suing her in the Second District Court, Jersey City, to recover the value of jewelry alleged to have been pawned by the plaintiff for the benefit of Miss Hindle when business was bad" ("Fact and Fancy Focused," *New York Clipper,* 23 Aug. 1879, p. 174). This note suggests that the relationship between Hindle and Berger went beyond that of employer and employee.

22. This affair is also discussed in chapter 2 of my dissertation. In this case, despite Mansfield's notoriety, national papers failed to comment on the story.

23. During Wesner's British tour (1876–80), London reviews noted her difference to the local male impersonators. During the 1876–77 theatrical season the thirty-five-year-old Wesner faced competition including St. George Hussey, who was then twenty-six;

Nelly Power, who was twenty-two; Bessie Bonehill, who was twenty; and Vesta Tilley, who was only eleven years old. The youth of the British performers and the tradition of casting male impersonators in feminized male roles in pantomime were two factors contributing to their more feminine performance style.

24. See, for example, "Why an Actress Cannot Wear Trousers Like a Man," *New York Journal,* 13 Feb. 1898; "Fascination of Masculine Garb for Ambitious Actresses," *New York Morning Telegraph,* 5 July 1903; "Stage Arts Adamless Eden," *New York Herald,* 10 July 1904; and Perriton Maxwell, "Stage Beauty in Breeches," *Theatre Magazine* 24 (Aug. 1916): 73, 75, 96.

25. *New York Journal,* 13 Feb. 1898.

26. Vesta Tilley, "The 'Mannish' Woman," *Pittsburgh Gazette Home Journal,* 3 Apr. 1904, p. 5.

27. Ibid. The American actress Katherine Grey made similar statements about women's "correct" social role in "My Beginnings," *The Theatre* 7 (Aug. 1907): 210–12. Almost all the most successful twentieth-century male impersonators highlighted their femininity in interviews and publicity material. Kathleen Clifford stressed her femininity from the beginning of her career, and she often asserted that her impersonations of men were unconscious and intuitive (see, for example, the interview in the *Dramatic Mirror,* 4 Mar. 1914, p. 23). The decency of Hetty King's act became a formulaic part of her advertising and reviews. King was also often photographed in female dress, and newspaper articles almost inevitably noted the length of her hair.

28. See Sarah Maitland, *Vesta Tilley* (London: Virago, 1986), 56.

29. There are a number of key works on theatrical cross-dressing and on the theatricality of gender. Prominent among these are collections such as Lesley Ferris, ed., *Crossing the Stage: Controversies on Cross-Dressing* (New York: Routledge, 1993); and Corinne E. Blackmer and Patricia Juliana Smith, eds., *En Travesti: Women, Gender, Subversion, Opera* (New York: Columbia University Press, 1995); and monographs such as Marjorie Garber, *Vested Interests: Cross-Dressing and Cultural Anxiety* (New York: Routledge, 1992); Judith Butler, *Gender Trouble: Feminism and the Subversion of Identity* (New York: Routledge, 1990); and Judith Butler, *Bodies That Matter: On the Discursive Limits of "Sex"* (New York: Routledge, 1993). The theoretical approaches in these and other works, however, either assume the existence of the category "lesbian" or work with constructions of femininity that are applicable primarily to the middle class. My own work has been significantly influenced by the work of Judith Butler, particularly *Bodies That Matter,* but I have found myself using her idea of "subversive reiteration" in relation to class rather than to gender and sexuality.

30. George Chauncey Jr., "Christian Brotherhood or Sexual Perversion? Homosexual Identities and the Construction of Sexual Boundaries in the World War I Era," in *Gender and American History since 1890,* ed. Barbara Melosh (New York: Routledge, 1993), 77.

31. George Chauncey Jr., *Gay New York: Gender, Urban Culture, and the Making of the Gay Male World, 1890–1940* (New York: Basic Books, 1994), 40–41.

32. A good summary of the emerging discourses around cross-dressing and lesbianism can be found in Carroll Smith-Rosenberg, "Discourses of Sexuality and Subjectivity: The New Woman, 1870–1936," in *Hidden from History: Reclaiming the Gay and Lesbian Past,* ed. Martin Duberman, Martha Vicinus, and George Chauncey Jr. (New York: Meridian, 1989), 264–80. Vern L. Bullough and Bonnie Bullough, *Cross Dressing, Sex, and Gender* (Philadelphia: University of Pennsylvania Press, 1993), provides a good starting point for those interested in nineteenth-century sexology and the changing construction of gender at the end of that century. The authors show the variety of reasons for cross-dressing by men and women and discuss the reactions of the medical establishment at the time. They also provide citations for most of the major sexological writings on transvestism.

33. Interview with Charles Young, n.d., clipping in New York Public Library at Lincoln Center, Robinson Locke Collection, ser. 2, vol. 299:184.

34. Fred W. Leigh and Kenneth R. Lyle, "Jolly Good Luck to the Girl Who Loves a Soldier" (London: Francis, Day and Hunter, 1905).

35. This recording has been rereleased in *The Golden Years of Music Hall* (Saydisc CD-SDL 380).

36. King apparently made several recordings in 1909 and 1910, but she seems to have avoided recording more of her songs until the 1930s, possibly because her voice and style of singing did not reproduce well in the earlier recordings (private correspondence with John Culme, 17 Feb. 1998).

37. See, for example, E. Anthony Rotundo, *American Manhood: Transformations in Masculinity from the Revolution to the Modern Era* (New York: Basic Books, 1993); and Chauncey, *Gay New York.*

38. Christina Simmons, "Modern Sexuality and the Myth of Victorian Repression," in *Gender and American History since 1890,* ed. Melosh, 29–30.

39. *New York Morning Telegraph,* Aug. 1910, in New York Public Library at Lincoln Center, Robinson Locke Collection, ser. 2, vol. 74:95.

40. Anthony Slide, *The Encyclopedia of Vaudeville* (Westport, Conn.: Greenwood, 1994), 463.

41. *New York Star,* 23 Feb. 1921, in New York Public Library at Lincoln Center, Robinson Locke Collection, envelope 2089.

5 TCHAIKOVSKY AND HIS MUSIC

IN ANGLO-AMERICAN CRITICISM, 1890s–1950s

MALCOLM HAMRICK BROWN

The proximity of two notable Tchaikovsky anniversaries—the sesqui-centenary of his birth in 1990 and the centenary of his death in 1993—had at last penetrated my consciousness and prompted me to start planning a class to commemorate the noteworthy near coincidence. What books, I wondered, belonged on the reading list for my students, most of whom would not be able to read Russian? I reached for the first volume in the Tchaikovsky section on my bookshelf and withdrew Gerald Abraham's collection entitled *Tchaikovsky: A Symposium,*[1] a book of essays by a number of critics. A note inside the cover reminded me that I had bought the book in April 1964. I had not read it since.

Opening to the introductory essay, "Tchaikovsky the Man," by the English critic Edward Lockspeiser, I started reading and soon encountered passages such as these: "Tchaikovsky had little reticence in describing his feelings. Even in the letters of his middle age he would sometimes gush like a schoolgirl." "Tchaikovsky's mind, seen for a moment from a scientific viewpoint, constitutes a text-book illustration of the borderland between genius and insanity." "The tragedy of Tchaikovsky was the denial, forced upon him, of normal love." "In Tchaikovsky's character . . . the neurotic elements are inseparable from his development as a composer. The man and his music are one—unsatisfied and inflamed."[2]

I hesitated at the somewhat snide innuendo but read on until the following description brought me up short: "Beginning with the Fourth Symphony, . . . Tchaikovsky's music now reflects all the indulgent yearning and the garish exteriorisation of a composer who can never refrain from wearing his heart on his sleeve—if, indeed, it is not music which suggests a less modest image than that."[3] Such commentary as this addresses not the music but the composer himself, and in a tone palpably ad hominem—scarcely what one expects from a professional music critic. Was this to be the nature of critical judgments found elsewhere in the volume? I flipped ahead to the next essay— Martin Cooper's discussion of the symphonies—and thought at first that the level of discourse had been upgraded. Cooper's comments seemed both more objective in tone and more technically adept. But then along came an account of Tchaikovsky's penchant for "the piling of climax upon climax in the top register of the strings, as in the first movement of the Fourth [Symphony], and the first and second movements of the Fifth."

> Such passages . . . do more than tear the heart (as indeed they are meant to do) but also affect the nerves like an exhibition of hysteria (with which they are very possibly related). This tendency reaches its climax in the last movement of the Sixth Symphony, where the perpetually descending phrase with which the strings open the movement is raised to a hysterical pitch of emotion. . . . There is something quite unbalanced and, in the last resort, ugly, in this dropping of all restraint. This man is ill, we feel: must we be shown all his sores without exception? Will he insist on our not merely witnessing, but sharing, one of his nervous attacks?[4]

Here again was an eminent English critic speaking about a piece of music as if he were speaking about the man who composed it, seemingly oblivious to the fallacy of such an equation. Moreover, given the frank tone of disapproval sounded here by Cooper no less than by Lockspeiser in the latter's preceding essay, one could only suppose that the two English critics shared an intense aversion both for the composer under discussion and for his music.

Had my political and social consciousness been so little raised thirty years ago that this invidious line of Tchaikovsky criticism simply had not registered? Had I been so unobservant as simply to miss equally blatant invocations of the biographical fallacy in the writings of other English music critics? What, I wondered, did Ernest Newman have to say about Tchaikovsky's Fourth Symphony?

Here are excerpts from an essay by Newman dealing with all the Tchaikovsky symphonies:

> The third and fourth symphonies . . . are in the main free from tragic suggestions of any kind. They are for the most part extremely impersonal, confining themselves to an expression of such generalized emotions as come more prop-

erly within the scope of the symphony pure and simple. . . . The extraordinary inventiveness of Tschaikowsky is nowhere more manifest than in these two works. . . . The fourth is big and masterly . . . throughout, the first and last movements being particularly vigorous; while the third . . . gives constant glimpses of the strong man's hand.[5]

Apart from his metaphorical aside about glimpsing "the strong man's hand," Newman speaks mainly about the music, not about the composer, and never equates the characters of the two. Moreover, the music strikes him as being mostly impersonal and confined to nonspecific emotions conventional to symphony. This is a far cry indeed from the hysteria, "indulgent yearning," and garish expression heard by Lockspeiser and Cooper.

Reassured by my reading of Newman, I turned to that most influential of all English critics, Sir Donald Francis Tovey, who, I remembered, had written a lengthy essay on Tchaikovsky's Sixth Symphony. Would I find that Tovey concurred in Martin Cooper's verdict that the symphony's finale exhibits the exposed "sores" of a sick man?

This is what the redoubtable Sir Donald maintains: "Nowhere else has [Tchaikovsky] concentrated so great a variety of music within so effective a scheme." Singling out the finale, "with its complete simplicity of despair" (as he so eloquently characterizes it), Tovey goes on to proclaim the movement "a stroke of genius which solves all the artistic problems that have proved most baffling to symphonic writers since Beethoven." Tovey unequivocally declares this symphony to be "the most dramatic of all [Tchaikovsky's] works," and the essay ends with this judgment: "Little or nothing is to be gained by investigating it from a biographical point of view; there are no obscurities either in the musical forms or in the emotional contrasts; and there is not the slightest difficulty in understanding why Tchaikovsky attached special importance to the work."[6]

Having just sampled Tovey's laudatory remarks about the work as a whole and his perception of the finale as "a stroke of genius," the reader should perhaps be reminded that this is the selfsame score that provoked Martin Cooper's ad hominem attacks.

How is it possible that recognized critics of established reputation arrive at such starkly disparate conclusions about the same music? "It happens all the time," someone will undoubtedly retort. And a contributory factor in the samplings at hand might well be that the two more positive critiques were written some forty years before the two decidedly negative ones. Certainly aesthetic perspectives change from one era to another and might well account for disparities in critical judgment.

But are differences in time and taste sufficient to account for the stark differences in tone between the critiques of Newman and Tovey, on the one hand, and of Lockspeiser and Cooper, on the other? Newman and Tovey, while not shying away from decisive and highly personal judgments about the work in question, nevertheless focus their remarks on the music itself, not its composer, and couch their observations in language that is comparatively matter-of-fact, straightforwardly descriptive, and relatively dispassionate. Lockspeiser and Cooper, by contrast, show little regard for the critical convention that places the artwork, not the artist, at the center of a reviewer's attention and takes for granted an analytical discourse on the cool and reserved side. Moreover, Lockspeiser and Cooper seem not merely unconcerned about but quite unconscious of having invoked the critical fallacy of suggesting that an artistic affect is, in some meaningful sense, an authentic image of an artist's real-life emotional experience, that "the man and his music are one," to use Lockspeiser's words, which lay bare this simplistic and reductive equation in all its muddleheadedness.

That Lockspeiser would posit such a conceptually crude formulation, to which Cooper also subscribes, might suggest that he was writing in an era more innocent of the insights of modern psychology and less responsive to modernist critical conventions than were Newman and Tovey, who favor a more objective tone. In fact, however, the opposite is true. The quoted passages from Ernest Newman and Donald Francis Tovey were published in the years 1902 and 1907, respectively, while those from Edward Lockspeiser and Martin Cooper appeared in 1945—quite the contrary of what might have been expected.

I reread the final two lines of Martin Cooper's comments about the finale of the Sixth Symphony: "This man is ill, we feel: must we be shown all his sores without exception? Will he insist on our not merely witnessing, but sharing, one of his nervous attacks?" And now an explanation suggested itself: Martin Cooper's critical judgment might well have been influenced by his awareness of Tchaikovsky's psychosexual orientation. Cooper was writing in the mid-1940s, by which time a view of homosexuality as a form of emotional illness had become widely accepted not only among psychiatrists and psychologists of various schools but also among the general public. Might Cooper have felt sanctioned by medical authority to declare Tchaikovsky ill and, as a corollary, to pronounce his music ill as well? If homophobic bias indeed played a part, conscious or unconscious, in Cooper's assessment of Tchaikovsky, how did his and Lockspeiser's response fit into the broader pattern of critical reaction to Tchaikovsky—a pattern that, could it be discerned, might reflect attitudes on the part of society as a whole?

These questions prompted me to undertake the admittedly limited and narrowly focused *Rezeptionsgeschichte* that follows. Samplings from Anglo-

American criticism on Tchaikovsky and his music are placed in the context of an emerging public awareness of the biographical facts about the composer's life relevant to his psychosexual orientation, and the resulting information is coordinated with contemporaneous public attitudes toward homosexuality. The emerging pattern suggests a plausible explanation for the striking disparity in response to Tchaikovsky encountered in the passages quoted from Newman and Tovey, who were writing in the first decade of the present century, and those quoted from Lockspeiser and Cooper, who were writing in the fifth.

One question loomed large: when exactly did it become public knowledge that Tchaikovsky was homosexual?[7] I found that the process of revelation occurred gradually, as one might expect, but it started much earlier than one might have imagined and was essentially accomplished in a surprisingly short time, at least within musical circles. Gossip in Moscow about the composer's difference in erotic tastes had circulated as early as the mid-1870s and contributed directly to his ill-considered decision to marry.[8] But if direct insinuations ever appeared in print during Tchaikovsky's lifetime—as they did about the composer's friend and schoolmate, the poet Apukhtin[9]—I have not succeeded in locating them.[10]

The earliest published intimation in English known to me—one densely veiled and ambiguous—appears in what may well be the first full-fledged biography of the composer published as an independent volume: *Tchaikovsky: His Life and Works,* "with extracts from his writings, and the diary of his tour abroad in 1888."[11] This early (if not earliest) biography was published in England, not in the composer's home country or elsewhere in Europe, and was written by Rosa Newmarch, an English music scholar with an avid interest in Russian music; her study of the subject in Russia had been sponsored by the illustrious Vladimir Stasov. Newmarch completed the biography in 1899, and the book was released almost six years to the day after Tchaikovsky's death (although the imprint date is given as 1900).

Newmarch was most probably made aware of the talk about the composer's heterodox erotic inclinations during her sojourns in Russia, although we cannot know what she made of the information. But consider these perhaps telling phrases in her biographical narrative: she describes the composer as a "gentle and sensitive artist, possessed with an almost feminine craving for approval and encouragement." Comparing him with the poet Pushkin, she suggests that "both had at times the gift of wearing their hearts on their sleeves in a very graceful, and not too unmanly, fashion." And when she comes to the marriage, this is how Newmarch sets the stage: "We have now reached the supreme crisis in the life of Tchaikovsky." She goes on to describe the composer's unusual secretiveness about his engagement, the shocked surprise of close friends when Tchaikovsky appeared at a social function with a wife on his arm, his increasing reserve and withdrawal from contact with friends and associates, and finally his precipitous trip to Saint Petersburg, followed immediately by reports of serious illness. Newmarch phrases her comments carefully: "Naturally his sudden departure gave cause for much gossip." She continues with this circumspect aside about the opinion of one of Tchaikovsky's closest friends, Nikolai Kashkin, "who knew his tenderheartedness and the almost feminine sensibility of his nature" and who was "filled with the gravest apprehensions which, as it afterwards proved, were not without some foundation." Newmarch concludes her account of the marriage and its aftermath with this statement: "Evidently for a short time [Tchaikovsky] was overwrought to the verge of insanity."[12]

It must be admitted, of course, that however one might interpret what could be discreet hints and veiled allusions, the matter of homosexuality as such remains unspoken and deep in the shadows. The very word found its way into English medical, legal, and social parlance only in the late 1890s, and even were Newmarch to have known it, the constraints of propriety would probably have prevented an English lady from acknowledging familiarity with the subject. All the same, a sense of something perplexing about Tchaikovsky seems to have been intuited by at least one reviewer of Newmarch's biography, who wrote in July 1900, "This book furnishes an interesting and valuable *resumé* of the somewhat mysterious, and, so far as we at present know, rather uneventful life of a remarkable musician."[13]

The reviewer's comments may prompt us to wonder what was being written about Tchaikovsky and his music by English and American critics during the composer's last years, toward the end of the century, when information about his life and personality was both scanty and enigmatic. The following are samplings from the last decade of the century:

An anonymous critic in the *American Art Journal* wrote of Tchaikovsky in 1891, "His example as a composer cannot be too highly commended . . . *first,* because it shows that the springs of melody have not yet run dry; *second,* because he demonstrates the fact that music can yet be written that will be fresh and original and yet be true to the fundamental principles of anti-Wagnerian times, without running into the dry pedantry of Brahms and his followers."[14]

An English critic had the following response in 1893 to Tchaikovsky's Fourth Symphony. The composer had traveled to England to accept an honorary doctorate awarded by Cambridge University. Saint-Saëns was being similarly honored at the same time, and a festive concert commemorating the occasion featured the two composers conducting their own music:

> The Russian master stood forward as, perhaps, the more significant figure of the two, not only because representing the newest influence upon European music—that of the Sclavonic [sic] race, but also because he brought with him a Symphony . . . [that exemplifies] much that is national in the composer's art. [The outer movements are] bustling, strenuous, at times extravagant, . . . *more an appeal to the judgment than the emotions;* but the *Andantino* came as an expression of pure feeling. . . . With this, the Russian master may fairly be allowed to have best vindicated his country's music.[15]

In 1936 Gerald Abraham, referring to the same work, would assert that "subjective emotion begins to force its way rather hysterically into the very stuff of . . . the music, . . . brutally . . . [forcing] it into a sort of expressiveness which it did not really possess."[16] Both the tone and the vocabulary employed by Abraham in this quotation anticipate by nine years the sort of judgments made by Lockspeiser and Cooper in 1945 and may well have provided the model. It is worth pointing out that by 1936, Abraham was well acquainted with a host of intimate details about Tchaikovsky's personal life at the time of the Fourth Symphony, including sensitive information about his failed marriage. But let us resist for a moment longer considering how those intimate details were revealed and turn our attention to one other noted critic at the turn of the century, well before these personal biographical facts were generally known.

The Irishman George Bernard Shaw also heard the Fourth Symphony conducted by the composer in 1893: "Of Tchaikovsky's symphony . . . I need only say that it is highly characteristic of him. In the first movement, the only one with a distinctly poetic basis, he is, as ever, 'le Byron de nos jours'; and in the later [movements], where he is confessedly the orchestral voluptuary, he is Byronic in that too. *The notablest merit of the symphony is its freedom from the frightful effeminacy of most modern works of the romantic school.*"[17]

A year later, following the composer's death, Shaw reviewed the first performance in England of Tchaikovsky's Sixth Symphony:

> The opening concert of the season on Wednesday last was a great success, thanks to Tchaikovsky's last symphony. . . . Tchaikovsky had a thoroughly Byronic power of being tragic, momentous, romantic about nothing at all. . . . [He] could set the fateful drum rolling and make the trombones utter the sepulchral voice of destiny without any conceivable provocation. This last symphony of his is a veritable Castle of Otranto, with no real depth of mood anywhere in it, but full of tragic and supernatural episodes which, though unmotivated, and produced by a glaringly obvious machinery, are nevertheless impressive and entertaining.[18]

In this review Shaw obviously cocks a skeptical eye at Tchaikovsky's music, wittily undercutting the sentiment and affect, yet nowhere does he interpret the score as crypto-biography, even though he is dealing with the *Pathétique* Symphony—a work already enshrouded by myth in the popular imagination of Shaw's time.

Space limitations preclude a detailed account of the background and preparation of Modest Tchaikovsky's prodigious three-volume documentary biography of his brother, the first volume of which bears the Russian imperial censor's date of 11 November 1900. This first volume includes the critical year of the composer's marriage, 1877. The two later volumes appeared in 1901 and 1902. Suffice it to say that this work was a landmark in the annals of composers' biographies on account of its extraordinary dependence on Tchaikovsky's own words—drawn from intimate letters, diaries, and other personal documents—as the structural basis for the biographical narrative. No earlier composer's personal life was so thoroughly revealed to the world as Tchaikovsky's was in the very words he himself had addressed to family members and intimate friends, within such a short time of his death. This is not to suggest that Modest practiced no editorial discretion with respect to his brother's erotic life (which Modest understood very well, since he too was homosexual). But the degree of frankness is remarkable for that time and place.

Rosa Newmarch translated, edited, and condensed the three volumes for the English market. Reduced to a single hefty tome, Newmarch's reworking of Modest's biography appeared in 1905 under the title, *The Life and Letters of Peter Ilich Tchaikovsky*.[19] Tchaikovsky was now exposed to English and American readers in his own translated words, which were interpreted by this new audience from a perspective formed quite naturally by Anglo-Saxon notions of the way men should conduct themselves both publicly and privately. Consider the following sample of what English readers in 1905 could learn from Modest's biography. This excerpt comes from a private letter Tchaikovsky wrote to his patroness, Nadezhda von Meck, explaining the circumstances of his engagement to Antonina Miliukova, who would become his wife: "When we met [for the first time in person] I told her again that I could only offer gratitude and sympathy in exchange for her love. . . . [I] told her frankly that I could not love her, but that I would be a devoted and grateful friend. . . . To live thirty-seven years with an innate antipathy to matrimony, and then by force of circumstance, to find oneself engaged to a woman with whom one is not in the least in love—is very painful. . . . I told her what she could expect from me, and what she must not count upon receiving."[20]

Some pages later Modest adds the following comment: "It was not until they entered into closer relationship that they discovered, to their horror, they were far from having told each other all."[21] Need the point be made that most readers in 1905, after having perused these tactfully discreet but plainspoken passages, would probably have understood quite clearly that Tchaikovsky did not conform to the masculine cultural stereotype sanctioned in contemporaneous English and American society?

The English in particular, arguably more so than Americans, have often displayed tender sensibilities on the matter of manliness in music, as is demonstrated by the following quotation from an 1889 article with that very title, "Manliness in Music":

> Few things have contributed more effectively to perpetuate in this country the prejudice against the musical profession . . . than the impression that musicians are as a class wanting in the manlier qualities. In a country like England, where devotion to athletics forms a cardinal tenet of the national creed, such an impression cannot fail to have operated greatly to the prejudice of the art. . . . We have the greatest sympathy for the healthy average well-born British male in his undisguised contempt for the effeminate young men whom his sisters too often view with favour on the score of their supposed artistic accomplishments. . . . No musician need be unmanly; and the best have almost invariably been remarkable for a robustness of mind and character. . . . There was no lack of virility in the character of Beethoven. Handel was made of sturdy stuff, capable of volcanic explosions of fury. . . . In our times the robust individuality of Brahms's music is the outcome of a thoroughly masculine nature.[22]

Keep in mind George Bernard Shaw's praise of Tchaikovsky's Fourth for its "freedom from the frightful effeminacy of most recent works of the romantic school." Recall the quoted review from 1891 that favors Tchaikovsky's music over the "dry pedantry of Brahms and his followers." And contrast these early affirmative critiques, both written before the publication of Modest's biography, with the one following, which appeared the year *after* Newmarch's English translation appeared. The critic, the Englishman Edwin Evans, is contrasting Tchaikovsky and Brahms: "On the one side, music calm, intellectual, raisonné, of careful and calculated symmetry; on the other, passion, the coursing of warm blood, violent reactions of an emotional temperament, fringing hysteria, both in its exuberance and in its depression."[23] The critic has invoked classic gender-coded vocabulary that bestows the label of masculine on Brahms's music and feminine on the music of Tchaikovsky.

The starkly contrasted and culturally loaded characterizations encountered in the quotation from Edwin Evans are nowhere to be found in the critical discourse of the American writer James G. Huneker, who reports on Tchaikovsky's participation in the concerts opening New York's Carnegie Hall in 1891. Huneker argues that "the barbaric swing of [Tchaikovsky's] work is tempered by European culture and restraint," and although he finds Tchaikovsky to be "not as profound as Brahms," he considers the Russian master to be "more poetic." "Above all [Tchaikovsky] paints better than the Hamburg composer," Huneker believes; "his brush is dipped into more glowing colors, his palette contains more hues." The critic then concludes the essay by declaring, "He is a strong man. He says great things in a great manner, and that is why I call him the greatest man at present in this broad and fair land."[24]

Huneker alters his critical discourse radically, however, once he learns more details about Tchaikovsky's personal life—details he shares with readers of his widely influential book from circa 1899, *Mezzotints in Modern Music: Brahms, Tschaikowsky, Chopin, Richard Strauss, Liszt and Wagner*. Here the critic somewhat abashedly confesses, "I once wrote of Tschaikowsky that he said great things in a great manner. Now I sometimes feel that the manner often exceeds the matter." Huneker goes on: "Clouded by an unfortunate and undoubted psychopathic temperament, [Tchaikovsky] . . . was denied even the joys and comforts of a happy home. . . . [His] entire existence was clouded by some secret sorrow, the origin of which we can dimly surmise, but need not investigate. . . . He was . . . morbid in his dislike of women." The critic's own squeamish response to having presented these unvarnished biographical details eventually prompts him to draw the line: "There is no need of further delving into the pathology of this case, . . . but it is well to keep the fact in view, because of its important bearing on his music, some of which is truly pathological."[25]

Music that is "truly pathological"? Facing critics such as this, who blithely invoke the biographical fallacy without a blush, composers risk indictment for indecent exposure merely by submitting their scores to public scrutiny.

Perhaps now is the appropriate moment to define as clearly as possible the critical fallacy to which I have already referred several times. I define the biographical fallacy as speaking about an artist's creative work as if it were straightforward autobiography or, by extension, attributing human emotions or characteristics to technical features, events, or configurations encountered in an inanimate artwork, suggesting thereby that the artwork somehow replicates an experience in the life of the artist who created it.[26] I agree with Alexander Poznansky's elegantly formulated observation that "a work of art nearly always obscures and transcends the experience that gives impetus to its composition"[27] but go still farther and claim that a true work of art *always* obscures and transcends its creative impetus, because viability as an artwork presupposes the conformity of its constituent elements to the laws, conventions, and semantic principles operative within the creative universe of the artform in question. Shakespeare's plays or Rodin's sculptures are no more passages from those artists' real-life biographies rewrit large in verse or stone than is Tchaikovsky's music his often troubled life translated into sound.

But the fundamental question remains: could the early exposure of Tchaikovsky's homosexuality have induced so powerful an antipathetic response in some music critics as to prejudice their evaluation of the composer's music in the period under discussion?

The question cannot be answered definitively. But the circumstantial evidence presented so far in favor of an affirmative answer gains additional plausibility when placed in the context of testimony about pervasive homophobia in English and American society from the 1890s through the 1950s. Many recent scholars agree on the critical importance of the 1890s in the formation of modern strictures against homosexuality, that is, the very moment when it emerged as a concept: "The social condemnation of male homosexuality increased. This is clearly seen in the development of harsher legal penalties in the last decades of the nineteenth century."[28] "The courts ordered the first English scientific text on homosexuality destroyed shortly after its appearance in 1898."[29]

For a characterization of the 1930s, 1940s, and 1950s, the period during which Abraham, Lockspeiser, and Cooper were writing their critiques of Tchaikovsky and his music, one can turn to C. S. Lewis. Writing in his autobiography about those years, Lewis ironically encapsulates the prevailing attitude of the period toward homosexuality:

> People commonly talk as if every other evil were more tolerable than this. But why? Because those of us who do not share this vice feel for it a certain nausea, as we do, say, for necrophilia? . . . We attack this vice not because it is the worst but because it is, by adult standards, the most disreputable and unmentionable, and happens also to be a crime in English Law. The world will lead you only to hell; but sodomy will lead you to jail and create a scandal, and lose you your job. The world, to do it justice, seldom does that.[30]

Moving forward to the decade immediately following World War II—at the start of which, it will be remembered, *Tchaikovsky: A Symposium* was published—the following three quotations offer perspective on the undiminished hostility in Britain toward homosexuals:

> In England the aversion to abnormal sex is so strong that a suspect homosexual can be pronounced guilty on circumstantial evidence that would be quite insufficient to convict a robber.[31]

The British view homosexuality with the same moral horror to-day as they always have. The attitude has hardly changed in hundreds of years.[32]

Few subjects evoke so great an emotional response as that of homosexuality. It must be admitted that for the average person an objective approach is impossible. When he considers the problem at all, the ordinary Briton does so with distaste that borders on horror.[33]

Given such deeply ingrained and persistent negative social attitudes toward homosexuality as sampled here, spanning the 1890s through the 1950s, mainly in Great Britain but in the United States as well, is it any wonder that critical judgments about Tchaikovsky and his music should have been affected?

In an article that has only recently come to my attention, and that provides an intriguing supplement to my own research, the Australian scholar Nigel Smith finds a further nuance in the composer's changing critical fortunes.[34] In the first decade of the century, Tchaikovsky's emotional expression was defended as powerfully sincere: "If he expressed the suffering phrases of humanity alone, he at least did so with all the truth and sincerity of an Ecclesiastes."[35] His gestures of personal exposure were seen as having universal meaning, as when Edwin Evans wrote about the Fifth Symphony: "It is like an eloquent sermon in which every man traces the allusion to his own shortcomings, and in which he seems to hear the expression of his secret thoughts."[36] Nonetheless, as we have seen with James Huneker, the same decade gave birth to the trend of viewing such effusions as signs of pathology. The language of medical diagnosis—terms such as *hypochondria, morbid perversity,* and *chronic hysteria*—became increasingly common. By 1919 Charles Buchanan could write in *Musical Quarterly:* "In the light of modern investigation we see Tchaikovsky for a clearly marked case of psychasthenia, and in remarking this fact one is merely recording a scientific phenomenon."[37]

Smith relates this trend to the newly current notion of homosexuality as an "identity which pervaded every aspect of an individual's life": in Foucault's words, as a "secret that always gave itself away."[38] What had once been seen as the composer's insight into the secret thoughts of humanity now became a deceptive split in his own psyche. Lockspeiser, for instance, in the article with which I began, speaks of his "forked sexuality condemning him to subterfuge and duplicity."[39] And this inner division scars the music as well: "He had to make a pose of his misery. He could not be himself. . . . But in the finale of his last symphony the mask dropped off, and the real tragedy of his life was written so plainly and directly that hardly anyone could fail to understand it. The pitiful incompleteness of Tchaikovsky's emotional system and of his whole life is laid bare."[40]

o   o   o

Tchaikovsky became a master in exploiting the familiar cycles of tension and release associated with the tonal and harmonic conventions of eighteenth- and nineteenth-century music. He understood the powerful expressive potential of telling reference to familiar musical topics encoded into his listeners' consciousnesses by the corporate compositional practices of classic and Romantic composers. He understood the semantic potential of these topics and these compositional conventions because he continually tested them on himself, if we are to believe half of what he writes in his letters about weeping as he played through this or that passage of music. We cannot doubt that he well understood how readily a listener's labile human emotions would respond to aural stimulus, how easily they would adhere to the surface of vibrant sonorities, and how natural it would seem to project the meaning of an immediate personal response onto the music itself.

The reception of this body of music in the early twentieth century became vulnerable to shifts in taste and prestige as the forbidding winds of modernism blew across the Continent. In Tchaikovsky's case, however, criticisms redolent of antiromantic prejudice were wrapped up in ad hominem attacks reflecting an insidious homophobia, and the effects of these unconscious discriminations linger in the critical literature to this day. From our perspective, over a hundred years later, we should be able to see them for what they are. The time is past when a swooning posture, an emotional assault, and a racing heart need to be construed as signs of illness.

NOTES

Earlier versions of this chapter were presented at the interdisciplinary conference "Tchaikovsky and His Contemporaries," Hofstra University, 7–9 Oct. 1993, and published in *Tchaikovsky and His Contemporaries: A Centennial Symposium*, ed. Alexandar Mihailovic (Westport, Conn.: Greenwood, 1999), 61–73. Reprinted by permission. I am deeply grateful to Chip Whitesell for helping me recraft this article for *Queer Episodes*.

1. Gerald Abraham, ed., *Tchaikovsky: A Symposium* (London: Lindsay Drummond, 1945).

2. Edward Lockspeiser, "Tchaikovsky the Man," in *Symposium*, ed. Abraham, 10, 12, 13, 14.

3. Ibid., 20.

4. Martin Cooper, "The Symphonies," in *Symposium*, ed. Abraham, 33–34.

5. Ernest Newman, "Tschaikowsky and the Symphony," *Monthly Musical Record* 32 (1 Aug. 1902): 146–47.

6. Donald Francis Tovey, *Essays in Musical Analysis*, vol. 2: *Symphonies (II), Variations and Orchestral Polyphony* (London: Oxford University Press, 1935), 85–86; the essay was originally published in 1907.

7. The term itself was, of course, unknown in Tchaikovsky's own day, and its present-day connotations and associations, so deplorably "essentializing," are utterly foreign to the composer's social milieu. I use the term here for its purely descriptive convenience, doing so reluctantly and fully conscious of its sociological anachronism.

8. "I would hope by marriage or, in any case, an open affair with a woman to shut the mouths of various contemptible creatures whose opinion I do not value in the least but who can cause grief to the people close to me" (Tchaikovsky to his brother Modest, 28 Sept. 1876, *Pis'ma k rodnym* (Letters to his family), vol. 1: *1850–79*, ed. V. A. Zhdanov [Moscow: Gosudarstvennoe muzykal'noe izdatel'stvo, 1940], 259).

9. See, for example, *Epigramma i satira; iz istorii literaturnoi bor'by deviatnadtsatogo veka, 1840–1880* (Epigram and satire: from the history of the literary war of the nineteenth century, 1840–80), vol. 2, comp. A. G. Ostrovsky (Moscow and Leningrad: Academia, 1932), 424.

10. On various occasions, published attacks on the Moscow Conservatory and its director, Nikolai Rubinshtein, hinted at scandalous behavior within the hallowed walls, and more than once Tchaikovsky interpreted innuendos about sexual misconduct as directly threatening himself. Take, for example, the following excerpt from a letter written to Modest in 1878: "At Fastov I got a newspaper (*Novoe Vremia*) and found in it 'A Moscow Feuilleton' devoted to a filthy, base, disgusting and slanderous *philippic* against the Conservatory. About me personally there's almost nothing. . . . But in one place the article touches on the amours of professors and girl students, and at the end adds: 'there are at the Conservatory also amours of another sort, but about them, for quite obvious reasons, I shall not speak' and so on. It's obvious what that refers to. . . . Let's suppose that the insinuation is not directed at me personally this time, but so much the worse. My [. . .] reputation falls on the entire Conservatory, as a consequence I am even more ashamed and distressed" (Tchaikovsky to Modest, 29 Aug. 1878, in *Pis'ma k rodnym*, 442). Notwithstanding Tchaikovsky's anguished assumption here and elsewhere that his "lost reputation" (see *Pis'ma k rodnym*, 259) was widely known and reflected badly on the conservatory, I have been unable to discover any reference to Tchaikovsky by name or even by veiled allusion in connection with published innuendos about sexual indiscretions at the conservatory during the composer's tenure as a faculty member.

11. Other early biographies of the composer include V. S. Baskin, "P. I. Chaikovksii," in the series *Russkie Kompozitory* (Russian composers) (Saint Petersburg: A. F. Marks, 1895); and Iwan Knorr, "P. I. Tschaikowsky," in the series *Berühmte Musiker* (Famous musicians), ed. H. Riemann (Berlin: Harmonie, 1900).

12. Rosa Newmarch, *Tchaikovsky: His Life and Works* (London: G. Richards, 1900), 25, 61, 69.

13. Unsigned review, *Musical Times* 41, no. 7 (1 July 1900): 474.

14. In "Facts, Rumours, and Remarks," *Musical Times* 32, no. 7 (1 July 1891): 403.

15. In the review of the Philharmonic Society, *Musical Times* 34, no. 7 (1 July 1893): 406–7 (emphasis added).

16. Gerald Abraham, with M. D. Calvocoressi, *Masters of Russian Music* (London, 1936; repr., New York: Knopf, 1944), 333.

17. George Bernard Shaw, *Music in London 1890–94*, 3 vols., rev. ed. (London: Constable, 1932; repr., New York: Vienna House, 1973), 3:3 (emphasis added).

18. Ibid., 3:178–79.

19. An American edition was published the same year, 1905, in New York. A New York reprint edition also appeared in 1970, issued in two volumes rather than in one, as originally.

20. Modeste [Modest] Tchaikovsky, *The Life and Letters of Peter Ilich Tchaikovsky*, 2 vols., edited from the Russian and with an introduction by Rosa Newmarch (repr., New York: Haskell House, 1970), 1:218–19.

21. Ibid., 1:224.

22. "Manliness in Music," *Musical Times* 30, no. 8 (1 Aug. 1889): 460–61.

23. Edwin Evans, *Tchaikovsky* (London: Dent, 1906), 39.

24. James Huneker, in his column "The Raconteur," *The Musical Courier*, 13 May 1891; in Elkhonon Yoffe, *Tchaikovsky in America* (New York: Oxford University Press, 1986), 120–23.

25. James Huneker, *Mezzotints in Modern Music* (New York: Scribner's; London: William Reeves, n.d. [ca. 1899]), 86–91.

26. I have been unable to pinpoint when or where I first saw the term "biographical fallacy," but it was most probably in reading theories of biography and autobiography, which occupied a large portion of my attention in the late 1970s and early 1980s. The concept had formulated itself in my mind, by analogy to the so-called pathetic fallacy, so thoroughly by the time I first encountered the term that I thought I already knew it and only later came to realize that someone had invented it before me.

27. Alexander Poznansky, *Tchaikovsky: The Quest for the Inner Man* (New York: Schirmer, 1991), 119.

28. Jeffrey Weeks, *Coming Out: Homosexual Politics in Britain, from the Nineteenth Century to the Present* (London: Quartet Books, 1977), 6.

29. Louis Crompton, *Byron and Greek Love: Homophobia in 19th-Century England* (Berkeley: University of California Press, 1985), 4.

30. In Alfred Gross, *Strangers in Our Midst* (Washington, D.C.: Public Affairs, 1962), 31.

31. D. J. West, M.B., and D.P.M., *The Other Man* (New York: Morrow, 1955), 69.

32. Gordon Westwood [Michael George Schofield], *Society and the Homosexual* (New York: Dutton, 1953), 104.

33. Tom A. Cullen, "Homosexuality and British Opinion," *New Republic* 132 (25 Apr. 1955): 13–15.

34. Nigel Smith, "Perceptions of Homosexuality in Tchaikovsky Criticism," *Context* 4 (Summer 1992–93): 3–9.

35. A. E. Keeton, "Peter Ilytch Tschaikovski," *Contemporary Review* 78 (July 1900): 78.

36. Edwin Evans, "Tchaikovsky Analyses 3: Symphony no. 6 in B minor, op. 74 ('The Pathetic')," *Musical Standard* 28 (Sept. 1907): 197.

37. Charles Buchanan, "The Unvanquishable Tchaikovsky," *Musical Quarterly* 5 (July 1919): 368.

38. Smith, "Perceptions," 6; Michel Foucault, *History of Sexuality*, vol. 1 (Harmondsworth: Penguin, 1976), 43.

39. Lockspeiser, "Tchaikovsky the Man," 21.

40. J. A. Westrup, "Tchaikovsky and the Symphony," *Musical Times* 81 (1940): 251.

6 TRANSCRIPTION, TRANSGRESSION,

AND THE (PRO)CREATIVE URGE

IVAN RAYKOFF

To consider replication degrading is, literally, homophobic:
afraid of the same.
—Wayne Koestenbaum, "Wilde's Hard Labor and the
  Birth of Gay Reading"

"I'd like to play something never before heard in public," announces
Franz Liszt (acted by Henry Daniell) in the 1947 Hollywood biographical film about Robert and Clara Schumann, *Song of Love:* "A paraphrase, arranged by myself, on a superb melody, 'Dedication,' by my esteemed
colleague, Professor Schumann."[1] (The film thematizes Schumann's "Widmung" as Robert's musical gift to Clara on the occasion of their engagement,
and throughout the film this "song of love" signifies the couple's romance.)
Although Liszt delivers a dazzling virtuoso arrangement of the tune to the mar-
veling guests at his recital, Clara remains unimpressed and whispers cattily (in
Katharine Hepburn's classic style of haughty dismissal), "Dedication to love?
Dedication to pyrotechnics!"

"You're a brilliant artist, Franz. I envy you," Frau Schumann confides to
Liszt after the ovation, as she sits down at the piano herself. "I wish I had the
power to translate the commonplace into such stupendous experience." She
plays her own simpler transcription of the same song for Liszt to consider.
"Once in a while, though, a little moment comes along, which seems to defy
such translation. Do you know what I mean, Franz? . . . *Love,* Franz, as it is.
No illusions, no storms at sea. No gilt, no glitter. Not the rustle of silk, and the
diamond garter, Franz. Just love, unadorned." Finishing her musical parable,
she asks, with arch significance, "Or do you know what I mean?" When Prin-

cess Hohenfels intercedes to support Liszt against her innuendo, he murmurs, chastened, "She did much worse than insult me, my dear. She described me!"

This scenario, Hollywood invention though it is, enacts a few quasi-musicological attitudes for its matinee audience, and even musically untrained viewers, coached by the accompanying dialogue, can hear the oppositional significance of the two arrangements performed. Clara's "unadorned" transcription—essentially the original song without additional embellishment—is clearly valued over the "stupendous" paraphrase (figure 6.1). Her seeming-

FIGURE 6.1. Transcription or Transgression? The climactic recapitulation in Liszt's arrangement of Schumann's "Widmung."

ly more authentic arrangement assumes the ability to represent love "as it is," in contrast to the implied superficiality and deceptive illusion of Liszt's virtuosic version. The scene also taps into certain recurrent notions about musicality and personality: it plays up the perceived excesses of the Romantic virtuoso style (flashy and popular with audiences yet deemed shallow by more "serious" musicians) as well as prevailing mythologies surrounding Franz Liszt. As the quintessential pianist-lover, Liszt gained a reputation for immoral amorous adventures and sexual promiscuity, an image contrasted here with the respectable virtues of bourgeois married life represented by Clara, Robert, and their "song of love."

David Wilde has asserted that "in his arrangements, Liszt often failed to capture the intimacy that lies at the heart of German song."[2] In both Hollywood portrayal and scholarly pronouncement, Liszt is an apparent outsider to true love—he misses the simple heart and soul of the matter. Liszt, it seems, needs to borrow another couple's dedication, either because he cannot create his own or because his own loves are not to be sung about in public. But when he usurps the matrimonial melody, he is rebuked for his transgressive appropriation. This playboy virtuoso is unworthy of the musical/matrimonial ideal, and his performative self-indulgence taints its purity. Liszt is compelled to exaggerate sincere feeling into dramatic spectacle, because he cannot limit himself to a normal—"commonplace"—love(song).[3]

Movie musicology notwithstanding, the scene demonstrates certain real-life attitudes concerning musical appropriation as involved in transcription and paraphrase. By 1947, when Song of Love premiered, the critical estimation of arrangements had completed a nearly absolute about-face from the earlier nineteenth-century tolerance (if not acceptance) of this repertoire and the wide circulation (if not ubiquity) of such music on recital programs. Authenticity was coming into fashion, and compositional or interpretive meddling of the Lisztian sort was regarded as a misled indulgence of the bygone Romantic era. In 1928 the pianist Artur Schnabel censured Liszt's arrangements of Schubert lieder: "To play these transcriptions nowadays is an offense against Schubert and a detriment to the taste of our time."[4] Arthur Loesser, discussing the declining reputation of piano arrangements during the early part of the century, asserts that "a greater purity of taste—one might almost call it prudishness—began to be evident" around this time.[5] Even in the early 1980s Alan Walker could still lament the long "conspiracy of silence" surrounding the Schubert-Liszt transcriptions. He pondered their omission from the 1936 Breitkopf und Härtel collected edition of Liszt's music ("a curious editorial decision . . . for which no satisfactory explanation was ever given") and the dearth of commercial recordings of these works.[6] Piano arrangements, transcriptions, and paraphrases had become a stealth repertoire, savored privately by a few aficionados while disappearing from public circulation in recitals, printed scores, and recordings.

Why this fall from grace? Why the apparent allergy to an important component of the Romantic piano repertoire after its vogue of popularity through the nineteenth and early twentieth century? Attitudes toward the compositional identity of the original musical work underlie the decades-long neglect, even suppression—as well as the recent renaissance—of this controversial repertoire. The continuing critical debate over piano transcriptions reveals a larger struggle over the "identity politics" of the compositional "body" and its reproduction, as well as the "moral" connotations inherent in this musical-physical analogy. Transcription is transgressive because of its potential not only to reconfigure an original musical text but also to rearrange the socially constructed ideals of originating (pro)creativity.

REARRANGING TASTES

> Few areas of musical activity involve the aesthetic (and even the moral) judgment of the musician as much as does the practice of arrangement.
> —Malcolm Boyd, "Arrangement," *The New Grove Dictionary of Music and Musicians* (1980)

Solo piano arrangements of instrumental and vocal material constitute a significant portion of the instrument's repertoire, both in quantitative and historical terms.[7] Piano transcriptions and paraphrases enjoyed their heyday from the 1830s (the era of celebrated virtuosi such as Liszt and Sigismond Thalberg) into the early twentieth century, when works such as the Verdi-Liszt *Rigoletto* paraphrase, the Bach-Busoni Chaconne, or Adolf Schulz-Evler's "Arabesques" on the "Blue Danube" waltz by Johann Strauss Jr. were still an integral part of the typical recital program. Even in the 1920s newly composed piano arrangements such as Igor Stravinsky's transcription of his own *Petroushka* (a showpiece for pianist Artur Rubinstein) or Manuel de Falla's "Ritual Fire Dance" (arranged by Rubinstein himself) found a sanctioned place in the concert repertoire.[8] Performed by latter-day virtuosi, such works continued the earlier Romantic-era piano tradition then still in vogue.

There were both practical and performative motivations for composing and playing piano arrangements in the nineteenth century. Simplified piano solos and duets provided the fodder for domestic entertainment and amateur music-making. Since mechanical means of sound reproduction were as yet undeveloped, and accessibility to large-scale orchestral and operatic performances remained limited, the piano reduction or transcription served as a primary tool for musical study and dissemination.[9] Arrangements also provided a means to promote new works and composers and to honor past masters. For virtuoso performers, highly elaborate and challenging paraphrases provided vehicles for concert entertainment and technical display. The nineteenth century was "the age of the piano," and transcribers explored the technical and sonic potential of the newly evolved instrument, striving to match pianistically the coloristic range of the orchestra or the dramatic glory of the opera singer. It was also the era of the pianist-composer, and this dual capacity as both musical creator and recreator enabled the virtuoso to fashion a substantial "homemade" repertoire, including embellishments and improvisations on material borrowed from other composers' works. Of Franz Liszt's entire compositional output of approximately two hundred solo piano works, only about half (or less, depending on how one catalogs it) consists of completely original compositions. Comments Philip Friedheim, "This rather embarrassingly leaves a large collection of arrangements, which even Liszt enthusiasts approach with some hesitation."[10]

Even those composers and performers deemed more "serious" engaged in a certain degree of musical borrowing and arranging for their performing or pedagogical needs. Robert Schumann turned a dozen Paganini caprices into piano études, and Johannes Brahms did likewise with compositions by Bach and Chopin. An 1842 review in the *Allgemeine musikalische Zeitung* asserts the value of arrangements (in this case, Johann Nepomuk Hummel's transcriptions of twelve Mozart concertos) for the dissemination of musical works but acknowledges the controversy they provoke: "If some voices are raised against these and similar transcriptions, if some declare—with more or less justification—that one should not profane holy works with strange and transparent guises, and so forth, it is still honorable and meritorious that such works have reached the greater public's awareness through sensible arrangements."[11] But "superficial" virtuosity was increasingly devalued, and along with it a concomitant portion of the arrangement repertoire.[12] Early in her career Clara Schumann performed a repertoire of virtuoso paraphrases and composed a set of flashy concert variations on a Bellini theme, but she later turned away from showpieces ("concert pieces like . . . Thalberg's Fantasies, Liszt, etc. have become quite repugnant to me")[13] and programmed more substantial works by Beethoven and the German Romantics. Partly as a result of her crusading efforts with this then less-popular repertoire, Schumann acquired something of a reputation as a musical priestess. "The reigning saint of music," the *Song of Love* script calls her, or "that dear old prig in petticoats," as Ernest Newman misogynistically puts it: "She and her associates honestly thought that they were the last bulwarks of the virtuous in art against the inroads of the immoral virtuosi."[14]

In the early twentieth century, significant critical opinion was already set against the piano-arrangement repertoire. Frederick Niecks, in a 1905 article on Liszt's piano works, notes that operatic arrangements "do not now enjoy the popularity they once enjoyed; the present age has lost some of its love for musical fireworks and the tricking-out and transmogrification by an artist of other artists' ideas."[15] In 1911, when Ferruccio Busoni performed his legendary series of Berlin recitals devoted to the music of Liszt (including numerous paraphrases, song transcriptions, and even Busoni's own versions of works by Liszt),[16] Edward J. Dent reported, "It can well be imagined how horrified the Berlin critics were at programs of this type; but they seem to have enjoyed them against their will."[17] Arrangements were also becoming less "necessary" as the phonograph provided new means for musical reproduction—and less "permissible" as international copyright agreements set in place legal restrictions on the adaptation or arrangement of musical compositions. Pianist-composers such as Ferruccio Busoni,[18] Leopold Godowsky, and Sergei Rachmaninoff continued the practice of transcription and paraphrase, but the rise of the modernist aesthetic and the consequent trend toward "authenticity" prompted a shift in the relationship between composer and performer and in attitudes about the creation and dissemination of musical works.[19] A division of labor between composer and performer became standard and expected, with the former regarded as musical creator and the latter as executant serving the composer's conception. Interpretation, previously a valued quality of individual Romantic expressivity, was deemed self-indulgent excess, indulging the ego of the performer over the original intentions of the musical work.

Thus the *appropriateness* of musical appropriation became an issue sparking a certain degree of heated opinion among composers, performers, and critics. Paul Hindemith, in his 1949 Norton lectures, sarcastically belittles the concert performer's urge to transcribe another composer's work: "The time comes in every serious performer's life, when he feels that it cannot be the final purpose of his existence to be some elevated form of public jester, that there must be some higher aim than a lifelong concentration on the question how to hit the right tone at the right time with the proper strength. . . . A very popular activity that satisfies such longings is producing arrangements of other people's creations."[20] Although Hindemith acknowledges the limited appeal of strict execution, he nevertheless mocks the creative performer's attempts to fashion an individualized (re)creative response to the musical work. On the other side of the debate, Kaikhosru Shapurji Sorabji, himself a deviser of eccentric pastiches on Chopin's "Minute Waltz" and Bizet's *Carmen*, ridicules the prevailing critical attitude regarding paraphrases in a 1932 essay: "Among the many works of Liszt misunderstood, malappreciated and derided by the average musician, whose mentality is invariably of the herd-type, slavishly following the lead of some pompous imbecile . . . and by the spurious-superior folk, whose temerity and impertinence in passing judgment upon matters of which they are utterly ignorant are only equalled by their ignorance of these same matters, the operatic fantasies come in for a very large share of abuse. They are virtuoso-music, display pieces of the worst type—vulgar, empty, tawdry, and so on."[21] Not only vulgar, some would say, but sacrilegious. Early in her career Wanda Landowska weighed in with a condemnation of transcriptions as profane creations: "'The harpsichord works of Bach,' said [Hans von] Bülow, 'are the Old Testament; Beethoven's Sonatas the New. We must believe in both.' And while saying that, he added several bars to the Chromatic Fantasy, changed the answer of the Fugue, and doubled the basses; thus he impregnated this work with an emphatic and theatrical character."[22]

Perhaps the shifting attitudes toward this repertoire are best illustrated by Hans Keller, who compares two dictionary entries on the term *arrangement* separated by a span of six decades: the definition in Hugo Riemann's 1882 *Musik-Lexicon* and another in Willi Apel's 1944 *Harvard Dictionary of Music*. Both begin identically ("the adaptation of a composition for instruments other than those for which it was originally written"), but whereas Riemann offers a case-in-point example (piano reduction vs. original composition), Apel feels compelled to remove the arrangement to neutral, nonmusical territory: "thus, in a way, the musical counterpart of a literary translation."[23] As Keller interprets this amendment, a twentieth-century anxiety motivates Apel, "no longer struck by any natural examples," to offer an extramusical rationale for the matter. What would constitute a natural example and why nature should be a factor in this discussion are issues not pursued by Keller. The repertoire itself holds clues to this anxiety over (un)natural forms of arrangement and to the larger moral issues surrounding the creative "urges" that motivate such musical reproductions.

THE WORK AS BODY

> "Took liberties with!" . . . The implication of it is that music is a sort of unprotected female who is never safe when a "fast" man is about.
> —Ernest Newman, "The Virtuous and the Virtuoso"

The debate over reproductive rights is a battleground of beliefs and values in our society, influencing political elections, motivating religious pronouncements, inciting antiabortion violence, and inspiring various national programs to encourage or limit population growth. The overarching questions in this cultural controversy concern the status and use of the body vis-à-vis personal desire and social convention: Is the body (particularly the female body) socially accountable or privately personal? What is the body's appropriate use or role in acts of pleasure or procreation? Closely related to these questions are issues concerning the control of reproduction (as with contraception or abortion) and the arrangements of sexual relation outside of legally approved practices (sodomy or polygamy, for example). Tradition is set in opposition to transgression, and the body becomes a contested site of personal identity, political power, and cultural struggle.

The reproductive-rights debate and the politics of the body can apply analogously to music and the other arts. The artistic work, like the human body, is an entity subject to a variety of manipulations—formal or substantive doctorings, social regulations, or intellectual deconstructions—from forces acting on it. Certain schools of literary criticism regard the written text as a conceptual body contingent on or influenced by the author or reader; a musical composition is likewise shaped through the composer's mind and the performer's physical body. But there are also regulations controlling actions on the musical body. Like the physical body, a composition is often regarded as a sanctified creative entity, and the bowdlerization of a masterwork, as tantamount to mutilation.

Landowska employs this analogy between the physical body and the musical work in the opening of her essay on transcriptions. She relates an anecdote about her 1908 visit to the sculptor Auguste Rodin, whom she describes as "a great lover of the music of the past." Together they tour his collection of antique sculpture; at one point

> he became ecstatic before a woman's torso mutilated by the centuries, "See, madame, the refinement, the suppleness of these lines! Ah! what a pity that parts are missing!" Out of curiosity I ventured to ask, "*Cher Maître,* why don't you try to reconstruct them?" He looked at me, amazed. It was obvious that this idea had never entered his mind; one had to be a musician to have such a thought. "But, madame, I do not feel able to do it; and even if I were, I should never dare." And I thought of all these small virtuosos and schoolmaster-composers who go tooth and nail at tampering, mutilating, and disfiguring our sublime works. . . . They put Bach, Mozart, and Handel back on the drawing board; and after slandering the most beautiful masterpieces, they dare to juxtapose their obscure names with those of our greatest masters. . . . What would sculptors say if some plasterer took it upon himself to shave off some marble from the Venus de Milo to give her a wasp waist or if somebody twisted Apollo's nose to give him more character?[24]

Landowska's characterization of the artwork as a vulnerable body informs her criticism of "the parasitic melodic line of the 'Ave Maria'" which Charles Gounod "grafted" onto Bach's famous Prelude in C Major from *The Well-Tempered Clavier*.[25] Other examples of "unnatural," even incestuous, musical matings are rife in the transcription repertoire: consider Busoni's combination of a Bach Prelude and Fugue into a single "Perpetuum mobile et infinitum" in his *Klavierübung* (1925), or Godowsky's quodlibets joining two Chopin études.

Because the term *transcription* is used broadly and inconsistently as a label for different kinds of pianistic adaptations, it will be useful to clarify definitional categories. Leonard B. Meyer distinguishes between two types of adaptation: the literal transcription, in which "means different from those of the original work are used to re-present it as accurately as possible," and what he calls the arrangement, or paraphrase, which "generally involves significant additions to, deletions from, or changes of order in the original" and demonstrates more idiosyncratic or improvisatory revisions with less adherence to the original work. According to Meyer, the primary difference between the two categories is the degree to which the work's original identity is maintained or modified: "the merit of a transcription . . . is measured by its ability to reproduce the character and 'tone' of the original; the merit of a paraphrase, on the other hand, depends not upon its faithfulness to a model but upon its inherent interest as a work in its own right." In short, the transcription "differs from its model in means and medium," while the paraphrase "differs from its model in significance as well."[26]

A key attribute in Meyer's definition invites closer consideration: the notion of *faithfulness*. Fidelity to the original work distinguishes the literal transcription from the more liberal paraphrase; it preserves the identity of the original and enables the transcription's "ability to reproduce" the original work. As Stephen Davies explains in his article on transcriptions and authenticity, a transcription's musical content must "adequately resemble and preserve" that of the original work. Although aspects of the original will necessarily be altered in the transfer, a transcription that revises too extensively "fails through its lack of faithfulness to the musical contents of the original."[27]

Franz Liszt's transcriptions of the Beethoven symphonies are oft-cited examples of this ideal of faithful reproduction. According to the biographer Frederick Corder, "Beethoven was the one composer towards whom any irreverent alteration was to [Liszt] unthinkable. . . . It is open to all to observe the scrupulous fidelity of his published Beethoven transcriptions, in marked contrast to the freedom of all his other ones."[28] Alan Walker praises these adaptations for "the challenge these symphonies presented in defying ten fingers to reproduce them without harming Beethoven's thought" and cites "the loving care, the meticulous attention to details, which shines out of every page of [Liszt's] Beethoven transcriptions" as evidence of his "single-minded devotion to the memory of Beethoven."[29] Regarding the Schubert-Liszt transcriptions, Derek Watson asserts that "critics of these song arrangements object to the innocent charm and simple sensitivity of Schubert's *Lieder* being wedded to the dazzling plethora of Lisztian effects. Yet he always remains faithful to the spirit of the originals."[30]

Whereas transcription strives for faithful reproduction of the original work, the *paraphrase* reconceives musical material through elaborative pianistic textures, new counterpoint and harmonies, improvisatory diversions (such "dished-up" revisions might include free-form "rambles," to borrow Percy Grainger's terms), or other compositional modifications. Walker defines the paraphrase as "a free variation on the original" that strives for "metamorphosis" rather than careful reproduction: "In a paraphrase, the arranger is free to vary the original, to weave his own fantasies around it, to go where he wills."[31]

Unconstrained by expectations of fidelity, the paraphrase invites a degree of compositional liberty, performative spectacle, and the expression of idiosyncratic identity, including even humor, irony, and parody. Discussing the Strauss-Godowsky *Die Fledermaus* paraphrase, Michel Kozlovsky notes that "every motive, harmony or contrapuntal line in this work is expressive of Godowsky's humor." He adds, "The place of this transcription in the piano repertoire is comparable to that of the clown among acrobats," an evaluation that recalls Hindemith's negative depiction of some performers as "public jesters." The work's ability to convey a high degree of personality is a function of its being a paraphrase: "Such jocular spirit could not have been produced in an original work; it is the distortion of a well-known piece of music which yields this result."[32] Critics often describe a paraphrase as a "distorted" or "perverse" musical arrangement, although ambivalent attitudes arise regarding the value or significance of such alterations. Kozlovsky notes that "this deliciously decadent 'perversion' of a simple harmonic idea is what makes Godowsky's [*Fledermaus*] paraphrase so charming." Discussing the Strauss-Godowsky "Symphonic Metamorphosis on 'Das Kunstlerleben,'" Maurice Hinson writes that "the simple Strauss waltz is completely transformed, imprisoned in a labyrinth of horrendous complexities. Every aspect of piano playing is utilized with exquisite decadence."[33]

Given the metaphorical correlations between musical work and creativity, on the one hand, and physical body and procreativity, on the other, critical attitudes toward "true" transcription and "perverse" paraphrase invite certain parallels to the arrangement of interpersonal and intimate relationships in society, particularly marriage and human procreation. If the creative relationship between composer and performer bears some analogy to the heterosexual procreative relationship (the male impregnates, and the female gives birth), then the virtue of "true" transcription mirrors the traditional social expectation of fidelity within marriage and the family. The transcription's fidelity is seen to preserve the hierarchy and sanctity of the creative musical union of composer and arranger-performer, unlike the compositional philandering associated with the paraphrase. The paraphrase writer is often accused of "taking liberties" with the composer's original creation, of "having his way with" the music. As a result, the paraphrase is often considered a bastardized version of the original that sacrifices fidelity to the composer for the sake of the adapter or performer's own gratification.

Identity and authority are the strategic concerns underlying the transcription versus paraphrase controversy, as they are in cultural debates over reproductive rights and the regulation of the body. This analogy between physical body and musical work can be carried further: new creation (of proud biological parents or inspired original composer) is often valued more highly than mere adoption or adaptation of another's (re)productivity. Furthermore, the original progenitor retains "rights" over the new body or work—at least until the child comes of age or the composition enters the public domain. The transcriber or paraphraser, however, is seen as a surrogate musical parent usurping the composer's distinct creative identity and his or her authority of authorship. The forced musical "marriage" between original composer and arranger makes for complicated legal designations in the naming of the parentage: consider the Schumann-Liszt and Chopin-Godowsky offspring (and the hyphenating complications of Saint-Saëns–Horowitz) or the other interlopers who, as Landowska puts it, "dare to juxtapose their obscure names with those of our greatest masters."

Anxieties over the appropriate regulation of (pro)creative "urges" affecting the work or the body also underlie both the cultural and the musical controversies. Hindemith, for example, rails against the metaphorical digestive urge of the "paracreative" arranger: "The irrepressible desire to arrange, to participate in the creative process, at least by nibbling, seems to belong in the same class—although on a higher level—with the cannibal's eating of his captured enemy in order to add the enemy's strength to his own."[34] Some critics claim that the composer's creation has been abused, resulting in a psychological disruption of the work's original identity. Paul Henry Lang detects "a weighty psychological problem" inherent in arrangements, which he regards as motivated by the narcissistic urge to perform: "the desire for improvisation and virtuosity arising from the identity of the composer and performer."[35] Sorabji credits a parapsychological urge when he notes Liszt's "power of seizing upon extraneous themes and so charging them with his own peculiar quality that, without actual alteration, they lose all semblance of their original physiognomy, and become 'controlled,' to use an expression borrowed from the spiritists, or 'possessed.'"[36] At stake is how the work/body may be handled in the course of its enjoyment and its perpetuation or reproduction.

(PRO)CREATING QUEERLY

> Things are being recycled so promiscuously these days. . . . Recycling requires no commitment, no point of view, for it's predicated on the emotions of mockery, knowingness and wit, not on those of earnestness or passion.
>
> —Michiko Kakutani, "Art Is Easier the 2d Time Around," *New York Times,* 30 Oct. 1994

Like a gay/lesbian perspective on social and sexual matters, a "queer" perspective on the musical work can provide further insights into the politics surrounding the urges of musical (pro)creativity and the processes of musical reproduction. The concept *queer* signals (in Moe Meyer's definition) "an ontological challenge that displaces bourgeois notions of the Self as unique, abiding, and continuous while substituting instead a concept of the Self as performative, improvisational, discontinuous, and processually constituted by repetitive and stylized acts."[37] What better précis for the distinction between true transcription and perverse paraphrase? The transcription, charged with fidelity to the patrilinear composer-progenitor's text/work/body, maintains the "unique, abiding, and continuous" identity of a musical work despite surface alterations of color and medium. The paraphrase, on the other hand, is idiosyncratic and unpredictable: it is performative in that it enacts a self-conscious display of technique, style, and personality; improvisational in that it veers off unexpectedly from the original score with flights of fantasy; and discontinuous because the arranger steps into the accepted reproductive progression, displacing to a significant extent the original ancestral forebear. In short, the paraphrase is *queerly and transgressively reproductive.*

One particular reproductive transgression of the paraphrase is that it oversteps the boundary of a work's unique and original content in pursuit of a newly configured outward expression. It disregards primary essence in favor of secondary appearance—a radical reevaluation of musical identity that privileges flexible (and possibly deceptive) outer style over apparently stable inner content. The paraphrase, Alan Walker writes, "is not interested in 'original thought,' it changes notation with impunity, and it does not reverence the sonic surface; indeed it often flits about, chameleon-like, donning the most outrageous acoustical disguises, defying us to say where the music's true identity is to be found."[38] Admittedly, it is sometimes difficult to locate the original musical self underneath its intricate contrapuntal disguises, as in the Schubert-Godowsky "Wohin?" paraphrase published in a Russian edition (figure 6.2).

The paraphrase could even be considered a form of musical *drag*, impersonating the original work while at the same time camouflaging that identity beneath a distracting array of surface appearances and surfeit personalities. Critics have not looked favorably on this tendency to disguise the identity of the original. Writes Arthur Briskier in his monograph on Bach transcriptions, "Adaptations with modifications are but vain accessories, which dress up this music and lessen its greatness" (recall Liszt's "gilt" and "glitter").[39] Hindemith engages the trope of cross-dressed music in his caricature of the arranger: "You take some older music written for harpsichord, organ, or any other relatively unattractive instrument or group of instruments, and dress it up with all sorts of more fashionable trimmings. For the connoisseur this is an artistic procedure of about the same value as providing a nice painted skirt and jacket for the Venus of Milo, or dolling up the saints of Reims and Chartres with tuxedos, mustaches, and horn-rimmed spectacles."[40] Hindemith's sartorial disapproval recalls Landowska's distress over Venus's "disfiguring" cosmetic surgery. He criticizes the paraphraser for doing precisely what the drag queen accomplishes: calling into question markers of identity by "dressing up" the true body/artwork with seemingly inauthentic gender signifiers.

Authenticity's esteem for the original text (hence, original musical self) also has a political aspect in terms of queer identity. Modern scholarship insists on the stable, fixed musical work as an object for historical interpretation, theoretical analysis, and faithful performance. The Urtext score, a carefully edited reproduction of manuscript sources, seems to best reflect the identity of the work and the original composer's musical conception. In discussing the transgressive potential of queer parody, however, Moe Meyer points out how "the relationship between texts becomes simply an indicator of the power relationships between social agents who wield those texts, one who possesses the 'original,' the other who possesses the parodic alternative." The queer—in his discussion, camp—copy becomes a transgressive vehicle when "the marginalized and disenfranchised advance their own interests by entering alternative signifying codes into discourse by attaching them to existing structures of signifi-

1. КУДА?

5

Свободная транскрипция для
фортепиано   Л. ГОДОВСКОГО

Ф. ШУБЕРТ, соч. 25

FIGURE 6.2. Schubert-Godowsky: Where is "Wohin?"

cation."[41] Having appropriated and revised the Schumanns' "song of love,"
Liszt is accused of transgressively rewriting the "musical text" of traditional
matrimony in just this way.

The power play over original text and its appropriate (re)creation is particularly evident when paraphrase is contrasted to another form of musical
replication, the theme-and-variations form. The typical variations form exhibits a reproductive mechanism that develops (or "paraphrases") the origi-

nal material numerous times. Busoni, however, has noted the general acceptance of a composer's decision to write variations on another composer's theme or musical model, unlike the stalwart resistance to writing free-standing paraphrases: "For some curious reason variation form is held in great esteem by serious musicians. This is odd, because if the variation form is built upon a borrowed theme, it produces a whole series of transcriptions, and the more regardless of the theme they are, the more ingenious is the type of variation. Thus, *arrangements* are not permitted because they change the original, whereas the *variation* is permitted although it *does change* the original."[42] The distinction might be explained by the fact that the variations' theme is stated at the outset as the origin(al); one rarely finds examples of a theme-and-variations form in which the original musical theme is given only at the close of a series of elaborations. This opening Ur-theme becomes the metaphoric father-progenitor of a series of musical offspring, mirroring the patrilinear model of procreation.

Just as queer political movements at the close of the twentieth century have fostered alternative structures of procreation and relationship (including adoption, artificial insemination, and broadened categories of the family), "queer" forms of cultural production similarly champion alternative forms of relationship between creator, re-creator, and audience. For example, the camp aesthetic—regarded as a hallmark of gay cultural expression in the twentieth century, at least in the tradition that venerates Oscar Wilde as inspirational forebear—readily employs copy, imitation, and parody for expressive effect. The paraphrase can provide a musical model of this aesthetic sensibility and this manner of creative (re)production. The "camp" paraphrase celebrates the primacy of an elaborately theatrical style, the exterior masquerade that enables interior expression, the indulgence in hidden "second" meanings ("the lie that tells the truth," to borrow Philip Core's title),[43] and the incongruous applause for a disfranchised object of devotion (the last element particularly applicable during the era of the paraphrase's critical denigration). In this sense, Liszt's voluptuous "Widmung" performance in *Song of Love* qualifies as a moment of camp expression.

Modernist criticism has typically regarded the imitative copy as an inferior simulacrum of the true original object. Walter Benjamin famously claims that the "aura" of the artwork "withers" through its mechanical reproduction and that "the technique of reproduction detaches the reproduced object from the domain of tradition. By making many reproductions it substitutes a plurality of copies for a unique experience." But this process of replication also "reactivates the object reproduced" for newly configured meanings.[44] Here "queer" (re)production begins its work. In a discussion of Oscar Wilde's post-trial prison writings, Wayne Koestenbaum considers Wilde's "fetishistic attention" to his own literary productions as an attempt to perpetuate gay identity via the reproductive mechanisms of modern publicity and publication. Koestenbaum asserts that Wilde "reclaimed aura for gay purposes by redefining mechanical production *as* aura and insisting that the copy bears the original's transcendence." The description of Wilde's philosophy on imitative copy can apply to the pianistic paraphraser's art as well: "Obsessed with copying, cannily undermining essences, Wilde entertained the glittering, seductive, and centerless play of surfaces, and refused to take essences earnestly."[45]

Other theorists present the concept of queer replication using different terminology: Jonathan Dollimore defines "transgressive reinscription" as "a turning back upon something and a perverting of it, typically if not exclusively through inversion and displacement."[46] Judith Butler considers "subversive repetition" a function of normative heterosexuality's assumption of original, true, and authentic identity in opposition to the stereotypical and homophobic understanding of homosexuality as a failed and perverse copy of that ideal.[47] Hans Keller's previously cited observation on the lack of "natural" examples of arrangement can be revealingly paired with Koestenbaum's consideration of the politics of cloning, typically considered an inherently *un*natural reproductive mechanism, in relation to post-Stonewall gay culture. As a slang term, *clone* is a mildly derogatory label for gay men who dress and groom themselves according to stereotypical images of masculinity. Since the more common meaning of the word carries associations of laboratories and scientific engineering, "it also subtly derides a gay male's non-procreative sexuality; it defines homosexuality as replication of the same."[48]

What sort of musical body does the queerly reproduced paraphrase represent? Consider again the subtly homophobic assessments of Liszt's bachelor-virtuoso character in *Song of Love*. Liszt's manner of musical (pro)creativity signifies sexual promiscuity. He is unable to experience intimacy, an apparent outsider to true love, a purveyor of tasteless insincerity and performative self-indulgence. Liszt's life contrasts with the Schumanns' model of (pro)creative order (composer Robert conceives what wife Clara brings forth to the world) and "correct" musical (re)production (exemplified by Clara's sincere and faithful transcription of her husband's original work). Liszt engenders his music differently (via unsolicited compositional appropriation and inauthentic replication) and enacts his music differently (via virtuoso performative gestures and seemingly spontaneous fantasy). Thus Clara's pointed barb—"Or do you know what I mean?"—carries a world of meaning.

In numerous critical treatments, too, Liszt presents a problematic figure as a composer who creates in an unorthodox manner. Indeed, his predilection for arrangements calls into question his ability to (pro)create at all. A review of Liszt's 1886 London performances in the *Monthly Musical Record* declares, "There can be no question that the genius of Liszt is reproductive [i.e., imitative] rather than creative."[49] Edward Baxter Perry, discussing Liszt's transcriptions in 1902, asserts that they demonstrate creative powers of a secondary rank, claiming that the "peculiar aptitude" required for transcription or paraphrase "may be a lower order of genius than the originally creative faculty."[50] In a 1905 article on Liszt as a composer, Frederick Niecks echoes Perry but brings out a fine distinction in this debate over Liszt's compositional capacities: yes, Liszt was "a creative genius," but a genius "qualitatively unlike" the great masters Mozart, Beethoven, or Schumann, for he was "inventive" (a cloner) rather than "creative."[51] Even some who concede that Liszt's compositional output is remarkable regard this as a sign of creative promiscuity: "For many historians and critics," writes Arnold Whittall in 1987, "Liszt's sheer productivity as a composer, coupled with the prominence of transcriptions and paraphrases of other men's music, has served to reinforce suspicions that he could not possibly have been either very serious or very discriminating in his creative work."[52]

At the same time, Liszt's fecund (re)creative urges (via the art of arrangement) and his unorthodox manner of handling a musical body (via paraphrase) elicit admiration from other commentators. Camille Saint-Saëns appreciates "how Liszt can take any bone and extract the marrow out of it, how his penetrating mind has cut through trivialities and platitudes and got to the hidden artistic germ, which he proceeds to fertilise."[53] Paul Henry Lang waxes poetic on the subject of Liszt's generative powers: "in Liszt's garden we see many noble plants which inclement circumstances prevented from bursting into bloom, but while many of them bear no flowers, not one of them is without deep roots."[54] Watson echoes the horticultural motif with curiously homoerotic imagery: "As a dramatist and a performer Liszt re-created a number of works distilled from the essence of other men's flowers."[55]

In this more positive light, the queerly reproduced paraphrase holds potential for a broadened understanding of the work or the body and its social and cultural relationships. Writing on the subject of queer cultural identity in 1994, Frank Browning asserts, "Some feel that being gay intimates not so much an aesthetic or a culture of identities as an entrée into a world of forbidden, transgressive desire, a manner of living that challenges overtly the heterosexual conventions of marriage and procreation in favor of a radical, collaborative exploration of pleasure and spirituality."[56] The paraphrase elicits pleasure in its humor, irony, and camp potential; it exercises spirituality in its transcendence over mundane literalness and its affirmation of metamorphosis over stasis. It celebrates the mutual "collaborative" relationship of the (re)creative process between composer and arranger-performer. And its transgressive treatment of the original text reminds one that the composer's authenticity may be as much an illusion as the virtuoso's spectacle.

OUT OF THE CLOSET

> I have the most hair-raising piano transcriptions of Strauss tone poems that you'll ever hear. I play them privately.
>
> —Glenn Gould, quoted in Payzant, *Glenn Gould*

If Liszt is a controversial, compositionally "queer" figure, what about his figurative pianistic progeny, the Romantic-style virtuosi of our own era? Twentieth-century pianists known for their repertoire of arrangements—the list includes Vladimir Horowitz, Jorge Bolet, Earl Wild, and Glenn Gould (and yes, Wladziu Valentino Liberace must be counted among them)—continued to perform transcriptions and "perverse" paraphrases during a time when prevailing attitudes looked down on such musical reproductions. Their repertoire of arrangements can be seen as a throwback to the Romantic era, compositional artifacts evoking musical tastes and values of the old-fashioned past. Even the titles of these works ("Fantasies," "Reminiscences," "Souvenirs," etc.) convey an aspect of nostalgic memory as performed—or in some cases camped—by these latter-day paraphrasers of the nineteenth-century virtuoso image.

More to the point, however, this repertoire could also serve a contemporary political purpose in signifying the *rearrangement* of social and personal texts through queer (re)production. The transcription and especially the paraphrase represent an apparent liberation from the established, apparently authentic texts of normative (pro)creativity. The paraphrase-playing pianist delights in this textual reconfiguration and can borrow its temporary disguise—the drag of a new-fashioned musical body—to enact his own personal rewriting of "moral" texts for public reception. The paraphrase can offer an expressive cover for presenting concealed (extra)musical meanings, as if in code, to an unsuspecting audience. Discussing Godowsky's free paraphrase of Bach's unaccompanied cello suites, Abram Chasins suggests that Godowsky intended "to probe inner meanings and hidden beauties; to give utterance to vaguely suggested thoughts and to project undivulged ideas."[57]

As Godowsky shows, one needn't be queer to indulge in the urge either to revise or to display and enact such subversive reproductions. But this communicative potential has been exploited and championed by numerous relatively queer pianists during the twentieth century. While Vladimir Horowitz publicly denied his homosexual tendencies,[58] his playing revealed the camp conflict between outer style and inner content. Harvey Sachs writes, "Vladimir Horowitz's phenomenal technique [read: phenomenal style, phenomenal spectacle] and questionable musicianship [questionable content, questionable sexuality] have made him the most controversial pianist of our time."[59] Glenn Plaskin asserts that Vladimir Horowitz conveyed "a flamboyant personal impression" via his arrangements. Horowitz himself admitted this repertoire influenced his own identity: through composing and performing paraphrases, he said, "my pianism started to change—it became more shrill, more brutal, so brilliant that I couldn't play certain kinds of music."[60] Indeed, one reviewer noted that in his concert paraphrases "the characteristic sound and fury would be turned loose [and] Horowitz would stop being respectful of the classics and start being his unafraid self."[61]

The paraphrase might also communicate certain disguised meanings. In Horowitz's seemingly patriotic paraphrase of John Phillip Sousa's "Stars and Stripes Forever" march, Detlef Gojowy hears both "a declaration of love for America, and at the same time a catastrophic caricature. . . . Horowitz, who had discovered America in the figure of Scott Joplin, made a grandiose, virtuosic, scurrilous ragtime out of Sousa's march—a music of the bordello, as Joplin's was. . . . The camouflage is as perfect as Horowitz's interpretation of it, at once ridiculous and monumental."[62] Was Horowitz merely being entertaining in his flamboyant paraphrase of themes from Bizet's *Carmen,* or might there have been a campy delight in the heroine's brash sexual promiscuity translated into his own act of musical (pro)creativity?

Glenn Gould also remained enigmatic on the subject of his sexuality, but his interest in transcriptions and paraphrases indicates some degree of a queer sensibility. Edward Rothstein—wondering "what, exactly, was the nature of Gould's sexuality?"—refers to one of his arrangements as an indication of Gould's inner urges: "Gould loved the spun-out desires of Tristan: once he began playing that work in his own piano transcription, we are told, there was no stopping him."[63] Kevin Bazzana asserts that Gould's arrangement of Maurice Ravel's "La Valse" provides a parodic commentary on the original work but that his performance of it also indicates a delight in ironic double meanings beneath the surface:[64] "It is difficult not to hear this sort of virtuosity— at once punishing and playful—as Gould's send-up of his own musical tastes and priorities. To make sly in-jokes (even album-length in-jokes) for listeners aware of his musical proclivities, to use a virtuoso's technique to poke fun at overt virtuosity—these are motivations highly unusual in a 'serious' classical performer, to say the least."[65] Friedrich Otto detects a queer (i.e., perverse, odd) sensibility in Gould's 1967 recording of a Beethoven-Liszt symphony: "Gould perversely brought forth from relative obscurity one of his oddest triumphs, the Liszt transcription of the Fifth Symphony. . . . Because he played this almost-laughable combination with the utmost seriousness, he brought it off with complete success. . . . This is Gouldian wit of a kind that only Gould could love. . . . The celebrated classicist was presenting, completely deadpan, a brilliant performance of Liszt's transcription of that most venerable of Romantic clichés, Beethoven's Fifth Symphony."[66] The juxtapositions Otto notes between comic and serious, or ironic and authentic, also indicate a camp sensibility enacted through the act of paraphrase.

In his own liner notes to the Beethoven-Liszt recording, Gould calls himself "extravagantly eccentric" and indulges in a form of scholarly drag by inventing four fictional authorities to comment on the project. The imaginary German musicologist Prof. Dr. Karlheinz Heinkel, for example, announces that "the transcription is from Liszt and we can leave the decision as to whether it fulfills the moral obligations pertaining to a transcription of German music to our colleagues in anthropological musikology [sic]."[67] In his "psychobiography," which explores the pianist's "suppressed" sexuality, Peter Ostwald notes that such role-playing impersonations were characteristic of Gould during a certain period of his life, and they provided an expressive outlet for inner states of being: "Glenn's make-believe characters allowed him to step outside of himself and give voice to inner doubts and conflicts. They provided a harmless, even ludicrous vehicle for bringing internal preoccupations out into the open."[68] In an analogous sense, Gould's transcriptions and paraphrases could also express these hidden secondary identities through musical means. Here, too, the body (or mind) could find its embodiment or expression through the creation and performance of musical (re)productions.

Niecks sees Liszt's manner of composition as "a defiance of conventional respectability, or a device for the dumbfounding and electrification of the gaping multitude."[69] The same could be said about Liberace, the popular twentieth-century pianist who fashioned his own extensive repertoire of pianistic paraphrases. Liner notes to Liberace's album *Candlelight Classics* (AVI Records AVL1023) mention the entertainer's "spectacular showmanship" and "his exceptional gift of totally captivating his audience through his multi-faceted musical talent." Liberace is also "a successful composer and arranger of music" with "many original compositions to his credit." Defying conventional standards of musical (re)production, however, all the compositions on this album are adaptions of "classical" works "totally reconstructed by Liberace." The first selection, for example, conflates Rachmaninoff's popular Prelude in

C-sharp Minor with the "Theme from *The Godfather.*" On his album *The Sound of Love* (Dot DLP25901, 1968), Liberace fits the melody of "Bye Bye Blackbird" to the arpeggiated figurations of Chopin's "Aeolian Harp" étude.

Liberace exemplifies queer camp and Dollimore's transgressive reinscription through his stylistic and performative border crossings. Marjorie Garber, for one, explores "category crisis" in relation to Liberace's onstage cross-dressing.[70] But just as the spectacle of Liberace's dazzling costumes was part of the open secret of his sexuality (he considered his outrageous outfits "just one tuck short of drag"), his repertoire of musical (re)creations constituted another mode of queer signification. Margaret Drewal, discussing Liberace's Radio City Music Hall concerts, describes how he dressed "Mack the Knife" in classical garb: "First, he played it 'straight.' Then he played 'Mack the Knife Sonata in C Major' by Mozart, 'Claire de Lune de Mack the Knife' by Debussy, and finally 'Blue Mack the Knife Danube' by Strauss. . . . 'Mack the Knife' is gendered male—definitely phallic. . . . A stylistic cross-dresser so to speak, 'Mack the Knife' [became] a transvestite tune."[71] Such "unnatural" musical matings prompted one critic to complain that "Liberace creates—*if that is the word*—each composition in his own image."[72] To hesitate granting Liberace creative ability (in this biblical turn of phrase, even a godly ability) bespeaks a larger uncertainty over his (pro)creative abilities, both musical and physical.

Times have changed since 1911, when James Huneker wrote regarding Liszt transcriptions and Thalberg paraphrases, "Bold is the man today who plays either in public."[73] Listeners and performers enjoying such works might feel compelled to apologize for their reprobate tastes and pleasures. "I must confess a weakness for some of the transcriptions of the romantic period," admitted *Musical America*'s Robert Sabin in 1959. "I sometimes enjoy a shamelessly pianistic and stylistically inexcusable elaboration. Morally, this is wrong, but pianistically it is great sport."[74] In a 1966 article on opera paraphrases, however, Raymond Lewenthal discusses the recently revived interest in bel canto opera and the plentiful piano arrangements it has inspired, innocently suggesting that "anything that has been kept in the closet long enough can eventually be brought out again as the height of fashion."[75]

Admittedly, the piano-arrangement repertoire has never completely disappeared from recital programs, even during the modernist and authenticist midcentury. But piano transcriptions and paraphrases have enjoyed a vigorous renaissance in recent decades, as witnessed by the increasing numbers of recordings and concert programs that feature these works. Evgeny Kissin included the Schumann-Liszt "Widmung" in his 1990 Carnegie Hall debut recital. Stephen Hough's *Piano Albums* of 1988, 1993 (both Virgin Classics), and 1999 (Hyperion) feature numerous transcriptions, including some of Hough's own.[76] Arcadi Volodos's 1997 debut album is composed *entirely* of arrange-ments, including a faithful copy of the Bizet-Horowitz *Carmen*.[77] Among the very few openly gay concert pianists, Jean-Yves Thibaudet recorded a 1985 Liszt album (Denon) including the Gounod-Liszt *Faust* and the Verdi-Liszt *Rigo-letto* paraphrases and a 1993 album (London) devoted to Liszt's opera tran-scriptions.[78] The market appeal of this audience-pleasing repertoire, the recent upsurge of interest in more obscure piano repertoire beyond the established canonical masterworks, and the continuing crossover trend breaking down distinctions between art music and popular music have all contributed to this recent revival. Perhaps this reparation can also be seen as the musical corre-late of the incipient but increasingly powerful identity politics that has devel-oped in American culture since the late 1960s and 70s. Personality is back in style; drag and camp are trendy politicized expressions of identity.

And yet this repertoire still elicits a certain degree of anxious justification. Accompanying the Volodos recording are liner notes by Harris Goldsmith that seem to anticipate some critical protest: "A recital of transcriptions such as the gifted young Russian pianist Arcadi Volodos offers here is guaranteed to raise the hackles of self-styled purists who regard a composer's printed text as sac-rosanct. Such keepers-of-the-flame will almost certainly take umbrage at this sort of 'Technique-in-excelsis,' with its extraordinary rhythmic vitality, its tactile approximation of orchestral sonority, and its glamorous bursts of col-or and excitement, finding it all impossibly inauthentic, and even hedonistic." Does one detect in the attributes *extraordinary, glamorous, inauthentic,* and *hedonistic* a recognition of the campiness of it all? Goldsmith goes on to ad-mit the destabilization of identity in such paraphrases, which "tend to reflect the stylistic fingerprints of the musicians who devised them," citing Volodos's "unlikely (and let us admit it, sinfully enjoyable) paraphrase" of Mozart's fa-mous "Rondo alla turca." Admitting the (queer) instability of such identities, Goldsmith acknowledges that these paraphrases are "often chameleon-like in their ability to change color, and they sound disconcertingly different when filtered through other fingers and sensibilities."

Since the era of Liszt, the perverse paraphrase has opened a compositional and performative space for queer musical liberation. The paraphrase carries political potential as a transgressive, counterhegemonic device offering a sub-versive treatment of a musical text and its performance; it disregards certain approved principles of (pro)creativity in favor of a more liberal and flexible attitude towards musical, compositional, and performative identity. Earl Wild comments about his 1981 Carnegie Hall recital series, *The Art of the Transcrip-tion,* by saying, "I admit that it is really an indulgence."[79] He adds: "I love to play transcriptions because they give the pianist so much more freedom. I can make my own interpretations." Liberation is achieved not only via musical reproduction but through the assertion of identity as well. "The pleasure in playing transcriptions comes from the projection of what they are," Wild admits.[80] He might also say that the pleasure comes from a projection of what the camp pianist himself represents: the queering of the original work/body and the transgressive potential for reordering the socially constructed "morality" of musical (pro)creativity.

The transformative urge inherent in the art of pianistic paraphrase has ramifications for all manner of musical creativity, even for interpersonal and social relationships. Encouraging and forward-looking words come from Percy Grainger, one of this century's most prolific transcribers for piano—"probably Liszt's only rival as a transcriber"[81]—and also a composer whose practices of bodily pleasure were somewhat "perverse" as well.[82] Grainger writes, "Later on I hope to publish my sketch books with free permission for anyone to use my themes, chords, ideas, etc. I should like to see every man tinkering with every other man's art; what kaleidoscopic, multitudinous results we should see!"[83]

NOTES

My gratitude to all those who have provided insights, criticism, and encouragement as this paper evolved to its current incarnation, especially Philip Brett, Jann Pasler, Chip Whitesell, Robert Tobin, Fred Maus, and Kevin Kopelson. An early version was read at the Sixth North American Gay/Lesbian Studies Conference, held at the University of Iowa in 1994.

1. *Song of Love*, film, dir. Clarence Brown (Metro-Goldwyn-Mayer, 1947). Pianist Arthur Rubinstein recorded the solo piano works on the film's soundtrack.

2. David Wilde, "Transcriptions for Piano," in *Franz Liszt: The Man and His Music*, ed. Alan Walker (New York: Taplinger, 1970), 201.

3. Certainly Liszt did "compose" love both in its unadorned virginal beauty and its low-cut evening wear: his famous "Liebestraum" (no. 3, in A-flat major) is a solo piano transcription of his own song "O lieb, o lieb, so lang du lieben kannst."

4. Artur Schnabel, "The Piano Sonatas of Franz Schubert," *Musical Courier* 97 (19 Apr. 1928): 9.

5. Arthur Loesser, *Men, Women and Pianos: A Social History* (New York: Simon and Schuster, 1954), 609.

6. Alan Walker, "Liszt and the Schubert Song Transcriptions," *Musical Quarterly* 67, no. 1 (Jan. 1981): 51.

7. For a comprehensive catalog of this repertoire, see Maurice Hinson, *The Pianist's Guide to Transcriptions, Arrangements, and Paraphrases* (Bloomington: Indiana University Press, 1990).

8. Arrangements in the other direction—from solo piano to symphony orchestra,

for example—were also popular. Maurice Ravel's 1922 orchestral transcription of Modest Musorgsky's *Pictures at an Exhibition* is now more familiar than the original solo piano version.

9. For a discussion of four-hand piano transcriptions as a medium of musical reproduction bringing "public" symphonic and chamber works into the domestic/amateur realm, see Thomas Christensen, "Four-Hand Piano Transcription and Geographies of Nineteenth-Century Musical Reception," *Journal of the American Musicological Society* 523, no. 2 (Summer 1999): 255–98. In an article on the homoerotics of four-hand piano duet playing, Philip Brett notes that "the piano duet also bears heavily the mark of the inauthentic because . . . it is the chief repository of the literature of transcription" (Brett, "Piano Four-Hands: Schubert and the Performance of Gay Male Desire," *19th-Century Music* 21 [1997]: 153).

10. Philip Friedheim, "The Piano Transcriptions of Franz Liszt," *Studies in Romanticism* 1 (1962): 83.

11. *Allgemeine musikalische Zeitung* 12 (23 Mar. 1842): 251–52.

12. For a discussion of Robert Schumann's attitudes toward the variations, fantasias, and arrangements of Liszt, Thalberg, and other Parisian virtuosi, see the chapter on virtuosi in Leon Plantinga, *Schumann as Critic* (New Haven, Conn.: Yale University Press, 1967), 196–218.

13. Cited in Nancy B. Reich, *Clara Schumann: The Artist and the Woman* (Ithaca, N.Y.: Cornell University Press, 1985), 264.

14. Ernest Newman, "The Virtuous and the Virtuoso," *More Essays from the World of Music* (New York: Coward-McCann, 1958), 161.

15. Frederick Niecks, "Liszt as a Pianoforte Writer," *The Etude* 23, no. 10 (Oct. 1905): 400.

16. Programs listed in Maurice Hinson, *Guide to the Pianist's Repertoire*, 2d ed. (Bloomington: Indiana University Press, 1994), 840–41.

17. Cited in James F. Penrose, "The Piano Transcriptions of Franz Liszt," *American Scholar* 64, no. 2 (Winter 1995): 272.

18. For an in-depth study of the group of composers, performers, transcribers centered on Ferruccio Busoni and Kaikhosru Shapurji Sorabji, see Marc-André Roberge, "The Busoni Network and the Art of Creative Transcription," *Canadian University Music Review* 11, no. 1 (1991): 68–88.

19. On the correlations between modernism and the authenticity movement, see Richard Taruskin, *Text and Act: Essays and Music and Performance* (New York: Oxford University Press, 1995).

20. Paul Hindemith, *A Composer's World: Horizons and Limitations* (Gloucester, Mass.: Peter Smith, 1952), 162.

21. Kaikhosru Sorabji, "The Opera Fantasies of Liszt," *Around Music* (London: Unicorn, 1932), 194.

22. Wanda Landowska, "Transcriptions," in *Landowska on Music,* ed. Denise Restout (New York: Stein and Day, 1964), 101.

23. In Hans Keller, "Arrangement For or Against?" *Musical Times* 110 (Jan. 1969): 22.

24. Landowska, "Transcriptions," 98–99.

25. Ibid., 103.

26. Leonard B. Meyer, *Music, the Arts, and Ideas* (Chicago: University of Chicago Press, 1967), 197–98.

27. Stephen Davies, "Transcription, Authenticity and Performance," *British Journal of Aesthetics* 28, no. 3 (Summer 1988): 216, 218.

28. Frederick Corder, *Ferencz Liszt* (New York: Harper and Brothers, 1925), 41.

29. Alan Walker, "Liszt and the Beethoven Symphonies," *Music Review* 31, no. 4 (1970): 302–3, 305. In other instances, Liszt seemed to be aware of the infidelities he may have been committing. Discussing his transcription of Beethoven's "Adelaida," Liszt wrote to his publishers Breitkopf und Härtel in 1840 about a "tremendous" cadenza and an additional coda he had inserted into the original work: "I will beg you to have the last Coda printed in small notes . . . so that purists may play the actual text only, if the *commentary* displeases them. It was certainly a very delicate matter to touch 'Adelaide.' . . . Have I done it with propriety and taste?" (in Corder, *Liszt*, 41–42).

30. Derek Watson, *Liszt* (London: Dent, 1988), 214.

31. Walker, "Liszt and Schubert," 52, 59.

32. Michel Kozlovsky, "The Piano Solo Transcription in the Romantic Period: Three Examples from Liszt, Godowsky and Busoni" (D.M.A. diss., Indiana University, 1983), 74, 86–87.

33. Hinson, *Pianist's Guide*, 136.

34. Hindemith, *Composer's World*, 162, 164.

35. Paul Henry Lang, *Music in Western Civilization* (New York: W. W. Norton, 1941), 866.

36. Sorabji, "Opera Fantasies," 195.

37. Moe Meyer, "Introduction: Reclaiming the Discourse of Camp," in *The Politics and Poetics of Camp*, ed. Meyer (New York: Routledge, 1994), 2–3.

38. Alan Walker, "In Defense of Arrangements," *Piano Quarterly* 143 (Fall 1988): 26.

39. Arthur Briskier, "Piano Transcriptions of J. S. Bach," *Music Review* 15, no. 3 (Aug. 1954): 191–202.

40. Hindemith, *Composer's World*, 162.

41. Meyer, *Politics and Poetics*, 10–11.

42. Ferruccio Busoni, *The Essence of Music, and Other Papers*, trans. Rosamond Ley (London: Salisbury Square, 1957), 88.

43. Philip Core, *Camp: The Lie That Tells the Truth* (New York: Delilah Books, 1984).

44. Walter Benjamin, "The Work of Art in the Age of Mechanical Reproduction," *Illuminations* (New York: Schocken, 1969), 221.

45. Wayne Koestenbaum, "Wilde's Hard Labor and the Birth of Gay Reading," in *Engendering Men: The Question of Male Feminist Criticism*, ed. Joseph A. Boone and Michael Cadden (New York: Routledge, 1990), 177.

46. "In the process of being made to discohere, meanings are returned to circulation, thereby becoming the more vulnerable to appropriation, transformation, and reincorporation in new configurations. Such in part are the processes whereby the social is

unmade and remade, disarticulated and rearticulated" (Jonathan Dollimore, *Sexual Dissidence: Augustine to Wilde, Freud to Foucault* [Oxford: Clarendon, 1991], 323, 87).

47. Butler argues that "the parodic or imitative effect of gay identities works neither to copy nor to emulate heterosexuality, but rather, to expose heterosexuality as an incessant and *panicked* imitation of its own naturalized idealization" (Judith Butler, "Imitation and Gender Insubordination," in *Inside/Out: Lesbian Theories, Gay Theories*, ed. Diana Fuss [New York: Routledge, 1991], 20–25).

48. Koestenbaum, "Wilde's Hard Labor," 182. Koestenbaum further asserts that whereas the scientific clone is a "faithful" reproduction of an organism, the gay clone is a "perverse" copy of hypermasculinity.

49. *Monthly Music Record* 16, no. 184 (1 Apr. 1886): 75.

50. Edward Baxter Perry, "Transcriptions for the Piano by Franz Liszt," *Etude* 20, no. 5 (May 1902): 172.

51. Niecks, "Liszt," 400.

52. Arnold Whittall, *Romantic Music: A Concise History from Schubert to Sibelius* (London: Thames and Hudson, 1987), 86.

53. Camille Saint-Saëns, *Portraits et Souvenirs* (Paris, n.d.), 20, in Ernest Newman, *The Man Liszt* (London: Cassell, 1934), 213.

54. Lang, *Music*, 873.

55. Watson, *Liszt*, 195.

56. Frank Browning, *The Culture of Desire: Paradox and Perversity in Gay Lives Today* (New York: Vintage, 1994), 9.

57. Abram Chasins, analysis of Godowsky's "Suite in C" (performed at Chasin's Carnegie Hall recital), *New York Times*, February 1935, in Rafael Kammerer, "Transcriptions," *Musical America* 79 (Feb. 1959): 138.

58. "I am not homosexual, you know, but I have too many women around me every day. I need male company" (in David Dubal, *Evenings with Horowitz* [New York: Birch Lane, 1991], 251). See also Glenn Plaskin, *Horowitz: A Biography of Vladimir Horowitz* (New York: William Morrow, 1983).

59. Harvey Sachs, *Virtuoso: The Life and Art of Niccolo Paganini, Franz Liszt, Anton Rubinstein, Ignace Jan Paderewski, Fritz Kreisler, Pablo Casals, Wanda Landowska, Vladimir Horowitz, Glenn Gould* (New York: Thames and Hudson, 1982), 13. Horowitz also did "true" transcription for musical and pianistic, rather than virtuosic, aims (e.g., his version of Musorgsky's *Pictures at an Exhibition*). See Plaskin, *Horowitz*, 251.

60. In Plaskin, *Horowitz*, 249, 247.

61. *New York Herald Tribune*, 9 Apr. 1946, in Plaskin, *Horowitz*, 248.

62. Detlef Gojowy, "Stars and Stripes Forever: Zur Transkription des Marschs von John Philip Sousa durch Vladimir Horowitz" (On Horowitz's transcription of Sousa's march), *Neue Zeitschrift für Musik* 147, no. 10 (Oct. 1986): 32–34.

63. Edward Rothstein, "Heart of Gould," *New Republic*, 26 June 1989, p. 28.

64. According to Geoffrey Payzant, Ravel's composition "is already a giddy parody of the sentimental Viennese waltz. Gould's transcription is a parody of those nineteenth-century piano transcriptions of orchestral and operatic masterpieces, and works

by Bach for organ, to which he objected in his youth" (Geoffrey Payzant, *Glenn Gould: Music and Mind,* rev. ed. [Toronto: Key Porter, 1992], 62).

65. Kevin Bazzana, *Glenn Gould—The Performer in the Work: A Study in Performance Practice* (Oxford: Clarendon, 1997), 114.

66. Friedrich Otto, *Glenn Gould: A Life and Variations* (New York: Random House), 140–41.

67. Gould's liner notes to *Glenn Gould Plays Beethoven's Fifth Symphony in C Minor, Op. 67, Transcribed for Piano by Franz Liszt* (Columbia Masterworks MS-7095).

68. Peter Ostwald, *Glenn Gould: The Ecstasy and Tragedy of Genius* (New York: W. W. Norton, 1996), 262.

69. Niecks, "Liszt," 400.

70. Marjorie Garber, *Vested Interests: Cross-Dressing and Cultural Anxiety* (New York: Routledge, 1992), 10–17.

71. Margaret Drewal, "Camp Traces in Corporate America," in *Politics and Poetics,* ed. Meyer, 155, 175.

72. In Bob Thomas, *Liberace: The True Story* (New York: St. Martin's, 1987), 81 (emphasis added).

73. James Huneker, *Franz Liszt* (New York: Scribner's, 1911), 63.

74. Robert Sabin, *Musical America* 79 (Feb. 1959): 228.

75. Raymond Lewenthal, "Who's Afraid of Lucrezia Borgia?" *Opera News* 31, no. 10 (31 Dec. 1966): 8–12.

76. Hough has also published a set of his *Song Transcriptions* (London: Josef Weinberger, 1999).

77. Arcadi Volodos, *Arcadi Volodos: Piano Transcriptions* (Sony Classical SK-62691). See Thomas Frost, "Trial by Horowitz," *International Piano Quarterly* (Autumn 1997): 40–44. Other recordings devoted solely to piano transcriptions and paraphrases include Kevin Oldham, *The Art of the Piano Transcription* (VAI), with works by Schubert-Liszt and Johann Strauss–Schulz-Evler, as well as Oldham's own transcriptions of Bach works; and Eric Himy, *The Art of the Transcription for Piano* (recorded 1992), with works by Mozart-Liszt, Saint-Saëns–Horowitz, Chopin-Michalowski-Rosenthal, and others.

78. Thibaudet was interviewed by a national gay and lesbian news magazine in 1994. Charles Isherwood, "Toujours Gai" (Always gay), *Advocate,* 17 May 1994, pp. 53–54.

79. In Harold C. Schonberg, "Earl Wild Harvests a Cornucopia of Liszt," *New York Times,* 10 Apr. 1988, p. 37.

80. In Raymond Ericson, "Piano Virtuosos Display Varied Art on New Releases," *New York Times,* 23 Jan. 1983, p. 21.

81. Kammerer, "Transcriptions," 7, 190.

82. See the discussion of Grainger's sadomasochistic tendencies in John Bird, *Percy Grainger* (London: Paul Elek, 1976), 42–51.

83. Letter to Scottish music critic D. C. Parker, *The Grainger Journal* 4, no. 1 (Oct. 1981), in Ronald Stevenson, "Grainger's Transcriptions," *Studies in Music* 16 (1982): 88.

7 MUSICOLOGY AND SEXUALITY

THE EXAMPLE OF EDWARD J. DENT

PHILIP BRETT

Imagine for a moment that music is a social problem. Or rather that it has for centuries been an outlawed or suspect activity whose practice leads to severe disapproval, sometimes punishment, except under certain circumstances that are, in a remarkable reversal, highly validated. Imagine, too, that in a newly industrialized society, driven by capital and depending for its stability on religion and the development of middle classes, no one quite knows how to deal with the rogue desire for music ingrained in each person.

What I have described is, in simple terms, the situation with regard to sexual activity in Europe beginning in the eighteenth century and intensifying in the nineteenth to such a degree that mechanisms had to be found to deal with it. And though it would be unwise to press the parallels beyond a certain point except out of pure mischief, those mechanisms bear a distinct family resemblance to the procedures brought to bear on music. For—let us be clear about this—unregulated music is potentially as dangerous as unregulated sex to the concept of order in capitalist society. That is paradoxically why *Messiah*, monumentalized out of all recognition to its original audience, could play a role in the control of the proletariat in nineteenth-century Britain.[1]

A prime solution for the sex problem was the invention of sexuality. "Situated at the point of intersection of a technique of confession and a scientific discursivity, where certain major mechanisms had to be found for adapting them to one another," as Michel Foucault puts it, "sexuality was defined as being 'by nature.'"[2] And so, believing itself to be a system of representation, this *scientia sexualis* that seemed to offer the most profoundly hermeneutic window on to the human soul was, as Foucault and others have argued, rath-

er "the operation of a subtle network of discourses, special knowledges, pleasures, and powers."[3] The enormously complicated taxonomy of these knowledges and pleasures was matched by a medical-psychiatric practice aimed at
regulating those conditions deemed perverse or deviant. Its most powerful
effect was to discover an inborn "instinct" that both generated a sexual identity and held open the promise of revealing the innermost being.

What happened in music during the same period was by no means so important in its effects, but it did move in similar directions and was, I believe,
affected by developments in the psychosexual field. The term *musicality,* of
which the *Oxford English Dictionary* records the first English use in 1853, replaced the older and more diffuse *musicalness* in a manner that offers a parallel to *sexuality.* Produced at the intersection of skill with the mystification
needed to invest art with religious status, this word suggests a special identity
defined apparently by nature but actually produced in musical institutions,
particularly conservatories. The taxonomic urge was satisfied by a new science,
that of *Musikwissenschaft,* or musicology, which was to embrace all possible
knowledge about music.

Opponents of the so-called New Musicology sometimes argue that since
its possibilities were envisioned by the founding fathers, they are not so new.
The point is not what possibilities were envisioned or, in the field of sexuality,
how many myriad perverse manifestations of the sexual drive were catalogued
but how both fields focused themselves upon certain particular issues. As Eve
Kosofsky Sedgwick has pointed out, "It is a rather amazing fact that, of the very
many dimensions along which the genital activity of one person can be dif-
ferentiated from that of another . . . , precisely one, the gender of object choice,
emerged from the turn of the century, and has remained, as *the* dimension
denoted by the now ubiquitous category of 'sexual orientation.'"[4] What she
calls the "rich stew" of components receded in importance as there gradually
distilled, out of models of Uranianism, sexual inversion, third sex, and the like,
the concept of homosexuality as a constitutive feature of certain types of human beings. Where homosexuality was established, heterosexuality could follow as the necessarily dominant term of a binary construction that became part
of the master narrative for identity and social organization in Western countries, along with categories of gender, class, nationality, and race. In a similar
way one might argue that a concept of European music founded upon German artworks arose from a widening knowledge of the alternatives, which were
all being busily discovered and equally efficiently minoritized around the turn
of the century.

Many of the early sexologists were, by later standards, decidedly liberal.

Several, like Karl Heinrich Ulrichs, Magnus Hirschfeld, and Edward Carpenter, were homosexual themselves or, like Havelock Ellis, worked closely with homosexuals.[5] The apologetics of these writers centered upon historical figures known to have had same-sex relations of one kind or another and upon classes of individuals in modern life thought to be particularly susceptible to homoerotic desire and therefore (in the eyes of these writers) to be given special consideration. In this essay, I restrict my discussion to the English-speaking world, but it should be noted that the German-speaking countries, dominant in music in the nineteenth century, were also the leaders in homoerotic culture as well as sexology. Winckelmann, the famous eighteenth-century classical scholar, is the key figure here, and Magnus Hirschfeld a worthy late nineteenth-century successor.[6] An argument comparable to mine could doubtless be developed from German or French materials also.

The sexologists had a good deal to say about the connections between the subject of their science and music. "This is certainly the art," wrote Edward Carpenter, "which in its subtlety and tenderness—and perhaps in a certain inclination to *indulge* in emotion—lies nearest to the Urning nature. There are few in fact of this nature who have not some gift in the direction of music." He is one of the first to name Tchaikovsky as a "thorough-going Uranian."[7] Havelock Ellis ventures a more startling thought: "It has been extravagantly said that all musicians are inverts." He then quotes Oppenheim to the effect that "the musical disposition is marked by a great emotional instability, and this instability is a disposition to nervousness," concluding that "the musician has not been rendered nervous by his music, but he owes his nervousness (as also, it may be added, his disposition to homosexuality) to the same disposition to which he owes his musical aptitude."[8] An agitation of the nerves, musicality, and homosexuality, in other words, are not related "tendencies" but one and the selfsame phenomenon.

Even more important in social effect than these remarks were the 1895 trials of Oscar Wilde, which made any further connection between illegal sexuality and music impossible. "You didn't mention it," said the ninety-one-year-old Virgil Thomson, speaking to his biographer about his homosexuality and offering this as ultimate explanation of his silence: "Of course everybody knew about the Oscar Wilde case."[9] I argue not only that people in the music profession, like those in dance and theater, were much affected by these events but also that musicology, seeking to detach itself from performance in order to attain academic respectability, was as actively shaped by them. Self-policing against the always present but never fully articulated threat of homosexuality would be a reasonable way of explaining some of the features of the discipline that have been characteristic of the last century: a steady emphasis on a rational scientific basis to both music history and theory; the search for fact at the expense of critical judgment; the avoidance of emotion or of the use of musicological studies to develop emotional maturity as opposed to power through knowledge; an escape from the gendered and dangerous present into the distant past, particularly a glamorized "Renaissance," with its aristocratic and male values; the recourse to formalism and immanent criticism in music analysis; an insistence on the autonomous, universal, and transcendent qualities of "music," a category usually left unmarked but referring exclusively to European high art music; and a denial of the subjective basis of all scholarly activity. All the considerable apparatus of a rational male scholarly discipline, together with an assumed heterosexuality, was deployed to ward off the evil spirit of femininity and the worse threat of effeminacy that lay beyond.

My account is obviously indebted to feminist critiques, but I particularly want to emphasize the point that, in this context, anxiety about women and the feminine is inextricably intertwined with anxiety about gender liminality within masculinity itself and the same-sex desire perceived to go along with it. Ellis's "nervousness," which he conflates or aligns with male homosexuality, is, after all, the chief *female* condition of late Victorianism. Much of what men in music feared during the twentieth-century was that they were broadly perceived as less than men, that is, as homosexuals.

Rather than venture further into what Sedgwick calls the "field of intractable, highly structured discursive incoherence at a crucial node of social organization,"[10] I want to pursue what did in fact happen to the homosexuals who, according to the sexologists, were abundantly to be found in music. Did *rigor scholasticus* achieve what a century's worth of aversion therapy was unable to effect? Did they remain in all walks of musical life but scholarship? Of course not. At least, not in the British Isles or North America. In tracking them and trying to develop thoughts about the difference they might have made, I have been looking for signs, however tentative, of what Foucault called a "reverse discourse." In the work of such figures as Carpenter and Hirschfeld, as he pointed out, "homosexuality began to speak in its own behalf, to demand that its legitimacy or 'naturality' be acknowledged, often in the same vocabulary, using the same categories by which it was medically disqualified."[11] If musicology, whatever its theoretical promise, had relapsed into a fairly well defined set of practices specifically designed, in my view, to ward off the threat of emasculation and effeminacy, then could such a set of practices, such a "discourse," bring forth an oppositional set of practices within its own field, using its own terms, as had happened to some extent in sexology?

I turn for my example to the life and work of Edward J. Dent (1876–1957), one of the early and long-term presidents of the International Musicological Society (1931–49). He is the only person to have combined that office with the presidency of the International Society for Contemporary Music, which he was, with others, instrumental in founding. The combination indicates not only the breadth of his interests but also his administrative skill and his determined antiparochialism.

Dent came from the landed gentry: the family house in Yorkshire was unbelievably grand. His father, whom he liked, was a Conservative Member of Parliament; his mother, whom he did not, was a county lady who could not imagine her son stooping to a career in music. He took the route from Eton to King's College, Cambridge, the year after Oscar Wilde's trials and fell in with the queer set in that haven for homosexuals at the turn of the century. Among his friends were the preposterous but kindly Oscar Browning, the idealist homosexual Hellenist Goldsworthy Lowes Dickinson ("Goldie"), and also E. M. Forster, Dent's near contemporary. At King's Dent breathed the heady, rebellious air that inhabits Forster's Cambridge novel *The Longest Journey.* His politics veered to the left, he embraced agnosticism, treating institutional religion all his life with irritation or amusement, and he became Socratic in his tendency to question fundamental assumptions, academic or musical. "Greek, too," as Hugh Carey gently puts it, "was the value he placed on the friendship of men."[12]

A portrait of a Cambridge circle of homosexuals centered on Dent and A. T. ("Theo") Bartholomew appears in a biography of Siegfried Sassoon that draws upon Dent's extensive World War I correspondence and other letters.[13] The don-dominated coteries I encountered at King's forty years later seemed little altered, but during those war years the Dent-Bartholomew orbit was augmented by servicemen, mostly officers in training like Sassoon. Dent showered his young friends with correspondence when they went to the front and sent parcels of jam. In return many of them were open with him about their intrigues and affairs; for Sassoon, Dent combined with Theo to arrange what seems to have been the thirty-two-year-old poet's first sexual encounter with another man, and he may have done likewise for others. The frightful carnage of the war meant that Dent lost many of these friends, including the composer W. Denis Browne, one of two younger men to whom he was especially attached, the other being Clive Carey, the singer and operatic director with whom he later worked at Sadler's Wells. Another close friend of the same generation was the excitable and brilliant professor of Spanish, J. B. Trend (1887–1958).

In my Cambridge days, most queer dons at the center of such circles appeared complacent; their full access to male and class privilege enabled them to become inured, at least so far as one could see, to the social disadvantages of their homosexuality and cushioned them from the fear of public exposure. There are hints that Dent was more politically aware as a homosexual. He intrigued one correspondent, for instance, with a description of the banned novel *Despised and Rejected,* which links the issues of musicality, homosexuality, pacifism, and socialism in a radical way.[14] Though Edward Carpenter's religiosity would surely have been anathema to Dent, he visited Carpenter in Derbyshire in 1913—about the same time as Forster: he not only returned in 1915 but also presented a copy of *Mozart's Operas* to the seer of Uranianism.[15] We cannot know, of course, to what extent Dent shared the two other men's interest in homosexual emancipation or their taste for young men of the working class, a strong feature of the social construction of homosexuality in Britain. Lost on Dent, most likely, was the epiphanic power of Carpenter's working-class lover, George Merrill, whose touch upon the novelist's buttocks ("I believe he touched most people's," commented Forster) triggered the creative spring for his one gay novel, *Maurice.*[16] Dent was, however, enthusiastic about the unpublished manuscript, which he was allowed to read early in 1915, and Forster wrote gratefully to him: "I am much dependent on criticism, and now, backed by you and some others, do feel that I have created something absolutely new, even to the Greeks."[17]

Dent remained a patrician, but a kindly one, despite his acid tongue. A combination of his attitudes toward class and religion can be sensed in his dismissal of Elgar, whom (as Winton Dean observes) "he despised as a professional musician bent on living the life of a country gentleman (a course exactly opposite to his own) and a Roman Catholic composer of oratorios to boot."[18] Dent commonly referred to *The Dream of Gerontius* as "Gerry's Nightmare," and his brief and disparaging account of Elgar in an article on modern English composers for Guido Adler's *Handbuch der Musikgeschichte* caused a public outcry.[19] He lived in a much more exclusively male world than Forster and probably would not have thought anything of the fact that musicology effectively excluded women themselves along with the feminine. He was also less discriminating over social issues than Forster, who would not likely have expressed his interest in Jamaicans and black Americans in the condescending and potentially racist language Dent used in letters to Clive Carey after visiting the United States for the International Musicological Society meeting in 1939.[20] Though something of a snob, Dent appears never to have become pompous or self-important, in spite of his leading position in so many spheres of musical life. And, as Philip

Radcliffe remarks, "his criticism, however severe, was never delivered with the uncompromising bluntness of Stanford."[21]

Like so many tentative Englishmen, he loved and romanticized Italy, partly as a way of evading his own identity and inbred inhibitions. When Forster went on his first visit in 1901, he did so with sheaves of suggestions from Dent, who already knew it well. Clive Carey's diary portrays Dent making aggressive, anti-English remarks on their Italian holiday in 1904. Ferruccio Busoni, whose socialist politics, elitist attitudes to art, antireligious sentiments, and combination of Italian directness with northern intellectualism struck a sympathetic chord, provided the English writer with a perfect contemporary subject.[22] Dent's biographers report that Philip Herriton, the Italophile hero of *Where Angels Fear to Tread,* was partly modeled on him; P. N. Furbank, Forster's biographer, sees more than a little of him in Cecil Vyse, the snobbish admirer who pins his artistic sensations on Lucy Honeychurch in *A Room with a View.*[23]

As a scholar, Dent was prolific, especially considering the extent of his other activities. More important, he was often able to see past a conventional view toward a new interpretation based on wider knowledge and keener perception. Modern work on Byrd's secular music, for instance, stems from an essay by Dent rather than from the more voluminous accounts of contemporary Tudor specialists, and his view of the key role of opera in the music of the eighteenth and nineteenth centuries was seminal.[24] His Enlightenment view of scholarship, balancing the rational with its opposite, is encapsulated in a sentence from one of his books: "We do not enjoy music as an art until we have learned to appreciate it rationally; but at the same time it cannot give us a real aesthetic emotion unless it confronts us forcibly with a further irrational element."[25]

My sense of his representing a reverse discourse within musicology is based not only on his opinions, which were unorthodox, but also upon the way in which they changed rather to oppose consensus than to accommodate it. In his early days, reacting against still prevalent Handel-worship in England, he elevated Alessandro Scarlatti on grounds that suggest the influence of Roger Fry's modernist aesthetic criteria. Later, he would adopt Handel partly in reaction to the increasing popularity of Bach, a feature that makes his *Notes on Fugue for Beginners* (Cambridge, 1941) a very lively or irritating read, depending on the reader's point of view, but usefully reminding would-be contrapuntists that practical and social concerns often produce genre effects. The quality of his prose, too, militates against a dull heterosexist conformity of the kind that became usual later, especially in the United States; Dent could turn a stylish phrase and liked to be mischievous.

His most serious moment of opposition, beyond even the remarks on El-gar that led to the public protest of 1931, was his contribution to the Beethoven centenary of 1927. Not a simple-minded dismissal, of course, Dent's was a careful attempt to put Beethoven in his place, which is to say to consign him to history—a history, moreover, in which his music is unfailingly interesting but not applicable to the present day. By insisting on his position as a histori-an, Dent allowed himself to speak with the double voice of judiciousness and aggression, but his contemporaries were not deceived: according to the obit-uary in *The Times* (23 Aug. 1957), many regarded his statements as "a stab in the back of genius":

> We know that the ethical element was perpetually present to the mind of Beethoven. At the present day we may very possibly wish that it had not been so present; it seems to be that insistence on ethical significance which has made musicians of to-day turn in revolt against their elders' adoration of him. But as historians we must admit the presence of ethical ideals, and it is indeed impos-sible fully to understand Beethoven unless we recognize his ethical intention and set ourselves to understand that too.

The failures of humanity over the hundred years in question, Dent reasonably claims, leave us waiting still for the Beethoven to show us the way to a happier world. "But it will have to be a new Beethoven. Ludwig lies in his grave."[26]

Dent's assault upon the cult of Beethoven was motivated in part by his love of the more human, life-sized genius of Mozart, who as an Italian opera com-poser was exempt from his distrust of the Teutonic. But even more opposi-tional than his critical opinions, perhaps, was the vision of a musical life Dent offered in practice. In this way he might be compared to his contemporary Charles Seeger—though to say that the American took himself more serious-ly would be a considerable understatement. In both cases, however, life and work were ultimately connected to social action. For all his patrician instincts and fluency in languages, Dent rejected the elitist notion behind John Christie's Glyndebourne and embraced opera in English (to which his many translations stand testimony), working hard for Lilian Baylis's enterprise at Sadler's Wells, with its commitment to opera for the people. Such action is today almost al-ways condemned as patronizing, but it was a strong part of the Fabian tradi-tion and remained part of Labour's program when it came to power after World War II. In the United States today, radio announcers' affected accents and the tinkling of Mozart or Vivaldi in expensive shops and restaurants sig-nal the almost exclusive connection of classical music to wealth and privilege. Dent would no doubt have been horrified by the mispronunciation and dismemberment of works characteristic of the British radio station Classic FM, but the astounding rise of musical literacy after World War II and the marketing of classical music in Britain today as a music of the people is the result of something for which he worked hard. It was no mean achievement.

Dent's various roles within and without musicology have a certain consistency as protest against orthodoxy from within the homosexual closet that not so much confined as defined lives like his. Such consistency became impossible for subsequent homosexual figures in the field as the effects of the self-policing I have described bit harder into modes of self-fashioning. Thurston Dart, for instance, a figure whose homosexuality was always more obscure than Dent's, used his tremendous prowess as harpsichordist and conductor to escape the stifling effects of professional musicology. While practicing within it, however, he adhered to its most rigorously philological and positivistic modes, latterly pouring scorn on the study of "music" and limiting his counterdiscourse to provocation of the kind that earned him the epithet "musicological harlequin" in Joseph Kerman's survey of the discipline.[27] A different but comparable divide characterizes the career of Howard Mayer Brown. Living openly with a male partner, he became a supporter of the lesbian and gay community and identified even more strongly with other social causes—his name is associated with an American Musicological Society scholarship for racial or ethnic minorities. Yet he would never allow any connection at all between these concerns and those of musical scholarship, which he romanticized as a sacred preserve to be protected at all costs from the "shrill." These thumbnail sketches cry out for greater elaboration than can be given here, of course, but they illustrate how impossible it gradually became, before the onset of "out" lesbian and gay scholarship in music, to subvert, let alone challenge, an academic discipline that had taken itself too seriously and had mistakenly excluded the real musical concerns as well as living personalities of the people within it.

In a sense, this was what Dent had been trying to tell everyone all along. At least, that is how I interpret his fashioning of a vision of musicology far different from the one characterized by the mainstream of professional work within the field since World War II. In a lecture delivered at Harvard in 1936, Dent laid out his beliefs in what he preferred to call "musical research." He spoke witheringly about the amount of "mere excavation" and "that atmosphere of the museum which is not much better than that of a prison," and he was as always scathing on the topic of the worship of "timeless" classics. "The real value of historical studies," he wrote, "lies in their being made a training for the imagination," and its chief pedagogical aim is to help students "to experience music emotionally, and to widen their emotional range."[28] A similar preoccupation with the exercise of imagination and a critical approach to the past surfaces in a set of lectures delivered at Cornell around the same time. Noting the duty impressed upon him in America to "discard my old typewriter . . . and buy the newest model," Dent comments:

> It is a principle which we ought to apply not only to our mechanical conveniences but also to our artistic experiences. Our minds are rendered sluggish by the constant habit of veneration; we must sharpen our critical faculties, so as to be able to discard past experience when it is no longer of real value to us, and then we shall have the mental space as well as freedom of judgment to welcome and enjoy the art of to-day and to-morrow.[29]

Dent was by this time an almost lone voice of provocation and wit set against an increasing orthodoxy that would not so much drown him out as pass him by; he would surely have been horrified by the resuscitation of the canonic nineteenth century in musicology that has occurred in the last thirty years. But in his life as in his provocation he exemplified an effective cultural politics. Making a space for opera, a genre against which late Victorians like Grove and Parry had campaigned, and working with populists like Lilian Baylis to achieve its acceptance at the level of what he often called "the ordinary music-loving public," he surely made a significant contribution to the vital and socially relevant British opera that sprang up alongside the welfare state in the immediate postwar years. If the cultural politics of musicology itself, busy finding respectability in the expanding university system of those years, ultimately obliterated Dent's scholarly profile, it is fitting that at the turn of the century another version of critical musicology has surfaced to undermine and replace the dominant scholarly ideology of the last half-century. I venture that he would not only have welcomed "New Musicology" but would also have worked hard to save it from dullness and conformity. He colluded in the nickname "the Old Serpent," picked up during the ground-breaking production of *The Magic Flute* in Cambridge in 1911. It was, of course, as the biblical serpent that he saw himself, always already outside the Judeo-Christian gender myth, offering serious diversion to those within it.

NOTES

This essay is in memory of Philip Radcliffe (1905–86), my principal teacher at King's College, Cambridge. His imitations conveyed a strong impression of the voice and wit of E. J. Dent, who was his teacher and therefore in some sense my scholarly grandfather. An earlier version was published in *Musicology and Sister Disciplines: Past, Present,*

Future: Proceedings of the 16th International Congress of the International Musicological Society, London, 1997, ed. David Greer (Oxford: Oxford University Press, 2000), 418–27.

1. Wilfrid Mellers unwittingly spots gender implications behind the political ones: "The eulogy of the Chosen Race (which so cunningly guides Popular Sentiment in the interests of the Ruling Classes) is at least sung in the *Messiah* with a manly gusto" (Mellers, *Music and Society* [London: Dobson, 1946], 99).

2. Michel Foucault, *The History of Sexuality,* vol. 1: *An Introduction,* trans. Robert Hurley (New York: Pantheon, 1978), 68.

3. Ibid., 72.

4. Eve Kosofsky Sedgwick, *Epistemology of the Closet* (Berkeley: University of California Press, 1990), 8.

5. Ellis collaborated with the prominent scholar and critic John Addington Symonds; see Wayne Koestenbaum's interesting account in *Double Talk: The Erotics of Male Literary Collaboration* (New York: Routledge, 1989), 43–67.

6. For recent work on Winckelmann and his era, see *Outing Goethe and His Age,* ed. Alice A. Kuzmiar (Stanford, Calif.: Stanford University Press, 1996).

7. Edward Carpenter, *The Intermediate Sex* (London: Allen and Unwin, 1908), repr. in *Selected Writings,* vol. 1: *Sex* (London: GMP, 1984), 235. In his article in the present volume, Malcolm H. Brown argues that Rosa Newmarch's biography of Tchaikovsky, released in 1900, appears to have made this knowledge available.

8. Havelock Ellis, *Studies in the Psychology of Sex,* vol. 2, part 2: *Sexual Inversion* (New York: Random House, 1936), 295. *Sexual Inversion* had a complicated publishing history, which is outlined by Koestenbaum in *Double Talk;* this passage on music appears with the revised and enlarged 3d ed. (Philadelphia: F. A. Davis, 1926).

9. Anthony Tommasini, *Virgil Thomson: Composer on the Aisle* (New York: W. W. Norton, 1997), 69.

10. Sedgwick, *Epistemology,* 90.

11. Foucault, *History of Sexuality,* 101.

12. Hugh Carey, *Duet for Two Voices: An Informal Biography of Edward Dent Compiled from His Letters to Clive Carey* (Cambridge: Cambridge University Press, 1979), 5. For biographical and personal details I have also relied on Philip Radcliffe, *E. J. Dent: A Centenary Memoir* (Rickmansworth, U.K.: Triad, 1976).

13. John Stuart Roberts, *Siegfried Sassoon* (London: Richard Cohen, 1999), 63–65, 135–36, 145, 161. In 1943 Dent presented much of his World War I correspondence to Cambridge University Library (Add. MS 7973), reserving the letters of his favorites, such as Denis Browne and Clive Carey, which may be found with the rest of his papers in the library of King's College.

14. A. T. Fitzroy [Rose Allatini], *Despised and Rejected* (London: C. W. Daniel, 1918), repr. with an introduction by Jonathan Cutbill (London: GMP, 1988).

15. Letter from Carpenter to Dent, 2 Oct. 1913, at King's College, and items C44-7 of

Cambridge University Library Add. MS 7973. Dent appears to have persuaded him to counsel an undergraduate composer, Frederick Seymour Bontoft (b. 1896).

16. See Forster's "Terminal Note" to *Maurice* (London: Edward Arnold, 1971), 235.

17. P. N. Furbank, *E. M. Forster: A Life,* 2 vols. (London: Secker and Warburg, 1978), 2:14.

18. Winton Dean, "Edward J. Dent: A Centenary Tribute," *Music and Letters* 57 (1976): 355.

19. Guido Adler, *Handbuch der Musikgeschichte* (Handbook of music history) (Frankfurt: Frankfurter Verlags-Anstalt, 1924), 937–38. A translation of Dent's account appears, together with the protesting letter (which came after the issue of the second edition in 1930 and was signed by Hamilton Harty, John Ireland, Augustus John, E. J. Moeran, Albert Sammons, George Bernard Shaw, Richard Terry, William Walton, and others), in Basil Maine's *Elgar: His Life and Works,* 2 vols. (London: G. Bell and Sons, 1933), 1:256, 2:277–78. Radcliffe (*E. J. Dent,* 18) attributes the invention of the nickname for *The Dream of Gerontius* to Donald Francis Tovey.

20. Carey, *Duet for Two Voices,* 161–62; Carey also alleges a "marked" anti-Semitism without furnishing any corroborating evidence of it (5–6).

21. Radcliffe, *E. J. Dent,* 17.

22. E. J. Dent, *Ferruccio Busoni: A Biography* (Oxford: Oxford University Press, 1933).

23. Furbank, *E. M. Forster,* 1:170.

24. E. J. Dent, "William Byrd and the Madrigal," *Festschrift für Johannes Wolf,* ed. Walter Lott, Helmuth Osthoff, and Werner Wolffheim (Berlin: M. Breslauer, 1929), 24–30.

25. E. J. Dent, *Terpander: Or Music and the Future* (London: Kegan Paul, Trench, Trubner, 1926), 83.

26. E. J. Dent, "The Choral Fantasia," *Music and Letters* 8 (1927): 111–121 (quotations, 113 and 121). For more on Beethoven in a similar vein, see Dent, *Terpander,* 71–72.

27. Joseph Kerman, *Contemplating Music* (Cambridge, Mass.: Harvard University Press, 1985), 117.

28. E. J. Dent, "The Historical Approach to Music," *Selected Essays: E. J. Dent,* ed. Hugh Taylor (Cambridge: Cambridge University Press, 1979), 189–206 (quotations, 194, 203, and 204).

29. E. J. Dent, *The Rise of Romantic Opera,* ed. Winton Dean (Cambridge: Cambridge University Press, 1976), 189.

PART 3
DOUBLE MEANINGS

8 CROSS-DRESSING

IN SAINT-SAËNS'S *LE ROUET D'OMPHALE*

AMBIGUITIES OF GENDER AND POLITICS

JANN PASLER

Today's interest in gender has encouraged us to ask new questions of the past. That a female character like Dalila or Carmen is "strong," at least strong enough to bring a male under her spell, and her male counterpart "weak," or at least willing to submit to female charm, may reflect fear of women's threat to the social order or be intended to evoke misogynous feelings in its listeners. But such characters may also be covers for other kinds of oppositions, even the inverse of what we expect. If we take gender to be a "floating signifier" whose "literal signification depends on metaphorical surplus-signification,"[1] we can use it to explore a network of possible meanings in a work.

With the orchestral premiere of his first symphonic tone poem, *Le Rouet d'Omphale* (Omphale's spinning wheel) at the Concerts Pasdeloup on 14 April 1872—the first such music composed in France—Camille Saint-Saëns made sure an explanatory text was printed in the program, even though there was little precedent for this.[2] This statement, also printed on the score, posits an unusual perspective on the idea of weakness: "The subject of this symphonic poem is feminine seduction, the triumphant struggle of weakness against force. The spinning wheel is only a pretext chosen merely from the perspective of the rhythm and the general character of the piece." What Saint-Saëns meant by triumph here is not self-evident. Was he being serious or ironic? Did he relish the idea, or was he troubled by it? How about his audiences? Are there moral or political implications in this program, and if so, what might they mean? Surely if he was to win support for the new genre inspired by Liszt and demonstrate the merits of "descriptive music," it was important that the subject attract listeners.

By calling the spinning wheel "only a pretext chosen . . . from the perspective of the rhythm," Saint-Saëns seems to divert attention from its traditional function as a symbol of domesticity associated with women, family life, and spatial confinement. Lawrence Kramer takes this dismissal as "an act of repression," an attempt to foreground the "formal integrity of the music" rather than the "feminine creativity" associated with the spinning wheel.[3] Although Saint-Saëns often spoke of the importance of form in his music, his note implies that he had some ambivalence about writing music inspired by such a device, perhaps misogynist misgivings. But what if Saint-Saëns was actually using the spinning wheel as a "pretext" to encourage listeners to expand their expectation of meaning beyond the domestic world of the woman and the home, and perhaps also beyond the imaginative space of their private lives?

Saint-Saëns's statement makes clear that the work's program, its "subject," lies not in its framing device but in "the triumphant struggle" allegorized by Hercules and Omphale, mythological characters who exchanged gender identities. For the Greeks, Hercules emblematized stoic virtue, strength, and heroism. Omphale was the Lydian queen thought to have bought him as a slave, his punishment from Zeus for committing a murder (possibly of his son). Omphale forced Hercules to exchange clothes and to spin wool with women of her court, while she wore his lion's skin, the symbol of his power.[4] Hercules is thus like the soul in the *Phaedrus* that Plato portrays as caught in an inner conflict between shame and desire.[5] In a sixteenth-century painting of Hercules and Omphale in Prague's Sternbersky Palace Museum, the closest representation I have seen of this story, Hercules has jewels in his hair and looks strangely feminine, as Omphale proudly wears the lion skin on her head. For both, the androgynous experience seems sensuous, even enjoyable.

In this chapter I argue for taking this gender inversion seriously. French history is full of symbols whose meaning is "multivalent" and, like androgyny, able to "transmit more than one message at once."[6] As Lynn Hunt explains, the meaning of Hercules fluctuated for the French depending on whether he was understood to represent the king or the people, a mighty "Colossus" or a "life-sized brother to Liberty and Equality."[7] Since the Revolution, the meaning of gender identity too has undergone flux in France. At one time the feminine might refer to the amazon seeking to save the country; at another time, to the moral guardian assigned to tame and civilize its citizens. The masculine has connoted qualities of either the men of the fields or those of the salons and courts. With the fall of the Second Empire and the devastation of the

Franco-Prussian War, the gender of allegorical figures representing the country was thrown into question. Gender ambiguities during this period shed light on the fluidity of identity in a culture struggling with inner conflict.

Saint-Saëns's works are ideal for studying these issues. Not only was he a staunch republican, in favor of a new political regime in the early 1870s, but he also was known to enjoy cross-dressing, that is, using clothes to question the fixed stereotypes of heterosexuality. As "simple" and "clear" as the work is formally, *Le Rouet d'Omphale* can be heard as a complex metaphor for exploring the ambiguities of personal as well as national identity at the time.

SAINT-SAËNS AND THE FEMININE

If we look to Saint-Saëns's personal life, we find reasons for him to explore the positive side of weakness and the feminine.[8] As a child he was frail and tubercular. As an adult he was short, spoke with a lisp, and suffered fragile health (his lungs finding solace only in the dry, warm climates of Algeria, the Canary Islands, and South Asia).

Saint-Saëns's father, a "sous-chef de bureau" (assistant department head) for the minister of the interior, died at age thirty-seven, just after Camille was born. The composer was raised by his mother, an amateur painter, and another recent widow, his great-aunt, who began teaching him piano when he was very young. James Harding points out that for decades his mother and great-aunt "cocooned" him at home "in loving comfort," even as his reputation as a formidable pianist, organist, and composer grew. "He was their sole interest. They saw themselves as the appointed custodians of genius. . . . Everything was arranged so that his home became a refuge from the exhausting tempo of his professional career and a haven where he was the object of unceasing feminine solicitude."[9]

In February 1875, three years after his great-aunt died, the thirty-nine-year-old Saint-Saëns impulsively proposed to and married Mlle Marie Truffot, the sister of one of his pupils. She once explained: "When I was 19 years old my brother had a very humorous letter from him . . . in which he asked whether Jean would like to be his brother-in-law." The next day Saint-Saëns wrote Marie's father formally requesting her hand. Little is known of their marriage. Saint-Saëns himself discouraged any reference to it. There was no honeymoon; the couple moved in with his mother. According to James Harding, "the marriage was not a success. Saint-Saëns's mother disapproved, and her son, irritable, highly strung, and capricious, was difficult to live with." The couple had two sons but in 1878 each died suddenly—the first at age 2½ by falling out a window of their rue Monsieur le Prince apartment; the second, an infant, six weeks later of a brain illness.[10] In 1881 Saint-Saëns abandoned his wife and returned to live with his mother, whom Harding considers "the only person he really cared for." When she died in 1888 at the age of eighty, he fled and, after disbursing their belongings, hid in Algeria under a pseudonym, Charles Sannois. Thereafter, without any permanent home, he "became a lonely nomad with only his pet dogs and his faithful manservant Gabriel to keep him company. He travelled ceaselessly and widely, either on long concert tours or on holiday."[11]

Saint-Saëns's biographers have been discreet about his private life. His friends say that "he looked like a parrot with his aggressively curved profile, hooked nose, and myopic but lively eyes," and when he walked, "he strutted like a bird and his bouncy gait was recognizable many yards away." Without implying anything about his sexuality, many point out his "gay, sunny nature" or his "gay self-assurance," which, some say, "helped to compensate for his lack of physical charm."[12] Harding admits that the composer was accused of "sharing the tastes of the Baron de Charlus," a homosexual in Proust's novel, and a more recent study unearths police records that suggest as much. But of this, so far nothing has been proven either way because of his own silence on the matter.[13]

Still, a few anecdotes suggest that Saint-Saëns liked to identify with the feminine, that is, to dress and act in drag. Charades were popular at the Sunday evening salons of his friend Pauline Viardot, and according to Harding, "he played a leading part in them, eagerly assisted by Turgenev."

> Their most applauded turn was one in which Saint-Saëns donned pink tights to impersonate a corpse while Turgenev mimed a doctor intent on dissection. The young composer's solo contributions included impromptu ballets. Paul Viardot . . . long remembered his [mimed] performance of the different temptations offered to Robert le Diable [represented by Romain Bussine] in Meyerbeer's opera. The spinning scene from Gounod's *Faust,* however, gave Saint-Saëns an opportunity to display his musical gifts. The makeshift curtains parted to reveal a Marguerite wearing a blue and white bonnet, two thick plaits of fair hair, a massive nose, and black beard. The creature began to sing in a falsetto voice of extraordinary agility and executed the most intricate trills and cadenzas with precision. At last she came to the Jewel song. . . . The perfection of Saint-Saëns's mimicry [of Madame Carvalho's rendition] lay in his uncanny reproduction of this flaw. He sang the whole aria just that shade too high exactly as his model did.[14]

Pauline's son, the violinist Paul Viardot, remembers these charades as the "favorite pastime of these evenings." He recounts once having pulled the curtain back to let the group "admire a Marguerite-Saint-Saëns at the spinning wheel, in costume, with two immense blond braids on his back, and hear him sing the jewel song with *points d'orgue* and trills that would render Mme Carvalho and la Patti jealous!" Another time, he notes, "Saint-Saëns, our prima donna assoluta, in the costume of Armide, sang Gluck's air, 'Flee, pleasures, flee,' (accompanied at the piano by his mother) and in a way not to have been dismissed by Mme Litvinne herself!"[15] In Moscow in 1875 Saint-Saëns also cross-dressed in an impromptu ballet, although this time before no audience. "With his long experience of impersonating Gounod's heroines," he mimed the sea nymph Galatea in a pas de deux with Tchaikovsky as Pygmalion.[16]

Cross-dressing was popular in bourgeois social circles at the time. Under the Second Empire and during the early years of the Third Republic, the Opéra sponsored masked balls, as did the wealthy in their homes. Some, however, took offense at these. In his novel *La Curée,* written at the same time as *Le Rouet d'Omphale,*[17] Émile Zola describes a "bal travesti" during which, stereotypically, women are preoccupied with their costumes, and men discuss politics and banking. Before it begins, the host's wife, Renée, and his son, Maxime, in the midst of an incestuous affair, exchange gender roles in miming *Les Amours du beau Narcisse et du nymphe Echo,* accompanied by a text and piano. The reader likely sees this as a metaphor for reality. Earlier Zola recounts a love-making scene in which Renée is "the man," on her knees "like a great cat," with the "blond and pretty" Maxime on his back, a *"fille manquée"* (sissy). "They had a night of crazy love-making. Renée was the man, with a passionate and active will. Maxime submitted. This neutral being, blond and pretty, limited [*frappé*] since childhood in his virility, became a big girl in the arms of the young woman. . . . He seemed born and grown for a sensual perversion. Renée enjoyed her domination; with her passion she made this creature yield whose sexuality was always hesitant. . . . He was the lover who adapted to the fashion and follies of the times." Later, after Maxime announces he will marry someone else, Renée reasserts her position: "It is I who am master . . . you don't have any more strength than a girl. . . . Let's not fight. I'd be the strongest."[18]

Set at the end of the Second Empire, the novel thus makes fun of what Zola called "*hommes-femelles,*" not necessarily homosexuals, but those who grew up "on or beneath" the skirts of women. Zola's point, however, is not to rub his readers' noses in their "crime." Instead he presents it as a product of the social perversions of the times. He wishes to denounce lives based on leisure (or idleness) and the focus on one's appearance (*coquetterie*), as well as the reign of fashion and incest. In his preface to *La Curée* he explains, "I wanted to show the premature exhaustion of a race that has lived too quickly and that leads to the man-woman of rotten societies."[19]

At the end of the Second Empire and the beginning of the Third Republic, people were fascinated with floating gender identities in part because the society itself was in flux—everything from the relation between church and state to the preeminence of men in the concert world.[20] The theater was a natural place to play out double identities and even double lives. Jann Matlock notes that, at least for a man, these "were acceptable to any who could master their challenges. His duplicity depended on his ability to bring the masquerades of others into his service."[21] Women too took part in the game. It was common for women composers to use male pseudonyms in public in part for more access to the institutions of power normally reserved for men. Vicomtesse Clémence de Grandval, who studied with Saint-Saëns, sometimes went by the name "Clément Valgrand." Saint-Saëns's friend and the person to whom he dedicated *Le Rouet d'Omphale*, Augusta Holmès, published her first songs under the name of "Hermann Zenta." Although active in the concert world (she nearly won the City of Paris prize in 1878), between 1870 and 1879 she also lived a double existence, successfully hiding five pregnancies from critics and the French public. And although she was beautiful, blond, and buxom during these years, she wanted her work to be known as "virile." Critics praised her music—full of marches, battle scenes, huge brass sections, and harsh dissonances—for its vigor, power, and grandeur. Later, to explain why she admired masculine values so much, she confessed, "I have the soul of a man in the body of a woman. How could it be otherwise? It was my father who raised me: a rough old soldier."[22]

Transvestism and other sexual inversions, literal or not, practiced in private and public by men and women alike, led to a large budding literature on the subject. In 1864 Karl Heinrich Ulrichs defined homosexuality, which he considered congenital, as the existence of a female soul in the body of a man. In 1869 Richard von Krafft-Ebing and C. Westphalin were the first to study the different forms of "sexual inversions" scientifically.[23] Westphalin defined "congenital perversion" as a woman who is physically female but mentally male and a man who is physically male and mentally female. Holmès's words suggest that such ideas were taken seriously. In the examples chosen and the case studies examined, transvestism often signaled homosexuality, but not always. In Greek mythology, Tiresias was a man for six months and a woman for six months. Caligula, Heliogabalus, and Nero were bisexual. L'abbé de Choisy remained heterosexual, although he was raised and dressed as a girl, as did Georges Sand, who dressed as a man. Agnes Masson considered Wagner a "closeted transvestite" who never crossed in public, except perhaps through the "androgynous character" of his music.[24]

AMBIGUITIES IN THE MEANING OF HERCULES AND OMPHALE

Saint-Saëns may have been attracted to the story of Hercules and Omphale because of the cross-dressing associated with the characters.[25] The meaning of the myth, however, has been constantly in flux, especially "the exchange of garments," which the art historian Frances Huemer notes was "one of the major problems associated with the Hercules-Omphale myth in ancient times."[26] From Greek into Roman times, it motivated comic plays, satires, and carvings that sometimes made fun of Hercules, victimized by love. In some works, however, he is a "god of fertility, she an earth goddess, in a cult, as in many Near Eastern religions in which the male was subject to a dominating female deity."[27] The clothing exchange may hark back to early marriage rites, particularly Dionysian ones.

The story was popular among painters, and a number of paintings at the Louvre Museum in Paris support an interpretation that does not add up to Hercules's humiliation even if Omphale is usually depicted somewhat above him.[28] One version adds a third character, an angel. For example, in an eighteenth-century Dutch painting (Louvre Museum, INV. 20770), Omphale, content and Madonna-like, leans on Hercules as he spins wool while a winged angel hovers over them. In a French painting from the same period (INV. 20394), Omphale also looks contentedly down on Hercules as he spins wool, but this time she is naked and white, whereas Hercules is bearded and darker, and the angel is on the left rather than the right. In a second version of the myth taken from Ovid's *Fasti* (2.331–58) and popularized by Tintoretto and other Renaissance painters, the cross-dressing leads to comedy. Hercules, mistaken for a woman, ends up in bed with a goat-legged faun that he then kicks out, rejecting this symbol of lust.[29] Rubens's painting of the two at the Louvre (ca. 1602; INV. 854) builds on Petrarch, who considered Hercules a victim of Cupid; as the strongest and greatest, his defeat is proof of the power of love. In this third version of the story, Hercules embraces his virility rather than giving it up. There is no cross-dressing. He is virtually nude, sexually tense, potentially dangerous, and associated with Dionysius. Omphale, more dressed than he, her hair ornamented with jewels and his lion's skin draped over her shoulder, is pulling his ear. Many have seen this as a story of his subjugation. As Huemer points out, however, emblems of fertility surround the couple, suggesting a marriage allegory, and many considered the myth an ironic depiction of Hercules's "thirteenth labor," that is, marriage.[30]

In France from the eighteenth century through the 1870s, Hercules had other meanings. Under the monarchy he was associated with the power of the

French kings. In their desire to find alternatives to the king's patriarchy, the early revolutionaries turned from him to female allegories, such as the goddess Liberty, to symbolize the state. In the major dictionary of iconology from 1791, the editor explains, "the iconologists represent Force with the figure of a woman covered by a lionskin and armed with the club of Hercules."[31] Everything changed in 1793, however, when Robespierre took over and the Terror set in. Looking to "the people" as the source of their power and seeking to remasculinize the Revolution, the revolutionaries again turned to Hercules, reinventing him as French rather than Gallic. A giant Hercules, representative of the people as awesome in its force, replaced Liberty on statues in public places and the seal of the republic. As Hunt puts it, "the Terror was the people on the march, the exterminating Hercules. Hercules, the people, was in the eyes of the radicals who had called it into being a potential Frankenstein." Opponents of the Terror wore masks and dressed up in women's clothes in their challenges to local authorities until the wearing of "clothes of another sex than one's own" was banned in 1797. After Robespierre fell, and as popular forces were eventually tamed, images of Hercules became domesticated. He was no longer represented as a giant but became the "brother of Liberty and Equality . . . [,] older, wiser, conciliatory, even somewhat paternal."[32]

In 1870–71, as Saint-Saëns was writing *Le Rouet d'Omphale,* these revolutionary antagonisms returned. The Third Republic was declared on 4 September 1870 amid war with Prussia; the siege of Paris began two weeks later and lasted through the winter. Paris capitulated and signed an armistice on 28 January 1871. Frustrated with the government, the city of Paris formed the Commune in March 1871 and revived the image of Hercules on its coins, just as the people had done during the popular rebellion of 1848. When the working class was again squashed in May as if a socialist "monster," Hercules disappeared. The reassertion of power by the Third Republic brought a return to female allegories, not just Marianne crowned with a Phrygian cap, but also Liberty wearing a lion's muzzle.[33] A sedate Liberty, a symbol of conciliation and moderation used from 1848 to 1851, appeared on stamps in the early 1870s. Simultaneously the conservative government under the bourgeois president Louis-Adolphe Thiers, elected in November 1871, focused on a peace treaty with the Germans. Germans occupied the country until July 1873, leaving only after five billion francs in war reparations were paid.

During this time school manuals taught children to refer to "la belle Alsace" as feminine. The painter Jean-Jacques Henner made reference to this in his famous depiction of Alsace as a simple peasant woman, sad, suffering, compassionate.[34] Many viewed the ceding of Alsace to the Germans in May 1871 as a serious injustice, "an abuse of force," since the region wished to remain French. She, and by extension the country, was weak, especially in the face of German force. The French scholar Mona Ozouf explains that the big question haunting all French thereafter was "should she, or shouldn't she, prepare to rectify this injustice, by force if it's necessary, that is, at the price of a war?"[35] While "the idea of revenge" preoccupied the far right for decades, opportunist republicans hoped for a peaceful solution.

Saint-Saëns was closely allied with the anticlerical, universalist-minded republicans who took over the government in 1870–71. So was Victor Hugo. The composer served in the fourth battalion of the National Guard of the Seine and, because of this, was forced to flee to London during the Commune. This political position complicates how he may have understood notions of strength and weakness, male and female, masculinity and femininity in the early 1870s. The war forced France to give up its imperialist pride and accept its relative weakness vis-à-vis its neighbors. Simultaneously the nation needed to rethink its strengths from a different perspective. In the preface to a book about Joan of Arc from 1876 by H. Wallon, the minister of public education, religious practices, and the fine arts, Pope Pius IX reflected on this issue. He described the popular French heroine as someone "weak" whom God had nonetheless chosen to "break down the force and efforts of the strong."[36] If the comparison of Omphale to Joan here seems a bit far-fetched, one should note that in the opening scene of Jules Barbier's libretto for the Prix de Rome cantata of 1871, *Jeanne d'Arc*, Joan appears "seated at her spinning wheel, her spindle fallen from her hand." Such an image suggests that the French were prepared to rethink conventional notions about weakness and strength, and perhaps the gender associations linked with them, in the aftermath of the Franco-Prussian war.

LE ROUET D'OMPHALE

In some ways *Le Rouet d'Omphale* is the inverse, or complement, of the work that immediately preceded it, Saint-Saëns's *Marche héroïque* (1871), composed during the Franco-Prussian War. The composer dedicated it to the memory of a close friend killed in battle, Henri Regnault, a successful academic painter who made his reputation with a portrait of Salomé for which Augusta Holmès sat. Also a singer, Regnault had recently sung Samson in a private performance of excerpts from Saint-Saëns's opera *Samson et Dalila*, with Augusta Holmès singing Dalila. The Société Nationale presented a two-piano reduction of the *Marche héroïque* at its inaugural concert on 25 November 1871 and repeated it on 13 January 1872 after a two-piano reduction of *Le Rouet d'Omphale,* his second work performed there. The orchestral version of the latter was evidently not completed until March 1872, the date on the final manuscript.

Both *Le Rouet d'Omphale* and the *Marche héroique* use ternary forms. The military march, replete with cadences that recall Beethoven's *Eroica,* symbolic of the musically heroic, encircles a lyrical interlude, possibly symbolic of domestic peace or the women back home the army aims to protect. In *Le Rouet d'Omphale,* by contrast, it is the heavy, "masculine" theme in the middle that provides the contrast, interrupting and encircled by lighter "feminine" material. The feminine has the last word in this tale; weakness holds strength within itself, and triumphantly so (Saint-Saëns's reference to triumph recalls a term associated with marches). To celebrate itself as feminine, then, could mean that even if apparently weak, France, like Joan of Arc, still had inherent power that, in the end, could triumph against force.

According to his biographers, the idea for *Le Rouet d'Omphale* came while reading a poem of the same name from Victor Hugo's *Contemplations* (1843), although not entirely so,[37] as Saint-Saëns points out in his program note. He admired Hugo in political exile and may have wished to render tribute to his triumphant return.

> In the atrium is Omphale's beautiful ivory spinning wheel.
> The agile wheel is white, and the distaff is black;
> The distaff is made of lapis-inlaid ebony.
> It is in the atrium on a sumptuous carpet.
>
> On its plinth, a worker from Egine sculpted
> Europa, whose plaintive cry a god is not heeding.
> The white bull is taking her away. Europa, hopelessly,
> Cries out, and, lowering her eyes, is terrified to see
> The monstrous ocean kissing her rosy feet.
>
> Needles and thread, half-closed boxes,
> Wool from Miletus, painted with crimson and gold,
> Fill a basket by the sleeping wheel.
>
> Meanwhile, horrible, horrifying, enormous,
> At the far end of the palace, twenty deformed ghosts,
> Twenty monsters covered with blood, only half-visible,
> Wander, crowded around the sleeping wheel:
> The Nemean lion, the hideous Lernean Hydra,
> Cacus, the black bandit from the black cave,

The triple Geryon, and the water typhoons
Which in the evening blow with thundering noise amid the reeds;
On their forehead all of them bear the horrible imprint of the club,
And all of them, keeping away, prowling with a terrifying look,
Stare at the spinning wheel, where hangs a flexible and bound thread,
From afar, in the shadows, and with a humbled eye.[38]

The ivory spinning wheel here is a metaphor (or memory) of a beautiful woman lying, like an Odalisque, on a "sumptuous carpet." It's asleep, as seductive as ever, surrounded by "needles and thread, half-closed boxes, / wool from Miletus, painted with crimson and gold"—colors associated with victory. And yet, on its plinth (a square base or baseboard that can also be interpreted as the base of the wall in the atrium) is sculpted a terrible tale, the rape of Europa (in old Greece, the name of a white moon cow), whose hopeless plaint the gods don't hear as she is carried off by a white bull, her feet kissed by the "monstrous ocean," as if in collusion. In the first half of the poem, the story of Europa interrupts the description of the spinning wheel, poetically piercing the silent beauty of the surrounding stanzas, while the spinning wheel and its related materials provide the frame for reading the story. These stanzas also pose a question: will we too, in the context of this rape, remain silent and oblivious, as does the spinning wheel?

In the second half of the poem, the situation reverses, echoing the manner in which the sculpted band on the plinth at its base frames the spinning wheel (or the plinth on the wall frames the wheel in the atrium). Everything that is awful lurks in the background, perhaps engraven on the outer walls—"twenty deformed ghosts, twenty monsters covered with blood," a dragon with seven heads, "water typhoons," and more.[39] Why are they here? They circle around the spinning wheel, as if haunting the palace, all staring at it through the darkness with humiliation. Are the monsters in the poem humiliated, as some have suggested, because their conqueror has been tamed, he whose club had left its "horrible imprint" on them all? Hercules is strangely absent, and the spinning wheel "sleeps," still unaware, unmoved by the terrible scene, intact.

There is a victory of sorts here—a moral one. It is brought on neither by the beautiful figure itself, whose thread remains undisturbed, nor by the protesting Europa, who is without hope. Rather the victory on which the poet counts is our reaction to the act itself, our response to an act in the past recalled by the sculpture at which the ugliest of spirits can look upon only as shameful. In 1871 French audiences may have imagined this as a reference to their country. Europa's rape and her abduction—like France's land taken away by another large white force—cannot be undone, but neither can we remain unaffected, the beauty of the spinning wheel reminding us of female beauty when it is untouched.

Following Hugo's example, Saint-Saëns builds his work with a motive inspired by the image of a spinning wheel. The opening measures render the big wheel as two sinusoidal curves, the violins in B♭ major arpeggios alternating with the flutes in D major arpeggios. Since two notes of the first curves (D, F, and B♭) are only one half step away from two of the second (D, F♯, and A), this creates the tension of micromovement, the necessary disturbance to get the momentum going. The "seduction" begins immediately.

Originally written as a composition for two pianos, the work is constantly playing with ever-mobile relationships between two sonorous entities—who leads, who accompanies, and when do they get together. (For his premiere of the work in this form, Saint-Saëns envisaged Augusta Holmès and himself performing together—a woman identified with male composers and a man who at home was dominated by women—which suggests that he may have wanted audiences to associate gender oppositions with the sounds, if not also gender ambiguities.) As the pattern accelerates "little by little," the 2/4 meter emerges and the flutes are "seduced" by the B♭ tonality of the violins, imitating them after four measures; with the momentum started, the range of the curve gradually reduces from a twelfth to a sixth to a second, and its reiterations decrease from a measure long to a half-measure. By the time the horns enter with chords that reinforce the turning pulsation every two measures, the relationship between the strings and woodwinds has changed, the strings reduced to an accompaniment of alternating seconds. The clarinets and flutes then share the rising arpeggios, until the woodwinds take over the repeated chords of the horns and the spinning wheel motive in the strings moves into the foreground, stretching up its own curve to a″ and then c♯‴ before settling back, diminuendo, as seconds ornamenting e′.

Like the spinning wheel in the Hugo poem (and the opening theme in a march), this A material thus sets the tone and functions as a framing device in the rondo-like ternary form, ABAB′A—CC′—AB″A. Emile Baumann points out that the regularity of the spinning wheel music "simulates indifference."[40] It lulls the listener into a sleepy state not unlike that of the spinning wheel in the poem. Is this the state Hercules was in as he reputedly spun wool with Omphale's maidens? Is this work a critique of the country as indolent when the Germans unexpectedly took their land?

The B section (at B) starts seamlessly in a new meter, 6/8. Also introduced by the violins and flutes, as in the A section but here in unison, the *grazioso* theme begins by arching up from d♯′(to e′), culminating at f♯‴ (to e‴), interrupted by rests every third eighth beat. This buoyant dance, a musical metaphor for Omphale,[41] establishes the tonality of A major—Daniel Fallon points out that the tonic of the piece is delayed until this point (m. 45), which musically makes everything before it a kind of prelude.[42] This dance also makes central the notion of orchestral interplay. That is, at the end of its phrases, the theme moves from one woodwind to the next and, at the end of the section, between the strings and various combinations of woodwinds in a show of orchestral virtuosity. With the return of the B section at *E*, this time in E major, the B' theme enters on the second eighth beat of the measure, suspensions replace what before were rests, and the ingenious use of the orchestra continues. In this section the theme moves from the clarinets and bassoons; then, with violins added, to the flutes, clarinets, and violins; to the same with bassoons; and finally to the alternation between strings and woodwinds that characterized the end of the previous B section. The return of the A material brings the spinning wheel through a series of modulations that end on an A major-minor seventh chord (which resolves obliquely to C♯), whereby the C section starts.

At this point the narrative underlying Saint-Saëns's music departs from that suggested by the Hugo poem, and the composer turns to exploring the myth inherent in the poem's title rather than Hugo's poetic ruminations on the spinning wheel as object. The notes for the second half of the music (indicated on the score but never, to my knowledge, in program notes at concerts) describe a scene absent from the poem, that is, Omphale and her slave Hercules. "People who are interested in seeking out the details will notice, at *J*, Hercules groaning in the bonds he cannot break, and, at *L*, Omphale laughing at the hero's futile efforts."

The masculine force in the music is different from that of the poem. It does not represent some rapist or vague collection of monsters,[43] imaginary or otherwise, nor is it one that dominates the second half of the piece and has the final word. Instead, Saint-Saëns writes music for Hercules as the male hero in bondage and places it in the middle of his work. This interjection resembles the way Hugo interrupts his description of the spinning wheel with the rape scene, only here the music is not about violence. What begins at *J* is an eight-measure theme played by the bassoons and contrabassoons, trombones, violas, cellos, and double basses, *espressivo e pesante*—a timbre not yet heard in the piece. Beginning in C♯ minor, that is, on three of the same notes as in the A major-minor seventh that ended the previous section, this theme arises pianissimo from under the spinning wheel's turning—or in Saint-Saëns's words, the "bonds he cannot break"—symbolized by the pulsing woodwind chords continuing from the A section. In its first statement, this theme stretches up a minor ninth to A (figure 8.1); then, repeating this same gesture as if weightlifting and confident of pushing further eight more times, it spans an eleventh to C♯, a thirteenth to E, and finally two octaves to G♯, where it climaxes forte at *K* before gradually descending. With its strength spent, it can do no more than utter long crescendos on the same note before cadencing finally to G. This section constitutes roughly one-fourth of the work. Other than the bassoons, the woodwinds never leave their accompanimental role; they never take part in Hercules's theme except to follow the lead of his crescendo and the harmonic movement upward.

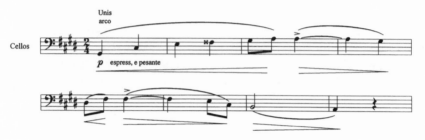

FIGURE 8.1. The Hercules (C) theme, at *J.*

The Hercules theme and its treatment recall Berlioz's *idée fixe* from the first movement of his *Symphonie fantastique.*[44] In both works the theme pushes higher with each repetition and subsides only after multiple attempts to begin again, giving musical form to longing and desire. In both the endlessly repeated chords of the accompaniment create constant tension. This musical similarity suggests that Saint-Saëns may have construed the C theme in *Le Rouet d'Omphale* as the loved one, although not Berlioz's seductively feminine loved one. Given the composer's feelings about Victor Hugo, perhaps the poet is part of the masculine force the composer is honoring here, his strength something Saint-Saëns hoped to appropriate. Michel Faure interprets the Hercules theme politically as representing "the monsters restored to life by Hercules's weakness." The absence of Hercules in the poem supports this interpretation, for Hugo in 1843, he points out, was nostalgic for Napoléon I— "a Hercules that conquered the terrifying forces of the Revolution." Saint-Saëns too may have felt nostalgic, possibly for "the dictatorship of Napoleon III, because the monsters of socialism were escaping."[45] In 1871, however, Parisians were more likely to associate Hercules with something else striking fear and envy—Germany. Michael Strasser has shown how envy of German strength and virtue was a potent force in the musical world of the late Second Empire.[46] The presence of German forces occupying Paris at the time might explain why

Saint-Saëns chose to give his Hercules a more tangible presence and wish him subdued by Omphale.

The theme that follows, C', is a mocking reiteration of C with the bass dropping out, the meter shifted to 6/8, and the accompaniment reduced to repeated seconds (see figure 8.2). At *L* the oboes and later the bassoons and flutes echo the rising fifths of the C theme's third phrase and imitate its arch up to an eleventh. But, as Saint-Saëns tells us, this variation suggests not that Hercules or his desire has undergone a transformation but rather that Omphale appears, in a way like Eve arising out of the ribs of Adam (as medieval painters sometimes depicted her). She does not wait until the end of the work to comment on Hercules's tune but immediately dislocates it by half a measure and interrupts it with rests every two eighth beats. Her response to Hercules's force is thus to seduce his desire and then render him silent, spent. If this is an unflattering portrait of a woman as neutralizing the male's power, perhaps even emasculating him, it does suggest that, having possessed masculine power as a woman sexually possesses a man, she is in the position to make light of it, to be proud—something like Renée felt after asserting her mastery over Maxime in *La Curée*. The playfulness of this section also raises another question: did the composer identify with Omphale, laughing and proud of his creation?

FIGURE 8.2. A mocking version of the C theme, at *L*.

The manner in which the work is conducted can strongly influence how these two aspects are perceived. Charles Dutoit, for example, conducts the masculine section at *J* as aggressive. For him, it should never really quiet down even at the end of the section. His interpretation of Omphale's reiteration of the theme is extremely quick and dismissive; the two forces remain distinct and opposed. By contrast, Leonard Bernstein conducts the masculine section as more lyrical. He also slows the final measures, as if Hercules gives in to Omphale, and uses a much slower tempo than Dutoit for Omphale's ironic retort, thereby underplaying its biting edge.[47] This interpretation suggests that the composer was seeking an interpenetration of opposites at this, the center of the work.

The structure of the work supports the latter performance. Formally and thematically it is a musical cross-dresser, for it uses many of the standard procedures in marches but in inverted ways. Omphale's celebration of her "triumph" is the inverse of that expressed in most marches. She affirms it piano rather than fortissimo, and in a light, graceful tone with staccatos. To underscore the confidence of this female, Saint-Saëns puts her theme in C major but slows the tempo somewhat and indicates that it is to be played *tranquillo*. It is the feminine material here that colonizes and takes over the masculine theme, that transforms its original nature (representing passionate force) and makes it become more like her (representing graceful charm). Unlike in marches, however, this process occurs on the new thematic terrain, that associated with Hercules (C) rather than with Omphale (B). Moreover, thematically C' suggests that she too was seduced. With C' based on C, Omphale and Hercules are structurally linked. This musical interdependence suggests a mutual attachment, for better or worse—an ironic reconciliation of opposites. Such an interpretation gives a new twist to the work as a political metaphor, possibly signaling hope for the peace negotiations with Germany in process during the writing of the work. For Saint-Saëns personally, it may also have expressed the nature of domestication. The passions of both C and C' are trapped in the middle of the work, surrounded by the music of the spinning wheel. One wonders whether a desire for such a synthesis drove the composer to marry four years later.

With neither Hercules nor Omphale returning, ultimately the seduction at the heart of this piece is performed by Saint-Saëns's music. The orchestra accomplishes this, and with clever craft and illusion rather than force. When the B material returns in the last quarter of the piece at *N*, the instrumental "sleight of hand" is utterly seamless: the orchestral interplay of woodwinds and strings earlier reserved for the ends of phrases here characterizes every quarter beat. Every two eighth beats bring a change in orchestration. No one part of the orchestra is accompaniment; no one part carries the melody. Instead different combinations of woodwinds, harps, and strings succeed one another so rapidly and artfully that the notes sound as if played continuously by a single set of instruments. Together they constitute the B" melody with ever-shifting timbres. The power of the final measures similarly comes from the almost imperceptibly subtle manner in which the composer slows the spinning wheel from six to four sixteenth notes per beat, from sixteenth notes to eighth notes to whole notes, and from one violin to another. Then the work ends as it had begun. In imitative interaction, the first and second violins echo the same figure a fourth apart, cleverly shift positions within the measure, share the final articulation of the A major chord, and alternately push the ascent to the high a''', finally reached by the first violins as a harmonic *ppp*. With such an ending the work seems to evaporate into what one critic called the "far reaches of the imagination [*des lointains imaginaires*]," not unlike the Adagio that ends Haydn's *Farewell* Symphony[48] or, one might add, Debussy's *Nocturnes*.

o   o   o

Some have insisted that the story of Hercules and Omphale is not necessarily "of great importance" and that as programs go, it is "*assez mince* [pretty thin]."[49] Over the next two decades, most critics focused on its easily accessible form, praising its "clarity" and "simplicity," aspects of the "Greek genius" the French believed they inherited "more than any other people."[50] Sometimes pointing to the "male talent" of the composer, critics implied that formal strength and integrity demonstrated virility and that this was what French music needed to recover from its decadence during the Second Empire.[51] Republicans, for whom artistic beauty was a metaphor for an ideal social order, considered clarity in language and form important as a way of suggesting the reconciliation, balance, and equilibrium of society's disparate realities.[52]

Perhaps Saint-Saëns relished this focus on form over content, as he did the apparent disparity between his straight public persona and his private pleasure in cross-dressing. Perhaps he counted on audiences' limited experience in interpreting instrumental music as if it were opera, that is, read against the background of current politics, to enjoy the freedom opera composers have to explore multiple ambivalences and ambiguities. On the surface Saint-Saëns appears to be moralizing, delivering a warning against woman's power and the seductions of feminine charm. This would be a message about male independence. Still, there are other ways to understand it. From a personal perspective, we might ask, was the composer caught in a conflict between desire for charm and shame for desiring it? From a political one, was he criticizing Hercules (and, by analogy, his country) for cross-dressing, for being too feminine, too lax as Germany attacked and the "rape of Europa" ensued? A new republic may have begun after the war, but, like Hercules in *Le Rouet d'Omphale*, its administrators, tamed and domesticated, were subject to the whims of the foreign other. Was he, as Faure suggests, regretting the weakness of what used to be strong in himself or others?

Alternatively, was Saint-Saëns more interested in what Omphale allowed him to explore (as when he played "Marguerite-Saint-Saëns at the spinning wheel" in that Viardot soirée), and did he hope his listeners would be likewise? Hercules may have allowed the composer to contemplate the pleasures of the masculine from the position of the seduced, but then, as I have already suggested, Omphale too expresses what it is like to be seduced. Since his earlier compositions were sometimes criticized for lacking charm,[53] it is possible that Saint-Saëns took on this subject to study and practice the art of musical charm as a way to enhance his own powers. He may also have thought that listeners would benefit from considering the merits of Omphale and her "triumphant struggle." During the early Third Republic, republicans were rethinking notions of femininity and refining their ideal of the republican woman. Educators preached that, to be good wives and good citizens, women must learn both "virile character," so they can "take the place of men if their husbands die," and, at the same time, "grace, charm, and delicacy," virtues understood as integral to French civilization.[54] When Omphale reiterates Hercules's music, transforming it with the addition of grace and charm, the masculine and feminine of the work momentarily fuse in her music: charm subdues force and force infuses charm. This interpenetration of virility and charm may have suggested to listeners how republican women could contain the passions of Eros within the framework of home and family. Heard this way, *Le Rouet d'Omphale* reflects a much more positive and productive view of cross-dressing and androgyny than Zola's pathologized decadence, one that could be manipulated to serve the interests of the new regime.

Studied in the context of the times, the work also can be read as a political metaphor, although the range of possible interpretations are as mutually exclusive as the political options open to the French people in the early 1870s. To the extent that the work reflects the republican spirit that seethed for change under the Second Empire, Hercules's music may represent the people, the beloved of Hugo forced into bondage by the weak, effeminate government of the monarchists. To the extent that it expresses republican sentiment during and immediately after the Commune, Hercules the character could signal the need to tame and contain the socialist monster, the music of the work's center. And to the extent that the expressive force of Hercules's music refers to German strength and virility—something the French both envied and feared—it suggests that charm may provide the French with what it takes to subdue the German intruder within. In the musical world, as Strasser has argued, the Société Nationale aimed to accomplish just that.[55] Saint-Saëns helped to found the organization beginning in February 1871, only one month after the signing of the armistice. With pieces such as *Le Rouet d'Omphale,* its members hoped an infusion of new French music would counterbalance the popularity of German music in their country. Composed during the confrontation of two political regimes, *Le Rouet d'Omphale* was thus a context for asserting the continuity of certain French values—formal clarity *and* feminine charm—and for reminding listeners that, as Saint-Saëns shows with the orchestra in the last part of his work, musical charm can be as effective as musical force.

It is important to ponder these questions given the works that followed. First, *Samson et Dalila,* premiered in 1877, tells a similar story. For Saint-Saëns as for Voltaire, Samson was a biblical Hercules. It may have been helpful for the composer to explore the charms of an Omphale before writing Dalila's beautiful seduction aria, "Mon coeur s'ouvre à ta voix," in *Samson et Dalila.*[56] The opera's meaning too needs reconsideration in the light of the politics and gender ambiguities previously discussed. Second, the composer's fourth and last symphonic poem, *La Jeunesse d'Hercule* (1877), and later *Déjanire* (1898) suggest that Hercules remained a multivalent symbol for the composer. The Hercules of *La Jeunesse d'Hercule,* however, changes back into his manly clothes. This work promotes a moral Saint-Saëns addressed in his second symphonic poem, *Phaeton* (1873), a Greek myth concerning retreat from the world of the passions to that of virtue and reason. Third, the composer's narrative for *La Jeunesse d'Hercule* inverts that of *Le Rouet d'Omphale,* the victory of strength over weakness. The score is prefaced with the following: "The story recalls how Hercules, at the beginning of his life, had two routes open to him: that of pleasure and that of virtue. Insensible to the seductions of the Nymphs and Bacchants, the hero enters upon the path of struggles and combat, at the end of which he glimpses the reward of immortality through the flames of the funeral pyre." In his analysis of the symphonic poem, Daniel Fallon notes that, unlike the account in the program of *Le Rouet d'Omphale,* "this love/duty conflict has no tangible root in the classical accounts of Hercules's youth,"[57] though it may have been a common accretion to the Hercules myth in baroque allegory. The musical structure of the work is also a kind of inverse of its predecessor's. Using a rondo form, ABACA (where A is Hercules's theme, B is a bacchanal that "tempts" him, and C represents the combat), Saint-Saëns again makes reference to the structure of marches; this time, however, as in marches, the "struggle" ends in the hero's "triumph." That he wrote it after he was married suggests that the fascinating and timely exploration of double lives/double identities in *Le Rouet d'Omphale* was over for the composer. Virtue had won, at least temporarily. The year he finished it a certain instability had also reached its end for the state. In the first universal male suffrage vote in France, republicans won their first majority in the Chambre des Députés, thereby ensuring the survival of the Third Republic. The composer and his country were ready to settle on a new identity, one they both hoped would have lasting value.

o   o   o

With *Déjanire* (1898), a tragedy in four acts adapted by Louis Gallet from Sophocles, Saint-Saëns returned to Hercules and the music of *La Jeunesse d'Hercule*. This time Hercules is poisoned by his jealous wife and dies consumed by flames. Neoplatonists thought of this story as the hero who needed fire to liberate his soul. For Saint-Saëns, it suggests a repudiation of the feminine. Did he think it was responsible for too much suffering within himself or society?

On 3 November 1901 Charles Lamoureux programmed *Le Rouet d'Omphale* with Tchaikovsky's last symphony (the *Pathétique*). Before performing them, his orchestra played Beethoven's First Symphony and Violin Concerto; afterward, it performed Berlioz's *Marche hongroise*. With works thought of as masculine encircling those associated with the feminine, this gesture makes its own statement about proper gender roles at the turn of the century.

NOTES

This chapter is part of my book *Useful Music, or Why Music Mattered in Third Republic France* (forthcoming from the University of California Press). An earlier version was written while I was a senior fellow at the Stanford Humanities Center in 1993–94. I am most grateful to the center for its generous support and to Philip Brett, Tom Grey, and Lloyd Whitesell for helpful comments on earlier versions of this chapter.

1. I am using gender here as one element of the "ideological field" Slavoj Žižek discusses in *The Sublime Object of Ideology* (London: Verso, 1989). For Žižek, such elements "are structured into a unified field through the intervention of a certain 'nodal point' (the Lacanian *point de capiton*) which 'quilts' them, stops their sliding and fixes their meaning" (87). In this chapter I explore a number of perspectives on the gender oppositions in *Le Rouet d'Omphale*, each of which suggests its own "quilt" of meaning.

2. As a regular practice, until the 1880s program notes were given for only a few works, such as Beethoven's *Pastoral* Symphony, Mendelssohn's *Midsummer Night's Dream*, and Berlioz's *Symphonie fantastique*.

3. Lawrence Kramer, "*Carnaval,* Cross-Dressing, and the Woman in the Mirror," in *Musicology and Difference,* ed. Ruth Solie (Berkeley: University of California Press, 1993), 324.

4. Thomas Bulfinch, *Bulfinch's Mythology* (New York: T. Y. Crowell, 1913), 147.

5. Jeffrey M. Muller discusses the allusions to Plato's *Phaedrus* in Rubens's painting *Hercules and Omphale,* connecting the bas-relief on the socle where Omphale stands (which shows Eros as a charioteer driving two horses) to a similar image in the Platonic dialogue. See Muller, "The Phaedran Charioteer and Two Early Paintings by

Rubens," *Essays in Northern European Art* (Doorspijk, the Netherlands: Davaco, 1983), 190–92.

6. Lynn Hunt, *Politics, Culture, and Class in the French Revolution* (Berkeley: University of California Press, 1984), 104.

7. Ibid., 107, 113.

8. Jean Bonnerot, *C. Saint-Saëns, sa vie et son oeuvre* (Saint-Saëns, his life and work) (Paris: Durand, 1914); Georges Servières, *Saint-Saëns* (Paris: Félix Alcan, 1923); and Arthur Dandelot, *La Vie et l'oeuvre de Saint-Saëns* (The life and work of Saint-Saëns) (Paris: Dandelot, 1930) are full of biographical detail. The most informative English-language sources are James Harding, "Saint-Saëns," in *The New Grove Dictionary of Music and Musicians*, 20 vols., ed. Stanley Sadie (London: Macmillan, 1980), 16:400–407; and idem, *Saint-Saëns and His Circle* (London: Chapman and Hall, 1965), based on interviews with many who knew the composer. A recent biography by Brian Rees, *Camille Saint-Saëns: A Life* (London: Chatto and Windus, 1999), draws heavily on these sources.

9. Harding, "Saint-Saëns," 16:401; idem, *Saint-Saëns*, 56.

10. See notes about these accidents reported in *Ménestrel*, 2 June 1878, p. 215, and 14 July 1878, p. 263.

11. Harding, "Saint-Saëns," 16:400–401. Saint-Saëns's relationship with Gabriel is unknown. According to Jeanine Huas in her *L'Homosexualité au temps de Proust* (Homosexuality in the time of Proust) (Paris: Danclau, 1992), "valets de chambre" were frequently homosexuals. In 1893 one doctor estimated that this was the case for one-third of such servants (23). In his article, "Vacation Cruises; or, The Homoerotics of Orientalism," *PMLA* 110, no. 1 (Jan. 1995): 89–107, Joseph Boone argues that in the nineteenth and twentieth century Algeria attracted many gay tourists such as Gide and Wilde. For more on sex as an aspect of tourism, see Robert Aldrich, *The Seduction of the Mediterranean: Writing, Art, and Homosexual Fantasy* (London: Verso, 1993).

12. Harding, *Saint-Saëns*, 57, 114.

13. Huas devotes a chapter of her book to Saint-Saëns as one of the three "notorious homosexuals" of the time. She publishes police records that contain bitter letters from a man who in 1893 accused him of being a "liar, thief, and pederast" and having "pederasts of your type that you maintain with pieces of bread" (in Huas, *L'Homosexualité*, 160–68; my translation—except where noted, all other translations from the French are my own as well). Harding also mentions the "theory" that the composer "indulged in Gide-like orgies with Arab boys and fellaheen [peasants]" but concludes that it can be "neither proved nor disproved" (*Saint-Saëns*, 202).

14. Harding, *Saint-Saëns*, 57–58. See also Paul Viardot, "Saint-Saëns Gai" (Cheerful Saint-Saëns), *Le Guide du Concert* (1914): 13. In this scene of *Faust*, Marguerite sings of discovering jewels and a mirror in the casket.

15. Viardot, "Saint-Saëns Gai," 13–14.

16. Modest Tchaikovsky, *The Life and Letters of Peter Ilich Tchaikovsky*, trans. and ed. Rosa Newmarch (New York: Haskell House, 1970 [1905]), 176; also cited in Rollin Smith,

Saint-Saëns and the Organ (Stuyvesant, N.Y.: Pendragon, 1992), 81; and Harding, *Saint-Saëns,* 141–42. Harding also notes that "there are also amusing stories that once in Algiers Saint-Saëns gaily donned a pink dress to receive the Archbishop of Carthage in a manner befitting his red robe" (202).

17. *La Curée*'s preface is dated 15 November 1871. The book was deposited at the Bibliothèque Nationale on 17 February 1872. Its second edition was published on 14 October 1872; its third, on 5 April 1873; and its fourth, on 12 June 1874. I am grateful to my research assistant, Jean-Louis Morhange, for encouraging me to read it.

18. Émile Zola, *La Curée* (The kill), in *Les Rougon-Macquart*, 3 vols., ed. Armand Lanoux (Paris: Fasquelle, 1960), 1:485–86, 568–70.

19. Ibid., 1:1581, 1604–5. The quotations in this paragraph come from the preface to *La Curée* and newspaper articles Zola wrote between 1868 and 1870.

20. Serious attention began to be paid to women musicians in the late 1860s, although for some this meant questioning whether they can express anything other than elegance and grace. See A. Vizentini, "Les Femmes compositeurs" (Women composers), *Art musical* (28 Sept. 1865): 349–52; idem, "Les Femmes compositeurs en France depuis 1694 à nos jours" (Women composers in France from 1694 to today), *Art musical* (22 Aug. 1867, 299–300); and the cover story by Ralph [*sic*], "La Musique et les femmes" (Music and women), *Art musical* (21 Jan. 1869): 57–58. Thereafter the Association for the Rights of Women, founded in 1870, set an ambitious agenda for the Third Republic and new journals such as *Le Droit des femmes* and *La Femme* advanced these ideas. Women's orchestras from abroad began to perform in Paris in 1874, and in 1876 a young woman petitioned to compete for the Prix de Rome in composition.

21. Jann Matlock, "Masquerading Women, Pathologized Men: Cross-Dressing, Fetishism, and the Theory of Perversion 1882–1935," in *Fetishism as Cultural Discourse,* ed. Emily Apter and William Pietz (Ithaca, N.Y.: Cornell University Press, 1993), 57.

22. In 1885 Holmès cut her hair and changed her appearance radically. Thereafter she often appeared in public dressed in a masculine style. For further discussion of these issues and their impact on her music, see my article "The Ironies of Gender, or Virility and Politics in the Music of Augusta Holmès," *Women and Music* 2 (1998): 1–25.

23. Richard von Krafft-Ebing, *Psychopathia Sexualis* (Sexual psychopathy) (1869), which was published in ten editions by 1892; C. Westphalin, "Die conträre Sexualempfindung" (The antipathic sexual sentiment), *Archiv für Psychiatrie und Nervenkrankheiten* 2 (1869): 73–108. Westphalin included a case study about a heterosexual man who liked to dress up as a woman. In his *Medical jurisprudence,* vol. 2 (1873), Alfred Swain Taylor describes a transvestite, the famous actress Elisa Edwards, who was discovered to be a man after her death. In *Les Perversions de l'instinct génital* (Perversions of the genital instinct) (Berlin, 1891; Paris, 1893), Albert Moll describes transvestites as fetishists who wear clothing of the opposite sex. Other studies include Jacques-Joseph Moreau de Tours, *Des aberrations du sens génésique* (Aberrations of the procreative direction) (Paris, 1883); Vanentin Magnan, *Des anomalies, des aberrations, et des perversions sexuelles* (Sexual anomalies, aberrations, and perversions) (Paris,

1885); Émile Laurent, *L'Amour morbide: Etude de psychologie pathologique* (Morbid love: a psychopathological study) (Paris, 1891); and idem, *Les Bisexués: Les fétichistes, pervertis, et invertis sexuels* (The bisexed: fetishists, perverts, and sexual inverts) (Paris, 1896). See the excellent study of this literature, which includes numerous case studies, in Agnes Masson, *Le Travestissement: Essai de psycho-pathologie sexuelle* (Cross-dressing: an essay on sexual psychopathology) (Paris, 1935); and Matlock, "Masquerading Women, Pathologized Men." According to Matlock, "after the 1880s, observers treated the line between cross-dressing and clothing obsession as ambiguous, though most saw both as sexual perversions" (34).

24. Masson, *Le Travestissement*, 11–31.

25. Saint-Saëns may also have been drawn to this story by Handel's *Hercules.* Handel was an important influence on the first act of his *Samson et Dalila*, a work in process during the composition of *Le Rouet d'Omphale.* Philip Brett reminded me that Dejanira's aria "Resign thy club," from Handel's *Hercules,* uses a spinning-wheel motive in the accompaniment and vocal part. For more on this and on Omphale in Handel's sources, see David Ross Hurley, "Dejanira, Omphale, and the Emasculation of Hercules: Allusion and Ambiguity in Handel," *Cambridge Opera Journal* 11 (1999): 199–213.

26. Frances Huemer, "A Dionysiac Connection in an Early Rubens," *Art Bulletin* 61, no. 4 (Dec. 1979): 565n10. This article traces the iconography and literary references to this myth in Greek and Roman sources.

27. Ibid., 565.

28. I am grateful to the Documentary Center Library of the Louvre Museum, Paris, for help in locating these paintings.

29. Tintoretto's painting *Hercules Expelling the Faun from Omphale's Bed* (now in the Museum of Fine Arts in Budapest) presents a subject he painted at least twice. I am grateful to Charles Cutter of the Department of Political Science, San Diego State University, for bringing it to my attention.

30. Huemer, "Dionysiac Connection," 568–74. See also idem, *Rubens and the Roman Circle: Studies of the First Decade* (New York: Garland, 1996), 67.

31. In Hunt, *Politics,* 103. An allegorical engraving of the first days of the Revolution published in Maurice Agulhon's *Marianne into Battle: Republican Imagery and Symbolism in France, 1789–1889,* trans. Janet Llody (Cambridge: Cambridge University Press, 1981), also shows a woman with a lion's skin tied around her waist (92).

32. Hunt, *Politics,* 66, 101, 94–117.

33. See the bust of Liberty reproduced in Agulhon, *Marianne into Battle,* 97.

34. The painting *Alsace* is presently in the Henner Museum, Paris.

35. Mona Ozouf, "Le Patriotisme dans les manuels primaires" (Patriotism in elementary-school manuals) and "L'Alsace-Lorraine, mode d'emploi. La question d'Alsace-Lorraine dans le *Manuel général,* 1871–1914" (The use of Alsace-Lorraine: the question of Alsace-Lorraine in the *Manuel général,* 1871–1914), *L'école de la France. Essais sur la Révolution, l'utopie, et l'enseignement* (The French elementary school: essays on the Revolution, utopia, and teaching) (Paris: Gallimard, 1984), esp. 207–10, 221.

36. In H. Wallon, *Jeanne d'Arc* (Paris: Firmin-Didot, 1876), ii. The pope's letter is dated 25 October 1875.

37. The poem was written in 1843 and published in *Contemplations* in 1856. In his *Saint-Saëns*, J. Bonnerot, the composer's "official biographer," claims that Victor Hugo's poem was the source for this work.

38. I would like to thank Jean-Louis Morhange for providing this translation.

39. Except for the Nemean lion, whose skin Hercules liked to wear, the meaning of these monsters is purposely vague. Since the Revolution, the French considered evils unleashed by the breakdown of traditional society to be "monsters." Hercules, for the Jacobins, was supposed to kill all of them, especially the hydra of federalism. Hunt, *Politics*, 41, 96.

40. Émile Baumann, *Les Grandes Formes de la musique. L'oeuvre de Saint-Saëns* (The great musical forms: the work of Saint-Saëns) (Paris: Éditions littéraires et artistiques, 1905), 310.

41. Baumann describes this section as the seductive dance of Omphale: "She brushes up against Hercules with subtle, intermittent touches . . . [;] she caresses him with suave and disconcerting sonorities. But the lascivious movements of her body resemble mocking gestures; mistress of herself, measuring her effects, she plays with the increasing desire of the hero; with the chromatic suppleness of the melody, she provokes him in disrobing herself; the indolence she pretends is more mockery" (ibid., 310–11).

42. Daniel Fallon, "The Symphonies and Symphonic Poems of Camille Saint-Saëns" (Ph.D. diss., Yale University, 1973), 234.

43. In his analysis of the work in *Musique et société du Second Empire aux Années Vingt* (Music and society from the Second Empire to the 1920s) (Paris: Flammarion, 1985), Michel Faure notes that he hears the music at *J* as symbolizing the groaning of the monsters to whom Hercules's weakness has given life again (120).

44. In its first appearance Berlioz's *idée fixe* is played by the flutes and violins, the same instruments that alternate seductively in the opening of *Le Rouet d'Omphale*.

45. Faure, *Musique et société*, 120.

46. Michael Strasser, "Virtue, Reform, and 'Pure' Music in Second Empire Paris," paper delivered to the Sixteenth Congress of the International Musicological Society, London, 16 Aug. 1997.

47. Charles Dutoit conducts the London Sinfonietta Philharmonia Orchestra in this work on Decca London 414 460-2, and Leonard Bernstein conducts the Orchestre National de France on Polydor International 400 070-2.

48. Baumann, *Les Grandes Formes*, 304, 312n.

49. James Harding, *Saint-Saëns*, 121; Maurice Silberblatt, "1835 Camille Saint-Saëns 1921," *La Vie française* (25 May 1935).

50. Amédée Boutarel, "Revue des grands concerts" (Concert review), *Ménestrel*, 21 Feb. 1892, p. 62.

51. Camille Bellaigue, *Le Figaro*, 26 Jan. 1889; Baumann, *Les Grandes Formes*, 304. More recently Kramer has interpreted Saint-Saëns's description of the spinning wheel's

formal function in the work as an attempt to "win back the masculinity his hero has lost" (*"Carnaval,"* 324).

52. For more on this see Miriam Levin, *Republican Art and Ideology in Late Nineteenth-Century France* (Ann Arbor: UMI, 1986).

53. See Paul Bernard's review of Saint-Saëns's first opera, *La Princesse jaune,* in *Revue et gazette musicale,* 16 June 1872, pp. 185–86.

54. E. Spuller, minister of public instruction and fine arts, in his speech (19 Oct. 1888) on the occasion of the inauguration of the women's high school, the Lycée Racine, reproduced in *Au Ministère de l'Instruction publique 1887, Discours, allocutions, circulaires* (At the ministry of public instruction, 1887: speeches, announcements, and memoranda) (Paris: Hachette, 1888), 247, 249.

55. Michael Strasser, "Ars Gallica: The Société Nationale de Musique and Its Role in French Musical Life, 1871–1891" (Ph.D. diss., University of Illinois, Champaign-Urbana, 1998).

56. The exact chronology of these pieces is unclear. According to the *Journal de musique,* 15 Dec. 1877, there was a private performance of act 2 of *Samson et Dalila* in Mme Viardot's salon in 1873.

57. Fallon, "The Symphonies," 332.

9 THE "DARK SAYING"

OF THE ENIGMA

HOMOEROTICISM AND THE ELGARIAN PARADOX

BYRON ADAMS

Videmus nunc per speculum in ænigmate; tunc autem facie ad faciem.
Nunc cognosco ex parte; tunc autem cognoscam, sicut et cognitus sum.
—I Cor. 13:12 (Vulg.)

On 12 February 1899 Edward Elgar, who was within eight days of completing the orchestration of his "Enigma" Variations, attended Quinquagesima mass at St. Joseph's Roman Catholic Church in Malvern.[1] As the former organist of St. George's Roman Catholic Church in Worcester, Elgar was familiar with the liturgy of the day, as well as with the Vulgate version of the epistle, drawn from St. Paul's first letter to the Corinthians, a verse of which appears as the epigraph to this chapter. Elgar certainly knew its translation in the Authorized Version: "For now we see through a glass darkly; but then face to face: now I know in part, but then shall I know even as also I am known." Elgar must have rendered *ænigmate,* a term with Greek origins, as "darkly," which in the passage from Corinthians means "obscurely" or "as in a puzzle."[2]

Elgar associated the word *darkly* with *ænigmate* as the cognate of *enigma.* In a letter to C. A. Barry, who quoted from it in the program note for the premiere of the variations on 19 June 1899, Elgar wrote: "The Enigma I will not explain—its 'dark saying' must be left unguessed."[3] The theme alone represents the "Enigma": the word *Enigma* appears in the manuscript of the variations only above the theme. The word is not in Elgar's hand but was written there by the composer's friend August Jaeger, a person whose relationship to the variations will be explored in this essay.[4]

It is clear that Elgar identified with the "Enigma" theme. Thirteen years after the premiere of the variations, the composer made this inner connection explicit in a revealing letter sent on 12 August 1912 to Ernest Newman, who had undertaken to write a program analysis for the premiere of Elgar's ode for mezzo-soprano, chorus, and orchestra, *The Music Makers*. In the course of a detailed discussion of the self-referential musical quotations that are interlaced throughout *The Music Makers,* Elgar wrote: "I have used the opening bars of the theme (Enigma) of the Variations because it expressed when written (in 1898) my sense of the loneliness of the artist as described in the first six lines of the Ode, and to me, it still embodies that sense."[5] Elgar associated himself so closely with the theme that he once used its first measure—marked "mesto"—as his signature in a letter posted on 10 October 1901 to Dora Penny, the "Dorabella" of the tenth variation.[6]

This brief précis of the history of the "Enigma" theme begins to point us toward the complex interaction, fraught with anxiety, between Elgar's art and what Arnold Bax called his "tormented life."[7] In the letter to Ernest Newman cited in the preceding paragraph, Elgar set forth a highly personal and self-referential aesthetic: "I am glad you like the idea of the quotations; after all art must be the man, & all true art is, to a great extent egotism & I *have* written several things that are still alive."[8] While such a confessional mode is scarcely unusual among late nineteenth-century composers, Elgar's relationship to his music is paradoxical. He wanted to write music that was self-referential but hoped to be protected from speculation concerning those references. To distract those seeking to pry into the personal sources of his more intimate scores, Elgar devised cunning diversions by using enigmas, epigrams (often in foreign languages he did not read), and other obfuscations. (This strategy has worked brilliantly, by the way: Elgar scholars have searched diligently for a "solution" to the "Enigma.") It is as if Elgar needed to obscure the inner origins of his art as much as he felt compelled to confess them. And yet, by strewing conundrums and clues throughout and around his music, Elgar seemed to invite speculation concerning his private life. As Diana McVeagh observes: "Has any other composer so *nearly* laid bare his sources, given so many hints, or been so provocative?"[9]

It is impossible to solve Elgar's provocative enigmas, of course; he was too elusive, and far too complex, to be neatly and finally explained. Thus this essay does not presume to move inexorably toward a full and all-embracing explication of Elgar's ambiguous and at times contradictory personality, of his "tormented life," or of the relationship between Elgar's music and his inner life. Rather, by placing the composer within a cultural context and by examining closely his relationships with his wife and his friends, I will open a perspective on Elgar that is as poignant and potentially illuminating as it is, perhaps, disturbing. If this essay asks more questions than it answers, that is by design.

McVeagh touches on an aspect of the composer's enigmatic behavior in an article entitled, after a quotation from Elgar himself that refers to the inner program of his cello concerto, "A Man's Attitude to Life." McVeagh strives to understand Elgar's frequent depressions by juxtaposing passages from his letters with lines she draws from the despairing sonnets of Gerard Manley Hopkins and Tennyson's *In Memoriam*. McVeagh compares Elgar and Hopkins in the light of their Catholicism, their shared sense of failure, and their bouts of depression. She does not mention, however, that one cause of Hopkins's depressions was his struggle to repress his carnal desires for young working-class men.[10] McVeagh then alternates lines from *In Memoriam* with sentences that Elgar wrote to August Jaeger on 11 November 1903 about the sudden death of Alfred Rodewald, a talented amateur conductor in Liverpool who had championed Elgar's music. Parts of Elgar's prose bear an uncanny similarity to Tennyson's verse. Here, first, is Elgar:[11]

> I found I could not rest so went up on Monday; did not go to the house but called a friends [*sic*] in the same street—they told me—I broke down & went out—& it was night—to me. What I did, God knows—I know I walked for miles in strange ways. . . . I know I went & looked at the Exchange where he had taken me—but it was all dark, dark to me although light enough to the busy folk around. . . . I went to my room & wept for hours—yesterday I came home without seeing anyone & am now a wreck & broken-hearted man." (Elgar to Jaeger, 11 Nov. 1903)

Compare this to Tennyson:

> Dark house, by which once more I stand
> Here in the long unlovely street,
> Doors, where my heart was used to beat
> So quickly, waiting for a hand . . .
> (*In Memoriam* 7:1–4)

> He is not here; but far away
> The noise of life begins again,
> And ghastly thro' the drizzling rain
> On the bald street breaks the blank day. (7:9–12)

> And I should tell him all my pain
> And how my life had droop'd of late,

And he should sorrow o'er my state
And marvel what possess'd my brain. (14:13–16)

McVeagh stops after comparing texts, but the connection offers a possible explanation for the melodramatic tone of Elgar's letter and the strange journey to Liverpool that it describes. In his letter Elgar tells how, arriving after Rodewald's death, he walked the streets for hours, dazed and weeping.[12] Elgar's biographers have long puzzled over this episode, but McVeagh's inspired comparison suggests a possible solution: Elgar, who like every literate Victorian had read *In Memoriam*,[13] felt impelled to reenact its basic plot, casting himself as the grieving protagonist and Rodewald as Arthur Hallam, Tennyson's beloved friend whose death inspired the elegy.

There are yet much greater implications that may be brought to bear on McVeagh's comparison of Elgar's letter with passages from *In Memoriam*. Many writers have recognized the erotic centrality of Hallam in Tennyson's poem. In an unsigned review of *In Memoriam* that appeared in the September 1850 issue of *Fraser's Magazine*, Charles Kingsley considered the elegy as a successor to "the old tales of David and Jonathan, Damon and Pythias, Shakespeare and his nameless friend, of 'love passing the love of women.'" Harold Bloom, writing of *In Memoriam* in his 1966 essay "Tennyson, Hallam, and the Romantic Tradition," asserts that it "need disturb no one any longer" that "Tennyson's Muse was (and always remained) Hallam."[14] Richard Dellamora observes: "In *In Memoriam*, erotic sentiment is free continually to expand precisely because—unlike subsequent works like *Leaves of Grass*—the poem is conceived in aesthetic, not sexual-aesthetic, terms. . . . As a meditation of the self, the poem moves not toward self-definition—as *Calamus*, for example, does—but toward self-expansion, an expansion of self in which Hallam, nature, God himself are assimilated into the poet's being—and to his poetry."[15]

Despite this common and persistent strain of textual criticism concerning Tennyson's elegy, McVeagh claims that "*In Memoriam* is not really about Hallam." To amplify this assertion, as well as protect Elgar from any unseemly inferences, she quotes the British psychologist Anthony Storr, who states reassuringly that "the Victorians were more, not less, tolerant of homosexual feelings, if not homosexual practices, than we are. . . . Those who are certainly predominantly heterosexual, as was Tennyson, seem to be allowed less latitude than formerly in expressing passionate friendship involving their own sex." McVeagh then cryptically suggests that "perhaps that throws some light on Elgar's friendship for Rodewald. Also it has a bearing on his feelings for Jaeger, and his expression of them in 'Nimrod.'"[16]

This is all quite disingenuous, of course. The Victorians encouraged social conformity, and their punishment for "homosexual practices" was swift and brutal. The "Labouchère Amendment," section 11 of the Criminal Law Amendment Bill of 1885, made all male homosexual acts liable to criminal prosecution: "Any male person who, in public or private, commits, or is party to the commission of, or procures or attempts to procure the commission by any male person of any act of gross indecency with another male person, shall be guilty of a misdemeanor, and being convicted thereof shall be liable at the discretion of the court to be imprisoned for any term not exceeding two years, with or without hard labour." Known colloquially as the "Blackmailer's Charter," this amendment, which remained on the statute books until 1967, led to a dramatic increase in the number of prosecutions for homosexual acts, as well as inciting intensified public homophobia.[17] The first prosecution under the Labouchère Amendment, resulting in the notorious Cleveland Street scandal of 1889, ruined the career of Lord Arthur Somerset, who was an officer in the Royal House Guards and a prominent courtier in attendance on the prince of Wales.[18] Twice during his lifetime Elgar witnessed the savage enforcement of English mores: the trials of Oscar Wilde in 1895 and thirty years later the disgrace of William Lygon, the seventh lord Beauchamp, the initials of whose sister—Lady Mary Lygon—stand above the thirteenth of the "Enigma" Variations.

Lord Beauchamp was the head of the noble Lygon family, which was ancient in lineage, distinguished in service, and Roman Catholic in religion. (Evelyn Waugh used the Lygons as a model for the aristocratic Flyte family in his *Brideshead Revisited.*) Lord Beauchamp and his sister made their estate, Madresfield Court, a center for social, cultural, and philanthropic activity in the area around Malvern and Worcester. Lady Mary Lygon was a keen musician and accomplished choral conductor, so she naturally extended encouragement and patronage to Elgar, a rising figure on the local musical scene who was also a Roman Catholic. Elgar participated as an adjudicator and conductor at the music festivals that Lady Mary organized at Madresfield Court. The Elgars dined with Lord Beauchamp and his family several times, both at Madresfield Court and in London. An apogee was reached in November 1913 when the Elgars were invited to spend a grand weekend at Madresfield Court.

Despite his successes as a politician and a courtier, Lord Beauchamp's position was imperiled several times by his interest in handsome young men. The waspish poet Hilaire Belloc alluded sardonically to both Lord Beauchamp's political aspirations and the "open secret" of his homosexuality in a poem that pillories Beauchamp as the effete "Lord Lundy":

Towards the age of twenty-six,
They shoved him into politics . . .
We had intended you to be
The next Prime Minister but three . . .
But as it was! . . . My language fails!
Go out and govern new South Wales! . . .
Good gracious how Lord Lundy cried!

Given the nature of gossip in provincial communities such as Worcester and Malvern, it is likely that some breath of the scandals surrounding Lord Beauchamp reached Elgar's ears at some point. Beauchamp had barely managed to weather an earlier brush with disgrace by a hastily arranged marriage and a period of retirement, but his public career and private life were irrevocably ruined in 1931 when he was forced to flee to New York to avoid prosecution for "homosexual offences."[19] Of this hapless peer George V is reported to have said, "I thought men like that shot themselves."[20]

As for Victorian tolerance of "homosexual feeling," one of the early reviews of *In Memoriam*, now usually attributed to the father of Gerard Manley Hopkins, attacked the poem in 1850 for its "strange manner of address to a man." The reviewer deplored that the main "defect which has painfully come out as often as we take up the volume, is the tone of—may we say so!—amatory tenderness." Expanding on his speculations, the reviewer suspected that both the "strange address" and "amatory tenderness" derive from Tennyson's "floating remembrances of Shakespeare's sonnets," which "present the startling peculiarity of transferring every epithet of womanly endearment to a masculine friend—his master-mistress, as he calls him by a compound epithet, harsh, as it is disagreeable."[21]

Despite a persistent popular contemporary belief to the contrary, this review evinces that the Victorians were well aware of the existence of homosexuality. Members of educated society shared a vocabulary, at once oblique and pejorative, that alluded to homosexuality while maintaining a proper degree of decorum. A typical, if paradoxical, strategy was to call attention to the absence of homosexuality from civilized discourse. An example of this strategy is the Latin phrase, first used by Sir Robert Peel during a debate in Parliament in 1826, decrying sodomy as the crime "inter Christianos non nominandum" (not to be named among Christians).[22] (A later, stronger variant of this same sentiment, dating from just after the Wilde trials and also in Latin, was "illum crimen horribile quod non nominandum est" [that horrible crime that is never to be named].[23] Latin, which almost all literate Victorian men learned at school, was a favored language for these descriptions.) In a passage from his monu-mental novel *A Dance to the Music of Time*, Anthony Powell aptly describes the reliance on sexual euphemism that the Victorians bequeathed to their Edwardian successors: "Lady Warminster represented to a high degree that characteristic of her own generation that everything may be said, though nothing indecorous discussed openly. Layer upon layer of wrapping, box after box revealing in the Chinese manner yet another box, must conceal all doubtful secrets; only the discipline of infinite obliquity made it lawful to examine the seamy side of life. If these mysteries were observed everything might be contemplated: however unsavory: however unspeakable."[24]

Elgar was most certainly aware of the price of difference in a society that went to such lengths to enforce conformity. As a Roman Catholic, as a musician, and as a tradesman's son without the benefit of either public school or university degree, Elgar felt himself an outsider looking into the closed world of Victorian middle-class society. To mitigate his feelings of exclusion, Elgar modeled his public persona on the popular image of the "English gentleman": his bearing was rigid and quasi-military; he strove for emotional reticence in society; his politics were Tory and staunchly imperialist; his clothing was immaculately tailored; and at times he disavowed any knowledge of, or interest in, his own unfashionable musical profession. Furthermore, he entered into a marriage that, however unorthodox in its origins,[25] was acceptably Victorian in that it was based more on shared piety and ambition than on desire.

Unfortunately Elgar went too far in his quest for respectability and came to be seen by some of the rebellious postwar generation as a caricature of an English gentleman. Siegfried Sassoon, who respected Elgar's music, noted the contrast between the public figure and the private man: "Elgar led me to the music-room and played the piano for nearly an hour. . . . It was splendid to see him glowing with delight in the music, and made me forget (and makes me regret now) the 'other Elgar' who is just a type of 'club bore.' At lunch, regaling us with long-winded anecdotes (about himself), he was a different man. The real Elgar was left in the music-room."[26] Osbert Sitwell derided him as a "plump wraith" who "looked every inch a personification of 'Colonel Bogie.'"[27]

Other descriptions of Elgar attest to the stress caused by maintaining such a facade, especially when the composer's highly emotional nature threatened to betray him at any moment. His friend Rosa Burley, who was the proper headmistress of a girl's school, thought him to be "one of the most repressed people it is possible to imagine."[28] Ernest Newman was just one of the many who observed Elgar's habit—as persistent as that of his continual nervous blinking[29]—of relieving his pent-up feelings with bursts of weeping: "This quick nervous response to life at its most salient and most energetic had a curious way of betraying itself in his gestures. . . . He could rarely listen to fine-souled music without tears coming into his eyes." As if uneasy over this revelation, Newman added that "[Elgar] was anything but a sentimentalist or weakling; his emotions were under the control, for the purposes of art, of a powerful and critical mind."[30]

Another eyewitness account is more candid about the composer's disposition. Charles Kenyon was a radical intellectual and music critic based in Manchester who wrote under the pseudonym "Gerald Cumberland." In an extensive article entitled "Elgar's Use of Literature," Brian Trowell has noted that "though [Cumberland] was a journalist, his work is not mere *reportage*: he knew a great deal about music, and admired Ernest Newman's critical writings almost as much as he admired Elgar's compositions. . . . His two books of reminiscences reveal a very wide acquaintance amongst composers and performers as well as theatre folk and artists."[31]

Cumberland interviewed Elgar twice, in 1906 and then at greater length in 1913. He would have often seen Elgar on the concert platform, and the two shared several mutual acquaintances, such as Ernest Newman. The earliest published version of these interviews was stiffly respectful, but later Cumberland drew on his extensive notes for a much less reserved portrait of Elgar in his book *Set Down in Malice*, published in 1919. Despite the promise of its title and an occasional arch remark, this volume is informed less by malice than by its author's probity.[32] Trowell aptly remarks that *Set Down in Malice* is a "book largely written on active service during the Great War, as the prefatory note tells us, 'in trenches and dugouts of Greece and Serbia,' in Port Said, Alexandria and Marseilles: it is the work of a sharp and highly intelligent observer who wished, no doubt in the face of possible death, to leave a true record of his experiences, and to say much that he had previously not been allowed to say."[33]

Cumberland's description of Elgar is striking and revealing. After remarking on Elgar's "curious fastidiousness of style that is almost finicking" and his "innate and exaggerated delicacy, an almost feminine shrinking," and after reporting Elgar's propensity for weeping while conducting his works, Cumberland concluded that "he is abnormally sensitive, abnormally observant, abnormally intuitive."[34] In addition to the feminizing aspect of this description, Cumberland's threefold insistence on the word *abnormally* is provocative. For Cumberland and for many of his readers, the term *abnormal* had a specific sexual implication.

In his *Nationalism and Sexuality*, a study of the ways in which attitudes toward masculinity and sexuality shaped national identity in Germany and

England during the late nineteenth and early twentieth centuries, George L. Mosse explores the sexual connotations that surrounded the word *abnormal.* Mosse writes that

> the appearance and character of each individual was classified as normal or abnormal: nervousness was supposedly induced by the practice of vice, while virility and manly bearing were signs of virtue . . . [;] those who could not control their passions were either considered abnormal to begin with or would inevitably drift into abnormality. . . . Masturbation was thought to be the root cause of all loss of control, indeed, of abnormal passion in general. . . . It was said to reflect an over-heated imagination, inimical to bourgeois sobriety, and was supposed to induce nervousness . . . [;] the masturbator's presumed passion for secrecy, it was asserted, easily led him to practice homosexuality. . . . That one abnormality led to another was common wisdom supported by the medical profession.[35]

In this context Cumberland's innuendo concerning Elgar is brutally clear; sophisticated readers, such as the radical audience for whom the book was presumably written, would have comprehended this instantly.

But an equally striking aspect of these insinuations is the way Cumberland conflates musicality with effeminacy and "abnormality" and then applies this belief to Elgar. The belief that musicality and homosexuality (or "inversion") are closely connected was widely retailed by "advanced" psychologists of the time. In *Sexual Inversion* (first published in 1897), the pioneering sexologist Havelock Ellis addresses this issue explicitly by writing that "it has been extravagantly said that all musicians are inverts." In language strongly reminiscent of that used by Cumberland, Ellis then proceeds to quote Oppenheim's opinion that "the musical disposition is marked by a great emotional instability, and this instability is a disposition to nervousness." Ellis suggests that "the musician has not been rendered nervous by his music, but he owes his nervousness (as also, it may be added, his disposition to homosexuality) to the same disposition to which he owes his musical aptitude."[36]

The connection, whether implicit or explicit, of musical ability with sexual inversion was scarcely original to either Ellis or Cumberland. To different degrees both authors mirror an undercurrent of anxiety concerning the presumed sexual irregularity of male musicians—or indeed any male involved in the arts—that pervaded British society during the Victorian and Edwardian periods. Such anxiety was often expressed by the use of such code words as *nervous, abnormal,* and *effeminate.* In a pointed memoir of his Victorian childhood, the composer and novelist Lord Berners wryly notes that "manliness was a virtue in which one had to be laboriously instructed. Like so many other virtues, it did not seem to correspond with the natural instincts of the human being. I came to the conclusion that 'manliness' was a very complicated ideal. . . . Why were music and painting held to be effeminate when all the greatest painters and composers had been men?"[37]

The presumption of sexual inversion by Victorian and Edwardian society concerning male musicians was exacerbated by the Wilde trials in 1895. A rapid change of aesthetics ensued after Wilde was sentenced to hard labor in Reading Gaol: decadent "aestheticism" was replaced by a more self-consciously "masculine" approach to art. As the English art historian William Gaunt wrote in 1945:

> The trial and conviction of Oscar Wilde had seemingly brought the aesthetic movement in Britain to a halt. It caused a wholesale literary and social fumigation. An exaggerated robustness was one of the consequences. Poets, no longer velvet-collared, absinthe-sipping, were now a hearty and virile race, tweed-clad, pipe-smoking, beer-drinking, Sussex-Downs-tramping. . . . The subject of sex was buried beneath fresh layers of discretion, beneath cryptic phrases and obscure turns of speech which might or might not conceal some romantic or extraordinary secret.[38]

Given this censorious climate, and the presumptive edicts of both medicine and society, is it any wonder that British composers responded by creating public personas that stressed their hearty virility? Among Elgar's contemporaries, Hubert Parry concealed his intellectual and sensitive disposition by emphasizing his status as an athlete and country squire. Aside from posing as an English gentleman, a designation that, as already noted, he had neither the education nor the class status to assume by right, Elgar affected the role of a tweed-clad sportsman. (Elgar's interest in the sporting life intensified after his marriage in 1889 and continued throughout the 1890s.) To maintain his status as a sportsman, Elgar obligingly demonstrated the requisite fascination with golf, billiards, and fishing, as well as hearty bicycling and robust tramping over the Malvern hills. He spent untold hours hanging about racetracks and betting on horses.

Concurrently Elgar manifested considerable shame at being associated with music at all. Rosa Burley comments that "it was one of Edward Elgar's peculiarities never to speak, even in the early days, of the teaching and playing by which he then really earned his living."[39] In his autobiography Arnold Bax writes of Elgar's "irritating pose of being interested in any topic rather than music." Bax illustrates his annoyance with the following painful anecdote:

The last time I met him was on his birthday in 1933. That evening Toscanini had given an ever-memorable performance of the "Enigma" Variations, and Harriet Cohen [the pianist] and I, with one or two others, repaired to the Savoy Grill after the concert for supper. There we discovered Elgar, characteristically surrounded by actors, Norman Forbes and Allan Aynesworth amongst them. Harriet, of whom Elgar was really very fond, rushed up to him and began vivaciously and charmingly to congratulate him upon the anniversary and the evening's wonderful music. With—as I thought—rather ridiculous affectation and ungraciousness, the old composer turned to his actor-friends and, spreading out his hands in mock mystification, exclaimed, "What on earth *are* these people talking about?"[40]

Perhaps the most poignant instance of Elgar's intermittent repudiations of his own musicality occurred in 1912, when he forced his reluctant wife to sell his violin in order to purchase that ultimate totem of Edwardian masculinity, a billiard table.[41]

Gerald Cumberland was not impressed by Elgar's social evasions and pretensions, however, and seems to have based his appraisal of Elgar's character on contemporary psychological theory. While there is no direct evidence that Cumberland had read Havelock Ellis when he wrote his chapter on Elgar, it would be surprising if an author who prided himself on his social and political radicalism had not investigated Ellis's theories. Cumberland may have discussed homosexual issues with acquaintances such as Edward Carpenter.[42] Carpenter, who lived openly with another man, was an early advocate of social tolerance for homosexuals. Carpenter and Ellis—who was not homosexual—were warm friends and frequent correspondents. Cumberland had read Carpenter,[43] whose theories concerning "inversion" were similar to those of Ellis,[44] and Cumberland and Carpenter were simultaneous houseguests of the composer Rutland Boughton. One notes in passing that Carpenter, who was nothing if not a polymath, was intensely interested in music and had published essays on the music of Beethoven and Wagner.[45]

Given his bitter reaction to Cumberland's article,[46] Elgar may well have grasped some of its imputations. As Elgar rose in society and gained in sophistication, he became increasingly aware of the homosexuality of those around him. Chief among these was the wealthy, generous Frank Schuster, the son of a German banker. Schuster was a close friend of Oscar Wilde and the notorious Count Robert de Montesquiou.[47] Schuster's sister Adela aided Wilde during his imprisonment by sending the disgraced author a thousand pounds.[48] Sassoon wrote of Schuster that "his hero-worship of Elgar was (justifiably) the most important achievement of his career, because he really did help Elgar toward success and recognition."[49] In return Elgar dedicated his concert overture *In the*

South to Schuster, writing, "[You will find] light-hearted gaiety mixed up in an orchestral dish [in] which[,] with my ordinary orchestral flavouring, cunningly blent, I have put in a warm cordial spice of love for you."[50]

At Schuster's lavish homes in London and at Bray-on-Thames, Elgar met houseguests including such homosexual artists as the novelist E. F. Benson and the painters Glyn Philpot and John Singer Sargent, as well as Wilde's first male lover, Robert Ross.[51] Through Ross, the Elgars met and befriended Wilde's youngest son, Vyvyan Holland. Also sure to be present were some of Schuster's "nephews," a euphemism then common in English high society for the younger lover of an older man. That Elgar was aware both of this term and of Schuster's homosexuality is confirmed by a comment he made in a letter to Alice Stuart-Wortley: "The de Meyers (now Americans) came over & Frank—*also* some extraordinary females, friends of the youth whom F[rank] introduces as his '*Nephew.*'"[52]

As might be expected, Elgar's relationship with Schuster was fraught with tension and ambivalence. The composer was capable of treating his patron with extraordinary coldness and ingratitude at times, practically repudiating Schuster as an acquaintance. Elgar's ungracious behavior stemmed from his envy of Schuster's wealth as well as his uneasiness concerning his friend's evident homosexuality.[53] Always high-strung and often awkward, Elgar could be very rude when he felt threatened or ill at ease socially. In his diary Sassoon records one such tense scene between Elgar and Schuster: "Elgar was grumpy and unkind to Frank Schuster (who has probably done more than anyone else to create his success) when he went 'behind' to see him at Queen's Hall. [Elgar] scarcely glanced at poor old Frankie. . . . There is no doubt that E[lgar] is a very self-centred and inconsiderate man."[54] Sassoon adds "I suppose he is very 'English'—always pretending and disguising his feelings."[55] Despite his keen appreciation for Elgar's musical gifts, Schuster was not blind to the composer's rudeness and social failings. Concerning the postconcert snub recorded by Sassoon, Schuster wrote a spirited letter to the conductor Adrian Boult, complaining that Elgar had greeted him "with the *coldest* of handshakes. I could have slapped him (and very nearly did)."[56] At least a part of Elgar's coldness on this occasion may have stemmed from his discomfort at Schuster's arriving backstage with Sassoon, whom the composer may have taken for one of his patron's "nephews." (Elgar eventually became quite fond of Sassoon and suggested to the poet on two separate occasions that they take a motor tour together in the composer's car.)[57]

While it was possible for a wealthy outsider like Frank Schuster to indulge his sexual tastes with discretion, the situation for the repressed and obsessively respectable Elgar was quite different—his social position was doomed to be precarious. Given the prejudice against homosexuality that pervaded English society and his own profoundly internalized investment in social propriety, it is highly unlikely that Elgar ever considered consummating his intense feelings for his male friends, if he indeed ever acknowledged to himself the merest possibility of such "abnormal" and, by the standard of the times, self-destructive behavior.

And yet it seems likely that Elgar, though a partner to a passionless marriage,[58] never attempted a sexual relationship with any woman other than his wife. Despite the romantic involvement with Alice Stuart-Wortley that some writers suppose to have occurred during the composition of the Violin Concerto in B Minor, Elgar's letters to her, while warm and intimate, are oddly devoid of eroticism and never exceed the boundaries of a chivalrous friendship.[59] In fact, he once described her to Schuster in distinctly unromantic terms as the concerto's "stepmother."[60] While it would be inappropriate to reduce the complexity of Elgar's personality by resorting to a reductive Freudian hypothesis, it is curious how often the composer used maternal terms to describe his female friends. Elgar describes the American socialite Julia Worthington as "motherly,"[61] and near the end of his life he informed Vera Hockman that she was "my mother, my child, my lover and my friend."[62] And then there is the nursery language that Alice and Edward Elgar used between themselves, which clearly reflected the wife's role as a nurturing mother while the husband played the part of a precocious, at times fretful, baby who composes "booful music."[63]

Disturbed, perhaps, by the ambiguous nature of Elgar's relationships with these women and his frequent declarations of love to men, some scholars have stretched the bounds of credulity to inflate Elgar's mildly flirtatious interest in his female friends and acquaintances into inspiring but nobly unconsummated love affairs.[64] (Elgar was prone to embarrassingly heavy-handed displays of flirtatiousness, but this was clearly a facet of his public personality: the lovable but harmless roué. In later years Elgar made sure that he was being observed when engaging in flirtatious banter with young women such as Vera Hockman.) Such tales are often based more on hearsay than established facts, and the recorded evidence of Elgar's life and published correspondence often contradict these romantic narratives. If Elgar loved Alice Stuart-Wortley so deeply, for example, why did the intensity of his relationship with her decline rather than increase—into a proposal of marriage, say—after the death of her husband in 1926?

Another telling instance of the way in which certain writers have transformed selected details of Elgar's life into tales of star-crossed romance is the lore that has gathered around Helen Weaver, the violin student from Worcester with whom the young Elgar is supposed to have fallen desperately in love.[65] There are only four references to her in Elgar's published correspondence, and these citations appear in four letters (two each from 1883 and 1884) sent to a single correspondent, the organist Charles Buck.[66] These letters allude to an informal engagement between Helen Weaver and Elgar that began in 1883 and was broken off the following year. Far from exhibiting an irreparable broken heart that would inspire future masterpieces, however, Elgar's initial allusion to this turn of events seems relatively muted for such a habitually self-dramatizing correspondent: "Miss Weaver is very well. I do not think that she will remain in Worcester much longer."[67] Given the impediments that stood in the way of a marriage to Miss Weaver, one wonders how Elgar could have seriously entertained such an unlikely idea. Helen Weaver was tubercular, as well as a member of a family whose financial status was far superior to that of the Elgars. Furthermore, the Weavers were strict chapel-going Nonconformist Unitarians who were appalled at the prospect of their daughter marrying a Roman Catholic. Given the many improbabilities surrounding this engagement, and the paucity of evidence, it is hard to see how this episode can be inflated into a star-crossed romance.

Despite the evasions of uneasy scholars, biographical evidence strongly suggests that Elgar's chief emotional outlet—one tolerated, if barely, by English society—was his intimate and passionate friendships with men such as August Jaeger, Frank Schuster, Ivor Atkins, and W. H. Reed. To these men he poured out his heart in letters filled with an almost "amatory tenderness," and to them he dedicated most of his music.

Homoeroticism, which Mosse defines as the "latently erotic aspects of personal relationships among men," runs as a persistent thread through Elgar's work, providing him with both subject matter and inspiration. Viewed in this light, Elgar's dramatic trip to Liverpool at Rodewald's death can be seen as a moving, instinctual protest against the conventional strictures that bound him, played out in the terms of one of the few homoerotic narratives available to him, Tennyson's *In Memoriam*.

The most important of these friends was August Jaeger, whom Rosa Burley described as "a lovable but rather typically commonplace little German." An excellent musician with discerning taste, Jaeger worked as an editor at Novello and championed Elgar's music in the firm. The friendship between the two men began in 1896 and ripened four years later with the composition of the "Enigma" Variations. Elgar's letters to Jaeger are playful and openhearted, and Jaeger amply returned Elgar's confidence and devotion. In his reply to Elgar's letter on the death of Rodewald, Jaeger listed the following qualities of the deceased: "his good nature, his enthusiasm, his love of you whom I love." The tone of the correspondence between the two men is unusually warm and intimate, far surpassing the warmth found in the letters of such Victorian authors as Thomas Carlyle, Matthew Arnold, or Charles Kingsley to male friends. Nor does the correspondence that passed between two of Elgar's younger contemporaries, Gustav Holst and Ralph Vaughan Williams, composers who were both close friends and staunch colleagues, approach the intimate tone of the letters Elgar and Jaeger sent to each other.[68] (One cannot imagine either Holst or Vaughan Williams starting a letter with a salutation like the one with which Elgar began a typewritten letter to Jaeger: "AUGUSTUS DARLING!")[69] If, as Harold Bloom declared in his article on *In Memoriam*, "Tennyson's Muse was (and always remained) Hallam," it is not too farfetched to suggest by way of paraphrase that Elgar's principal Muse was (and always remained) Jaeger.

Elgar's friendship with Jaeger inspired the ninth of the "Enigma" Variations. By a process similar to the one used to derive from *ænigmate* both the words *dark* and *enigma*, Elgar devised a cunning bilingual pun that transformed the German word *Jaeger* ("hunter") into the name of the mighty hunter from the Bible, *Nimrod*. As the ninth in a set of fourteen variations, "Nimrod" represents both the structural and expressive climax of the work.

Its formal placement and emotional import set the "Nimrod" variation in striking contrast to the variation bearing the initials of Elgar's wife, "C.A.E." (Caroline Alice Elgar). As the first variation of the set, "C.A.E." is the least elaborate, merely an ornamented and slightly extended variant of the theme itself. Thus "C.A.E." is musically and structurally much less prominent than the climactic "Nimrod." Material from these two variations is juxtaposed later in the work, and the result is telling. When the "C.A.E." is recalled in the finale, which is a musical self-portrait of the composer entitled "E.D.U.,"[70] it is menaced by ominous trumpet calls and brusquely whisked aside to prepare for the grand restatement and extensive return of "Nimrod." Unlike the "Nimrod" music, which pervades the finale, "C.A.E." is granted a single, twenty-measure return in a movement consisting of 237 bars.

In comparison to a great deal of Elgar's earlier music, the "Nimrod" variation, and indeed the "Enigma" Variations as a whole, carries an astoundingly vivid emotional impact. This release of creative energy is surely the consequence of an aesthetic discovery. Three days after he improvised a theme and some variations for his attentive wife on the evening of 21 October 1898, Elgar posted a letter to Jaeger that contained a new insight into the paradox of his own creative process: "I have sketched a set of Variations (orkestry) on an original theme. . . . I've liked to imagine the 'party' writing the var[iation] him (or her) self & have written what I think they w[oul]d have written." On 16 February of the following year, Elgar explained to the editor of *The Musical Times* that "in each variation I have 'looked at' the theme through the personality (as it were) of another."

The conceptual strategy that Elgar first employed in the "Enigma" Variations permitted his imagination to make two strategic moves. The first was to recognize the "Enigma" theme as a symbol of his own essential nature. The second enabled Elgar to imagine himself "looking at"—as through a glass darkly—that symbolic theme as refracted through the prisms of his friends' personalities. Of the many paradoxes surrounding this enigmatic composer, this is perhaps the most mysterious: Elgar liberated himself from the weight of his inhibitions, and thus developed his own individual voice as a composer, by imaginatively projecting himself into the souls of other persons. This paradoxical strategy also permitted him to express homoerotic feelings safely by shifting responsibility for such feelings away from himself. In his symphonic study *Falstaff* (1913), for example, Elgar may have conceived of himself as Shakespeare's eponymous character, a device that would have enabled him to displace his own homoerotic yearning onto the aging knight who loves Prince Hal and is sternly rejected.

Elgar transformed the hesitant "Enigma" theme (figure 9.1a) into the ardent "Nimrod" variation (figure 9.1b) by using his empathetic imagination to become the loving and loyal Jaeger, just as he may have imagined himself as the hero of *In Memoriam*. Elgar made a further use of the "Nimrod" variation in a musical context at once touching and revealing. Four years after Jaeger's death in 1909, Elgar paid tribute to his friend in *The Music Makers,* a frankly autobiographical setting of a poem by Alfred O'Shaughnessy for mezzo-soprano, chorus, and orchestra (figure 9.1c). In a work filled with self-quotation, one section is particularly notable. Elgar quotes the "Nimrod" variation in the chorus and orchestra, while soaring above them, the mezzo-soprano sings these Tennysonian lines:

But on one man's soul it hath broken,
A light that doth not depart;
And his look, or a word he hath spoken,
Wrought flame in another man's heart.

In the previously quoted letter to Ernest Newman concerning *The Music Makers,* Elgar touches on this passage in a moving but conflicted manner:

a.

b.

c.

FIGURE 9.1. (a) "Enigma" theme, "Enigma" Variations; (b) "Nimrod" variation, "Enigma" Variations; (c) recall of "Nimrod" variation, *The Music Makers*.

"Here I have quoted the Nimrod Variation as a tribute to the memory of my friend, A. J. Jaeger: by this I do not mean to convey that his was the only soul on which light had broken or that his was the only word, or look that wrought 'flame in another man's heart'; but I do convey that amongst all the inept writing and wrangling about music his voice was clear, ennobling, sober and sane, and for his help and inspiration I make this acknowledgement."[71]

In the light of the composer's conflicted statements and the potent conjunction of text and music at this point in *The Music Makers,* the question arises: whose point of view does Elgar seek to express through the mezzo-soprano's voice and the poet's words? Is it the composer's own voice or Jaeger's voice that we are meant to hear? Or does the singer represent a confluence of both Elgar and his departed friend? Does Elgar's confession to Newman imply that other men besides Jaeger inspired this music? Who were they? Do they, too, speak through these words and this music? Perhaps Elgar's own confusion was the result of a profound inner conflict, for this passage, which McVeagh describes as the "marvelous, aching recall" of the "Nimrod" music,[72] may well be the closest he ever came to an explicit declaration of love for Jaeger or, indeed, for any other man.

Elgar's choice of a mezzo-soprano for this portion of *The Music Makers* is significant in this context, for it recalls his choice of the same type of voice for the Guardian Angel in his oratorio *The Dream of Gerontius.* Elgar composed this setting of Cardinal John Henry Newman's poem in 1900, almost immediately after finishing the "Enigma" Variations. Elgar's choice of Newman's poem, despite opposition from his publishers and in defiance of British anti-Catholicism, sheds further light on his predilection for subjects dealing with passionate male friendship.

Like *In Memoriam, The Dream of Gerontius* is dedicated to the memory of a beloved friend, Newman's "*fratri desideratissimo*" Father John Joseph Gordon. Newman was deeply moved by his visit to Gordon's deathbed: "He was anointed and then said 'I am so happy.' I said 'Go to sleep' and he is now trying to do so. . . . Remember me, O God, for the bitter things Thou bringst on me. . . . The anointing had an almost miraculous effect on him. All nervousness and anxiety is gone—he is cheerful, smiling and happy."[73] Memories of Father Gordon's exemplary death in 1853 haunted Newman so deeply that he enshrined them twelve years later in *The Dream of Gerontius.*[74]

But another person, far more dear to Newman than Gordon and still living at the time *The Dream of Gerontius* was written, also provided inspiration for the poem. Ambrose St. John was Newman's faithful disciple and most beloved friend. Both Newman and St. John had been Anglican clergymen who converted to Roman Catholicism and took priestly vows in 1845; they were inseparable companions at the Birmingham Oratory until St. John's death in 1875. Newman wrote movingly of St. John in his *Apologia pro Vita Sua* of 1864: "Dear Ambrose St. John; whom God gave me, when He took every one else away; who are the link between my old life and my new; who have now for twenty years been so devoted to me, so patient, so zealous, so tender; who have let me lean so hard upon you."[75] In a letter written shortly after St. John's death, Newman confided that "from the first he loved me with an intensity of love, which was unaccountable. . . . At Rome 28 years ago [in 1847] he was always so working for and relieving me of all trouble, that being young and Saxon-looking, the Romans called him my Angel Guardian."[76] Ambrose St. John inspired the Guardian Angel of Newman's poem just as surely as Hallam inspired *In Memoriam*—or August Jaeger inspired Elgar's "Nimrod" variation.

On 12 January 1900 Elgar traveled to the Birmingham Oratory to ask Newman's literary executor, William Neville, for permission to condense *The Dream of Gerontius* into a suitable libretto for his oratorio.[77] Neville had been Newman's secretary and infirmarian at the oratory and thus had observed Newman and St. John at close quarters for many years. Perhaps the otherworldly Father Neville, who used Newman's study to receive visitors, regaled Elgar with tales of the touching mutual devotion that his priestly companions shared for twenty-eight years. Elgar may well have seen the intimate double portrait of Newman and St. John that presently hangs in the oratory. Like most English Catholics, Elgar had read the *Apologia pro Vita Sua*,[78] which concludes with a magnificent, loving apostrophe to St. John.

Aside from owing its inspiration to a male muse, certain passages in Cardinal Newman's *Dream of Gerontius* possess a homoerotic strain comparable to certain stanzas of *In Memoriam*. The Guardian Angel's veiled narration of St. Francis of Assisi's reception of the Stigmata expresses religious sentiment through words that hint at the underlying possibility of a more carnal kind of embracement:

> There was a mortal who is now above
> In the mid glory; he, when near to die,
> Was given communion with the Crucified,—
> Such, that the Master's very wounds were stamped
> Upon his flesh; and, from the agony
> That thrilled through body and soul in that embrace,
> Learn that the flame of the Everlasting Love
> Doth burn ere it transform . . .[79]

At the conclusion of the poem, as he dips the soul of Gerontius into the lake of Purgatory, the Angel takes leave of his precious charge with the following words:

Softly and gently, dearly ransomed soul,
In my most loving arms I now enfold thee. . . .
Be brave and patient on thy bed of sorrow;
Swiftly shall pass thy night of trial here,
And I will come and wake thee on the morrow.[80]

In Newman's text the protagonist's guardian angel is unambiguously assigned a male gender. In his extensive condensation of the poem, Elgar retained two clear references to the angel's gender as Gerontius sings: "I will address him. Mighty One, My Lord, My Guardian Spirit, all hail!"[81] By assigning the angel's words to a woman's voice, Elgar created an androgynous figure whose duality invites an ambiguous response from the listener. (This ambiguity makes one of Elgar's recent biographers so uncomfortable that he erases it completely. In an otherwise accurate and enlightening discussion of *The Dream of Gerontius,* Robert Anderson inexplicably states that "Elgar, with a mezzo-soprano in mind, eliminated references to the maleness of the angel.")[82]

Perhaps it is too fanciful to suggest that Elgar's choice of mezzo-soprano for both *The Dream of Gerontius* and *The Music Makers* implies that he selected this plangent vocal timbre to connect Newman's Guardian Angel with the fallen Jaeger. But the use of a mezzo-soprano to voice the sentiments of the male angel may well have provided Elgar with a precedent for the expression of a male viewpoint through the medium of a woman's voice in *The Music Makers.* Whether or not this was Elgar's intention, the dual nature of the angel certainly reflects Elgar's own divided personality. Once he discovered the "Enigma" strategy for entering alternate personae and portraying himself as if through their eyes, Elgar was free to develop his creative personality in many directions, including the feminine; indeed, five of the "Enigma" Variations bear women's initials.

Elgar was at least vaguely aware that his creative identity had both masculine and feminine aspects, as indicated by a hint he dropped in a letter about the cryptic Spanish quotation he affixed to his self-referential violin concerto. Elgar chose a little phrase from the eighteenth-century French author Alain René Lesage's picaresque novel *Gil Blas;* it reads "Aquí está encerrada el alma de . . ." ("Here is enshrined the soul of . . .").[83] This mystification, so typical of the composer, has led scholars on a merry chase ever since: there are even long disputes of the possible profound significance in the number of ellipsis points after the quotation. (Are there three dots or five? And what—or whom—does this signify?) Numerous highly romantic guesses have been put forward as to whose soul is enshrined in the concerto. Alice Elgar told Dora Penny that it was the Elgars' American friend Julia Worthington.[84] One scholar nominates young Worcester violinist Helen Weaver as the primary inspiration for the concerto,[85] but as previously noted, most commentators agree that the score is a portrait of Alice Stuart-Wortley, with whom Elgar is supposed to have been infatuated. (Those who propose Stuart-Wortley are divided as to whether she and Elgar actually consummated their putative affair.) That Elgar was intensely fascinated with Alice Stuart-Wortley is without doubt, but she may well have had a much more complicated relationship to the concerto than that of mere muse.

The most persuasive testimony regarding the concerto is offered by a reliable eyewitness, Elgar's friend Stanford Terry.[86] Terry helped Elgar proofread the concerto and attended the earliest rehearsals of the work. As a gesture of thanks, the composer presented Terry with the proofs of the score; Terry later gave this score to a friend who deposited the valuable document in the British Library (Add. MS 62000). For his friend, Terry wrote an extended private preface that records many of the spontaneous remarks about the concerto that Elgar made as the two men worked side by side. Terry was a distinguished and scrupulous musicologist whose specialty was J. S. Bach, and although writing privately, he was concerned that he leave an accurate record of his work with Elgar.

Concerning the epigraph from *Gil Blas,* Terry writes:

> I did not attempt to obtain any solution of the mystery of the Spanish motto. At the same time[,] I have not the slightest doubt that it is his own soul which the Concerto enshrines. In the first place it will be noticed that he originally wrote "del" before the blank, an indication that the name to follow was a masculine one.[87] True, while I was looking over his shoulder he wrote "de la" in red ink under the "del," but thereafter he took the trouble to consult a Spanish friend, M. de Navarro, as to whether the word "del" would leave the sex of the soul's possessor undetermined. Receiving an assurance that it did[,] he retained it and deleted the "de la."[88]

The proof copy of the score confirms Terry's description of this process; the curious aspect of this anecdote is that Elgar made such a private gesture in front of another person. Terry continues: "There is evidence of a particular intimate relation between the Concerto and its creator . . . I have never heard Elgar *speak* of the *personal* note in his music except in regard to the Concerto, and of it I heard him say more than once when he was playing it over before it was produced 'I *love* it.' Then there is a fact for which Ivor Atkins of Worcester is my authority. Speaking of the concerto[,] Elgar said to him one day that he would like the Nobilmente theme in the Andante [six measures after rehearsal 53 in the full score] inscribed on his tomb."[89] Terry fails to appreciate the irony of Elgar's request to Atkins that a theme from the concerto's slow movement provide his epitaph, for, in Lesage's novel, the Spanish phrase that the composer appended to his score is itself found on a tombstone.[90]

At no point in his narrative does Terry mention the name of Alice Stuart-Wortley. She may have played a crucial role in the creation of the concerto, however, one that is not inconsistent with Terry's assertion that the work is a self-portrait. It is conceivable that Elgar, using the paradoxical strategy that he first employed in the "Enigma" Variations, imagined himself as Stuart-Wortley and composed a self-portrait through "the personality (as it were) of another"—in this case the lovely woman whom he nicknamed "Windflower." This would explain Elgar's cryptic comment to his early biographer, Basil Maine, who wrote that "the composer once went so far as to tell the writer that it was a feminine spirit he had in mind when he wrote those words at the beginning of his work."[91] By portraying himself through the eyes of Stuart-Wortley, Elgar may have gained access to his own "feminine spirit," just as he had done earlier in the five variations headed by women's initials in the "Enigma" Variations. (Moreover, Elgar hardly needed to have consummated a love affair with Isobel Fitton, Winifred Norbury, or the rest to do so.) Such a hypothesis also places Elgar's description of Stuart-Wortley as the concerto's "stepmother" in a new and interesting light.[92] Finally, this creative subterfuge may have been the only way that the inhibited, self-consciously "masculine" composer could have written a concerto for violin, an instrument that was an emblem of his own shameful musicality—a signifier of femininity so embarrassing that he sold his own to buy a billiard table.[93]

The credibility of this hypothesis is enhanced by Terry's report of Elgar's effort to ensure that the Spanish epigraph was left both ambiguous and androgynous. In a letter of 9 October 1910 Elgar wrote to Antonio de Navarro: "If I want it to refer to the soul of a feminine sh[oul]d it be—de la . . . ?" It is surely significant that Elgar does not write "soul of a woman" here, but rather "soul of a feminine." A feminine what, exactly? In another letter from this period concerning the violin concerto, Elgar offered an elaborate translation of the little phrase to his correspondent, the amateur conductor Nicholas Kilburn, and then teasingly wrote "the final 'de' leaves it indefinite as to sex, or rather gender. Now guess."[94]

But neither Kilburn or anyone else did guess, of course; Elgar made sure that most of his enigmas—the crucial ones—were impenetrable, and given his times and social ambitions, he may have had every reason to favor leaving riddles unguessed, even his own. And yet, as he scattered clues, he may have hoped that his secrets would be uncovered eventually and liberate him from his disguises and evasions. The greatest Elgarian riddle can never be fully answered, however: how did this repressed, perpetually blinking man, corroded by envy and tormented by depression, find the courage in his forty-second year to transcend his limitations and make the leap of imagination that freed him to create a series of imperishable scores? In the dark presence of this insoluble enigma, the words of St. Paul echo as a caution and as a reminder: "For now we see through a glass darkly; but then face to face: now I know in part, but then shall I know even as also I am known."

NOTES

This essay is the fruit of seven years of constant thought and intermittent labor. Many helpful friends and colleagues have offered advice, suggestions, and criticism; I must particularly express thanks to William Austin, Stephen Banfield, Philip Brett, Ruth Charloff, Lauren Cowdery, Richard Dellamora, Jennifer Doctor, Geoffrey Ford, Sophie Fuller, James Hepokoski, Christopher Kent, Susan McClary, Charles McGuire, Mitchell Morris, Oliver Neighbour, Sir Roger Norrington, Lucy O'Brien, and Elizabeth Wood. I also want to express my gratitude to the helpful staffs at the Elgar Birthplace Museum, the Worcester County Record Office, the Music Library of the University of Birmingham, and the British Library. This essay first appeared in *19th-Century Music* 23, no. 3 (Spring 2000): 218–35 (© 2000 by The Regents of the University of California; reprinted by permission). That year it received the Philip Brett Award (sponsored by the Gay and Lesbian Study Group of the American Musicological Society) for exceptional work in the field of queer musicology.
For Captain Raymond Keith Norman, in memoriam.

1. Alice Elgar diary, 12 Feb. 1899 ("E. to S. Joseph's"), held at the Music Library, University of Birmingham. Alice Elgar's appointment diary for 1899 had the various feasts of the Roman Catholic church printed next to the date.

2. These deductions are an extension of those first made by Ian Parrott in his *Elgar* (London: Dent, 1971).

3. In Jerrold Northrop Moore, *Edward Elgar: A Creative Life* (Oxford: Oxford University Press, 1984), 270.

4. A careful examination of Jaeger's distinctive cursive script leaves no doubt that he wrote the word *Enigma* on the manuscript of the Variations.

5. Jerrold Northrop Moore, ed., *Edward Elgar: Letters of a Lifetime* (Oxford: Clarendon, 1990), 248.

6. Mrs. Richard Powell (neé Dora Penny), *Edward Elgar: Memories of a Variation*, 4th ed. (Aldershot, U.K.: Scolar, 1994), 52–53.

7. Sir Arnold Bax, *Farewell, My Youth and Other Writings,* ed. Lewis Foreman (Aldershot, U.K.: Scolar, 1992), 26.

8. Moore, ed., *Letters of a Lifetime,* 249.

9. Diana McVeagh, "A Man's Attitude to Life," in *Edward Elgar: Music and Literature,* ed. Raymond Monk (Aldershot, U.K.: Scolar, 1993), 2.

10. See Richard Dellamora, *Masculine Desire: The Sexual Politics of Victorian Aestheticism* (Chapel Hill: University of North Carolina Press, 1990), 42–57.

11. Rodewald had rapidly become one of Elgar's closest friends; his name features frequently in Alice Elgar's diaries during 1902. Rodewald traveled with Elgar several times and spent Christmas Day with the composer and his family. The following extract represents an expansion of comparisons from McVeagh, "A Man's Attitudes," 5–6. The poem's text is quoted from Alfred Lord Tennyson, *In Memoriam,* ed. Susan Shatto and Marion Shaw (Oxford: Oxford University Press, 1982).

12. Elgar posted an equally emotional (but less Tennysonian) letter concerning Rodewald's death to Frank Schuster on 10 Nov. 1903, the day before he wrote to Jaeger: "I have just [returned] home from Liverpool and can *only* send you thanks for your letter. It is [all] too dreadful about my dear Rodewald: he passed away peacefully yesterday. O my God; it is too awful. I had a card from him last Wednesday quite cheerful saying he was 'over the influenza'—he became unconscious on Thursday & he never recovered. I could not rest & fled to Liverpool yesterday only to be told all was over. I will write again soon but this is [all] too cruel and horrible for I can only grieve over the awfulness of it." This letter is missing from Jerrold Northrop Moore's edition of Elgar's correspondence. Alice Elgar's diary entry of 10 Nov. 1903 confirms her husband's extreme distress: "E[dward] away at N. Western Hotel, Liverpool. A[lice] dreadfully anxious about him. . . . E. dreadfully sorrowful" (permission to quote from both letter and diary granted by the Elgar Will Trust).

13. Moore, ed., *Letters of a Lifetime,* 337.

14. Harold Bloom, "Tennyson, Hallam and Romantic Tradition," *Ringers in the Tower* (Chicago: University of Chicago Press, 1971), 149–50.

15. Dellamora, *Masculine Desire,* 39.

16. McVeagh, "A Man's Attitude," 5, 7. Even with McVeagh's obliquity and discretion, the implications of her essay troubled E. Wulstan Atkins, son of Elgar's friend Ivor Atkins, who provided an introduction for the volume in which McVeagh's essay appears. Atkins writes: "It is difficult for those born after the First World War to understand that for Victorians who were brought up not to show their emotions in public, it was normal for them to express these feelings in written word and poetry, and that friendship between men could be deep and affectionate without in any way suggesting a sexual relationship." Given McVeagh's strenuous attempts to diffuse the potentially explosive topic of sexual relations between men, one wonders why Atkins felt compelled to conjure up the specter of homosexuality at all. See E. Wulstan Atkins, introduction, in *Edward Elgar: Music and Literature,* ed. Monk, xvii.

17. Jeffrey Weeks, *Coming Out: Homosexual Politics in Britain from the Nineteenth Century to the Present* (London: Quartet Books, 1977), 14–15.

18. Theo Aronson, *Prince Eddy and the Victorian Homosexual Underground* (London: John Murray, 1994), 132–33.

19. Ronald Hyam, *Empire and Sexuality: The British Experience* (New York: St. Martin's, 1991), 33, 52n31. See also A. L. Rowse, *Homosexuals in History* (New York: Carroll and Graf, 1983), 222–23 (the Belloc poem is quoted on 222). Of Lord Beauchamp, the circumspect *Dictionary of National Biography* states that "in 1931 he suddenly resigned all his offices but one and went to live abroad." Rowse asserts erroneously that Lord Beauchamp "died in New York in 1938," when in fact the hapless nobleman quietly returned to England near the end of his life and died at Madresfield Court.

20. Michael De-la-Noy, *Elgar the Man* (London: Allen Lane, 1983), 76.

21. In Christopher Craft, *Another Kind of Love: Male Homosocial Desire in English Discourse 1850–1920* (Berkeley: University of California Press), 47. The reviewer's final allusion to Shakespeare is drawn from sonnet 20: "the Master Mistress of my passion, / A woman's gentle heart but not acquainted."

22. Colin Spencer, *Homosexuality in History* (New York: Harcourt Brace, 1995), 263; and Weeks, *Coming Out*, 14.

23. Richard Davenport-Hines, *Sex, Death, and Punishment: Attitudes to Sex and Sexuality in Britain since the Renaissance* (London: William Collins, 1990), 142.

24. Anthony Powell, *A Dance to the Music of Time: Second Movement: At Lady Molly's* (Chicago: University of Chicago Press, 1995), 211.

25. Alice Elgar was some years older than her husband, enjoyed a markedly higher social station, and converted to Roman Catholicism for his sake.

26. Siegfried Sassoon, *Diaries 1923–1925*, ed. Rupert Hart-Davis (London: Faber and Faber, 1985), 151–52.

27. Osbert Sitwell, *Laughter in the Next Room* (Boston: Little, Brown, 1948), 220.

28. Rosa Burley and Frank Carruthers, *Edward Elgar: The Record of a Friendship* (London: Barrie and Jenkins, 1972), 25.

29. Sassoon, *Diaries 1923–1925*, 152.

30. Ernest Newman, "Elgar: Some Aspects of the Man in His Music," (*The Sunday Times*, 25 Feb. 1934), repr. in *An Elgar Companion*, ed. Christopher Redwood (London: Ashbourne, 1982), 156.

31. Brian Trowell, "Elgar's Use of Literature," in *Edward Elgar: Music and Literature*, ed. Monk, 195.

32. Cumberland's portrait of Vaughan Williams is complimentary, for instance; the author stressed what he perceived as that composer's heartily British and downright masculine nature. See Charles F. Kenyon [Gerald Cumberland], *Set Down in Malice; a Book of Reminiscences* (London: Grant Richards, 1919), 255–56.

33. Trowell, "Elgar's Use of Literature," 196.

34. Kenyon, *Set Down in Malice*, 79, 87. It is interesting to note that tears are used as a signifier of Lord Beauchamp's supposed effeminacy in the previously quoted poem by Belloc.

35. George L. Mosse, *Nationalism and Sexuality: Respectability and Abnormal Sexuality in Modern Europe* (New York: Howard Fertig, 1985), 10–11.

36. Havelock Ellis, *The Psychology of Sex: Sexual Inversion*, 6 vols. (New York: F. A. Davis, 1910), 2:295. For an exploration of the connections between the constructions of "musicality" and "homosexuality," see Philip Brett, "Musicality, Essentialism and the Closet," in *Queering the Pitch: The New Gay and Lesbian Musicology*, ed. Philip Brett, Elizabeth Wood, and Gary C. Thomas (London: Routledge, 1994), 9–26.

37. Lord Berners, *First Childhood* (Chappaqua, N.Y.: Turtle Point, 1998), 82.

38. William Gaunt, *The Aesthetic Adventure* (New York: Harcourt, Brace, 1945), 214–15.

39. Burley and Carruthers, *Elgar: The Record of a Friendship*, 73.

40. Bax, *Farewell, My Youth*, 26–27. One of the actors mentioned by Bax, Norman Forbes Robertson (Norman Forbes was his stage name), became quite close to Elgar in the composer's later years. The two men had met through Frank Schuster.

41. Moore, *Elgar*, 641.

42. Kenyon, *Set Down in Malice*, 260.

43. Ibid., 132.

44. Spencer, *Homosexuality in History*, 304–5.

45. Ibid., 302.

46. Atkins, introduction, xxvi. Elgar's angry reaction to Cumberland's essay, as well as its scandalous nature, was fodder for gossip in British musical circles of the day, especially among supporters of Elgar's great enemy, Sir Charles Villiers Stanford. In a diary entry dated 26 April 1919, the young composer Herbert Howells—Stanford's favorite student at the Royal College of Music—recorded meeting Elgar at Schuster's house in London: " [W. H.] Reed introduced me to the famous man, who looked fairly afraid of me—as tho' I were possibly a Bolshevik or a Gerald Cumberland" (in Christopher Palmer, *Herbert Howells: A Celebration* [London: Thames, 1996], 81).

47. Montesquiou was the principal model for both the Baron Charlus in Proust's *A la recherche du temps perdu* and Des Esseintes in Huysmans's *A Rebours*.

48. Richard Ellman, *Oscar Wilde* (New York: Knopf, 1988), 523.

49. Siegfried Sassoon, *Diaries 1920–1922*, ed. Rupert Hart-Davis (London: Faber and Faber, 1981), 293.

50. Moore, *Letters of a Lifetime*, 144.

51. In addition to being acquainted with homosexual men such as these, the Elgars knew Radclyffe Hall, the author of the pioneering lesbian novel *The Well of Loneliness*. (It is highly unlikely, however, that Elgar ever dipped into *The Well of Loneliness*.) One of Elgar's favorite mezzo-sopranos, Agnes Nicholls, was the first of Radclyffe Hall's lovers. After the death of her husband, Lady Maud Warrender, who was a staunch supporter of Elgar and his music, lived in a lesbian relationship with the singer Marcia van Dresser. See Diane Souhami, *The Trials of Radclyffe Hall* (New York: Doubleday, 1999), 21, 30, 59, 266.

52. Jerrold Northrop Moore, ed., *Edward Elgar: The Windflower Letters* (Oxford: Oxford University Press, 1989), 245.

53. Elgar was certainly not prejudiced against Schuster's Jewish heritage, as the composer did not share the casual anti-Semitism that pervaded English society at the time. Furthermore, Elgar was appalled by Hitler's discriminatory policies against Germany's Jewish population. See Elgar's anguished letter of 17 Mar. 1933 to Adela Schuster in Moore, ed., *Letters of a Lifetime*, 466–67.

54. Sassoon, *Diaries 1920–1922*, 79–80.

55. Ibid., 80.

56. In De-La-Noy, *Elgar*, 191.

57. Sassoon, *Diaries 1923–1925*, 151, 282. Sassoon, who was a handsome war poet, did not take up Elgar on either of his offers.

58. Sexual relations between Elgar and his wife seem to have ceased after the birth of their daughter, Carice, in 1890. See Trowell, "Elgar's Use of Literature," 191, 298, n. 48.

59. Of the friendship between the two, Michael Kennedy writes: "Edward Elgar and Alice Stuart-Wortley were souls in harmony as far as his music was concerned, and this understanding was one of deep affection involving no disloyalty or infidelity to either of the other married partners" (Kennedy, *Portrait of Elgar* [London: Oxford University Press, 1968], 130). Kennedy expanded on this observation in his article "The Soul Enshrined: Elgar and His Violin Concerto," in *Edward Elgar: Music and Literature*, ed. Monk, 75.

60. Letter of 27 May 1910, in Moore, *Elgar*, 581.

61. Moore, ed., *Letters of a Lifetime*, 235.

62. In Moore, *Elgar*, 795.

63. Although the use of a private, intimate language was not uncommon among Victorian couples, I am unaware of any other examples from the period of a husband and wife consistently using baby talk to communicate throughout the course of their entire marriage. On Alice Elgar's motherly attitude toward her moody husband, see Moore, *Elgar*, 561.

64. One musicologist has even suggested to me the unlikely scenario of Elgar's having had an affair with the brisk and practical Rosa Burley.

65. Note, for example, how the usually scrupulous Brian Trowell becomes breathlessly speculative whenever he mentions Helen Weaver in his valuable essay "Elgar's Use of Literature," 217–24.

66. Moore, ed., *Letters of a Lifetime*, 6–7, 10–11. In *Elgar* (104) Moore cites a fifth, more expansive and self-pitying reference to Helen Weaver from the same period in one of Elgar's letters to Buck.

67. In Moore, *Elgar*, 104.

68. See Ralph Vaughan Williams and Gustav Holst, *Heirs and Rebels: Letters Written to Each Other and Occasional Writings on Music by Ralph Vaughan Williams and Gustav Holst*, ed. Ursula Vaughan Williams and Imogen Holst (London: Oxford University Press, 1959).

69. Jerrold Northrop Moore, ed., *Elgar and his Publishers: Letters of a Creative Life*, 2 vols. (Oxford: Clarendon, 1987), 1:377.

70. "E.D.U." is derived from Alice Elgar's nickname for her husband, "Edoo," from the German form of his Christian name, "Eduard."

71. Moore, ed., *Letters of a Lifetime*, 249–50.

72. McVeagh, "A Man's Attitude," 7.

73. In Meriol Trevor, *Newman: The Pillar of the Cloud* (London: Macmillan, 1963), 630–31.

74. Father Gordon was the first of the priests in the oratory to die.

75. Newman, *Apologia pro Vita Sua: Being a History of His Religious Opinions*, ed. Martin J. Svaglic (Oxford: Clarendon, 1967), 252.

76. Letter to Lord Blachford dated 31 May 1875, in Wilfrid Ward, *The Life of John Henry Cardinal Newman*, 2 vols. (London: Longmans, Green, 1913), 2:410.

77. Moore, *Elgar*, 296.

78. Kenyon, *Set Down in Malice*, 86.

79. John Henry Newman, *The Dream of Gerontius*, ed. Winterton (Oxford: A. R. Mowbray, 1986), 34.

80. Ibid., 54–55.

81. Elgar uses this text one measure after rehearsal number 17 in the full score, 90–91.

82. Anderson, *Elgar*, 212. Anderson makes a similar but less sweeping assertion in his *Elgar in Manuscript* (London: British Library, 1990): "Elgar eliminated lines emphasizing the male pronouns Newman used of the Angel" (46).

83. As Jerrold Northrop Moore notes, this phrase is "quoted at the beginning of William Earnest Henley's *Echoes*, where Elgar probably found it" (*Elgar*, 586n170).

84. Powell, *Memories*, 105–6.

85. Trowell, "Elgar's Use of Literature," 244–45. In a newspaper article entitled "The Mysterious Mrs. Nelson" (*Sunday Telegraph*, 15 Nov. 1992), Michael Kennedy reports on a curious rumor about Elgar spread by the notoriously waggish composer William Walton. According to this imaginative scenario, Elgar fathered an illegitimate daughter with a young actress (later a cook for the art historian Lord Clark, with whose wife Walton once had an affair), and this woman, a Mrs. Nelson, is the true inspiration for the violin concerto. Kennedy concludes his report of this rumor on a proper note of interrogation, if not skepticism.

86. Terry heard Elgar play sketches for the concerto in 1909 at Frank Schuster's house, 22 Old Queen Street, Westminster, in London.

87. It is surely significant that, as Terry notes, Elgar's initial impulse was to write a masculine article.

88. Elgar ultimately drops the article, leaving only the ambiguous preposition. That Terry is unsure about Spanish grammar hardly compromises the gist of his observation.

89. The italicized words are also underlined in Terry's typescript. On 8 May 1910 Elgar wrote to Frank Schuster: "I have the Concerto well in hand & have played (?) it thro' on the P[iano] F[orte] & it's *good!* Awfully emotional! too emotional but I love it" (Moore, ed., *Letters of a Lifetime*, 220).

90. The full quotation from *Gil Blas* reads: "Aquí está encerrada el alma del Licenciado Pedro Garcias" (Here is enshrined the soul of the licentiate Pedro Garcias). See Trowell, "Elgar's Use of Literature," 244.

91. Basil Maine, *Elgar: His Life and Works* (Bath: Cedric Chivers, 1933), bk. 2, 141.

92. This theory may also offer a rather sad rationale for the gradual cooling of the friendship between Elgar and Stuart-Wortley: once he had finished with the violin concerto, he had less need either of her encouragement or proximity. It is telling that Elgar never completed the piano concerto that Stuart-Wortley urged him to compose for her; the piano was not "his" instrument, after all.

93. Basil Maine writes that the violin "by consent of composers, interpreters and public, is of all our instruments the queen" (Maine, *Elgar*, bk. 2, 141).

94. Letter of 5 Nov. 1910, in Moore, *Elgar*, 587. Elgar dedicated *The Music Makers* to Kilburn.

10 "AN ANTHOLOGY OF FRIENDSHIP"

THE LETTERS FROM JOHN IRELAND
TO FATHER KENNETH THOMPSON

FIONA RICHARDS

On 25 November 1943 the composer John Ireland wrote to his close friend Father Kenneth Thompson:

My music does not appeal to *women:* who form the majority of listeners. They know instinctively that it is not inspired by their charms—and for the same reason, I do not think what I write is acceptable to the majority of men.

Well, when you return from your present trip, or, at any rate, when the war is over, you must take a country living . . . in a small town, where we can work up a large choir & I will be your organist & choirmaster. I really mean this. I will live with you in the Rectory or Vicarage. You will not be such a fool as to marry the good lady who is thirsty for your blood. Marriage is not for Uranians. It only creates the most ghastly strife and horrible unhappiness for *both* parties, believe me.

. . . Although living here is by no means ideal, it might be much worse. I shall have to try to put up with it till hostilities cease. You must not think I am being quite idle. I have nearly completed a Fantasy-Sonata for Clarinet and Piano—it is in one movement, & will last 14 or 15 minutes. I have been at it for quite 6 months! The clarinet is a remarkable instrument, & I have been most impressed by the playing of Thurston—hence the choice of this combination. . . . I'm afraid it will have very few performances—works for wind instruments are seldom heard. I will have to concoct some "bread-&-butter" (ie uninspired) works. Life without romance is really dull—one lives only on memories, and even these are marred by the fact that one did not make the most of one's opportunities. "Gather ye rosebuds while ye may" is a maxim to be instilled into the young—though I know this to be contrary to ecclesiastical principles!

Part of a longer letter and belonging to a sequence of letters to Thompson, these three paragraphs, which run consecutively, give away all sorts of little details about the composer. Ireland's reasons for feeling that his music lacks a popular appeal, his throwaway lines about marriage and Uranians, and his allusions to memories and lost chances leave the reader with no doubt that this correspondence was a platform for disclosures about his own sexuality.

John Ireland (1879–1962) is perhaps best known as an English composer of piano miniatures and songs, a lyricist influenced by his native landscapes (figure 10.1). He was part of the British music establishment and for many years was a professor of composition at the Royal College of Music. He was also a man who suffered problematic relationships throughout his life. His childhood in the company of bullying siblings, a frail mother, and an elderly father, the latter aged seventy when John was born, must have contributed to the difficulties he suffered. Despite his brief and ultimately unsuccessful relationships with women, there is no doubt that Ireland was considerably more interested in men, specifically much younger men. There is, however, no direct evidence that Ireland ever had a close sexual relationship with a man or a boy, and he did not particularly mix in homosexual circles. He was a very private figure, and because of this and the problems involved in extracting relevant information, there has never been any truly open discussion of Ireland's personal life. In particular, there has been little written about his religious convictions or his sexuality.

Articles that were published during the composer's lifetime said nothing about these important aspects of his personality, curious omissions given that they are determining factors in his music. Crossley-Holland, in the fifth edition of Grove's *Dictionary of Music and Musicians,* although very perceptive about other aspects of Ireland's life and music, made only a few veiled hints. The two posthumous biographies that appeared in 1969 and 1979 contained little discussion of Ireland's sexuality and no allusion to the possibility that the composer may have been drawn to beautiful young men.[1] Both these books portrayed Ireland as a kindly figure let down by other people. Norah Kirby (1898–1982), housekeeper to Ireland in his later years, sponsored the second biography and thereby almost certainly exerted control over its contents. Kirby is partly responsible for the mystery that surrounds Ireland's sexuality. Details of his early life remain elusive because of a lack of biographical evidence, some of which she destroyed in an attempt to create in death the figure she venerated in life, although some was lost at an earlier stage, during World War II. Hugh Ottaway, in the 1980 edition of *Grove,*[2] preserved the silence, even going so far as to avoid any mention of the more personally weighted works

FIGURE 10.1. John Ireland (courtesy of Derek Longmire).

such as *The Land of Lost Content,* a song cycle setting texts by A. E. Housman. Indeed, the issue of Ireland's sexuality was never addressed until 1985, when Stephen Banfield wrote that unless we recognize the pederastic side of Ireland's nature, "we cannot fully understand the songs, which must surely be seen as a personal testament."[3] Since then the references to Ireland's sexuality have either been subtle but honest (Alan Rowlands), included only as an evasive footnote (Barbara Docherty), or rather facetious (Ken Russell).[4] Humphrey Carpenter chose to present Ireland as lecherous drunkard.[5] The picture of the composer up to the year 2000 was therefore a rather curious one:[6] remembered with fondness as a benign old man but also presented as a cantankerous alcoholic. Wishfully turned into a disappointed heterosexual by protective friends, his real desires have been ignored and camouflaged.

Even with no supporting biographical evidence, the programmatic and literary nature of Ireland's output suggests an innate homosexuality. Just as Housman's poetry has often been treated as a cryptic diary, so is Ireland's music inherently autobiographical, described by Stephen Banfield as "having an intense, highly organised personal bearing, even though one often encounters problems in defining it."[7] The intention behind this chapter is to move closer to an understanding of the personal nature of John Ireland's music. Even before one looks at the notes of the music, there are many clues to his sexuality, including obvious signs, such as the composer's interest in symbols such as the goat-god Pan and in the poetry of Housman and Rupert Brooke. Then there are more suggestive indications in the musical expression of homoerotic passions aroused by World War I and by the Anglican church. There are hints and ambiguities in his choice of words by the homosexual icon John Addington Symonds for use in a public celebratory context. There are song settings of the highly charged, secretive love poetry of Philip Sidney and Aldous Huxley. And there are also enigmatic dedications and carefully chosen literary descriptors attached to many of his works.

Although much can be gleaned about Ireland's emotional life from the music alone, there is other evidence, including one peculiarly revealing and illuminating source of information. This is the collection of correspondence from Ireland to his friend Kenneth Thompson (1904–91), which spans the period 1936–61. Although one cannot be sure that this is the complete correspondence, it does seem to have been painstakingly preserved by Thompson, who gave the material to the British Library in 1979.[8] Into this correspondence Thompson has periodically inserted explanatory notes or diary entries of his own on brown paper, some written retrospectively and some concurrent with the letters they accompany. The correspondence, which began on 18 May 1936, was extensive, comprising 143 letters and cards, often long and detailed. On average Ireland wrote once a month, although there were also periods, the 1950s in particular, when he wrote much more frequently. And there were times when there would be a gap of a few months, for example in 1942, when there were only two letters, and in 1948 and 1949. From August 1960, when his eyesight was deteriorating, he was forced to use a typewriter, and from 1961 Norah Kirby had to write on his behalf. Sadly the archived Ireland-Thompson correspondence is almost entirely one-sided: few letters from Thompson to Ireland survive, with just five held by the John Ireland Trust. The tone of these five letters is warm and reassuring, the church presiding over the discussion. They also include a number of references to Ireland's sexuality. In addition to these, there are two letters from Thompson to Colin Scott-Sutherland, dated 1976 and 1981,[9] in which he talks at length of his relationship with and knowledge of the composer.

Given the expansive and regular nature of the correspondence, the letters to Thompson stand as a unique body of information on Ireland's life and music and serve as an analytical tool for uncovering his identity. Although he wrote to many other friends and musicians, there was no one else with whom he corresponded on such a continuous basis over such a long period, and indeed Ireland himself described the friendship as being "firm & of long standing" (12 Dec. 1954). There was also no other individual to whom he revealed so many different facets of his character. His letters to performers tended to focus only on music; those to publishers, on business matters. Letters to other friends, such as composer John Longmire (1902–86) and critic Edwin Evans (1871–1945), spoke of his music and other matters but were neither so broad-ranging nor so open in manner. There is only one other source that carries similar references to religion and sexuality. These are letters to another friend, the ex-cleric Arthur Robert Lee Gardner (dates unknown), but these are limited in number and in date span.

It seems that the combination of Kenneth Thompson's position as a cleric and his obvious empathy with Ireland's music and feelings acted as a springboard for the composer, allowing him to unload the more secret and intimate aspects of his life. Thompson, in a confessorial role, somehow legitimized Ireland's feelings for young boys, and this collection of letters contains many references, some veiled, some explicit, to his homosexuality.

Kenneth Thompson first met the composer around 1932, when he was the priest-in-charge at St. Cuthbert's, Kensington, a church occasionally attended by Ireland, who was at this time living close by, in Gunter Grove, Chelsea. At this time Ireland was fifty-three and Thompson was just twenty-eight, a striking age gap separating the two. It is clear from the letters that Thompson also had homosexual leanings and that the two men enjoyed a close, emotional relationship. There were a few years in which, according to Thompson, the two men spent many evenings together, the younger one cycling to the composer's house. There are therefore no letters from these early years of acquaintance, as Ireland and Thompson saw one another regularly. The years 1933–36 were a difficult time for Ireland, for he was suffering from the disintegration of an intense relationship, and this much younger man was probably a replacement for the composer's previous young protégés and confidants.

In 1936 Ireland rented a flat in Deal, dividing his time between the Kent coast and London. The first surviving written communication to Thompson, a short card, was from this year. In 1936 Thompson also moved, leaving London for Sussex, to be the assistant chaplain at Lancing College, taking in addition the post of lecturer and librarian at Chichester Theological College in 1937. In 1941 he became a chaplain in the navy, drafted to HMS *Cabbala*, HMS *Blenheim*, and then, in 1942, to HMS *Sandhurst*. During these war years he was at one point in Alexandria and then, in 1945, in Caserta, Italy. He remained in the services in 1946, based first in Flixton and then in Rochester, and on leaving the navy he became the vice-principal of Ely Theological College for a brief period. After a few years traveling, he settled in Swansea in 1951, after which he worked at Stonyhurst College, in Lancashire. The next few years were complicated, with Thompson moving frequently, working first at Cottesmore School, in Crawley, and then at Harrow School before returning to Swansea. In 1957 he became a temporary librarian at Cowley Fathers, Oxford, a city in which he settled after a somewhat checkered career.

The letters from Ireland to Thompson cover diverse subjects. The composer often wrote of his own music. Comments were sometimes about work in progress, with Ireland telling his friend about current projects, as well as the grief the composing process caused him, and mentioning recent performances. He also wrote retrospectively, categorizing and evaluating his own output, often expressing a feeling of failure and worthlessness. Similar judgments were applied to other composers, with Debussy, Ravel, Stravinsky, Berg, and Boulez rated highly and many of his British contemporaries dealt with harshly. He wrote extensively and descriptively of places he lived in or visited, with Sussex frequently extolled and used as the standard against which to measure all other locations. The general tittle-tattle in the letters offers a picture of domestic issues, health concerns, and niggling worries. From the war years there are Ireland's thoughts on the world situation, accompanied by declarations of depression and a sense of futility. At other times the tone is passionately effusive, Ireland adopting the language of an arch Romantic. There are references to friends—notably the composer Geoffrey Bush (1920–98), whom Thompson introduced to Ireland in 1936 and whom Ireland mentioned many times, and Lawrence Norcross (b. 1927), a teacher who went on to found the John Ireland Society—but only very rarely to family.

Given that Thompson was a cleric, it is hardly surprising that throughout the correspondence Ireland refers to his own religious doubts and self-questioning. He was strongly attracted to the ritual and ceremony of the Anglo-Catholic church, an attraction common to many homosexual men in the early part of the twentieth century, as discussed in Ellis Hanson's *Decadence and Catholicism.*[10] It was this love of the formality and detachment of High Church rites that caused Ireland to waver between the Anglican and the Roman Catholic church, although his equally strong distaste for Marian devotions prevented his actual conversion. Thompson played an important role in this, for he himself switched from the Anglican to the Catholic church and back again. In 1947 he became a Roman Catholic but by 1949 had already reverted to Anglicanism. He worked at a Catholic school in 1951 before once more affirming his faith in the Church of England. After the death of his mother in 1956 he was again tempted to return to Rome.

Despite the lure of the Roman Catholic church, Ireland was to have associations with the Anglican church and its music for much of his life, and like many musicians of his generation, he began his professional career as an organist. His first post was in 1896, as assistant organist at the recently consecrated Holy Trinity Church, Chelsea, followed by an appointment at St. Jude's, Chelsea, in 1900. Ireland's period at St. Jude's is interesting because it was at this time that he began a series of regular visits to the Channel Islands, where the striking juxtaposition of the islands' Christian churches and pagan sites reinforced the connection in his own mind between Christianity and paganism. For Ireland, the Anglo-Catholic church's appeal both resonated and conflicted with his attraction to a pagan celebration of religious belief, an opposition to which he tended to allude at times of extreme stress. The best example of this came in July 1936, when his close friend Percy Bentham (1884–1936) died, causing Ireland to write:

> I have not got over it—& will never get over the loss of this friend. The loss of him is inconceivable to me—& so far as I can see, his death was absolutely casual & unnecessary, & I cannot in any way attribute it to some imaginary deity which, we are told, takes account of even a sinner's death. He had much more work to do here, on this planet, & his death is a severe disaster to all—he was only 52. As you know, I am rather a bad sort of Catholic—not a . . . practising one, tho' it is here in my heart & mind. It is the only thing which represents & presents what is permanent—and age-long. As one grows older, & ambitions fade, & one becomes rather lacking in fire and significance, one's heart must turn towards what represents permanence. I do not wish one to lose this. I am a Pagan, a Pagan I was born, & a Pagan I shall ever remain. That is the foundation of religion. (17 July 1936)

The appeal of both Christian and pagan rituals was prevalent among homosexuals in the early part of the twentieth century, and one only has to look at contemporary writers to see this. E. F. Benson, for example, converted to Roman Catholicism while writing of homoerotic experiences set against a backdrop of pagan landscapes and Pan worship.

Ireland's most significant appointment as organist and choirmaster was at St. Luke's, Chelsea, in 1904, a position he held until 1926. During this time he wrote the major part of his church music. St. Luke's also introduced him to people who were to play important roles in his life. Although Ireland continued to attend church services, there was a gap in his employment as an organist between 1926 and 1940. In 1939 he left England for Guernsey, ostensibly to consider settling on the island, and early the following year he renewed his links with the church as director of music at St. Stephen's, St. Peter Port. The formal elements of the services here appealed to Ireland, and he wrote to Thompson soon after taking the job that ritualistically "they do the Mass rather well, with everything, including incense and the Gospel" (1 Mar. 1940). Ireland had other, less important, connections with another of Guernsey's churches, St. Saviour's, where he performed as organist from time to time. From this period came his only work dedicated to Kenneth Thompson. This was the short, simple mass *Sancti Stephani,* which remained in manuscript until after Thompson's death.

Ireland's association with the church was one of the most obvious ways in which his attraction to the beauty of youth could find an outlet, and during his time at St. Luke's he came in contact with three boys who were to become closely involved with his work. The first of these was Charles Stafford Markes (1900–85), who joined the choir in 1908, exchanging singing for organ duties when his voice broke in 1915. In 1911 Ireland took him on as a piano pupil and contributed financially to his schooling. The two developed a close friendship, with Markes spending much time in his teacher's company and commenting on his work. A musical misunderstanding led to a rift between the two after World War I, the friendship lying dormant until 1948. One of Markes's friends was Robert Glassby (ca. 1900–34); brought into the choir on Markes's instigation, he became another of Ireland's protégés and may have been the youth behind Ireland's piano piece "The Holy Boy." The most significant of the choirboys encountered at St. Luke's was Arthur George Miller (1905–86), the son of a local antiques dealer and someone who was to be of enormous importance and a source of creative inspiration to Ireland in the 1920s.

Apparently religion, sex, ritual, and sensuality intermingled in Ireland's mind. In his letters to Thompson, a remark on the subject of boys often followed or preceded a comment on the church. For example, in May 1940 he wrote from Guernsey that he was attending Mass most days and described the manner of service, following this with a reference to a young boy he had met on the island. This mixing of the sacred and the profane is evident in Ireland's potent anthem *Ex ore innocentium* ("from the mouths of innocents"), written in 1944. This piece was the last of three anthems, all of which were settings of religious texts relating to the Passion.[11] For *Ex ore innocentium* Ireland chose the topic of the symbolism of sacrifice, using Bishop W. W. How's text "It is a thing most wonderful." Although this chapter is not the forum for extensive discussion of meanings in Ireland's music,[12] *Ex ore innocentium* is a good example of the way in which the composer's musical structures and motifs carry expressive meaning.

In terms of its genre, the piece is unusual, being a curious blend of solo song, unison song, and anthem. The subject of Christ's Passion—sacrifice, suffering, and love—is associated with the innocence of the angelic choirboy, and Ireland's references to the first performance of this work made great play of the appearance of the boys in the choir, who looked "perfectly ravishing, in light blue cassocks and ruffs" (6 Sept. 1944). The music itself is deeply sentimental, the artless, diatonic quality of the opening melody sentimentalized by appoggiaturas and chromatic chords (see figure 10.2).

FIGURE 10.2. *Ex ore innocentium* (© 1944 by Boosey and Co., Ltd.; reproduced by permission of Boosey and Hawkes Music Publishers, Ltd.).

In the central section the narrative voice muses on Christ's sacrifice, the music swiftly moving from simple minor oscillations to a swooning climax, musical juxtapositions mirroring the mixed sentiments of the words. As a whole the piece draws together elements of Ireland's hymnody style and aspects of his love songs: his complex feelings about the Anglo-Catholic church are captured in this tiny but many-layered anthem.

In his letters to Thompson, Ireland supported his discussion of religious matters with references to relevant literature. The two men exchanged books and recommended reading matter to each other, and the nature of this literature provides another indicator of Ireland's "personal bearing." On a number of occasions Thompson and Ireland read and commented on books that were concerned with religious or even occult issues. Some of the literature they discussed dealt with homoerotic issues. In 1955 Ireland read Broad's *The Friendships and Follies of Oscar Wilde,* finding it very interesting and commenting that Lord Alfred Douglas must have been "a worthless & ruthlessly selfish character" (15 May 1955). This subject must have been topical, for in November 1955 Parliament voted on revising the sex laws; Ireland mentioned this event, merely noting that there had been no change (23 Oct. 1955). More often the literature discussed dealt specifically with the beauty and comradeship of young males. One of the writers they read was Forrest Reid, whose works often explored close male friendship. His novel *The Garden God* depicts a dream world in which two boys experience an intense, fleeting friendship, spending their days together in a haze of sensual pleasure.[13] In November 1936 Ireland read Reid's newly published *The Retreat,* part of a trilogy of novels, although he was not particularly taken with the book. Nevertheless, in December he read *Uncle Stephen,* another volume of the trilogy, and liked this much better.

Like *The Garden God, Uncle Stephen* creates a dream world of close male friendships superimposed on a countryside that retains elements of wilderness. The main protagonists are a young boy, Tom, and his Uncle Stephen, aged sixty-three, who has a mysterious past involving a young man. Tom forms close relationships with his uncle, with a local poacher, and with a strange boy named Philip, who is a manifestation of the young Stephen. The book abounds with descriptions of sensation, and references to Greek gods run throughout it; for example, Uncle Stephen sleeps beside an ancient statue of Hermes, "he who cares for boys"[14] (interestingly, on one occasion Thompson sent Ireland a photograph of a representation of Hermes). Ireland would have found this book appealing for its deeply intimate nature, its mingling of adolescence, paganism, and sentiment, and its implicit homoeroticism:

> Tom bent down till he could see on the sleeping boy's cheeks and upper lips a faint down composed of minute silken hairs, invisible at a distance, but which now showed like a velvet film on the smoothness of his skin. With the tip of his finger he tested his own skin, brushing it lightly to and fro.
>   He held the syringa over Philip's mouth, but, though he touched him with the utmost carefulness, the blossom left a golden stain of pollen. Tom moistened his finger and tried to remove it without wakening him.[15]

Reid narrowly escaped being branded as a Uranian writer. At the turn of the century a group of writers who came to be termed "Uranian" were producing Romantic works concerned with the beauty of young boys and their appeal to adult males. These writers, many of whom were members of the church, included Lord Alfred Douglas, Horatio Forbes Brown, John Gambril F. Nicholson, and Charles Kains Jackson. Their precursors were John Addington Symonds, author of *A Problem in Modern Ethics* (1891),[16] and Edward Carpenter, whose *Homogenic Love* followed in 1894. The subject matter of the Uranians was the theme of comradeship between an older man and a youth, usually a middle-class man and a working-class youth, a theme dear to Ireland's heart. Most of his significant relationships were with much younger men and, in the case of his choirboys, with youths from working-class backgrounds. Other Uranian topics were the evanescence of boyhood, the angelic face of youth, eroticism mingled with religion, and guilt at a forbidden passion. Many of these poems looked back to the pederastic culture of classical Greece and featured Greek figures, with Hyacinthus, Apollo, and Narcissus considered appropriate subjects. Works were given suggestive titles such as *Ladslove Lyrics* and *A Garland of Ladslove.*

The figure of Narcissus, the youth who falls in love with his own reflection, was of long-standing and symbolic interest to Ireland and featured a number of times in his output. Narcissus appeared mainly via Ireland's settings or evocations of A. E. Housman's verse, many of whose poems held a personal appeal for the composer on account of their homosexual resonances. In the early 1920s, long before Ireland met Thompson, he set one of Housman's Narcissus poems, giving it the title "Ladslove" in the song cycle *The Land of Lost Content.* In 1941 he returned to the same poem, discussing it with Thompson, and this time created a piano piece with the title *A Grecian Lad,* prefaced with a quotation from Housman.

While there is no evidence that Ireland read any of the overtly Uranian, usually privately printed works, he was certainly aware of the use and meaning of the term *Uranian* and did read related subject matter, including Carpenter's *Iolaus.* A figure on the fringes of the Uranian circle was Martin Donisthorpe Armstrong. In 1938 Ireland wrote to Thompson that he had come across an interesting poem by Armstrong called "The Young Bather" (1 May 1938).[17] In this poem Armstrong watches a young swimmer and mourns that his youth and beauty must pass. Youths stripped for swimming constituted a topos for much Uranian verse, the voyeurism always tinged with regret for the passing of boyhood.

Down by the water a boy stood there,
Stripped to bathe, on a rock shelf narrow,
   Sweet-curved, spare,
   With clustering hair,
Pure as a lily-bud, slim as an arrow.

More significant than the Armstrong poem was Thomas Mann's *Death in Venice,* which appears almost as a leitmotif in the letters. The first reference was in 1938, at the same time that Ireland was reading "The Young Bather," when he described the story as a "forbidden subject, . . . treated with great beauty and skill" (1 May 1938). The following month he wrote again: "'Death in Venice' is an absolutely unique study, carried out with supreme skill, of an emotion, which, so far as I am aware, has never been dealt with in literary form before—it may have been analysed pathologically by Havelock Ellis as a 'case,' but this is a work of Art!" (15 June 1938). In 1946 Ireland once again returned to the subject of *Death in Venice,* this time trying to legitimize its content, saying that "surely the idealistic rapture called fate by the beautiful and unattainable [was] not dangerous" and telling Thompson that this sort of emotion was surely not "contrary to God's will" (23 Jan. 1946). Later that year he wrote again, in answer to Thompson's dislike of the work, saying "I have re-read the story, & can see why you would dislike it—having not experienced the passion so wonderfully depicted—that the author has experienced it cannot be doubted!" (17 Oct. 1946). The following month Ireland again discussed the book, mentioning that he reread it often. During these same years the composer's musical works were increasingly focused on the subject of youth, with piano pieces such as "The Boy Bishop" and the orchestral overture *Satyricon.*

In July 1939 Ireland's move to Guernsey prompted letters that frequently alluded to the charm and beauty of the island's numerous small, lovely bays. These letters also hint at the appeal of its young boys. Many of these comments have been effaced by Thompson, although most are still legible; they are mainly references to boys aged between nine and thirteen, generally fairly innocuous comments on their attractive looks. In April 1940 Ireland took up residence in the Birnam Court Hotel, St. Peter Port. The hotel's proprietor was George Rayson, who had a young son, Michael (b. 1930). Ireland was drawn to the boy, whom he described as "beautiful, clever & alert, with perfect manners—& being educated at one of the best schools here. Not, alas, musical. But lovely, long, curling eyelashes. Here comes out the stifled paternal instinct!" (29 Apr. 1940). In a slightly later letter Ireland enclosed a photograph of the boy, saying that he was "attractive, but not at all affectionate, wh: is perhaps as well!"

(18 May 1940). For Ireland this was a powerful encounter, and the intensity of the experience was to produce one of his most luscious tone poems for piano, "In a May Morning."

Sadly for Ireland the heady experience of Guernsey was brought to an abrupt end with the German invasion of the island in June 1940. Ireland was on one of the last ships to leave the island, the SS *Antwerp*. On his return a period of retrospection and nostalgia for the months on the island led to the production of a number of pieces. One of these was "In a May Morning," the second movement of the piano suite *Sarnia*, which he completed in 1941. *Sarnia* (the Latin name for Guernsey) is made up of three movements: "Le Catioroc," "In a May Morning" and "Song of the Springtides." Individually each movement is about an aspect of Ireland's time on the island; as a whole the suite reflects Ireland's paganism, sexuality, and pantheism, topics that were captured in many of his other works but that are here specifically located on Guernsey. Ireland originally wanted to call the second movement "Boyslove," another name for the plant southernwood (the Uranians often used the term as a title, as in Nicholson's *Chaplet of Southernwood*), but feared that this would cause comment. Although he felt the words "in an April garden" situated the piece accurately, in the event he transposed his April meeting to May, dedicating the piece to Michael. Ireland wrote to Thompson that Michael Rayson was

> just a part of the whole flood of beauty in Guernsey—those last 6 or 7 weeks were really an extraordinary revelation—there was *everything at once*—the unbelievable beauty of the Channel Islands in Spring, the delightful surroundings and feeling of heart's ease—the joy of that lovely Church where I played the organ—and Michael constantly about the house and garden, fitting in so well with everything—it was almost too wonderful to be true & certainly far too wonderful to last. . . . alas, how fragile, how transitory! And yet, how eternal & true! Well, I have expressed some of it in my new piano work, "SARNIA." (26 June 1941)

Ireland prefaced the piece with a passage from Victor Hugo's novel *Les Travailleurs de la mer* (1866). Hugo himself spent some time living in exile on Guernsey, where he wrote and situated this work. *Les Travailleurs de la mer* is at once a detailed, realistic depiction of daily life on Guernsey and a work imbued with symbolism and mystery, portraying the island as a place where Pan still hovers. Ireland selected several sentences from a passage near the end of the novel where Hugo describes a day in May in sensuous terms, including the following:

Partout une divine plénitude et un gonflement mystérieux faisaient deviner
l'effort panique et sacré de la sève en travail.
  Qui brillait, brillait plus; qui aimait, aimait mieux . . .

[Everywhere a divine fullness and a mysterious swelling suggested the pagan and
sacred effort of the sap at work.
  What shone shone more fully; who loved, loved better . . .][18]

The work has strong formal similarities with "April" (1925), an earlier piano piece concerned with analogous experiences of landscape and season. In
both works the outer sections feature a single musical idea that, ballad-like, is
presented several times, altering slightly with each reappearance. Whereas
"April" is a lyrical embodiment of early spring, "In a May Morning" is a richly nostalgic musical version of the essence of a late spring day poised on the
brink of summer. The opening section of this work (see figure 10.3), fundamentally tonal but richly chromatic, embodies all that is sentimental in Ireland's writing, a sentimentality sometimes but not exclusively associated with
the pieces written for boys.

FIGURE 10.3. "In a May Morning," from *Sarnia* (© 1941 by Hawkes and Son, Ltd.; reproduced by permission of Boosey and Hawkes Music Publishers, Ltd).

Essentially a slow-moving love song, it is melody driven, with long-drawn
phrases and multiple appoggiaturas, slow to resolve. And always present are
faint hints at previous works by the composer, musical wafts of bygone times.
Both "April" and "In a May Morning" have rhapsodic central sections that

move away from their opening melodic material. In "April" this central section offers an opportunity for piano figuration and roulades, whereas in "In a May Morning" the mood moves from sentiment to pantheistic ecstasy. Ireland's way of expressing this rapture is to use many parallel chords and moving semiquavers, now with modal undertones.

The new theme of "In a May Morning" is used as the main material of the last movement of *Sarnia.* "Song of the Springtides" is concerned with the heady side of nature, its title taken from Swinburne's *Songs of the Springtides* and its prefacing quotation coming from "Thalassius" (1880), one of the poems contained in this collection. Swinburne's works had appealed to Ireland from an early stage in his career on account of their nature ecstasy and perhaps for the ambiguous nature of Swinburne's expressions of sensuality. Like Hugo, Swinburne spent some time in the Channel Islands, partly because of his reverence for Hugo's writing, and was especially drawn to Sark and Guernsey, writing of the latter that he knew nothing "perhaps to match it for the very romance of loveliness; and the sea, with its headlands like the Hebrides and its coves like South Cornwall, has surpassed itself just here."[19]

With "In a May Morning" Ireland attempts to recapture in music the atmosphere of a momentary but powerful experience. This experience was relived in September 1941 when, on leave from the navy, Thompson visited Ireland in Banbury. They spent the evening with Ireland playing piano music while incense burned, a picture of Michael enjoying pride of place on the piano. Thompson wrote his own description of the piece on the back of a letter from Ireland: "In Michael's piece (No 2) a beautiful meditative melody full of . . . emotional yearning. . . . It works up to climaxes of emotion which recede again. In middle a light shaking movement . . . 'a beauty too fragile to touch'—then a lighthearted playful bit in irregular time—'Michael playing about the garden,' I suggested" (12 Sept. 1941; letter dated 10 Sept. 1941).

Although Michael Rayson was the most important of the Guernsey boys, there were others who were mentioned in the letters or who inspired pieces of music. One of these was Peter Lihou, who sang in Ireland's island choir for just a few months. The composer dedicated his school song "Boys' Names" to Lihou, although never told the boy that he had written a piece for him. Sentiment and nostalgia contributed to Ireland's personality, and this was manifested in part through songs for children, either unison or partsong. During this period in the 1940s Ireland became interested in Eleanor Farjeon's verse for children, specifically her volume *Over the Garden Wall* (1933), which has the same disingenuous, lissom quality as Walter de la Mare's verse, and he set five of her poems as unison songs for equal voices and piano. These were "The

Boy," "Boys' Names," "Joseph Fell a-Dreaming," "The Bell in the Leaves," and
"Autumn Crocus." All the settings are simple diatonic songs matching the
artless nature of the poems. However, the one dedicated to the young Peter
Lihou is curious. The Farjeon poem is a reflection on boys' names, bearing the
opening line, "What splendid names for Boys there are!" and making reference to the sound of specified names, for example, "Peter like a piper's tune."[20]
Musically this song is similar to Ireland's other Farjeon settings—diatonic and
lyrical—and the poem may seem an innocuous one, preceded in *Over the
Garden Wall* by a parallel poem on girls' names. The words, however, have
strong Uranian resonances. In 1892 John Gambril Nicholson produced a bal-
lade with the title "Of Boys' Names." His poem is remarkably similar to that
of Farjeon:

> Old memories of the Table Round
>   In Percival and Lancelot dwell,
> Clement and Bernard bring the sound
>   Of anthems in the cloister-cell,
> And Leonard vies with Lionel
> In stately step and kingly frame,
>   And Kenneth speaks of field and fell,
> And Ernest sets my heart a-flame. . . .[21]

Whether or not Ireland recognized these connections, the fact that he set a
poem so similar to Nicholson's eulogy, dedicating the song to a youth he barely
knew, is striking. He was quite unhappy in this period of hostilities and of exile
from his homes, frequently expressing sentiments of discontent or fantasiz-
ing about ideal situations that were impossible to create. This was accompanied by regrets for opportunities now lost, such as the post as organist at St.
Luke's (which he had given up sixteen years earlier). The year 1944 was filled
with backward glances, including further references to Michael Rayson, and
the following year Ireland and Thompson once again met, this time back at
Gunter Grove, for another impromptu evening of music and talking. Ireland
played his piano pieces *Sarnia*, "April," "Bergomask," "The Boy Bishop," and
"Puck's Birthday." Thompson returned the photograph of Michael in 1946,
arousing in the composer "poignant memories of a happy and very vivid
time—a combination of various factors, including Spring in the Channel Islands, which is more violent than English Spring—constant attendances at a
Catholic Church—all pervaded by the glamour of Contact with Beauty in its
finest human form. Too good, alas, to last—excellent in memory. Imperfectly
recorded, maybe, in music" (15 Nov. 1946).

Although his letters to Thompson often refer to his interest in youths, whether in brief, sometimes camp, asides or in more extensive and heartfelt discussion, Ireland never mentioned the two adults, one woman and one man, with whom he had had long-standing personal relationships and to whom he dedicated a number of works. Given the letters' intimate and open nature, these significant omissions might seem curious. Perhaps Ireland was not happy to write about people whom he had truly loved, while he was willing to express his dreams and fantasies. Maybe the nature of his own relationship with Thompson was such that he simply did not wish to refer to earlier, deeper passions.

Of these two affairs the first, and probably the most important, was with the aforementioned Arthur Miller, who became known to Ireland on joining St. Luke's choir. From 1922 to 1929, starting when Miller was seventeen and Ireland forty-three, the composer dedicated a series of works to "AGM." These were nearly all intended as birthday gifts, with the date 22 February, Miller's birthday, given at the end of several works. The first was a piano piece bearing the dedication "Pro amicitia," specific both in its title—*On a Birthday Morning*—and in its precise dating of 22 February 1922. The next was dated 1924: the Prelude in E-flat for piano. In 1925 there were two pieces for Arthur Miller. The first of these was the usual birthday present for 22 February, "Bergomask," for piano. The second Miller piece of this year assigned place as well as person in the dedication. This was the song "When I Am Dead, My Dearest," labeled "To A.G.M.: Cerne Abbas" and dated June 1925. The two men had toured Dorset in 1923, and it is most likely that this song was written in memory of this holiday (figure 10.4).

In 1926 the birthday gift was a set of three songs: "Love and Friendship," "Friendship in Misfortune" and "The One Hope." This song cycle expresses in both its words and its music the ephemeral nature of romantic love and the sturdier type of love that is friendship. From 1927 the dedications became increasingly poignant. The birthday work of that year was the song cycle *We'll to the Woods No More*, consisting of two Housman settings, "We'll to the Woods No More" and "In Boyhood," and a piano epilogue, "Spring Will Not Wait." The dedication in the printed music merely reads "To Arthur," while the manuscript offers a fuller dedication, "To Arthur: in memory of the darkest days." Evidently, as I will show, 1927 was a crisis year, and Ireland wrote nothing for Miller in 1928. In 1929 Ireland offered his final Miller dedication, "February's child," for piano.

Quite clearly Arthur Miller was someone of the deepest significance to Ireland, although the nature of Ireland's feelings remains uncertain. There is only one known surviving letter from Miller to Ireland, none from Ireland to Miller,

FIGURE 10.4. John Ireland in Cerne Abbas, Dorset, 1923 (reproduced courtesy of the John Ireland Trust).

and tantalizingly little other concrete evidence of this friendship. Just a few photographs and assorted documents remain, from which it is clear that there were ambiguities, uncertainties, and tensions in this relationship. Despite the fact that throughout his life Ireland enjoyed a problematic relationship with women, on 17 December 1926 he made the disastrous move of marrying a young pupil, Dorothy Phillips (b. 1909), with Arthur Miller acting as his witness. There are all sorts of reasons why he may have done this. In 1926 he gave up his post at St. Luke's, quite possibly because of his close relationship with a former choirboy, and the marriage was presumably an attempt to block and disguise his increasing self-knowledge. Miller himself then married, in St. Luke's church, on 26 June 1927, this time with Ireland as witness. Ireland divorced his wife on 5 March 1928, and anecdotal evidence attests to the marriage as having been unconsummated. Miller's marriage lasted much longer, and the couple had a daughter. He remarried in 1940, and this partnership produced two further daughters and two sons. The two men continued to stay in touch, Ireland purchasing businesses for Miller in the 1930s and 1940s and continuing to support him financially into the 1950s. It is curious, then, that Miller never features in the Thompson letters.

Ireland's next significant relationship with an adult began in 1927, soon after Miller's marriage. In the autumn of that year he was introduced to the young and very beautiful pianist Helen Perkin (1909–96). In 1925, at the age of sixteen, she had entered the Royal College of Music (RCM) on a scholarship, and two years later she was assigned to Ireland for composition lessons. He thought she showed talent but even greater promise as a pianist. She became a close companion of the composer, spending much time in his company from 1928, and the friendship was perhaps another attempt by Ireland to make a heterosexual partnership work for him. Her early recital programs included his works, and in 1929 one of the songs in the cycle *Sacred and Profane,* "Hymn for a Child," was dedicated to her. In 1930 she was the soloist in the RCM performance of Prokofiev's Piano Concerto no. 3, conducted by Sargent, and began to broadcast on the National Programme. The year was significant as well in terms of her association with Ireland, for his piano concerto received its first performance at the Promenade Concerts (the Proms) in 1930, with Perkin as soloist and dedicatee.

The concerto is closely and irrevocably linked with this woman. When Ireland knew her, she was very young and beautiful, her youth and talent appealing to the composer, and just as "In a May Morning" is about the whole experience of Michael Rayson and the Guernsey spring, the concerto is about the experience of knowing Helen Perkin. The piano part was designed specifically to suit her small hands, and the main theme of the first movement is a transformation of a motif from one of her compositions, *Phantasy* for string quartet, broadcast earlier that year. Ireland deeply admired her performances of his concerto, describing her playing in almost rapturous terms in letters to Edward Clark. However, again there is no evidence that this friendship was anything other than a purely platonic one, one that came to an abrupt and bitter end. In 1934 Perkin married. Ireland was angered at the marriage, as their relationship had been an intense and possessive one, and the two ceased to communicate. The split caused him considerable torment, an anguish that he expressed at length several years later, although not to Thompson. When Ireland and Perkin did resume contact by letter, it began on cordial terms but became increasingly vitriolic on Ireland's part. Eventually the dedication was removed from the concerto.

Ireland's developing antipathy to Perkin in the late 1940s is mirrored in his letters to Thompson, and from about 1950 onward the intermittent, usually rather brief references to women in the letters are often quite acerbic and disparaging, with women viewed as a breed apart. They are seen as either an irritation or a complication. On reading the works of Alberto Moravia, Ireland found the stories "quite *horrid* in places, where the sensuality of the females is described" (30 Dec. 1952). He frequently expressed his feelings that women were not suited to performing his music, particularly disliking the sound of female voices in church (14 July 1938). In his later years he often came out with statements such as the following: "Experience has taught me that my music is seldom understood by women performers" (15 May 1955) (on hearing that Gina Bachauer was to play the piano concerto at the Proms), and "Very few of my songs are suitable for female voices—and none for a *real* contralto" (Feb. 54).

Ireland never referred to either Miller or Perkin in his letters to Thompson, but he did mention his unfortunate marriage, although never at any length. For a number of years Thompson himself toyed with the idea of marrying. From the outset Ireland advised him against this move, as the letter of 1943 quoted at the opening of this chapter shows. The following year Ireland was equally vociferous in his condemnation of marriage, and again in 1946 he advised against this step. Evidently whatever Thompson had been considering did not come to fruition, as there are no further warnings until ten years later, in 1956. In December of this year Ireland wrote that matrimony is "very easy to get into, but excessively difficult to get out of" (23 Dec. 1956). These counsels continued for the next three years, with Ireland becoming more and more vociferous in his statements: that of May 1958 baldly declaims, "If you cannot see clearly how disastrous it would be (for you or anyone of our temperament) nothing I could say would convince you" (4 May 1958). From December 1959 to July 1960 there are no letters—and then suddenly there is a short note belatedly congratulating Thompson on his approaching marriage (17 July 1960), a marriage that came as a surprise to those who knew Thompson well. This was the last handwritten letter.

Ireland's problematic and disappointing personal relationships and his separation from his family had left him without an heir. It has been suggested that he had a will drawn up in 1932, leaving everything to Arthur Miller, and certainly there is some evidence that this may have been the case.[22] The John Ireland Trust holds a document dating from around 1940–42 and written in the hand of Herbert Brown, Ireland's solicitor; it lists the potential recipients of Ireland's estate and names Miller as the main beneficiary. In 1952 Ireland wrote to Thompson, saying, "[I have] long postponed making a fresh will, which is essential, since the death of my sister. . . . I shall hate the idea of all my papers, letters, etc. passing through the hands of a normal (heterosexual) person" (30 Dec. 1952). On 17 July 1953 Ireland drew up his new will, leaving everything bar a small sum of money to Norah Kirby, whom he had known for only a few years, since 1947. Shortly after this he wrote to Thompson, discussing his will. The empty envelope (postmarked 12 Aug. 1953) that bore this letter survives, accompanied by a tantalizing note from Thompson saying that he chose to destroy a very private letter about Ireland's will, as requested by the composer. Ironically, then, Ireland's fortune and estate were left to a woman. Although Kirby undoubtedly did much for Ireland in his later years, this seems curious. He had two nephews living and had enjoyed good relations with one of them; in addition, there was Arthur Miller, as well as Kenneth Thompson himself. Maybe Ireland chose Kirby because she had cared for him in the later part of his life, when no one else did. Or perhaps Ireland thought that he could rely on Kirby to destroy his most personal and explicit effects. Appropriately, Thompson officiated at Ireland's funeral (figure 10.5).

We therefore have to thank Thompson for his bold decision not to destroy his letters and for choosing to donate correspondence of such intimacy to a public institution. The collection of letters from Ireland to Thompson stands as a unique body of information on the composer. In their openness and through the observations on people and places, they reveal much about his nature. They were his forum for presenting himself, warts and all, and one of the few outlets for discussion of his sexuality in conjunction with his religious beliefs. In their diversity and frankness they also shed light on his music. Thompson must have felt that those who would listen to Ireland's music in the future might benefit from knowing more of his private personality, and this material is a unique way in which we are able to do this.

FIGURE 10.5. From l. to r.: Kenneth Thompson, John Ireland, Norah Kirby (reproduced courtesy of the John Ireland Trust).

NOTES

1. John Longmire, *John Ireland: Portrait of a Friend* (London: John Baker, 1969); Muriel Searle, *John Ireland: The Man and His Music* (Tunbridge Wells, U.K.: Midas, 1979).

2. Reprinted in Stanley Sadie, ed., *The New Grove Dictionary of Music and Musicians*, 29 vols., 2d ed. (London: Macmillan, 2001), 12:568–70.

3. Stephen Banfield, *Sensibility and English Song* (Cambridge: Cambridge University Press, 1985; repr., 1988), 167.

4. Alan Rowlands, "John Ireland: A Significant Composer?" *RCM Magazine*, Summer, 1992, pp. 18–24 and Spring, 1993, pp. 13–19; Barbara Docherty, "The Murdered Self: John Ireland and English Song 1903–12," *Tempo* 171 (Dec. 1989): 18–26; *A Portrait of the Final Years of Sir Arnold Bax*, film, dir. Ken Russell (a Dreamgage Production for LWT in association with RMArts, 1992). This film, written by Russell, includes a fleeting glimpse of Ireland at the cinema, lusting after boys rather than the blond picture-house girl favored by Bax.

5. Humphrey Carpenter, *Benjamin Britten: A Biography* (London: Faber, 1992), 40. Although Carpenter presents anecdotes rather than real supporting evidence, Ireland did go through a period of depression and heavy drinking in the late 1920s.

6. My book *The Music of John Ireland* (Aldershot, U.K.: Ashgate, 2000) includes a chapter on the subject of Ireland and love.

7. Banfield, *Sensibility*, 161.

8. British Library additional manuscripts (Add. MS) 60535–6. Permission to quote from the letters granted jointly by the John Ireland Trust, London, which owns the copyright, and the British Library, which holds the letters.

9. Held at the John Ireland Trust.

10. Ellis Hanson, *Decadence and Catholicism* (Cambridge, Mass.: Harvard University Press, 1997).

11. The other two anthems were *Vexilla regis* (1898) and *Greater Love Hath No Man* (1912).

12. Instead see Richards, *Music of John Ireland,* where I consider Ireland's output within six topics: Anglo-Catholicism, paganism, country, city, love, and war.

13. Forrest Reid, *The Garden God: A Tale of Two Boys* (London: David Nutt, 1905).

14. Forrest Reid, *Uncle Stephen* (London: Faber, 1931; repr., London: GMP, 1988), 121.

15. Ibid., 129.

16. Symonds wrote the lyrics that Ireland set in 1937 in one of his best-known pieces, *These Things Shall Be,* a work of typically confusing messages. Written as a celebration of the coronation of George VI, it includes a quotation of the "Internationale," which then served as the Soviet national anthem. The words ostensibly allude to a future utopia, but there are decided ambiguities in Symonds's references to manhood and youth dwelling in happiness together.

17. Martin Donisthorpe Armstrong, "The Young Bather," *Exodus and Other Poems* (London: Lynwood, 1912), 41–42.

18. Hugo quoted in John Ireland, *The Collected Piano Works,* 5 vols. (London: Stainer and Bell, 1976), 4:28; the translation is my own.

19. In Philip Henderson, *Swinburne: The Portrait of a Poet* (London: Routledge, 1974), 256.

20. Eleanor Farjeon, "Boys' Names," *Over the Garden Wall* (London: Faber, 1933), 91.

21. John Gambril F. Nicholson, "Of Boys' Names," *Love in Earnest* (London: Elliot Stock, 1892), 61–62.

22. Stewart Craggs, *John Ireland: A Catalogue, Discography, and Bibliography* (Oxford: Oxford University Press, 1993), 68.

PART 4

QUEER LISTENING

11 TRISTAN'S WOUNDS

ON HOMOSEXUAL WAGNERIANS
AT THE FIN DE SIÈCLE

MITCHELL MORRIS

In Richard von Krafft-Ebing's *Neue Forschungen auf dem Gebiete der Psychopathia Sexualis* (New investigations in the field of sexual psychopathy), a slim supplement to his vast, influential taxonomy of late nineteenth-century sexual deviation, there is a fragmentary case study of more than passing musical interest. A patient who suffers from *konträre Sexualempfindungen,* or "contrary sexual instincts," makes the following remark while describing his love life and emotional history: "As little as I am interested in politics, so I passionately love music, and am an enthusiastic devotee of Richard Wagner's, which partiality I have noticed most homosexuals have; I find that this music corresponds so precisely to our natures."[1] Krafft-Ebing's patient was in truth one of a much larger crowd, if the composer Alban Berg can be believed. Writing to his fiancée soon after a trip to Bayreuth in 1909, Berg summarized the experience and remarked in passing: "Bayreuth couldn't kill *Parsifal* for me, nor could the ghastly horde of homosexual Wagnerians spoil Wagner."[2] The letters Berg wrote from Bayreuth suggest that he might have been referring to the circle gathered around Wagner's son Siegfried, who was conducting at Bayreuth that year, and whose conduct between the acts of *Parsifal* struck the rather priggish Berg as concentrated on fashion and society at the expense of an appropriate reverence.[3] But Siegfried's active homosexual life, however many acquaintances it may have brought him to compensate for his troubles with the police, cannot be the only thing to have drawn the "ghastly horde" of which Berg complained.[4] A better answer would surely be found in responses like that of Krafft-Ebing's patient: an allegiance to Wagner and his works strong enough to constitute a subculture within a subculture. The Wagnerians, it seems, included a group of listeners who understood their devotion to *der Meister* and his works as a way of making sense of their own transgressive sexual desires and gender identifications.

What shape would this particular Wagnerism have taken, and for what reasons would it have done so? Admittedly something about Wagner's music, and the discourse and institutions surrounding it, makes the idea plausible; by contrast, there is something strange about imagining a homosexual Verdi cult. We might suppose that a homosexual Wagnerian association would have been an international phenomenon, like Bayreuth itself, predominantly composed of men of the aristocracy or the high middle classes. Its members' rarefied socioeconomic positions would have protected the group somewhat from social opprobrium and police persecution. At the same time, however, it must surely have gained strength and an important opportunity to test its formulations and experimental identities in semipublic from the complex, active subcultures of the festival's host country.

Historical circumstances had led to the formation of the first-ever homosexual emancipation movement in Germany, increasingly active from the later 1890s until it was suppressed by the Nazis at the end of the Weimar Republic. This movement, including two central male sociocultural groupings devoted to gay and lesbian rights and sensibilities, developed different rhetorical strategies to counter a strong current of conservative social commentary most apparent in the publications and other activities of the Allgemeine Konferenz der deutschen Sittlichkeitvereine (General Conference of German Moral Societies).[5] Moreover, the German homophile movement exerted considerable influence on emerging theories of gay and lesbian identity in other Western homophile traditions.

On one side was the Wissenschaftlich-humanitäres Komittee (Scientific-Humanitarian Committee], founded by Dr. Magnus Hirschfeld and his associates to bring about the repeal of German penal code §175, which prohibited male homosexual relations. The committee's name clearly indicates its principal interest: to use the prestige of disinterested science, as embodied in advanced and authoritative sexological studies, to counter prejudice and bring about enlightened legal change. Hirschfeld's activities further included the foundation of the Institut für Sexuellewissenschaft (Institute for Sexual Science) in Berlin, along with its important publication, the *Jahrbuch für sexuelle Zwischenstufen* (Yearbook for intermediate sexual types; this ran from 1899 to 1923); Hirschfeld even made an appearance in an early gay rights film, *Anders als die Anderen* (Different from the others).[6] The institute also made common cause with a number of groups active in the women's suffrage movement, or *Frauenbewegung*. As is indicated by the name of their journal, and perhaps their support of the feminist movement, Hirschfeld and his allies adhered to a theory of homosexuality as a gender-transitive phenomenon: that is, gay men and lesbians alike were understood as members of *das dritte Geschlecht* (the third sex), innately intersexed in mind and to at least some extent in body and, because of the unique sensibilities derived from their liminal status, likely to be especially expressive and creative. In addition to publishing scientific and anthropological studies of same-sex activity as it occurred in various geographically discrete instantiations, the *Jahrbuch* also sought articles on historical forebears (mostly great artists but a few political leaders and religious reformers as well).

On the other side were the homosexual-rights activists who participated in the Gemeinschaft des Eigenen (Fellowship of individuals), founded in 1902 by Adolf Brand, Benedikt Friedländer, and others. This group's principal periodical was *Der Eigene* (variously translated as "The special" or "The self-owner"). Although Brand had begun the journal in 1896 to promulgate anarchist politics, by the end of the decade it had been transformed into a completely homophile publication with strong ties to the growing reform movements associated with physical education, nutrition, hiking, and other physical and moral activities. It also promulgated a fervent ideology of masculinity in which the idealization of ancient Greece and German nationalism were conflated as the ne plus ultra of maleness. The focus on this understanding of masculinity usually counterposed itself to the theories offered at Hirschfeld's institute. The writers of *Der Eigene* tended to claim that all people are inherently bisexual, that homosexual feeling among men arises ideally out of a deep spiritual admiration for masculine virtues, and that in consequence genital activity is a mere accessory to the more important task of cultivating deep bonds of friendship between men. The Gemeinschaft des Eigenen was thus less concerned than the institute with the revocation of §175.[7]

Even this brief description of the homosexual emancipation movement in Germany shows that it was complicated by the contradictory overlaps Eve Kosofsky Sedgwick has noted between minoritizing and universalizing definitions of homo- and heterosexuality, between separatist and transitive definitions of gender.[8] Is same-sex desire biological or, as it were, rhetorical? Is a homosexual person to be conceived as an "intermediate sexual type" or as one who expresses a general human tendency that helps weld together the society? Homophile-accented versions of Wagnerism were drawn completely into these contradictory positions, so that the Wagnerian framework became arguably a central means through which sexuality could be constructed and articulated. In the ongoing project from which this chapter is drawn I will describe the process as it operated across a wide spectrum of historical moments, artistic genres and styles, nationalities, and associations; in this chapter, however, I will concentrate on a few of the most striking manifestations of Wagnerian homosexuality in early twentieth-century Germany.

o   o   o

The nineteenth-century stereotypes of homosexual character—the artsy, nervous, effeminate man, for instance—are familiar to everyone and, despite a quarter-century of vigorous disputation, still constitute a kind of folk knowledge about homosexuals. It is not mere historical duration that makes revising this kind of image difficult, for the reigning sexologists who promulgated these stereotypes as keys to the essential nature of homosexuals took them only slightly more seriously than did homosexuals themselves. The writers associated with the Gemeinschaft des Eigenen, which battled the medicalization of homosexuality as fiercely as possible, often conceded a certain amount of ground to the doctors, and the Institute for Sexual Science accepted contemporary medical views of homosexual behavior much more fully. Magnus Hirschfeld, although distrustful of Krafft-Ebing for his view of homosexuality as pathological, depended on the information supplied in the case studies of *Psychopathia sexualis* to argue for the concept of the third sex. Such profiles filled not only the learned treatises but also the literature of the subculture. (See, for instance, Radclyffe Hall's *Well of Loneliness,* in which Stephen Gordon first recognizes her true nature through a reading of *Psychopathia sexualis.*)[9] Even into the 1920s, the notion of exceptional homosexual artistry was promulgated by influential sexologists such as Albert Moll:

> Uranists often distinguish themselves by their passion for music and the other arts. Coffignon has already cited this love for music as one of the peculiarities of the Uranist character. . . . They often possess a remarkable talent for acting. . . . I believe that this talent must be attributed in large measure to the habit of lying which clings to the Uranist during his entire life. I also believe that their ability to place themselves in another situation and enter completely into another role also depends on a certain disposition of the central nervous system as does sexual perversion itself.

Unsurprisingly, Moll argued that this exaggerated empathy cast its feminizing influence further, inducing among other things an intense love for clothes, jewelry, perfume, and so on.[10]

Of course, if one were to look for a nineteenth-century culture hero to match such characterological traits, the hero who appears first and most powerfully is Richard Wagner: voluptuary, moral transgressor, actor-liar, musician. Indeed, many of the criticisms that help define not only the course of Wagner's career but also his posthumous reception contain in hindsight a distinctively gay-centered aura. Consider these remarks by Nietzsche, late in his career, in the context of Dr. Moll's description of "Uranists" (also called "Urnings"): "Was Wagner a musician at all? In any case he was something else to *a much greater degree*—that is to say, an incomparable *histrio,* the greatest mime, the most astounding theatrical genius that the Germans ever had, our *scenic artist par excellence.* . . . As a musician he was no more than what he was as a man: he *became* a musician, he *became* a poet, because the tyrant in him, his actor's genius, drove him to be both."[11] As an actor, Wagner was most convincing playing women's roles, according to several of the singers whom he rehearsed for Bayreuth's opening productions.[12] And there was a famous set of letters Wagner wrote to the Viennese seamstress Berthe Goldwag specifying the precise amounts and colors of expensive satins she should acquire for the various dressing gowns she was to make for him. The letters were eventually acquired by Daniel Spitzer, a Viennese journalist, who published them in 1877 with mocking commentary in the *Neue Freie Presse.* Spitzer prefaced the collection with an out-of-context quotation from *Die Walküre,* act 1, that says it all: "*Wie gleicht er dem Weibe!*" (How like the woman he is!). But even this obvious gibe did not suffice—Spitzer also introduces the letters with further insinuating commentary: "Could [the letters] be vows of friendship to his dear Buelow, messages of love, or were they written to some German maiden or youth? Wagner's personal letters to a German youth are sure to be unusual, we thought, considering his extremely peculiar printed statements on the subject."[13] Wagner's famous taste in apparel was the topic of cartoons as well (figure 11.1).

This set of commentaries suggests a strong set of cross-gender identifications at work in Wagner's character, thus setting him up as a potential Hirschfeldian ally. But Wagner could equally be seen as a precursor of the Gemeinschaft des Eigenen—those writings on German youth that Spitzer was so keen to mention, for instance, are fulsome with Greek idolatry and praise of manly virtue. Moreover, for members of this group, there was above all the matter of Wagner's complicated and intense homosocial relationships.

In 1903 Hanns Fuchs, a turn-of-the-century novelist and homosexual-rights activist, published a study entitled *Richard Wagner und die Homosexualität,* in which he sets out the case for a universalizing, gender-separatist view of

Frou-Frou Wagner.

FIGURE 11.1. Caricature from Daniel Spitzer, "Briefe Wagners an seine Wiener Putz-macherin," *Neue Freie Presse*, 1877.

Wagner. Fuchs begins with a typical "A. L. Rowse" defense, discussing the role of what he termed "spiritual homosexuality" (*geistige Homosexualität*) in the lives of a number of "great men" in history: not only Michelangelo, Shakespeare, Goethe, and August Platen but also, when he comes to talk about music, Jean-Jacques Rousseau, Beethoven, Weber, and others. Fuchs cites texts and historical anecdotes wherever possible, but he also depends on the kind of characterological traits that would have been mentioned by the sexologists. (To the usual list he also adds vegetarianism, which he asserts homosexuals share with other sexually irregular types!) This definition of a homosexual type allows him to move to a consideration of Wagner; Fuchs finds evidence of spiritual homosexuality in Wagner's ancestry (including an uncle who Fuchs claims was probably queer), in various biographical incidents that reveal to Fuchs the deeper truth, and in Wagner's operatic characters, who are understood to embody features of Wagner's sexual and emotional life. But nowhere is spiritual homosexuality more in evidence than in Wagner's relationships with King Ludwig II and with Nietzsche.[14] Fuchs reprints numerous letters from the respective correspondences to make these points.[15]

Wagner's appeal to his fin-de-siècle homosexual audience can be explained by the ways in which they could understand his character. Wagner was not a full-fledged Urning in Fuchs's terms, but he was certainly a spiritual sympathizer. His effeminacy and other marginal characteristics did not stand in the way of his becoming a German institution, however; on the contrary, he made his personality and work into an unparalleled force chiefly by managing to reconstitute a significant segment of German culture and society around him. Fuchs and other writers of the time often seem to be asking by implication whether this Wagnerian strategy could work for homosexuals. The possibility that Wagnerism could provide a template for homosexual political struggle is at least part of the reason the image of Wagner mattered to Hirschfeldians and Brandians alike. If the composer's biography were the sole locus of homophile claims to a Wagnerian legacy, however, then Wagner's appeal as a tutelary figure would have been limited. The music, and the kinds of experiences it underwrote, helped keep composer and works in the midst of a lively contest for interpretive priority.

o   o   o

Wagner's operas are filled to bursting with dissident sexualities, and innumerable nineteenth-century critics repeatedly worried about the resulting moral problems.[16] (Hanns Fuchs, who was not at all worried, was delighted to be able to find homoerotic subcurrents in many characters, not least of whom are King

Mark and all the inhabitants of the Grail castle.)[17] For mainstream critics, however, the difficulties had a way of multiplying. Although incest was the most distressing irregularity to be managed, the sexual danger present in Wagner's work was not only a matter of the onstage characters' actions; many listeners found the music itself, with its heavy sensuality and insistent claims on the attention of the audience, to be equally perverse. Consider, for instance, the famously interrupted love duet in act 2 of *Tristan und Isolde*, where, after building up musical and dramatic tension to the point of delirium, Wagner refuses to resolve. The orgasmic impulses that were finally on the verge of being released slam up against a stony blockage in a frankly sadomasochistic maneuver in which what is most desired is exactly what is (partially) withheld. Many analytical discussions of *Tristan* have been sparked by Wagner's mauling of listener expectations here and elsewhere. Such moments are a species of the sublime and have required methods that themselves have enabled many extraordinarily nuanced and resonant interpretations.[18] Nonetheless, the critical and scholarly need to establish a cognitive framework around these disruptions can blunt us to a simple fact. Wagner's affective design at points such as these can succeed only by claiming total power over its listeners. We must simply surrender to the music's Dionysian flow, or we risk hearing nothing but painful, assaultive noise. The consequences of such a refusal seem to me to be the most important subtext of the famous caricature from *L'Éclipse* in 1869 (figure 11.2). Although the ostensible complaint represented is Wagner's noisiness, the image of violent defloration provides a resonance so crucial as to claim center stage, especially when considered in the light of Wagner's durable association with sexual irregularities. The gender neutrality of the ear merely ups the ante.[19]

The effect of Wagner's music on the listener might have been understood to accord with the inner natures of its homosexual partisans in at least two closely related ways. First, the character and motion of the music underwrote the stage action, thus justifying the actions of dissident and perverse operatic characters who could be proclaimed as ultimately superior role models; second and even more important, the music could be understood as acting directly on the bodies of the listeners, helping them to internalize the appropriate character traits and attitudes. Life could imitate art according to a theory best described as a kind of antinomian Platonism.[20]

It is possible to envision something like this as a development from the philosophical milieu within which Wagner's music established itself. Nietzsche in particular, during his pro-Wagner days, writes in terms that can easily be turned toward the exigencies of homophile apologetics. A particularly

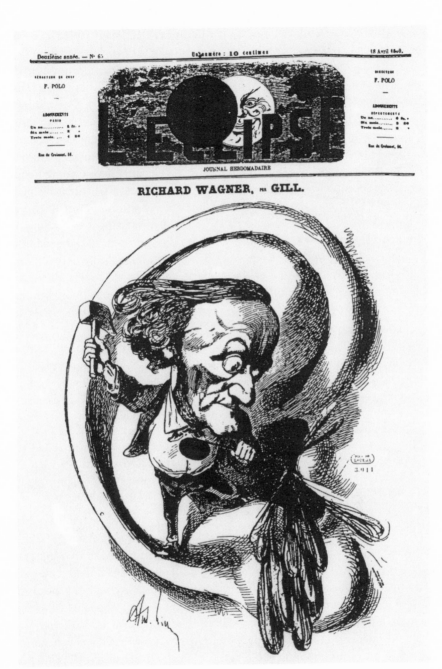

FIGURE 11.2. Caricature from *L'Eclipse,* 18 April 1869.

interesting example of this occurs in the middle of "Richard Wagner in Bayreuth," part 4 of the *Unzeitgemässe Betrachtungen* (Untimely meditations).[21] After offering a series of reflections on the meaning of the first Bayreuth festival, Nietzsche launches into a discussion that departs from Schopenhauer as read through Wagner, as well as from Nietzsche's own interpretation of Wagner in *Die Geburt der Tragödie* (The birth of tragedy), in placing Wagner's musical work at the center of a large-scale project to reclaim those metaphysical and ethical powers of music that had been lost since the ancient Greeks. This reclamation can be understood as a process of synthesis and consequent simplification, and its keystone is an aspect of the sublime that Nietzsche calls the sense of the tragic. Music's crucial role here still seems to arise from its nature as the incarnation of Schopenhauer's *Wille*, leading Nietzsche to declare flatly that the relationship between music and life is "not only that of one kind of language to another kind of language[;] it is also the relationship between the perfect world of sound and the totality of the world of sight."[22] The dissociation of these things in the modern world critically damages both, but this harm can be repaired through the actions of a particular kind of person:

> In this world of forms and desired misunderstanding there now appear souls filled with music—to what purpose? In noble honesty, in a passion that is suprapersonal, they move to a grand, free rhythm, they glow with the mighty tranquil fire of the music that wells up out of inexhaustible depths within them— all this to what purpose?
>
> Through these souls music reaches out to its corresponding necessary shape in the world of the visible, that is to say to *gymnastics:* in its search for this it becomes judge over the whole visible world of the present. This is Wagner's second answer to the question as to what significance music can have in this age. Help me, he cries to all who can hear, help me to rediscover that culture whose existence my music, as the rediscovered language of true feeling, prophesies; reflect that the soul of music now wants to create for itself a body, that it seeks its path through all of you to visibility in movement, deed, structure, and morality![23]

Although Nietzsche's historical and metaphysical justification of Wagner's work is exceedingly complex and abstract, it can easily be condensed into an argument that could merge with the versions of popular homophile Platonism found in nineteenth-century Europe. According to such points of view, the musical bodies of which Nietzsche speaks with respect to Wagnerian situations begin to be located not only in the physiques of the actual singers but also in fantasy figures projected on some kind of "image track" accompanying the music. This type of Wagner interpretation in its specifically homophile inflections helped lead to the extensive body worship found in expensive Wagnerian art but even more in varieties of commercial art (figure 11.3), all the way down to the steamy sword-and-sorcery comic-book illustrations of artists such as Frank Frazetta or Boris Vallejo.[24] The body consciousness I have described is undoubtably related to Wagner's dramaturgy, which often displays a liking for the suffering, preferably wounded male body on display (most obviously Tristan and Amfortas but also, to some extent, Wotan, Siegmund, and Siegfried, whether alive or dead), but it is related as well to Wagner's fantastic ability to manipulate the ebb and flow of musical desire. The music's effect on the body apparently intensified the stage action to an unbearable extent, whatever gestural language dominated the production. Cosima Wagner's productions at Bayreuth were notoriously stylized; especially in the case of *Tristan,* her taste for statuesque poses helped move the focus of the drama far away from physical action toward nearly pure *innigkeit* (interiority).[25] But such stasis also meant that small gestures counted enormously; if Tristan, say, should follow Wagner's directions and suddenly rip off his bandage to reveal his bare chest, the effect would be enormous.[26]

This can all be understood as a way of imagining subjectivity as constituted primarily through male suffering. To be sure, Wagner's taste for men in pain can seem to some writers terribly Christian—if the display of the crucified Jesus does not always provide the direct model for the treatment of Wagnerian heroes, then surely they are built around the type of erotically appealing saints such as Sebastian—and to that extent not altogether novel. Nevertheless, the prima donna's usual function was not typically taken over by a man.[27] It is possible, furthermore, that this complicated interweaving of religious and erotic sentiment contributes to the evolving antipathy Nietzsche had begun to feel toward his greatest mentor by 1876. Nietzsche welcomed men's agonistic self-constitution by force of will, understanding this as a remedy for the ills caused by Christianity. But Wagner's work often required Christianity as a ghostly but nonetheless real presence. Nietzsche found this unbearable for several reasons, but one of the most powerful causes of his revulsion was his awareness of the attraction he found in Wagner's glorification of suffering. The late work *Nietzsche contra Wagner* contains passages in which Nietzsche means to condemn Wagner's work by calling him "a miniaturist" and presenting the music as springing almost purely from human abjection. In Nietzsche's terms, particularly during his earlier "heroic" period, it would be healthy to despise such unaristocratic music as the work of priestcraft in the service of weakness. Even as Nietzsche sets out such an analysis, however, he seems unwilling to forsake a kind of backhanded admiration, and his critique is unbalanced by its own eulogistic undertones. Moreover, after the experience of symbolist and

Figure 11.3. Caricature from *Le Don Quichotte*, September 1891.

Decadent writers and artists, it becomes close to impossible to hear Nietzsche's criticisms as anything other than perversely positive. I will quote a passage at length for the sake of its Wagnerian sense of extension:

> Here is a musician who is a greater master than anyone else in the discovering of tones, peculiar to suffering, oppressed, and tormented souls, who can endow even dumb misery with speech. Nobody can approach him in the colors of late autumn, in the indescribably touching joy of a last, a very last, and all too short gladness; he knows of a chord which expresses those secret and weird midnight hours of the soul, when cause and effect seem to have fallen asunder, and at every moment something may spring out of nonentity. He is happiest of all when creating from out of the nethermost depths of human happiness, and, so to speak, from out of man's empty bumper, in which the bitterest and most repulsive drops have mingled with the sweetest for good or evil at last. He knows that weary shuffling along of the soul which is no longer able either to spring or to fly, nay, which is no longer able to walk; he has the modest glance of concealed suffering, of understanding without comfort, of leave-taking without word or sign; verily as the Orpheus of all secret misery he is greater than anyone, and many a thing was introduced into his art for the first time by him, which hitherto had not been given expression, had not even been thought worthy of art— the cynical revolts, for instance, of which only the greatest sufferer is capable, also many a small and quite microscopical feature of the soul, as it were the scales of its amphibious nature—yes indeed, he is the master of everything very small.[28]

That is to say, Wagner was the master of the art of coming out, understood in this context as the process of finding words for what hurts. (And coming out acquires, as I have indicated, a distinctly Decadent quality—this passage might have been written by a German Huysmans.) But mobilizing previously silent pain is not simply a spectacle as in the film *Philadelphia,* feeding listeners with sentimental approbation at the expense of those sufferers on stage; on the contrary, this pain could empower the sufferers who were now noisy with discourse. If there is no immediate cure for suffering, why not turn it to one's own uses? Many of the homosexual identities forming themselves at the fin de siècle could not help but employ such a potent tool as suffering, such an effective solvent as Wagner, to consolidate their senses of individuality further. Tristan or Amfortas had already provided a pattern for homosexual subjectivity.

o   o   o

That this could be so is apparent in a 1909 novel by Hanns Fuchs, *Eros zwischen euch und uns* (Eros between you and us), which tells the story of Georg von Brenckendorff, an army officer of noble family whose homosexuality is a source of suffering, not because he has moral qualms about his erotic and affectional status, but because his irregular desire leads to a terrible lack of fit between his emotional life and the cold incomprehension of the world. On the one hand, the novel seems to have an apologetic function, seeking to convince readers who might be straight that the love separating "them and us" is a worthy thing deserving sympathy rather than condemnation; on the other hand, it seems designed to advocate a particular style of homosexuality, one based on equal parts of Wagnerism and suffering, to the extent that those things can be distinguished. I should note, however, that despite Fuchs's evident desire that this subjectivity be taken to be universalizing and male separatist, it mirrors the complexities of its partially Wagnerian origin by sliding on occasion into the minoritizing, gender-transitive world it works so hard to avoid. In general, the prose style is rather overheated, aimed at a general public and all the more interesting for that reason. (Its interest and its unfamiliarity lead me to devote a considerable amount of space to it.) But I think that the book's aesthetic problems derive as well from its dependence on Wagner: Fuchs aims at Wagnerian suffering but must leave the necessary, all-too-necessary soundtrack to his readers' imaginations; the prose, however, with its melodramatically obsessive unhappiness, is unbearable without the mediation of Wagner's music.

The officer's miseries are set out from the very beginning of the novel: Georg is on an extended leave from the service to recover from a nervous breakdown. Early on the novel portrays the crisis as stemming from a deep unhappiness with his occupation; at one point he flatly states that he has ended up a lieutenant by default, because all he knows otherwise is how to play the piano. But the stigmata of his real affliction begin to multiply rapidly. Georg has used his time to travel to Italy, visiting friends—"a totally international group . . . mostly aristocrats and artists"—in Rome and Florence.[29] He plans to conclude his journey with a short trip to Venice, although a Russian prince whom he meets in Florence (and who, as the novel later makes clear, is a member of the third sex) objects that Venice is only for the sad and tired: "It's like the last act of *Tristan*, my dear—pain, nothing but pain" (8). When Georg arrives in Venice, the prince's remark carries over to a visit to Wagner's *Sterbehaus* (death site), conveyed by a handsome young gondolier named Luigi. (All of this happens, portentously enough, during Holy Week.)

The heavy emphasis on sadness and death is entirely appropriate to the portrait we are offered of Georg's internal world, which is overwhelmingly centered on loneliness, alienation, and Wagner. Every stage of his journey back to assume his army post seems to provide him with another opportunity to reflect on his suffering. Even his reunion at the post with Fritz Wendelin, an old friend from his youth, fails to offer him any solace: Fritz, an aspiring composer, tells Georg that he has received critical attention for a symphony he had written and that the army is sending him to Berlin to study composition (!). When Fritz leaves, Georg is left in solitude. But finally a Wagnerian destiny intervenes. Fritz sends Georg a letter from Berlin, describing in glowing terms a performance of *Tristan* he has seen. He finds his thoughts on Georg, however:

> "In the middle of the second act I had to think of you, and I really wished you were here. I believe if you had been here, everything would have been even more beautiful."
>
> Georg had thought the same way. When he had heard *Tristan* in Munich, in the beautiful house in which poor King Ludwig had had this work performed for himself alone, he had pictured to himself how glorious it must be to be able to enjoy the work without interruption. But he could not be alone with such trembling. O no! A beloved person, a good friend must be there, with whom he could share the happiness of such hours. (90)

From thoughts of *Tristan* Georg turns back to his near-omnipresent thoughts of loneliness and alienation. He reads on and finds that Fritz has invited him to Berlin to see, if not the entire *Ring* cycle, at least *Siegfried*—Fritz would love to share the experience of Brünnhilde's awakening with him. As Georg takes up pen to accept Fritz's invitation, however, he suddenly realizes that he cannot go to *Siegfried*, because his friendship with Fritz is simply not intimate enough to bear the musical experience. Filled with conflicting emotions, Georg goes over to the piano, where the score of *Tristan* sits.

> Without thinking, he began to play. He had arrived at the song satirizing Morold. Now he proceeded. He was always inflamed by the great scene between the two women. Kurwenal came to announce Tristan. Isolde answered: the melody reared up in magnificent defiance. Then again the feverish dialogue of the two women.
>
> A little knock at the window and a voice.
>
> "Is anybody in there?"
>
> That's Gasberg, Lieutenant Gasberg.
>
> He doesn't interrupt his playing and he doesn't look away.
>
> "Yes, the door is open."
>
> Kurwenal reported to the hero. Isolde: "Lord Tristan may draw nigh."
>
> And now the *Blickmotiv*. How it shrieks in maddest pain! How it protests!
>
> And now the door opposite the grand piano opens, and an unknown, beautiful man stands at the threshold. Next to him, Gasberg's smiling, youthful face.
>
> "I've brought Wandelsloh along."

And again the *Blickmotiv.*
And the two pairs of eyes that dive deep into one another. . . . (92–93)

However much his interior dialogue may emphasize a kind of male separatist ideal of brotherhood in the earlier pages of the novel, Georg's meditations at the piano have raised up the specter of gender-transitive identification. Georg has temporarily become Isolde and will occupy that role at least subliminally for the rest of the novel. The man who at this moment plays Tristan, Hans Wandelsloh (another German army officer of noble family), turns out to be the love of Georg's life; significantly enough, the conversation that follows their fateful introduction is almost entirely about Wagner. In the days that follow, the friendship deepens. Georg plays Wagner all through the night while Hans listens in rapture. It happens that the family Wandelsloh had planned a summer trip to Bayreuth, but Hans's sister must instead take their mother to Karlsbad for her health. Georg was also planning a trip to Bayreuth, so the two end up going to the festival together.

This Wagnerian romance is interrupted, however, by the rude return of the world and its social pressures. An army captain accused of *sittliche Verfehlungen* (moral lapses—a euphemism for sex crimes) flees to Holland, and the resulting scandal, accompanied by more desertions and a few suicides, sends Georg into a brief nervous relapse.[30] Meanwhile Hans is sent away on duty; by the time he returns, Georg is caught up in his own social obligations. The two finally become free to journey to Bayreuth, however, with an initial trip to Munich to see Ludwig's grave, Wagner's house, and the Hoftheater. No sooner has Georg begun to stroll around Bayreuth than he runs into the Russian prince and his companion, whom Georg had last seen in Florence (on page 8). The two quiz Georg about his life and invite him to pay them a visit: lots of their acquaintances will be coming to Bayreuth from Paris, Rome, Vienna . . . They also explain that they will not be going to *Das Rheingold* but will start at *Die Walküre;* and in any case, they are more interested in *Parsifal* than anything else.

The superficial chatter of the Russian prince and his companion heightens the intensely sacral character of the love between Georg and Hans and makes explicit that love's grounding in music. True Wagnerians, they are planning to see everything. Moreover, not only do they experience the bliss of their idol's work in performance; they make the operas the basis for extensive (and usefully protohomophile) discussion. Consider part of the conversation that takes place on the rest day between *Die Walküre* and *Siegfried;* a meditation on Siegmund and Sieglinde leads the apparently straight Hans to a furious antinomian declaration.

"What is the Norm? What everybody does. Why is the Norm? Exactly because everybody does it! A fine point of view! Is it also a Norm to cheer all of the time just because everybody else does? Or to believe in some ultimate future state? 'Everybody' does that, too. Oh, these everybodies and everymen! But is it such a great thing to appeal to them? And it naturally flatters the crowd, always taught differently, whenever they see themselves suddenly made into an authority."

"You place the rights of the individual before the rights of the crowd?"

"Yes and no. It is a question of who the individual is. The person who has come to consciousness, the cultured person, if you will, must have the right to develop his personality." (180–81)

The discussion inevitably proceeds to Plato's *Symposium* and eventually to an ever-intensifying declaration of true friendship between Hans and Georg.

All this nobility finds its contrast in the inverts, represented chiefly by the Russian prince, who dominates the novel's next scene. He invites Georg to his house for a party and greets him draped in Indian silk, an effeminate outfit that is "a fantastic mixture of a nightshirt and a kimono" (188). The other guests are effete and upper class, richly bejeweled, perfumed, and powdered, and for the most part equally orientalesque. They smoke only cigarettes (at that time an effete choice for a man), and their attitude toward Wagner and Bayreuth favors decoration and sociability over elevated thoughts:

> A tall, very slim man with wonderful hands showed off a fine piece of embroidery he had made: Parsifal stood before Kundry, who had spread out both arms in longing.
>
> The young artist explained the technique of the work. The lids of his almond-shaped eyes never lifted completely. He spoke with a tired and drawling voice.
>
> "I have made this piece for my friend in Odessa. His birthday is in three weeks, and he doesn't want anything that isn't handmade." . . .
>
> "How long did you work on it, Blanche?"
>
> "Three months, my dear." (190–91)

Not only is the party graced with drag names such as "Blanche"; eventually, various guests slip into an adjoining room to change into dresses. The final condemnation of the inverts comes when the Russian prince mentions in passing that he knew Oscar Wilde. Georg is excited by this, since he thinks highly of Wilde's courage in remaining in London for trial; the prince, however, shows himself to be shallow and deficient in political consciousness when he scoffs at the value of "a martyr's crown" (196–97). As a result Georg returns to Hans thoroughly discouraged and in need of a few glasses of beer and the purer Wagnerism he shares with his friend.

At last the Bayreuth season comes round to *Tristan*. Georg is captivated by the sound of the opera in its full orchestral incarnation as he sits hand in hand with Hans, leaning slightly against him (201). As the opera progresses, his identifications pass from the Isolde of act 1 over to the wounded, lonely Tristan of act 3, and at every point his previous miseries are transformed by his attraction to the notion of love-death. What he finds appealing in opera will in fact be his in life, for the relationship with Hans naturally cannot last. Following the death of his mother, who has been the chief advocate of heterosexual conformity in the novel, the heartbroken Georg goes off to attend to family matters. At this point it may seem as if he will finally be free to pursue his friendship with Hans, but the catastrophe now arrives. Hans, on a visit to his sister, meets one of her old friends, falls in love, and proposes. Georg hears rumors of this but cannot credit them; when Hans writes him with the news, however, Georg's always precarious health shatters once and for all. He takes another extended leave and travels Italy again, coming with his last strength to Munich. What's wrong with him? As a doctor tells his host, yet another homosexual nobleman:

> "He wants to die, Prince. His will is unconquerably resistant to all techniques."
> "I think you're right . . ."
> "There might be one thing . . ."
> "Tell me!"
> "If he could see his friend again. He is with him in his thoughts continuously. That would bring healing—or swift death." (255–56)

Of course, poor ignorant Hans comes to visit, alarmed that his good friend Georg is so ill. Of course, the mere sight of him sends Georg spiraling further downward. After a deeply felt deathbed speech—"cling to your wife . . . [;] in her womb is the future," and so on ad nauseam—Georg dies. As he breathes his last, Hans leans over the bed and kisses him on the lips "*noch einmal*" (once more). In fact, however, this is the first mention of the intimacies of kissing, which apparently have been occurring throughout the novel, and it is only the second description of any physical contact. Only death, it seems, is an event expensive/expansive enough to allow Fuchs to show his heroes touching.

Despite all these melancholy plot twists, it is clear that Fuchs means for us to enjoy our vicarious participation in Georg's suffering. His death is a triumph all the more spicy because it is accompanied by the sharp promise of physical gratification without actually receiving it. *Tristan*'s moments of "rapturous unfulfillment," as Lawrence Kramer has called them, seem to have provided Fuchs's hero with his favorite way of (almost) getting off, and it's a kinky twist he means to teach all his readers.

Plainly the ecstasies of Fuchs's heroes would not have been possible without the powerful ideological support of the cult of manhood and "spiritual homosexuality" that had grown up in the circles that patronized *Der Eigene*. Since the emotional ties between men were held always to take precedence over any vulgar bodily contact, representing a physical relationship was totally unnecessary. It is certain that for Hirschfeld and his *Zwischenstufen*, by contrast, the question of bodies and their characteristics was always present and in need of serious consideration. There were two possible Wagners, one for each framework.

Of course, the two schools of thought I have pictured as struggling over Wagner's legacy could not be separated from each other completely, just as in the image and work of Wagner himself the incoherences of minoritizing/universalizing and gender-separatist/gender-transitive notions of sexual identity are thoroughly mixed. But apparently for some, separating the camps was not all that difficult; when the Nazis came to power, Wagner's distressing irregularities of sexuality and gender were hidden by a normalizing reinterpretation of his works driven by musicians and cultural critics, by the government's praise of his German nationalism and virulent anti-Semitism, and by the enthusiastic collaboration of his widow, his children, and the institution of Bayreuth in creating an idealized composerly portrait. Hirschfeld was forced to flee for his life, and the Institut für Sexuellewissenschaft's library, with its priceless collection of materials, was burned to the ground. Friedländer and his allies were not persecuted. They tended to marry and become youth counselors and *Wandervogel* leaders. They were safe as long as their spirits were manly and their bodies didn't matter.

NOTES

This chapter is part of an ongoing study entitled "Wagnerian Homosexualities, 1880–1920." The initial version was written for the conference "Representations of Gender and Sexuality in Opera," held at SUNY-Stony Brook in September 1995. Many thanks to Katrin Sieg, Robert Fink, Susan McClary, and Robert Tobin for their suggestions and support.

1. Quoted in Hanns Fuchs, *Wagner und die Homosexualität* (Wagner and homosexuality) (Berlin: H. Barsdorf, 1903), 129.

2. Alban Berg, *Letters to His Wife*, ed., trans., and ann. Bernard Grun (London: Faber and Faber, 1971), 90.

3. Berg, *Letters*, 85–86.

4. Siegfried Wagner's homosexuality, while not uncommonly acknowledged in the literature, clearly deserves much more research.

5. These societies, incidentally, concerned themselves with a predictable congeries

of issues surrounding a perceived breakdown of traditional gender roles and attendant sexual license. See John C. Fout, "Sexual Politics in Wilhelmine Germany: The Male Gender Crisis, Moral Purity, and Homophobia," in *Forbidden History: The State, Society, and the Regulation of Sexuality in Modern Europe*, ed. John C. Fout (Chicago: University of Chicago Press, 1992), 274–76.

6. See especially John Lauritsen and David Thorstad, *The Early Homosexual Rights Movement (1864–1935)* (New York: Times Change, 1974); and James D. Steakley, *The Homosexual Emancipation Movement in Germany* (New York: Arno, 1975).

7. The best historical account of the Gemeinschaft des Eigenen, along with a number of translated primary sources, appears in *Homosexuality and Male Bonding in Pre-Nazi Germany*, ed. and intro. Harry Oosterhuis, trans. Hubert Kennedy, special issue of *The Journal of Homosexuality* 22, nos. 1–2 (1991).

8. See Eve Kosofsky Sedgwick, *Epistemology of the Closet* (Berkeley: University of California Press, 1990), esp. 88–90.

9. Radclyffe Hall, *The Well of Loneliness* (London: Jonathan Cape, 1928), 207.

10. Albert Moll, *Perversions of the Sex Instinct: A Study of Sexual Inversion Based on Clinical Data and Official Documents,* trans. Maurice Popkin (Newark: Julian, 1931), 65–79.

11. Friedrich Nietzsche, *The Case of Wagner,* trans. Anthony M. Ludovici (London: T. N. Foulis, 1911), 23.

12. See also Joseph Horowitz, *Wagner Nights: An American History* (Berkeley: University of California Press, 1994), 221.

13. Daniel Spitzer, ed., *Richard Wagner and the Seamstress: First Publication in the English Language of a Collection of Letters,* trans. Sophie Prombaum (New York: Frederick Ungar, 1941), 17.

14. Incidentally, the Wagner-Ludwig connection provides much more material than I can present here. A minor example of this would be a novel by Catulle Mendès, *Le Roi vierge,* which parodies the relationship between Wagner and Ludwig.

15. Reprinted Wagner-Ludwig letters also show up in the *Jahrbuch.*

16. See also Frederic Spotts, *Bayreuth: A History of the Wagner Festival* (New Haven, Conn.: Yale University Press, 1994), 73.

17. On Mark's relationship to Tristan, Fuchs may know something about the medieval sources. See Judith Peraino, "Courtly Obsessions: Music and Masculine Identity in Gottfried von Strassburg's Tristan," *repercussions* 4, no. 2 (Fall 1995): 59–85. Richard Mohr makes a similar argument about *Parsifal* in "'Knights, Young Men, Boys': Masculine Worlds and Democratic Values," *Gay Ideas: Outing and Other Controversies* (Boston: Beacon, 1992), 129–218.

18. On the question of the sublime and musical interpretation, see Mitchell B. Morris, "Musical Eroticism and the Transcendent Strain: The Works of Alexander Skryabin, 1898–1908" (Ph.D. diss., University of California at Berkeley, 1998).

19. In response to this essay, several scholars have pointed out that this particular ear is reminiscent of a vulva. Nevertheless, it remains relatively ungendered, and perhaps this gender-slippage heightens the anxiety underwriting the cartoon's humor.

20. I say "antinomian" here to emphasize the disorderly nature of Wagnerian protagonists. Platonism, of course, already had a long and influential role in the justification of same-sex affections, and this nineteenth-century version diverged from the Platonic homophile tradition only slightly. In the contexts I am discussing here, a significant role might have been played by Schopenhauer's startling defense of same-sex relations in the appendix to "The Metaphysics of Sexual Love," one of the supplements to the fourth book of *The World as Will and Representation*.

21. This section of the *Betrachtungen* was published in 1876, approximately a year before the breach between Nietzsche and Wagner became apparent. Some scholars have argued that features of the text demonstrate that Nietzsche was already troubled by philosophical, musical, and characterological aspects of his mentor, but any reservations Nietzsche may have had at the time tend to vanish so far beneath his panegyric as to make such arguments doubtful.

22. Friedrich Nietzsche, "Richard Wagner in Bayreuth," *Untimely Meditations*, trans. R. J. Hollingdale, intro. J. P. Stern (Cambridge: Cambridge University Press, 1983), 215.

23. Ibid., 216–17.

24. I describe the historical development of this comic-book Wagnerism in a paper in preparation entitled "Conan the Wagnerian."

25. Spotts, *Bayreuth*, 96.

26. In fact the effect was enormous on at least one occasion. Albert Niemann performed *Tristan* in New York and caused a sensation: "When, in Act 3, he tore the bandage from his bloody wound, it was too much. Krehbiel wrote: 'An experienced actress who sat . . . at my elbow grew faint and almost swooned. . . . [Niemann] never again ventured to expose the wound in his breast, though the act is justified, if not demanded, by the text'" (Horowitz, *Wagner Nights*, 119 [quoting Henry Krehbiel, *Chapters of Opera*]).

27. See Sedgwick, *Epistemology*, 140–48.

28. Friedrich Nietzsche, *Nietzsche contra Wagner*, trans. Anthony M. Ludovici (London: T. N. Foulis, 1911), 57–58.

29. Hanns Fuchs, *Eros zwischen euch und uns* (Berlin, 1909), 7. Further page references will be given parenthetically in the text. All translations from the novel are mine.

30. There are deliberate echoes here of a set of scandals at the beginning of the century in which important public figures and close associates of Kaiser Wilhelm II were exposed as homosexuals. The controversies began with the outing of the wealthy industrialist Alfred Krupp and culminated in the Eulenburg affair, which revealed extensive homosexual activity among many of the Kaiser's closest military and diplomatic advisors. The scandals disturbed German politics from 1902 to 1907 and at one time or another involved nearly every important public figure concerned with homosexual rights.

12 WHEN SUBJECTS DON'T COME OUT

SHERRIE TUCKER

Let's say you're a feminist researcher working on a women's music history project that involves interviewing living sources. You are committed to an analytical approach that takes gender to be constructed, historically contingent, and inextricably intersected by other social categories such as race, class, and sexuality. You are sensitive to, and do not wish to reproduce, the all-too-common tendency for historical work on gender to be short on sexuality and historical work on sexuality to be short on gender.[1] For the sake of argument, let's just say your topic is all-woman big bands during World War II. You conduct oral histories with women musicians who played in these jazz and swing aggregations (called "all-girl" bands in those days), women who bent the gender expectations of their audiences in numerous ways.

The women you interview played instruments associated with men: trumpets, saxophones, trombones, and drums. In addition, they developed musical skills associated with men: improvisation, fat timbres, loud volumes, and hot styles. They went on the road in homosocial groupings, carried union cards, drew professional wages, and participated in jam sessions, all at a time when embodying the image of "ideal womanhood" would have meant playing the "sweetheart waiting at home"—writing letters to soldiers, planting a Victory garden, and perhaps taking a defense job—but assuredly not taking a hot ride chorus on a tenor sax. Yet the women you interview did not just wistfully sit by their Philco radios, gazing at a photo of GI Joe to a Glenn Miller pulse, nor did their musical citizenship stop at loaning their bodies and smiles to the local USO club as patriotic dance partners for the troops. No, the women you interview stood together on bandstands, producing the energetic jump tunes, big-band boogie-woogie numbers, blues, and sweet romantic ballads to which other people danced. Some of these women had been professional musicians before the war, many playing in all-woman bands in the 1930s and even the 1920s. In the 1940s, however, they helped to fill the wartime demand for dance music and the band shortage caused by the draft vulnerability of male musicians. Others had high-school band training and welcomed the opportunity to make some money, travel, experience a degree of independence, boost the morale of citizens and soldiers, or establish themselves in musical careers that many hoped to continue when the war ended.

The women you interview packed up their horns and took to the road in what, for the most part, were racially segregated all-female bands, operating on either black or white performance circuits. After sleepless nights on buses they ascended bandstands in dance halls, tobacco barns, quonset huts, and make-shift outdoor stages where, decked out in high heels, gowns, and hairdos, they blasted out the hits of the day popularized by male bands such as those of Jimmie Lunceford, Count Basie, and Harry James. Women's bands rarely recorded, yet they barnstormed ballrooms, theaters, and military camps coast to coast, as men's bands did, often confounding, titillating, and astounding the music reviewers. Favorable reviews were usually not framed in terms of musical excellence; rather, they were crafted along the lines of ubiquitous amazement that women could play at all. Language in the trade publications indicates that all-woman bands challenged common notions of both musicians and women. Women's bands were advertised as sex-spectacles: "sultry sirens of swing," "lovely loreleis of rhythm,"[2] or (my own personal favorite) "gingervating, glamorous gorgeous gals."[3] At the same time, skilled women musicians were described as cross-dressers of sorts: "the female Louis Armstrong" or "a Gene Krupa in girls' clothes."[4] No matter which way the hyperbole blew, women musicians did not have the option of being received as musicians who happened to be women. In both favorable and unfavorable press, they were portrayed as imitation musicians and as alternative (sexually excessive or freakish) women. As a feminist historian, your motives are worlds apart from those of the alliterative wordsmiths of the 1940s (you assume these women were competent musicians, for starters). Nonetheless, because you are committed to recovering lost histories and incorporating sexuality as a salient category of analysis, you, too, begin to wonder: *how else might these women be nontraditional?*

During the interview process, in fact, you begin to notice that many of these women musicians continue to live with another woman musician whom they met during their band careers. Someone else answers the phone, and you recognize her name as that of yet another drummer or tenor star from a band that folded fifty years ago. Ah, you think, all-woman bands, of course! Perhaps these all-female environments provided safe havens for lesbians in the 1940s (and earlier, perhaps, since there were many all-woman bands in the 1920s and 1930s as well), a way to earn a living, to meet one another, and to form communities. Perhaps for some women they served as sites for same-sex romantic/sexual exploration, as Allan Berube and Leisa D. Meyer have found the military to have been during World War II.[5] John D'Emilio observes:

> [World War II] severely disrupted traditional patterns of gender relations and sexuality, and temporarily created a new erotic situation conducive to homosexual expression. It plucked millions of young men and women, whose sexual identities were just forming, out of their homes, out of towns and small cities, out of the heterosexual environment of the family, and dropped them into sex-segregated situations—as GIs, as WACs and WAVEs, in same-sex rooming houses for women workers who relocated to seek employment.
>
> The war freed millions of men and women from the settings where heterosexuality was normally imposed. For men and women already gay, it provided an opportunity to meet people like themselves. Others could become gay because of the temporary freedom to explore sexuality that the war provided.[6]

Could all-woman bands have provided social spaces for some women musicians to explore new sexual freedom and identities during this time of relative mobility and loosened gender and sex roles and rules? The field appears rich in historical opportunities for exploring sexually nontraditional women musicians' lives.

Only there's one hitch. No one "comes out." You conduct dozens of interviews. The women musicians to whom you talk are happy to discuss their nontraditional careers and explain how they managed to achieve and maintain identities as jazz and swing musicians; they talk about various obstacles that hounded them throughout their years on the road in all-woman bands and the survival strategies they developed to deal with them; African American women describe the difficulties of traveling and performing in the Jim Crow south (sometimes in bands that broke the color line by hiring one or two white women); and women of all races talk about the burden of proving they could "really play," a job requirement that most attribute to sexism. But sexuality—any form that fails to rate the Ozzie and Harriet seal of approval—turns out to be a volatile, unwelcome subject. In fact, interviewees appear to be on guard about the likelihood that questions about nontraditional sexuality will come up and are ready to head them off at the pass before you even ask. Some narrators agree to be interviewed under the condition that only musical questions will be asked, not "personal" ones. Other interviewees punctuate their stories with disclaimers such as "other all-girl bands were wild, but the girls in our band were good all-American girls—nobody smoke or drank."

Nearly one hundred interviews later, subjects continue to speak candidly about sexism, racism, work and travel conditions, their families' feelings about their careers, hardships and opportunities on the road, methods of converting skeptical audiences and reviewers, their means of acquiring musical expertise, the way they got their jobs, and their evaluations of their band experiences.

But no one comes out.

Well, that isn't entirely true. A number of women come out as straight, including some of the women who live with another woman. Many explain why they never married, and you haven't even asked. An alarming number of women musicians out other women musicians—"So and so is a lesbian"—and then quickly add, "But don't tell her I told you and don't write about it." In numberless indirect ways, you are the recipient of fuzzy hints (and firm protestations) of lesbian existence, traces of homophobia (narrator homophobia? the historical presence of public homophobia reflected in narrators' impulses to deflect the topic of nontraditional sexualities before it comes up?), and abundant between-the-lines clues about the dangers of nontraditional gender roles, but no one comes out. No one offers direct, personal, authorized testimony about lesbian existence in the all-woman bands. Sexuality is topic and nontopic, messily present and urgently denied. You are left with too much and nothing at the same time. You contemplate your hundreds of pages of transcripts and notes and find nothing about nontraditional sexuality that you can ethically write. Not one of your occupationally nontraditional (and proud of it) female big-band narrators outs herself as a sexually nontraditional woman.

Which brings me to the "title cut," so to speak, my guiding question, the theme song to my eight years of research on the "hypothetical" topic just delineated: what do you do when subjects don't come out? That is, what do you do when the topic or subject of sexuality doesn't surface or when coy openings you, a conscientious researcher, have engineered fail to result in at least some of the interview subjects coming out of the closet? What do you do when you enter the project with the conviction that your project will succeed to the extent that a certain percentage of the narratives you collect will be from out lesbians and you will be able to write them into jazz history, and then you leave reeling with dilemmas, not the least of which is: did anyone come out? What are the signs? You find yourself asking whether you are so time- and culture-bound that you are unable to recognize and appreciate nontraditional sexual identities that deviate from your own expectations. And what about all those retracted statements ("Don't write about that")? I mean, *what do you do?*

Do you ignore sexuality and allow the heterosexist presumption that everyone is straight to shape the way your feminist history is read? Do you pry and risk losing contacts with a relatively small group of living artists on whom you depend for information? Do you take third-party outings ("So-and-so is a lesbian, but don't tell her I told you") as reliable evidence, and if so, evidence of what? Lesbian existence? Homophobia? The powerful contours of the closet in the 1940s? Do you attempt to read and interpret social codes across differ-ence? In my case this means cross-generationally, and often cross-culturally—a white middle-class woman who attended high school in the early 1970s (think antiwar movement, second-wave women's movement, gay liberation move-ment) interviewing African American and white women jazz musicians whose young adulthoods occurred during World War II. Do you gingerly describe relationships in purposefully ambiguous terms? Do you conclude that sexu-ality must not have been that important an aspect of women musicians' lives? Or do you simply wait in the closet wings for someone to come out confidently and perceptibly? And *then* what do you do? Foreground the words of that long-awaited out narrator as the voice of lesbian jazz America in everything you write, as if the disclaimers, betrayals, silences, and other complicating factors of other interviews do not also speak of sexuality?

Although this chapter does not present answers, it will, I hope, raise ethi-cal questions, suggest theoretical maneuvers, and invite dialogue.[7] By reliving some of the twists and turns of my own interviews with women musicians, I hope to represent a kind of complexity and flexibility to theorizing sexuality in musical discourses that may not always be so obstinately unavoidable when we do so without living sources: when we speculate about deceased historical figures and their work, for instance, or when we bypass the lives of composers and musicians altogether and "sex the grooves," setting our focus on musical works themselves. Working with differently positioned living narrators can provide, as no amount of deep listening, musicological analysis, or archival research can, a humbling education about one's own ethnocentrism around sexuality (case in point: my yearning for subjects to come out). By mention-ing sexual ethnocentrism, I'm talking not just about queer vs. straight identi-ty politics but about recognizing the way our own cultural and historical un-derstandings of a range of traditional and nontraditional female sexualities at a particular time and place shape our expectations, our research goals, and our scholarly desires, if you will. If interview subjects possess different cultural and historical understandings of sexualities, does it make sense to expect them to conform to a model we value (to wait for them to come out, for instance, in-stead of attending to the information they might share about their historical, social, political, and cultural reasons for choosing discretion over disclosure)? Or is it more scholarly, more culturally sensitive, and more tolerant of sexual difference to work toward understanding different modes of constructing and inhabiting sexual identities in particular musical fields?

But how do you analyze sexuality when nobody tells you what it is?

Perhaps a more useful starting question is this: why do I yearn for interview subjects to disclose their sexuality? Where did I get the idea that my sexuality-sensitive intersectional analysis must involve classifying women musicians into clearly delineated, immutable categories of sexual desire? Is there a way of analyzing sexuality in the context of these interviews that does not require the outing of individuals? Are the subjects who are not coming out indeed telling me something about sexual identities, rules and regulations of sexual behavior, and the relationship between sexuality and musical performances, between sexuality and musical careers and survival, if only I can listen more carefully to their differently positioned frameworks and recognize the historical specificity of my own? While my interviewees don't come out, they do reveal the power of a structure that conceals, shapes, and imperfectly contains sexual contents ("Don't write about that"). A closer historical look at this closet is in order. What does the closet mean to me as a particularly situated interviewer in the late twentieth century? And what did the closet mean to the female musicians who in the 1990s narrated their experiences as jazz and swing musicians in all-woman bands fifty years earlier?

Eve Kosofsky Sedgwick urges an analysis of the closet as more than a metaphor with two diametrically opposed possibilities—out or in (and all the meanings that may reverberate from this unforgiving binary: Is the subject honest or secretive? Is she heroic or tragic, courageous or cowardly? What values do I, as researcher, attach to what may also be looked at as agency, discretion, privacy, and hard-won survival tactics of interviewees?). Although Sedgwick advocates recognizing the limitations of the closet as metaphor, she also encourages us to examine the closet as a "regime of knowing," a not superseded one at that. She exposes the closet not just as something to exit and be done with but as a factor shaping the daily lives of even openly out lesbians and gay men: "Every encounter with a new classful of students, to say nothing of a new boss, social worker, loan officer, doctor, erects new closets whose fraught and characteristic laws of optics and physics exact from at least gay people new draughts and requisitions of secrecy or disclosure."[8]

What about the new researcher who says she is writing a book and dissertation on all-woman bands?[9] Does this situation demand secrecy or disclosure? What grounds these choices? Is there no space between them? What does it mean to expect full disclosure from women to whom I am a stranger—a stranger with a tape recorder, a notebook, and publishing ambitions, no less? Think-

ing of the closet as an unobliterated character always needing to be confronted, whether one is in or out, is useful in thinking through interview scenarios.

o   o   o

I sit on a couch with two white women at their apartment in a seniors' hous-
ing complex. One woman is in her late sixties; she is a trumpet player and my
interview subject.[10] The other is older, nearly eighty, and I am told that she is
"not a musician but a good musician's friend." We spend the afternoon together talking, laughing, and watching videotapes of bands from the 1940s.
Occasionally the older woman puts her arm around the younger one. Just as
I'm thinking, "Yes! I've found my lesbian subjects at last," they take me on a
tour of their two-bedroom apartment, lingering in the two bedroom doorways
where each neatly made bed is plainly visible. "Now this is a sure sign of something," I say to myself, pretending to admire the paint in the second bedroom.
"Either it is a sign that they are not lesbians but they know that I think they
might be lesbians, or it is a sign that they are lesbians who are showing me their
beds so that I will think they are not lesbians."

Several days later, while still trying to figure out the signs of that visit, I receive in the mail an unnecessary but polite attempt to pay for a tape I had giv-
en them. Before returning the check I notice with glee that it is from a joint
checking account. "Aha!" I think. "A clear sign!" I feel deliriously happy. When
I describe this artifact to my professor, however, she tells me that what is interesting is that I read "joint checking account" as a code for sexuality. It is interesting, I agree, but then I realize that I still know nothing. It's not like I can go
back for another interview based on this new information. "Um, yes. I want to
thank you for revealing that 'joint checking account.' May I ask you some rather
frank questions? Did other members of your band have 'joint checking accounts'? Did you join an all-woman band in order to open a 'joint checking
account,' or did you find that you wanted a 'joint checking account' after you
joined the band and met others who had 'joint checking accounts,' or . . . ?"

It appears that the metaphor of bravely coming out of the closet is no less
problematic than the metaphor of the closet itself, which provides only the most
extreme possibilities of in or out, public or private, secrecy or disclosure. I wonder whether the conflicting but related signs of joint bank account and separate bedrooms can be most lucidly read as a dance of negotiation with the unforgiving structures of the closet that is required of women who live together
in a society ever-curious about gay self-disclosure (Sedgwick adds that "invol-
untary" gay self-disclosure is especially titillating to "the fine antennae of public
attention").[11] While the check with two names and the apartment with two beds

may not necessarily point to a particular lesbian relationship that I can recon-struct from these shards of information, they do point, I believe, to the pres-ence of the closet as a shaping factor in the lives of women who live nontradi-tionally, be it with a woman lover, a woman friend, a roommate, alone and unmarried, or on a bus with fifteen other women jazz and swing musicians.

John D'Emilio argues for historical specificity over mythological models to produce new, more accurate theories of gay history. Two oft-used myths he indicates are "the myth of the abysmal past" (life was terrible for gay people before gay liberation, after which they could come out) and the myth of the "eternal homosexual," who always was and "always will be." "These myths have limited our political perspective. They have contributed, for instance, to an overreliance on a strategy of coming out—if every gay man and lesbian in American came out, gay oppression would end—and have allowed us to ig-nore the institutionalized ways in which homophobia and heterosexism are reproduced."[12] As Sedgwick has noted, the strategy of coming out of the clos-et (a specific and important oppositional tactic of the gay liberation movement in the United States) did not obliterate the epistemological structure of the closet experienced by Western gay people, nor did it dampen public interest in gay disclosure. D'Emilio agrees that the strategy had "a positive political function in the first years of gay liberation,"[13] a usefulness that is evident in a range of legal and social reforms (repeals of sodomy laws, etc.). Yet he asks whether it makes sense to bank on this strategy and the myths that propel it and advocates specificity when engaging in historical inquiries into sexuali-ties in specific times and places. When narrators requested to talk only about music, not personal matters, or when they outed a colleague in the course of a story and then instructed me not to write about that, I was reminded again and again that coming out had not yet been valorized in a political movement when these women were playing and that African American women, who al-ready suffered racial discrimination, may have felt particularly protective of additional stigmas (and particularly excluded from the gay liberation move-ment of the 1960s and 1970s). What does it mean to assume that the privacy that narrators continue to protect is and was "abysmal"? Can we assume that women musicians in same-sex relationships in the 1940s, whose all-woman band communities included women musicians who were not in same-sex re-lationships and who were constantly sexualized by reviewers and advertise-ments, *want* to be historicized as lesbian foremothers? Certainly many wom-en from that generation were active in the gay liberation movement, but might there be others, including some of the women musicians who don't come out, who understand their sexual identities in different terms? My own struggles with narrators concerning how to talk about these issues suggests that they harbored conceptions of identity, privacy, and disclosure, and investments in what a history of all-woman bands should include, quite different from the ones I was prepared to recover and write into history.

o   o   o

I wind up a long, productive interview with an African American guitarist who has shared with me detailed remembrances about musical styles, specific band histories, and the effects of racism and sexism on black all-woman bands. Before I leave, the narrator, who is committed to having these histories written and told as accurately as possible, gives me several phone numbers of other women she thinks I should interview. At home I follow up, reaching first a friend of hers who played in some of the same bands, but at different times, an African American alto saxophonist who seems enthusiastic about my project and agrees to a telephone interview. When I call the saxophonist at the appointed time, however, she tells me that she is very sorry, but her son won't let her do the interview. I don't press the issue, but I'm saddened that she feels she must take orders from her son and that the son wishes to suppress his mother's story. The next summer, while visiting the guitarist, I mention that her friend's son had told her to cancel the interview.

"That's interesting," says the guitarist. "She doesn't have a son."

She pulls the phone onto her lap and dials. I know I should leave the room, but my feet refuse to move. "What's this about your canceling your interview with Sherrie? Oh, no, Sherrie isn't like that. She isn't interested in that. Sherrie is not the type to exploit your personal life. She only wants to hear about your music."

She hangs up and tells me that the interview is back on. Her friend made up the story about her son. In fact, she made up the son. "Her girlfriend doesn't want her to do the interview because they've been together for thirty-five years and they own a house together. Everyone knows. But no one talks about it. Don't ask her any personal questions and don't tell her I told you."

My interview with the alto player goes well, other than the fact that I can't ask her any questions that might help me to learn what function the all-woman bands had for women with nontraditional sexual identities. She graciously narrates her career with great detail and pride, but she does not mention her personal life outside music, either past or present. The identity she willingly offers is that of a serious musician who had worked steadily for fifty years. She is humble about her own abilities but wants me to write about the talented women with whom she worked and who have received little attention for their skills. I come away from the interview feeling both the importance of the narrative she offered me and the significance of her silence. I am also curious as to why her friend outed her in the first place.

Feminist ethnographer Kamala Visweswaran has theorized silences and betrayals as "defining parameters of women's agency and identity."[14] Looking for productive ways to read and write about the silences and betrayals that abound in my interviews with women musicians, I have thought a great deal about the alto saxophonist's invented son. The decision to present a male authority figure who could veto her interview tells me something about the alto player's and her partner's limited access to power. Did the "son" help them buy the house? The invented son also shows me a tactic that she has developed to augment her authority when the decisions of two grown women don't carry enough weight to be taken seriously. This information seems extremely important to my research, but even to write about it here, with names protected and instruments scrambled, feels like a betrayal of trust and of privacy. The alto player didn't know that I knew the son was invented. And she didn't know that I knew why he canceled the interview.

I relate the story of the saxophonist's bossy son here not only because it reveals a great deal about the daily inventiveness that nontraditional women have deployed to protect themselves in a heterosexist, racist, sexist system but also because it illustrates the lengths to which nontraditional narrators may go to protect their privacy in interviews with researchers who want them to come out. Narrators' perceptions of me as a product of my historical locatedness often accurately pegged me as someone who would be interested in lesbian "herstories," as well as in certain other anticipated topics that many narrators preferred not to address (e.g., sexual harassment, unwanted pregnancy on the road, and sex discrimination by popular male bandleaders or by the musicians' union). Visweswaran advocates a stance for feminist ethnography in which identities are understood as "partial(ly) revealed and strategic." Rather than seek full disclosure (a tall—well, impossible—order), we can ask the following: What is revealed, when is it revealed, and why? When do silences fall, and what purposes do they serve? These questions are useful alternatives to both the ruthless in or out possibilities of the closet and a related mythology of the second-wave women's movement—namely, that silence is invariably the antithesis of empowerment.

As Paula Ebron and Anna Tsing point out, the assumption that silence must always be broken comes from a particular feminist discourse that is not applicable to all women at all times. Sometimes silence is powerful.[15] If I think about silences in my interviews as acts of limited agency, or even of resistance, how might that change the ways in which I theorize and narrate the gaps in my informants' stories? Can the silence that produces and is protected by the invented son be considered resistant? I have to admit that, invented or not, the alto player's son effectively negotiated the terms of this particular interview. The boundaries were clear, and I didn't dare cross them in our conversation. But is there a way of writing about the terms, the silences, the betrayals, and the boundaries, a way of theorizing them without breaking them?

As Visweswaran notes, that which "cannot be spoken" gets "betrayed." Dozens of narrators shared unspeakable information with me via third-party betrayals and then asked me not to use it. I am left with the diametrically opposed options of silence or betrayal as well, neither of which seems ethical or feminist. I can conceal or out nontraditional women musicians. Is there another option? Is there a way to reveal, partially and strategically, what narrators taught me through betrayals and silences without spilling their secrets? This is what I am trying to do.

A white female drummer speaks fondly of the woman with whom she lived for fifty years. She also comes out as straight several times during our interview, yet I have asked no questions that I can recognize as having to do with sexuality. When I do get up the nerve to pose a question clearly about nontraditional sexualities, my consciously nonthreatening language is painstakingly careful. How do I ask without upsetting the delicate balance she presents to me: the lifetime primary relationship with a woman, on the one hand, and the direct appeals to straight identity (normalcy? privacy?), on the other. I search for words that may open another door without insisting that anyone come out or even be inside. "Did all-woman bands provide a safe environment for women who weren't, say, living by societal norms? Women who had romantic relationships with other women, for instance?"

She begins her answer with a list of facts. Interestingly, they are facts about sexual stigmas, not sexual identities or behaviors. "In those days," she tells me, "it was very important not to be taken for a lesbian, whether one was a lesbian or not, because it could hurt one's own career as well as the careers of one's friends." Everyone passed as straight, she explains, because "girl musicians" were already considered to be sexually deviant, and care had to be taken to disprove this at all times, to perform popular versions of femininity while simultaneously performing big-band hits of the day and to keep performing traditional femininity offstage, at least in public. Personal reputations affected professional opportunities. "The big New York agencies would blacklist you if rumors got out that you were a loose kind of woman, or you drank, or you were a lesbian. *All* girl musicians," she adds, "had to be careful not to be seen in public in pairs too often. *Even I* had to be careful not to be seen in pairs with my friends," she says in a firm voice, looking me in the eye.

That look haunts me when I consider these issues. It is painful to imagine myself as a parody of a feminist historian: rooting for narrators to exercise agency in their pasts, urging them to tell their own stories in their own words, then getting baffled when narrators' agency turns out differently than I'd planned. Yes, I was hoping she would come out. And here she was, aware of my modus operandi but resisting—skillfully, I might add—refusing to pin down her own sexual identity to meet my needs. Instead she offered a compelling set of reasons about not only why lesbian musicians passed as straight in the 1940s but why straight women musicians passed as straight. The closet, in this formulation, shaped the daily existence of all women musicians, lesbian or not, and in fact, when carefully utilized, increased their work opportunities. My mind spins. Could the sexual stigmatization attached to women musicians (and other women in traditionally male occupations) constitute one of the important factors that D'Emilio suggests is lost when we "overrely" on a strategy of coming out? If *all* female jazz and swing musicians had to pass as straight, regardless of sexual orientation, then it appears that sexual reclassification was based not only on one's lovers but also on occupation, big-band genre (with sweet styles considered more feminine and "hot," more masculine), and perhaps instrument choice (with brass, saxophones, drums, and bass considered masculine in this particular cultural and historical context and piano, flutes, violin, and harp considered feminine).[16] Although she refuses to disclose her sexual identity (to talent agents of the 1930s and 1940s and to feminist music historians in the 1990s), this narrator, like many others, insists on her identity as a "real musician." This is the identity she wants to come out in her history. It is an identity she fought for all her life.

o   o   o

A white pianist, one of many narrators who still play professionally, tells stories populated by straight women and at least two kinds of "lesbians": "lesbians" and "terrible lesbians" (neither of whom I am supposed to discuss). Studying the transcripts later, it appears that the distinction has everything to do with different negotiations of the closet. Terrible lesbians were those who "did not care what people thought," who flirted with audience members. Terrible lesbians could lose a band its bookings. Even if a terrible lesbian got only herself fired, she left the band with a chair to fill, a hardship that could also affect the sound, professionalism, opportunities, and reviews of a band that already was expected to sound amateurish since the musicians were "girls."

Lesbians who weren't "terrible," however, were discreet: "Nobody would ever know that's what they were." They protected the band's reputation, as well as its sound. This narrator admires the women in the latter category, women who didn't come out, a reversal of the way value tends to operate in contemporary lesbian and gay histories.

Elizabeth Lapovsky Kennedy and Madeline D. Davis's *Boots of Leather, Slippers of Gold* (1993) is an example of a history of pre-gay-liberation lesbians that relies heavily on the closet as metaphor. Although the book is based on oral histories of lesbians who attended gay bars in Buffalo, New York, in the 1930s, 1940s, and 1950s, the authors' stakes are reflected in a hierarchy of value implicitly crafted into the text, in which out butches are valorized, femmes (who can pass and so cannot be considered as out as out butches) are somewhat less valued, and lesbians who were not out are completely omitted. Such a formulation leaves no room for the pianist's admiration for lesbians who passed as straight in some areas of their lives to keep their bands together or for the drummer's recollection that all women musicians, regardless of sexual identity, passed as straight to claim careers and identities as competent musicians. Nevertheless, contradictions in Kennedy and Davis's text indicate that a more complex analysis might have added to the historical accuracy of their study. In their discussion of the 1940s, the authors mention that the war was liberating for lesbians because they "were no longer easily identified when they went out together dressed in trousers without male escorts."[17] In other words, out lesbians felt liberated by the extra privacy afforded them because straight women were also working jobs, hanging out with women, and wearing pants. They could be out and pass at the same time. Yet the authors do not allow this slip in the closet discourse to unsettle their celebration of brave "out butch" visibility. Might feminist historians of nontraditional sexualities learn useful frameworks, as well as data, from subjects who don't come out? Even if we don't adopt the frameworks as our own, if we find them homophobic (a major dilemma in my own attempts to work with what narrators do offer about sexuality), might we find ways to incorporate contradictory voices that reflect historical complexities of narrators' positions and our own?

When I approached women musicians from the 1940s, I had often been preceded by other researchers from my generation of feminist-oriented women's historians. To my surprise, some musicians referred directly to the film *Tiny and Ruby: Hell Divin' Women*, Greta Schiller and Andrea Weiss's documentary film about trumpet player Ernestine "Tiny" Davis and her partner, pianist and drummer Ruby Lucas, two African American women musicians who performed in the 1930s, 1940s, and 1950s.[18] Some musicians cited the film as an example of the exploitation of women musicians' personal lives they wished to avoid. Although I had found the film quite sensitive and respectful, these concerns challenged me to rethink both my research goals and the narrators' concerns more historically. A conversation with Andrea Weiss about the controversies surrounding the making of *Tiny and Ruby* was enlightening, particularly her comment that although she and Schiller were careful never to describe the relationship in words that Tiny and Ruby did not themselves use (they didn't use the word *lesbian,* for instance) and to let Tiny and Ruby define their own relationship on the screen, they could not prevent enthusiastic critics from hailing the documentary as a "lesbian film."[19] The film's reception was overwhelmingly positive, but the fact that it was received as a film about lesbians distressed even Tiny and Ruby, who appear out as they discuss their relationship within the frame of the film and who, according to Weiss, participated in the film knowing that their relationship would be its focus.

Watching the film again, I am aware of a valuation of outness despite subtle contradictions (that, admirably, were not left on the cutting-room floor). Trumpet player Tiny Davis (then in her eighties) speaks openly and outrageously about her love for women, laughing a lot and using a multitude of high-shock-value words, such as *pussy.* I have seen this film many times, and it is very entertaining. What I failed to notice in earlier viewings, however, was that the off-camera filmmakers' questions make no bones about what kinds of answers are being sought. "What made you so wild and crazy?" someone shouts offscreen. "I always was kind of different!" says Tiny, mugging as if she were onstage in a vaudeville show, elongating the word *different* in a way that seems to give it particular sexual meaning. Despite the fact that her performance in this film is right out of the 1920s and 1930s blues continuum of double-entendres and raucously uttered unspeakables, Tiny comes off as a veritable advertisement for the liberation that comes from being out in the 1970s sense of the word. Usually Tiny steals the show. But it is her partner, Ruby Lucas, who interests me this time.

While Tiny is busy pleasing the audience of interviewers who are unabashedly eager to cast her as the eternal out lesbian, Ruby appears more critical of her documenters and of Tiny's behavior. At one point she chastises Tiny onscreen for saying *pussy.* The film further manipulates our impression of Tiny by the use of voiceovers in which first-person poetry by Cheryl Clarke assumes the persona of Tiny Davis. The poet reads lines such as "And I was butch on the horn" and "I used my tongue" while images of Tiny's career flash on the screen. I had not previously noticed the extent to which this portrait of Tiny Davis is purposefully constructed. She is valorized in much the same way as the out butches of *Boots of Leather* (except that, interestingly, Tiny describes herself onscreen as a femme). Ruby, on the other hand, down to earth and out of the limelight, offers a historical contextualization of nontraditional sexuality in the 1940s that presents an alternative to the gay-liberation assumptions that characterize much of the film: "It wasn't quite as open as it is now. It wasn't at all. But people done what they wanted to then. You understand what I'm saying? But it was just, they were more, you know, kind of cool with it." This statement doesn't transplant 1970s lesbians into the 1940s, but neither does it promote an "abysmal past" model. Public and private function quite differently in Ruby's explanation than they do in strict closet metaphors, where public equals liberation and private translates into tragic isolation. Being "cool with it" sounds quite different from "abysmal past," and it also appears to be Lucas's explanation of her less out stance during the filming.

If the different historical context that Ruby describes had been further developed in the film, would the women musicians I interviewed have liked it any better? Would second-wave feminists and gay-liberation-oriented gay and lesbian viewers have liked it less? Does the controversy surrounding the film point to historical tensions between traveling women musicians with a range of sexual identities and conflicting modes of inhabiting them? Were the communities of all-woman bands sites of internal conflicts regarding sexuality, as well as sites for sexual exploration? Are these conflicts and tensions also unspeakable by women who wish to be taken seriously as jazz and swing musicians?

In their efforts to be perceived as "real musicians," women in all-woman bands in the 1930s and 1940s pushed against stigmas that sought constantly to sexualize them and mark them as deviant. Fifty years later along comes a new set of historians wanting to write about all-woman bands, and this group is also interested in their sexual identities, including (or especially) nontraditional ones. Is it any wonder that so many narrators quizzed me about the way I planned to write their stories? That so many offered opinions regarding whether to address the existence of same-sex romantic or sexual relationships?

"Well, you have to write about it because it was there," an African American pianist advised, adding quickly, "but don't *emphasize* it. It takes away from the musicality."

"I don't care if it happened or not. It isn't *history*," insisted a white trombonist.

"There have been gays and lesbians in all occupations. Why pick on all-girl bands?" This challenge came from a white clarinetist who had been playing professionally since the 1920s.

Women musicians from the 1940s are well aware that the historical inability of reviewers, audiences, and historians to hear all-girl bands as musically substantive resulted in their omission from the most lucrative and lasting circuits of the industry, as well as from jazz and swing history. Their sexualization in trades, newspapers, and advertisements did indeed detract from their "musicality," for audiences arrived expecting novelty bands. Mainstream jazz and swing histories have routinely omitted both all-woman bands and nontraditional sexualities. Colleagues assume that my study will include lesbian identities and communities, although historians of male big bands are not expected to include sexuality (or gender) as an important category of analysis. The "real" jazz and swing histories focus on male instrumentalists who are presumed straight. Is it reasonable to expect nontraditional women musicians to come out when their identities as "real musicians" are still under siege? Narrators' strategies to reveal musical identities and to conceal sexual ones make a certain kind of institutional sense that I have to respect. Yes, my motives are different, but I have to take seriously the place at the table I inherit as someone who writes about women jazz and swing musicians. It is a fraught historiographical field.

Still, if women musicians don't want me to know that there were lesbians in all-woman bands, why do they keep telling me who they were? Is it another function of fighting the stigmas attached to being a woman musician? Is pointing away from oneself merely a strategy for maintaining a "respectable" reputation? If this is the case, however, why do the women who do this point to women so nearby—to friends and to women they have known for years? Despite all the cautions, I can't help but wonder whether there is something communicated here that I am allowed to acknowledge. Were all-woman bands safe havens for women with nontraditional sexualities during the 1930s and 1940s as long as the lesbians were discreet? Is third-party betrayal the only way that this information can emerge? Perhaps it is a way of telling me, yes, nontraditional sexual identity existed in the bands, but it was dangerous, unspeakable: *don't write with a post-gay-liberation sensibility because it wasn't like that.*

Finding a way to write is another matter.

What would you do?

NOTES

1. For discussion of the tendency of historical research about lesbians to insufficiently theorize connections between gender and sex and for a model analysis that develops these links in a specific historical context, see Leisa D. Meyer, *Creating GI Jane: Sexuality and Power in the Women's Army Corps during World War II* (New York: Columbia University Press, 1996), 148–78.

2. Both of these catchphrases were used in the entertainment pages of *Chicago Tribune* to describe a performance of Ada Leonard and Her All-American Girls (advertisement, *Chicago Tribune*, 20 Dec. 1940, p. 24).

3. Description of Eddie Durham's All-Star Girls in Ted Yates, "Greatest Aggregation of Girl Stars Have Plenty of Zing When It Comes to Swing," *New York Age*, 4 Dec. 1943, p. 10.

4. Dozens of woman trumpet players were dubbed "the female Louis Armstrong"; drummers, "the female Gene Krupa." A *Downbeat* article in 1937 described the drummer in the Ingenues all-girl band as "a Gene Krupa in girls' clothes." Another drummer was described in 1940 as a "skirted Krupa" ("They Have A Gene Krupa In Girls' Clothes!" *Downbeat*, Apr. 1937, p. 21; "Anne Wallace Weds, Quits," *Downbeat*, 1 Sep. 1940, p. 8).

5. Allan Berube, *Coming Out under Fire: The History of Gay Men and Women in World War II* (New York: Free Press, 1990); Meyer, *Creating GI Jane.*

6. John D'Emilio, "Capitalism and Gay Identity," in *The Lesbian and Gay Studies Reader*, ed. Henry Abelove, Michèle Aina Barale, and David M. Halperin (New York: Routledge, 1993), 471–72.

7. I am grateful to the many people who have engaged in such dialogue with me over the years, especially my dissertation adviser, Angela Davis, as well as Donna Haraway and the members of the "Feminist Writings, Global Connections, Positioned Subjects" writing seminar at UC Santa Cruz and Inderpal Grewal and members of the "Queer Theory" reading group at San Francisco State. Chinosole, Ronni Sanlo, Maylei Blackwell, Isa Velez, and Andrea Weiss also offered invaluable feedback on this yet unsolved dilemma. I eagerly await Ronni Sanlo's book on nontraditional women in all-girl bands of the 1930s.

8. Eve Kosofsky Sedgwick, "The Epistemology of the Closet," in *Lesbian and Gay Studies Reader*, ed. Abelove, Barale, and Halperin, 45, 46.

9. See my book *Swing Shift: "All-Girl" Bands of the 1940s* (Durham, N.C.: Duke University Press, 2000).

10. The interviewees' instruments have been changed to protect their privacy.

11. Sedgwick, "Epistemology," 45.

12. D'Emilio, "Capitalism," 467–68.

13. Ibid.

14. Kamala Visweswaran, "Betrayal: An Analysis in Three Acts," in *Scattered Hegemonies: Postmodernity and Transnational Feminist Practices*, ed. Inderpal Grewal and Caren Kaplan (Minneapolis: University of Minnesota Press, 1994), 105.

15. Paula Ebron and Anna Lowenhaupt Tsing, "In Dialogue? Reading across Minority Discourses," in *Women Writing Culture*, ed. Ruth Behar and Deborah A. Gordon (Berkeley: University of California Press, 1995), 390–441. See also Kamala Visweswaran, "Refusing the Subject," *Fictions of Feminist Ethnography* (Minneapolis: University of Minnesota Press, 1994), 60–72.

16. These gender constructions of genre, style, and instrument are not universal but historically and culturally specific to the jazz and swing bands of the 1930s and 1940s.

Linda Dahl traces notions in which drums are considered masculine and strings considered feminine to both European and African traditions but cautions that gender organization and its markers (including musical ones) vary from culture to culture and must be related to specific contexts (Dahl, "My Sax Is a Sex Symbol," *Stormy Weather: The Music and Lives of a Century of Jazzwomen* [New York: Limelight Editions, 1989], 35–44). For more on gender and music theory, see various issues of *Women and Music: A Journal of Gender and Culture;* Susan McClary, *Feminine Endings: Music, Gender, and Sexuality* (Minnesota: University of Minnesota Press, 1991); and Susan C. Cook and Judy S. Tsou, eds., *Cecilia Reclaimed: Feminist Perspectives on Gender and Music* (Urbana: University of Illinois Press, 1994).

17. Elizabeth Lapovsky Kennedy and Madeline D. Davis, *Boots of Leather, Slippers of Gold* (New York: Routledge, 1993), 38–39.

18. *Tiny and Ruby: Hell Divin' Women,* film, dir. Greta Schiller and Andrea Weiss (Jezebel Productions, 1986).

19. I am grateful to Andrea Weiss for her candid remarks about the controversies surrounding the making and reception of *Tiny and Ruby.*

CONTRIBUTORS

Byron Adams, Professor of Composition and Musicology at the University of California, Riverside, was awarded the first Ralph Vaughan Williams Research Fellowship in 1985 and has published widely on the subject of twentieth-century English music. His articles and reviews have appeared in *19th Century Music, Music and Letters, MLA Notes, Current Musicology,* and *The Musical Quarterly,* as well as *Vaughan Williams Studies;* his entries for the revised edition of the *New Grove Dictionary of Music and Musicians* include those on Husa and Walton. Adams has been named to the editorial board of *American Music* and in 2000 was awarded the American Musicological Society's Philip Brett Award for two essays dealing with the intersection of nationalism and homoeroticism in twentieth-century English music.

Philip Brett, Distinguished Professor in the Department of Musicology at the University of California, Los Angeles, is the general editor of *The Byrd Edition;* the compiler of *Benjamin Britten: Peter Grimes* (Cambridge University Press, 1983); and a coeditor of *Queering the Pitch: The New Gay and Lesbian Musicology* (Routledge, 1994), *Cruising the Performative: Interventions into the Representation of Ethnicity, Nationality, and Sexuality* (Indiana University Press, 1995), and *Decomposition: Post-Disciplinary Performance* (Indiana University Press, 2000).

Malcolm Hamrick Brown, Emeritus Professor of Music (musicology) at Indiana University in Bloomington, is the founding editor of the scholarly series Russian Music Studies and the author of articles and essays on Russian music of the nineteenth and twentieth centuries.

Sophie Fuller, Lecturer in Music at the University of Reading, is the author of *The Pandora Guide to Women Composers: Britain and the United States, 1629–Present* (Pandora, 1994). Her research on British women composers and musicians has appeared in various essay collections, dictionaries, encyclopedias, and journals. She and Nicky Losseff are editing a collection of essays on the idea of music in Victorian fiction, to be published by Ashgate in 2003.

Mitchell Morris teaches in the Department of Musicology at the University of California, Los Angeles. He has written on American popular music, Russian and Soviet music, opera, and musical ethics. Forthcoming work includes an edited collection of essays on disco and a study of representations of nature in American music at the turn of the century.

Jann Pasler, Professor of Music at the University of California, San Diego, helped found the first music research center at the Centre National de la Recherche Scientifique, Paris, in 1983–84; in the fall of 1994 she and Philip Brett ran the "Retheorizing Music" project at the UC Humanities Research Center. She has published on French music and cultural life, as well as modernist and postmodernist issues in music, and has produced two video documentaries, *Taksu: Music in the Life of Bali* and *The Great Ceremony to Straighten the World*. She is completing a monograph entitled *Useful Music; or, Why Music Mattered in Third Republic France*, for the University of California Press.

Ivan Raykoff, a Ph.D. candidate at the University of California, San Diego, is writing a dissertation on the mythology of the Romantic pianist in twentieth-century popular culture. In 2000 he received the AMS 50 Dissertation Fellowship from the American Musicological Society. He has studied piano at the Eastman School of Music and at the Liszt Academy of Music in Budapest on a Fulbright grant and performs regularly with new music ensembles and as a soloist, in addition to pursuing research and teaching interests in contemporary music and film studies.

Fiona Richards, Lecturer in Music at Britain's Open University, completed a doctoral thesis entitled "Meanings in the Music of John Ireland," which was published as *The Music of John Ireland* (Ashgate, 2000). Her research also focuses on the British pianist and composer Helen Perkin and on British music and performance issues.

Eva Rieger, Professor of Musicology at the University of Bremen from 1991 to 2000, has lived in London, Berlin, and Göttingen and now resides in Zürich and Vaduz, Liechtenstein, where she works as an independent scholar. Her most recent books are *Alfred Hitchcock und die Musik: Zum Verhältnis von Film, Musik und Geschlecht* (Kleine, 1996) and *Bibliographie Frau und Musik 1970–1996* (Olms, 1999). Forthcoming publications include an edition of the letters of Marie Fillunger to Eugenie Schumann and, with Monica Steegmann, a collection of autobiographical texts by women singers. She is also working on gender roles in opera and a biography of Minna Wagner.

Gillian Rodger, Visiting Assistant Professor of Musicology at the University of Michigan, completed her Ph.D. from the University of Pittsburgh with a dissertation entitled "Male Impersonation on the North American Variety and Vaudeville Stage, 1868–1930," which received the 1998 Philip Brett Award for exceptional work in the field of queer musicology. Before moving to Ann Arbor, she worked on the *Garland Encyclopedia of World Music* for two years.

Sherrie Tucker, Assistant Professor of American Studies at the University of Kansas at Lawrence, is the author of *Swing Shift: "All-Girl" Bands of the 1940s* (Duke University Press, 2000). Her articles on women, gender, and jazz have appeared in numerous anthologies and journals, including *Unequal Sisters: A Multicultural Reader in U.S. Women's History* (Routledge, 2000), *Women and Music: A Journal of Gender and Culture*, *Black Music Research Journal*, *American Music*, *Oral History Review*, and *Frontiers: A Journal of Women's Studies*.

Lloyd Whitesell teaches at McGill University in Montreal. He has also taught at the University of Virginia, the University of Southern California, the University of Minnesota, and the State University of New York at Stony Brook. He has published articles on Benjamin Britten, Joni Mitchell, minimalism, modern tonality, and the anxiety of influence. Previously he served as cochair of the Gay and Lesbian Study Group of the American Musicological Society and for three years was coeditor of the *GLSG Newletter*.

INDEX

Abraham, Gerald, 134, 140, 144
Ada Leonard and Her All-American Girls, 309n.2
Adams, Maude, 106, 107
Adler, Guido, 182
Aebi, Gertrud, 36, 37
Aestheticism, 4, 15, 55, 69, 70, 72, 73, 225
Allan, Maud, 90, 95, 100n.63
Allatini, Rose (pseud. A. T. Fitzroy): *Despised and Rejected*, 2–3, 182
Allitsen, Frances, 81; vocal compositions, 93–94
American Musicological Society, 5
Amos, Tori, 7
Anderson, Mary, 90
Anderson, Robert, 235
Androgyny. *See* Gender: transitivity
Apel, Willi, 156
Apollo, 255
Apukhtin, Aleksey, 138
Arbuthnot, Lady, 79
Armstrong, Louis, 294
Armstrong, Martin Donnisthorpe, 255–56
Arnold, Matthew, 230
Asquith, Herbert, 90
Asselin, André, 72–73
Asselin, Lucienne, 72–73
Atkins, E. Wulstan, 239n.16
Atkins, Ivor, 229, 236–37
Attwood, Clare, 88
Audley, John, 58
Auerbach, Nina, 87, 88
Aynesworth, Allan, 226

Bach, Johann Sebastian, 153, 154, 156, 157, 158, 162, 167, 183, 236

Bachauer, Gina, 264
Bachelorhood, 10, 65, 70, 72, 73, 165. *See also* Marriage: avoidance of
Ball, Harry, 119
Balzac, Honoré de, 38
Banfield, Stephen, 247, 248
Barbedette, Gilles, 57
Barbey d'Aurevilly, Jules, 57, 65, 70, 72
Barbier, Jules, 199
Barnard, Charlotte Alington. *See* Claribel
Barney, Natalie, 58
Barry, C. A., 216
Barthes, Roland, 7
Bartholomew, A. T., 181
Basie, William "Count," 294
Batten, Mabel Veronica, 84–85, 86, 87, 88, 91, 96
Baudelaire, Charles, 57, 65, 70
Baumann, Emile, 202
Baumann, Liberta (née Sterchi), 44
Bax, Arnold, 217, 225–26, 266n.4
Baylis, Lillian, 184, 186
Bazzano, Kevin, 168
Beauchamp, Lord William, 220–21, 240n.34
Bech, Henning, 5
Beethoven, Ludwig van, 136, 142, 154, 156, 158–59, 166, 169, 184, 200, 210, 226, 277
Bellini, Vincenzo, 154
Belloc, Hilaire, 220
Benjamin, Walter, 164
Benkert, Karoly Maria, 3
Benson, E. F., 227
Benstock, Shari, 4
Bentham, Percy, 251
Berg, Alban, 250, 271
Berlioz, Hector, 204, 210

Berners, Lord Gerald, 224–25
Bernhardt, Sarah, 54, 106
Bernstein, Leonard, 205
Bertrand, Aloysius, 70
Berube, Allan, 295
Big bands, all-women, 293–310: incorporating
    sexuality in histories of, 293–99; sexualiza-
    tion of musicians in, 300, 303–4, 307–8; spec-
    ulation about lesbian presence in, 294–95,
    299, 303, 308
Bizet, Georges, 155, 168, 171
Blackmer, Corinne E., 7
Bloom, Harold, 219, 230
Blunt, Wilfred Scawen, 84
Bolet, Jorge, 167
Bonehill, Bessie, 119, 132n.23
Boughton, Rutland, 87, 226
Boulanger, Nadia, 60
Boulez, Pierre, 250
Boult, Adrian, 227
Boyd, Malcolm, 153
Boys, love of, 55–57, 62–64, 246–47, 249, 252,
    255–63. See also Uranianism
Bradby, Barbara, 7
Brahms, Johannes, 25, 26–27, 30, 33, 34, 139, 142,
    143, 154
Brand, Adolf, 273, 277
Brett, Philip, 5–6, 8, 14, 241n.36
Bright, Dora, 81
Briskier, Arthur, 162
Britten, Benjamin, 14
Broad, Lewis, 254
Brontë, Charlotte, 27
Brooke, Rupert, 248
Brown, Herbert, 265
Brown, Howard Mayer, 185
Brown, T. Allston, 118
Browne, Horatio Forbes, 255
Browne, W. Denis, 181
Browning, Frank, 166
Browning, Oscar, 181
Buchanan, Charles, 145
Buck, Charles, 229
Bülow, Hans von, 156, 275
Bulton, Ernest, 55–56, 58
Burlesque, 106, 109, 115
Burley, Rosa, 222, 225, 229, 242n.64
Bush, Geoffrey, 250
Bush, Kate, 7
Busoni, Ferruccio, 153, 155, 158, 164, 183
Bussine, Romain, 194

Butler, Judith, 132n.29, 165
Butt, Clara, 94
Byrd, William, 183
Byron, Lord, 140

Caird, Mona: The Daughters of Danaus, 82
Caligula, 196
Camp, 162, 164, 166, 168–72
Carassou, Michel, 57
Carey, Clive, 181, 182, 183
Carey, Hugh, 181
Carlier, F., 56–57, 60
Carlyle, Thomas, 230
Carpenter, Edward, 179, 180, 182, 226, 255
Carpenter, Humphrey, 14, 248
Carvalho, Mme., 194–95
Casadesus, Gaby, 73
Castle, Terry, 4, 7, 46n.15
Catholicism, 10, 233–34, 251–52. See also Elgar,
    Edward: Catholicism of; Ireland, John: and
    religion
Chabrier, Emmanuel, 55
Chappell, Arthur, 33
Chasins, Abram, 167
Chauncey, George, 4, 58, 126
Choisy, L'Abbé de, 196
Chopin, Frédéric, 154, 155, 158, 160, 170
Christian, Prince, 33
Christian, Princess, 33
Christie, John, 184
Claribel (Charlotte Alington Barnard), 92
Clark, Edward, 264
Clarke, Cheryl, 306
Clarke, Robert Coningsby, 84
Classic FM (British radio station), 185
Cleveland Street scandal, 221
Clifford, Kathleen, 121, 123, 126, 127, 132n.27
Closet, the, 185, 296–300, 302–8; positive uses of,
    304, 305, 308. See also Secrecy
Cocteau, Jean, 15, 54, 60, 69
Coffignon, 274
Coffin, Charles Hayden, 94
Cohen, Harriet, 226
Communities, lesbian, 37, 80, 88, 96
Compton, Edward, 89
Cook, Blanche Wiesen, 44
Cook, Susan, 310n.16
Cooper, Martin, 135–38, 140, 144
Corder, Frederick, 158
Core, Philip, 164
Corelli, Marie, 94

Craig, Edith, 87, 88
Craig, Gordon, 87
Crane, Hart, 5
Crevel, René, 52
Cross-dressing, 7, 13, 37, 87, 88, 106, 128–29, 162, 167, 170, 192–93, 194–95, 197, 198, 206, 207, 212nn.16, 22–23, 287; and homosexuality, 106, 122–23, 129, 196
Crossley, Ada, 94
Crossley-Holland, Peter, 246
Cumberland, Gerald. See Kenyon, Charles
Currid, Brian, 7
Cushman, Charlotte, 106
Cusick, Suzanne, 6, 7

Dahl, Linda, 310n.16
Dandyism, 10, 64, 65, 69–70, 72; as depicted by male impersonators, 113–14, 125. See also Ravel, Maurice: dandyism of
Daniell, Henry, 150
Dart, Thurston, 185
Daudet, Lucien, 54
Davies, Stephen, 158
Davis, Ernestine "Tiny," 305–7
Davis, Madeline D., 305, 307
Dean, Winton, 182
Debussy, Claude, 15, 70, 170, 207, 250
Decadence, 4, 10, 69, 70, 87, 95, 225, 283
Dellamora, Richard, 219
de Meyer, Baron, 227
de Meyer, Baronne, 227
D'Emilio, John, 295, 300
Dent, Edward J., 14, 87, 155, 181–86; on Beethoven, 184; and counterdiscourse within musicology, 183–88; on Elgar, 182, 184; and music for the people, 184–85, 186; on musicology, 185–86; and opera, 183, 184, 186; and religion, 181, 182
Deslandes, Baroness "Elsie," 60
Diaghilev, Sergei, 54, 60
Dickinson, Goldsworthy Lowes, 181
Dietrich, Marlene, 128–29
Difference, personal experience of, 2, 64, 72, 306
Docherty, Barbara, 248
Dollimore, Jonathan, 165, 170
Domestic partners, 27, 30, 35, 36, 38, 41, 79, 80, 86–87, 89–90, 294, 299–300, 301, 303, 305–7
Doner, Kitty, 121, 123, 125, 126
Douglas, Lord Alfred, 99n.55, 254, 255
Dresser, Marcia von, 99n.49, 241n.51
Drewal, Margaret, 170

Dutoit, Charles, 205
Dyer, Richard, 7

Ebner, Ottilie, 26
Ebron, Paula, 302
Eddie Durham's All-Star Girls, 309n.3
Edward, Prince of Wales, 220
Edwards, Bella, 95
Effeminacy. See Femininity; Gender: transitivity
Elgar, Alice, 228, 230, 236, 239nn.11–12, 240n.25
Elgar, Carice, 242n.58
Elgar, Edward, 182, 184, 216–38; attitude toward himself as musician, 222, 225–26, 237; Catholicism of, 216, 218, 220, 229; and class, 222; and the creative process, 217, 230–33, 235–38; The Dream of Gerontius, 233–35; and enigmas, 15, 217, 237–38; "Enigma" Variations, 216–17, 219, 220, 226, 229, 230–33, 234, 235, 237; and homoeroticism, 216–44; The Music Makers, 217, 231–33; violin concerto, 228, 235–37
Ellicott, Rosalind, 81
Ellis, Havelock, 3, 81, 179, 224, 226, 256
Elman, Mischa, 84
Enigmas, sexual, 15, 60, 72–73, 168, 299, 303–4. See also Sexual categories
Eulenburg affair, 4, 291n.30
Evans, Edwin, 142, 145, 249

Falla, Manuel de, 60, 72, 153
Fallon, Daniel, 203, 209
Fargue, Léon-Paul, 52
Farjeon, Eleanor, 259–60
Fauré, Gabriel, 85, 87
Faure, Michel, 52, 204, 207
Femininity, 142, 180, 191–92, 193, 200, 208, 210, 224, 274, 303; construction of, 81, 106. See also Gender
Feminism, 6, 37, 81, 123, 180, 273, 297, 302, 305, 307. See also New Woman; Women
Feminization, fear of, 126, 180, 237; in music profession, 3, 142. See also Music: association with the feminine; Women: and music profession
Ferguson, Valentine Munro, 90
Fillunger, Marie, 9, 13, 28; conflict with Clara Schumann, 31–33; financial independence, 32, 35, 36, 37; relationship with Eugenie Schumann, 25–45; as singer, 25–26, 30, 34
Fiske, Col. James, 118
Fitton, Isobel, 237

Fitzroy, A. T. *See* Allatini, Rose
Flaubert, Gustave, 65
Forbes, Norman, 226
Forster, E. M., 10, 181, 182, 183
Foucault, Michel, 4, 12, 145, 177, 180
Fox, Della, 121
Franco-Prussian War, 193, 198–99, 201, 202, 204, 208
Frazetta, Frank, 281
Friedheim, Philip, 154
Friedländer, Benedikt, 273, 289
Fry, Roger, 183
Fuchs, Hanns, 275–78; *Eros zwischen euch und uns,* 283–89

Gabriel, Virginia, 92
Gallet, Louis, 210
Ganz, Adelina, 83
Garber, Marjorie, 170
Gardner, Arthur Robert Lee, 249
Garland, Judy, 7, 129
Gaunt, William, 225
Gautier, Théophile, 57
Gender: crisis in modern understanding of, 3, 4, 5, 11, 12, 295; as key to musical interpretation, 191–93, 200, 202–10; and political meanings, 192–93, 197–99, 200, 202, 206, 207–9; separatism, 273, 275, 284, 286, 289; transitivity, 12, 64, 65, 69, 88, 91, 92, 94, 180, 192–93, 194–96, 202, 205–6, 207–8, 235–37, 273–75, 277, 284, 286, 287, 289. *See also* Femininity; Masculinity
George V (king), 221
Gerhard, Similde, 41
Gerschner, Augusta, 117
Gide, André, 52, 62–64, 69, 211nn.11, 13
Gilbert, Sandra, 5
Gill, John, 7
Glassby, Robert, 252
Gluck, Christoph Willibald, 34, 37, 195
Glyndebourne Opera, 184
Godowsky, Leopold, 155, 158, 159, 160, 162, 163, 167
Goethe, Johann Wolfgang von, 277
Gojowy, Detlef, 168
Goldsmid, Louisa, 79, 80, 96
Goldsmith, Harris, 171
Goldwag, Berthe, 275
Gomperz, Caroline (née Bettelheim), 30
Goncourt, Edmond, 57, 65
Goncourt, Jules de, 57, 65
Gordon, Father John Joseph, 233
Gould, Glenn, 167, 168–69

Gounod, Charles, 158, 171, 194, 195
Grable, Betty, 129
Grainger, Percy, 84, 159, 172
Grandval, Vicomtesse Clémence de, 196
Grey, Katherine, 132n.27
Grove, George, 186
Gubar, Susan, 5
Guérin, Daniel, 52, 60

Hadleigh, Boze, 6
Hahn, Reynaldo, 60
Hajdu, David, 7
Hall, Radclyffe, 83, 84, 86, 88, 241n.51; relationship to music, 84; *The Well of Loneliness,* 4, 274
Hallam, Arthur, 219, 230, 234
Hallé, Charles, 25, 33–34, 35
Hallé, Lady. *See* Norman-Neruda, Wilma
Hamilton, Stella, 90
Handel, George Frideric, 6, 142, 157, 183, 213n.25; *Messiah,* 177
Hanson, Ellis, 251
Haraucourt, Edmond, 94
Harding, James, 193–94
Harvey, P J, 7
Haydn, Franz Joseph, 207
Heliogabalus, 54, 196
Henley, William Earnest, 243n.83
Henner, Jean-Jacques, 198
Hepburn, Katharine, 150
Hercules and Omphale, 13, 192, 197–98, 200–210
Hermes, 254
Herzogenberg, Elizabeth, 25, 27, 41
Herzogenberg, Heinrich, 25, 27, 41
Heyse, Paul, 38
Hichens, Robert, 90
Hindemith, Paul, 155, 159, 160, 162
Hindle, Annie, 109, 110, 112, 115, 116, 118, 119, 125, 130n.1; depiction of swell, 114; marriages, 116–17; realism in impersonation, 110, 112; singing range, 112
Hindley, Clifford, 14
Hinson, Maurice, 159
Hippius, Zinaida Nikolayevna, 87–88
Hirschfeld, Magnus, 179, 180, 272–74, 275, 277, 289
History: oral, 293–310; oral, ethics in, 296–99, 302, 303, 308; queer perspective on, 8, 9, 17, 80, 88, 95–96, 273, 294–99, 300, 307–8; and sexual ethnocentrism, 297–98, 304, 307
Hoch Conservatory (Frankfurt), 30
Hockman, Vera, 228

Hohenfels, Princess, 151
Holland, Vyvyan, 227
Holme, Vera, 88
Holmès, Augusta, 196, 199, 202, 212n.22
Holst, Gustav, 230
Homoeroticism, 254; Edward Elgar and, 216–44; in Newman's *The Dream of Gerontius,* 234; in Tennyson's *In Memoriam,* 219, 221, 229, 234
Homosexual emancipation movement, German, 272–74, 275–77, 289
Homosexuality: and abnormality, 223–24; and blackmail, 56–57, 60, 220; at Cambridge, 181–82; earliest use of term, 3, 4, 12, 139; in literature, 38, 182, 220–21, 254–56; as modern identity type, 3–4, 12, 13, 144, 145, 178; and modernism, 3, 5, 8; and modernity, 4–5; openness about, 26, 43, 54, 63, 88, 141, 299–300, 305–7; and police arrest, 55–56, 58, 60; prejudice against, 13, 16, 26, 37, 79–80, 129, 144–46, 165, 221, 228, 296, 305; and prosecution, 4, 56, 220, 254, 291n.30; Victorian awareness of, 221–22. *See also* Music: and queer sexuality; Sexual categories; Wilde, Oscar: trials of
Hopkins, Gerard Manley, 218
Hopkins, G. W., 51
Hopper, DeWolf, 121
Horowitz, Vladimir, 11, 160, 167–68, 171
Hough, Stephen, 170
Housman, A. E., 247, 248, 255, 261
How, W. W., 253
Howells, Herbert, 241n.46
Huas, Jeanine, 56, 211nn.11, 13
Huemer, Frances, 197
Hugo, Victor, 199, 200–204, 208, 257–58
Hummel, Johann Nepomuk, 154
Hundoegger, Agnes, 41, 42
Huneker, James G., 142–43, 145, 170
Hunt, Lynn, 192
Huret, Jules, 55
Hussey, St. George, 131n.23
Hutchinson, Cecilia, 35
Huxley, Aldous, 248
Huysmans, Joris-Karl, 69, 70, 95, 241n.47, 283
Hyacinthus, 255

Improvisation, 10–11, 63, 159, 161
Interlaken, 25, 36, 44
International Musicological Society, 181, 182
International Society for Contemporary Music, 181
Invert. *See* Gender: transitivity; Sexual categories

Ireland, John, 245–66; "April," 258–59, 260; "Boys' Names," 259–60; *Ex ore innocentium,* 253; and Guernsey, 252, 256–59, 263; "In a May Morning" (*Sarnia*), 257–59, 260, 263; *The Land of Lost Content,* 247, 255; love of boys, 14, 246–47, 249, 252, 255–63; and marriage, 245, 246, 263, 264–65; and nostalgia, 246, 257, 258, 259, 260; and paganism, 251, 257; piano concerto, 263–64; privacy of, 246; and religion, 246, 250–54; sexuality reflected in his music, 14, 246, 247–48, 253, 256, 257–60; and women, 245, 246, 263–64; works dedicated to Arthur Miller, 261

Jackson, Charles Kain, 255
Jacob, Naomi, 88
Jaeger, August, 216, 218, 219, 229–35
James, Harry, 294
James, Henry, 5
Jazz, 16, 293–308
Joachim, Joseph, 27
Joan of Arc, 199, 200
Joplin, Scott, 168
Jourdan, Alecia, 110
Jourdan-Morhange, Helen, 52

Kakutani, Michiko, 161
Kashkin, Nikolai, 139
Keller, Hans, 156, 165
Kennedy, Elizabeth Lapovsky, 305, 307
Kennedy, Michael, 242n.59, 243n.85
Kenyon, Charles (pseud. Gerald Cumberland), 223–24, 226
Kerman, Joseph, 185
Kilburn, Nicholas, 237
King, Hetty, 121, 124–25, 126, 127, 128, 132n.27
Kingsley, Charles, 219, 230
Kirby, Norah, 246, 248, 265, 266
Kirchner, Theodor, 41
Kissin, Evgeny, 170
Klimt, Gustav, 95
Koestenbaum, Wayne, 7, 150, 165
Kopelson, Kevin, 7
Kozlovsky, Michel, 159
Krafft-Ebing, Richard von, 3, 81, 196, 271, 274
Kramer, Lawrence, 6, 192, 288
Krupa, Gene, 294

La Comtesse, 62, 64
"La Mara." *See* Lipsius, Marie
Lamoureux, Charles, 210
Landowska, Wanda, 156, 157–58, 160, 162

Lang, Paul Henry, 160, 166
Lehmann, Liza, 81, 84, 90, 100n.58
Lesage, Alain René: *Gil Blas*, 235–37
Lesbian: definition of, 44, 79–80. *See also* Communities, lesbian
Levi, Hermann, 41
Levi, Mary, 30, 34, 41
Lewenthal, Raymond, 170
Lewis, C. S., 144
Leybourne, George, 112, 131n.15
Liberace, 11, 167, 169–70
Lihou, Peter, 259–60
Lingard, William Horace, 112
Lions comiques, 109, 112, 114
Lipsius, Marie (pseud. "La Mara"), 38, 40, 41
List, Emilie, 31
Liszt, Franz, 12, 26, 38, 150–56, 158–59, 160, 161, 162, 163, 164, 165–66, 167, 169, 170–72, 174n.29, 191
Litvinne, Mme., 195
Litzmann, Berthold, 36
Loch, Emily, 33
Lockspeiser, Edward, 134–38, 140, 144, 145
Loesser, Arthur, 152
Long, Marguerite, 49–51, 64–65, 72
Long, W. W., 117
Longmire, John, 249, 266n.1
Lorrain, Jean, 54–55, 60
Lucas, Ruby, 305–7
Ludwig II (king), 70, 277, 290n.14
Lunceford, Jimmy, 294
Lygon, Lady Mary, 220
Lygon, William. *See* Beauchamp, Lord William

Maassen, Maria, 36
Maddison, Adela, 81, 83, 84, 85–87, 88, 91, 96; songwriting, 92, 94–95
Maddison, Frederick, 85, 86, 87
Mahler, Alma, 69
Maine, Basil, 237, 244n.93
Maitland, Sara, 125
Male impersonation, 11, 105–30; audiences for, 106, 114–15, 118, 121, 122, 125, 126; characters in acts, 113–14, 116, 119; issues of class in, 115–16, 118, 125–26, 129–30; performance style, 112–13, 119, 129; realism in, 110, 121, 122, 123; songs in acts, 116, 124, 126; spoken commentary in acts, 113, 119, 123–24; structure of acts, 110, 118–19, 129
Mann, Thomas: *Death in Venice*, 64, 256
Manns, August, 25
Mansfield, Helen Josephine, 118

Marchesi, Matilde, 25, 26
Mare, Walter de la, 259
Markes, Charles Stafford, 252
Marriage, 10, 80, 82, 83, 95, 116–17, 152, 160, 163, 166, 193, 197, 206, 221, 222, 228, 289; alternatives to, 83; avoidance of, 89, 91. *See also* Bachelorhood; Ireland, John: and marriage
Martindale, Bertha, 90
Marx, Eleanor, 83
Masculinity, 69, 142, 165, 192, 196, 200, 203, 207, 210, 273; construction of, 81, 106, 115–16. *See also* Gender
Masson, Agnes, 196
Matlock, Jann, 196
Maupassant, Guy de, 57
Mauriac, François, 52
Max, Edouard de, 54
McClary, Susan, 6, 310n.16
McVeagh, Diana, 217, 218–19, 233
Meck, Nadezhda von, 141
Meeting places for homosexuals, 55, 57–61; bars, 57–58; bath houses, 5, 56, 57; brothels, 56, 60–61; railway stations, 1, 5; restaurants, 57–58, 60, 63; urinals, 5, 60. *See also* Salons
Mellers, Wilfrid, 187n.1
Mendès, Catulle, 55, 290n.14
Merezhkovsky, Dmitri Sergeyevich, 87, 88
Merrill, George, 182
Meyer, Leisa D., 295, 308n.1
Meyer, Leonard B., 158
Meyer, Moe, 161, 162
Meyerbeer, Giacomo, 194
Michelangelo, 277
Miliukova, Antonina, 141
Miller, Arthur George, 252, 261–63, 264, 265
Modernism: and homosexuality, 3, 5, 8; in music, 2–3, 12, 146, 155, 170
Modulation, 12–13
Moll, Albert, 274–75
Montague, H. J., 131n.16
Montesquiou, Count Robert de, 55, 58, 59, 60, 69, 70, 226
Moore, Jeremy Northrop, 243n.83
Moravia, Alberto, 264
Moreau, Gustave, 95
Morris, Louise Sutherland, 93, 94
Morris, Mitchell, 6
Mosse, George L., 223–24, 229
Motherhood, 80, 95
Mozart, Wolfgang Amadeus, 34, 154, 157, 166, 170, 171, 184; *The Magic Flute*, 186
Muddocci, Eva (Hope Evangeline Muddock), 95

Munch, Edvard, 95
Mundt, Marta Gertrud, 86–87, 96
Music hall, 105, 109, 119, 121, 125, 127, 128
Music: association with the feminine, 81; and
    authenticity, 16, 152, 155, 158, 162, 167, 170, 171;
    as code for sex, 1–2; as conceptual model for
    queer studies, 8; as dangerously revealing, 15–
    16, 135, 145; and desire, 13, 32, 79, 92, 150, 152,
    202, 204, 205, 278, 281, 286, 288; as ineffable, 9;
    as lingua franca, 11–12; and metaphors of the
    procreative body, 153, 156–61, 163–68, 171–72;
    and morality, 152–53, 155, 156, 167, 169, 170, 191,
    207, 209, 277; as polymorphous, 16–17; and
    queer listening, 6–7, 11, 16–17, 30, 37, 46n.15,
    92–93, 122, 272, 277–78, 283–89; and queer
    sexuality, 2–3, 6, 8, 14, 91, 167–72, 179–80, 224–
    25, 246, 247–48, 253, 257–60, 271, 274, 277–78,
    284–88; as threat, 177; and virtuosity, 150–56,
    157, 159, 161, 165, 167–69, 171; voice-types, 93–
    94, 112, 123–24; women's education in, 26–27,
    92. See also Feminization, fear of
Musicality: as suspect, 2, 8, 178–79
Musical performance: and queer meaning, 6–7,
    11, 92, 161–72, 194–95
Musicians: and class, 82, 91; in literature, 82, 84,
    182. See also Male impersonation: issues of
    class in; Women: as composers; Women: and
    music profession
Musicology, 178, 179–80, 185–86; counterdis-
    course within, 14, 180, 183–86; New Musicol-
    ogy, 178, 186; queer studies in, 5–7, 185;
    shaped by attitudes toward homosexuality,
    179–80
Musique de placard, 15
Musset, Alfred de, 87

Näcke, Paul, 57, 60
Napoléon I, 204
Napoléon III, 204
Narcissus, 255
National Police Gazette, 108, 113, 115, 117
Navarro, Antonio de, 236, 237
Nazimova, Alla, 95
Nero, 196
Neville, William, 234
Newman, Cardinal John Henry, 233
Newman, Ernest, 135–38, 154, 156, 217, 222–23,
    231, 233
Newmarch, Rosa, 89, 138–39, 141–42, 187n.7
New Woman, 3, 10, 81, 83, 95. See also Feminism;
    Women
Nicholls, Agnes, 84, 241n.51

Nicholson, John Gambril F., 255, 257, 260
Niecks, Frederick, 155, 166, 169
Nietzsche, Friedrich, 275, 277, 278–83
Nikisch, Arthur, 84
Nilsson, Christine, 117
Norbury, Winifred, 237
Norcross, Lawrence, 250
Norman-Neruda, Wilma, 25, 33–34, 35

Obscurity, stylistic: and sexuality, 15, 20n.43. See
    also Elgar, Edward: and enigmas
Omphale. See Hercules and Omphale
Opera, 7, 154–56, 170, 171, 183, 184, 186, 194–95,
    199, 207, 209, 271–89
Oppenheim, Hermann, 179, 224
Orenstein, Arbie, 53
O'Shaughnessy, Alfred, 231
Ostwald, Peter, 169
Ottaway, Hugh, 246
Otto, Friedrich, 168–69
Overbeck, Ella, 81, 87–88, 91, 95
Ovid, 197
Ozouf, Mona, 199

Paganini, Niccolò, 154
Palmer, Christopher, 14
Pan, 248, 257
Pantomime, 106
Paraphrase, 150–72; and perversity, 159–72. See
    also Transcription
Parrot, Ian, 238n.2
Parry, Hubert, 186, 225
Passing: lesbians as straight, 299, 303–4, 305;
    women as men, 37, 109, 110
Pastor, Tony, 110, 112, 118, 119
Patti, Adelina, 195
Peel, Robert, 221
Peniston, William, 58
Penn, Donna, 88
Penny, Dora, 217, 236
Perkin, Helen, 263–64
Perry, Edward Baxter, 166
Petrarch, 197
Phillips, Dorothy, 263
Philpot, Glyn, 227
Piano, 6, 7, 11, 150–72, 193, 195, 202, 284, 285–86
Pius IX (pope), 199
Plaskin, Glenn, 168
Platen, August von, 277
Plato, 192, 287
Poe, Edgar Allan, 70
Polignac, Princesse de, 16, 60, 85, 86, 87, 91, 96

Popular Concerts (London), 25, 33
Poulenc, Francis, 52, 60
Powell, Anthony: *A Dance to the Music of Time,* 222
Powell, Eleanor, 129
Power, Nelly, 132n.23
Poznansky, Alexander, 143
Private domain, 9, 14–16, 51, 54, 58, 65, 81, 84, 122, 192, 194, 207, 295, 300–304, 305, 307; concerts in, 81, 84–85. *See also* Salons; Secrecy
Prokofiev, Sergei, 263
Proust, Marcel, 52, 54–55, 57, 60, 63; *In Search of Lost Time,* 1–2, 5, 55, 59, 61, 63, 194, 241n.47
Pushkin, Alexander, 138

Quilter, Roger, 90

Rachmaninoff, Sergei, 155, 169
Radcliffe, Philip, 183, 186
Ramann, Lina, 38, 39
Ravel, Maurice, 15, 49–54, 55, 60, 61, 64–73, 168, 250; as bachelor, 49, 51, 53, 64–65, 73, 77n.60; and creative process, 51, 72; dandyism of, 15, 53, 65–70, 73; evading sexual classification, 51, 53, 72–73; *Gaspard de la Nuit,* 15; privacy of, 49–53, 61, 70, 72–73; and prostitutes, 52–53, 61; as solitary type, 49, 72–73; speculation about sexuality of, 51–53, 73, 74n.15
Rayson, George, 256
Rayson, Michael, 256–59, 260, 263
Reed, W. H., 229, 241n.46
Regnault, Henri, 199
Reid, Forrest, 254–55
Reynolds, Margaret, 7
Richter, Hans, 25
Ricoeur, Paul, 51
Riemann, Hugo, 156
Rimbaud, Arthur, 52, 54, 70
Robespierre, Maximilien de, 198
Rodewald, Alfred, 218–19, 229, 230
Rodin, Auguste, 144, 157
Roland-Manuel, 49, 65
Romantic friendship, 37, 80, 219, 229, 233–34
Romanticism, 140, 142, 146, 152–55, 167, 169, 170
Rosenthal, Manuel, 52–53, 74n.12
Ross, Robert, 227
Rothstein, Edward, 168
Rotundo, Anthony, 126
Rousseau, Jean-Jacques, 277
Rowlands, Alan, 247
Rowse, A. L., 277
Royal Academy of Music (London), 89

Royal College of Music (London), 246, 263
Royal College of Music (Manchester), 25, 35–36
Royal Musikhochschule (Berlin), 27
Rubens, Peter Paul, 197
Rubinstein, Artur, 153
Rubinstein, Ida, 95
Rudorff, Ernst, 27
Russell, Ken, 248
Ryan, Annie, 117, 119
Rycenga, Jennifer, 7

Sabin, Robert, 170
Sachs, Harvey, 168
Sadler's Wells Theatre, 181, 184
Saint-Saëns, Camille, 139–40, 160, 166, 191–210; *La Jeunesse d'Hercule,* 209–10; *Le Rouet d'Omphale,* 12–13, 191–93, 196, 198, 199–210; *Marche héroique,* 199–200; *Samson et Dalila,* 199, 209
Salome: as Decadent icon, 95
Salons, 4, 16, 58, 59–60, 84–85, 88, 91, 192, 194. *See also* Private domain: concerts in
Samain, Albert, 94
Santley, Charles, 93
Santley, Edith, 89, 93
Sargent, John Singer, 227
Sargent, Malcolm, 263
Sassoon, Siegfried, 181, 222, 226, 227
Satie, Erik, 15
Sayn-Wittgenstein, Carolyne von, 38
Scarlatti, Alessandro, 183
Schiller, Greta, 305
Schlichting, M. de, 58
Schnabel, Artur, 152
Schopenhauer, Arthur, 280
Schreiner, Olive, 83
Schubert, Franz, 6, 43, 152, 159, 162
Schulz-Evler, Adolf, 153
Schumann, Clara, 9, 25, 27, 30, 34, 35, 36, 38, 41, 43, 44, 150–52, 154–55, 165; conflict with Marie Fillunger, 31–33
Schumann, Eugenie: *Erinnerungen,* 25, 30, 36; financial independence, 34, 35, 36; relationship with Marie Fillunger, 9, 25–45
Schumann, Marie, 25, 27, 31–33, 34, 36, 43, 44
Schumann, Robert, 9, 25, 27, 36, 43, 150–52, 154, 160, 163, 165, 166, 170
Schuster, Adela, 226
Schuster, Frank Leo, 90, 91, 226–27, 228, 229, 239n.12, 241nn.40, 46, 243nn.86, 89
Schwob, Marcel, 55
Scott, Cyril, 2

Scott-Sutherland, Colin, 249

Searle, Muriel, 266n.1

Secrecy, 49, 56, 61, 143, 145, 194; and enforced silence, 14–15, 17, 80, 90–91, 179, 221–22, 237–38, 246, 295–308; and resistant silence, 302, 308; and strategies of disguise, 1, 14–15, 29, 51, 54–55, 57, 60–61, 69–70, 167, 168, 196, 274, 301–2, 305. See also Closet, the

Sedgwick, Eve Kosofsky, 5, 74n.6, 178, 273, 298, 300

Seeger, Charles, 184

Selwyn, Blanche, 110, 112; depiction of swell, 114

Sexology, 3–4, 8, 37, 57, 62, 81, 139, 144, 178–79, 180, 196, 271–73, 274–75, 277

Sexual categories, 131n.20; as makeshift, 10, 63; in medical-scientific terminology, 3, 61–63, 178; in slang terminology, 62–63; in transition, 12, 64, 83. See also Boys, love of; Enigmas, sexual; Solitary type; Uranianism

Sexual inversion. See Gender: transitivity; Sexual categories

Sexuality: crisis in modern understanding of, 3, 12, 14; invention of, 177–78. See also Homosexuality

Shakespeare, William, 144, 277

Shattuck, Roger, 15

Shaw, George Bernard, 140–41, 142

Sheridan, John, 110

Sheridan and Mack company, 110

Sherwood, Grace, 108

Shields, Ella, 121, 127–28; performance style, 127–28

Showalter, Elaine, 4, 95

Sidney, Philip, 248

Simmons, Christine, 126

Sinfield, Alan, 4, 69

Singer, Winnaretta. See Polignac, Princesse de

Sitwell, Osbert, 222

Smeroshi, Caroline, 26

Smith, Nigel, 145

Smith, Patricia Juliana, 7

Smyth, Ethel, 6, 41, 43, 60, 81, 83, 84, 88, 91, 99n.53

Solie, Ruth, 6

Solitary type, 15, 57, 61, 63–64, 72–73. See also Sexual categories

Solomon, Maynard, 6

Somerset, Lord Arthur, 220

Song of Love (film), 150–52, 154, 164, 165

Sophocles, 210

Sorabji, Kaikhosru Shapurji, 155, 161

Sousa, John Philip, 168

Spitzer, Daniel, 275

Stanford, Charles Villiers, 25, 183, 241n.46

Stasov, Vladimir, 138

Stein, Gertrude, 20n.43, 59–60

St. John, Ambrose, 233–34

St. John, Christopher, 83, 88

Storr, Anthony, 219

Strasser, Michael, 204, 208

Strauss, Johann, Jr., 153, 159, 170

Stravinsky, Igor, 85, 153, 250

Strayhorn, Billy, 7

Stuart-Wortley, Alice, 227, 228, 236–37

Sullivan, Arthur, 25

Swell. See Dandyism: as depicted by male impersonators

Swinburne, Algernon, 94, 259

Swinton, Elsie, 85

Symbolism, 87, 281

Symonds, John Addington, 10, 187n.5, 248, 255

Taormina (Sicily), 88, 90

Tchaikovsky, Modest, 141–42

Tchaikovsky, Pyotr Ilich, 179, 195; and "biographical fallacy," 135–37, 143–44, 146; criticism of his music, 13, 16, 134–46; as homosexual, public knowledge of, 137–44; pathologized by critics, 134–47; symphonies, 134–37, 139–42, 145, 210

Temple, Hope, 100n.58

Tenant, Margot (later Asquith), 90

Tennyson, Lord Alfred, 230, 231; In Memoriam, 218–19, 221, 229, 231, 234

Terry, Ellen, 87

Terry, Stanford, 236–37

Thalberg, Sigismond, 153, 154, 170

Thibaudet, Jean-Yves, 171

Thiers, Louis-Adolphe, 198

Thomas, Gary C., 5

Thompson, Father Kenneth, 245–66; career of, 250

Thompson, Victoria, 62

Thomson, Virgil, 7, 20n.43, 179

Thurstone, Frederick, 245

Tilley, Vesta, 119, 120, 121–22, 123, 124, 126, 127, 128, 130nn.1, 9, 132n.23; performance style, 119, 123, 124

Tintoretto, 197

Tiresias, 196

Toklas, Alice B., 60

Tommasini, Anthony, 7

Toscanini, Arturo, 226

Tovey, Donald Francis, 136–37

Transcription, 9, 11, 150–72; and fidelity, 158–60, 165. *See also* Paraphrase
Transvestism. *See* Cross-dressing
Trend, J. B., 181
Trouser roles. *See* Cross-dressing
Trowell, Brian, 223
Truffot, Marie, 193
Tsing, Anna, 302
Tsou, Judy S., 310n.16
Turgenev, Ivan, 194

Ulrichs, Karl Heinrich, 179, 196
Uranianism, 10, 178, 179, 182, 245, 246, 255, 257, 260, 275, 277. *See also* Boys, love of; Sexual categories

Vallejo, Boris, 281
Vance, Alfred, 112
Variety, 105–30
Vaudeville, 11, 105–30, 306
Vaughan Williams, Ralph, 230, 240n.32
Verdi, Giuseppe, 153, 171, 272
Verlaine, Paul, 54, 94
Viardot, Paul, 194–95
Viardot, Pauline, 37, 194, 207
Vicinus, Martha, 95
Victoria (queen), 33
Viñes, Ricardo, 70–72
Visetti, Alberto, 84
Visweswaran, Kamala, 302, 303, 309n.15
Vivaldi, Antonio, 184
Vivian, Charles, 112, 115; marriage to Annie Hindle, 116
Volckmann, Ida, 38, 39
Volodos, Arcadi, 171
Voltaire, 209
Vyver, Bertha, 100n.63

Wagner, Cosima, 281
Wagner, Richard, 11, 12, 16, 26, 34, 95, 139, 196, 226, 271–89; and male suffering, 281–89; music of, and homosexuals, 271–72, 277–78, 283–89; *Tristan und Isolde,* 3, 70, 168, 278, 281, 283, 284–86, 288
Wagner, Siegfried, 271
Wakefield, Mary, 89–90, 93, 96

Walker, Alan, 152, 158–89, 162
Wallon, H., 199
Walton, William, 243n.85
Warrender, Lady Maude, 99n.49, 241n.51
Watson, Derek, 159, 166
Waugh, Evelyn: *Brideshead Revisited,* 220
Weaver, Helen, 229, 236
Weber, Carl Maria von, 277
Weber, Jean, 60, 69
Weiss, Andrea, 305–6
Wesner, Ella, 109–10, 111, 112, 116, 117–18, 119, 121, 125, 127, 128, 130n.1; depiction of swell, 114; realism in impersonation, 110, 112; singing range, 112
West, Shearer, 95
Westphalin, C., 196
White, Emmie, 90
White, Maude Valérie, 81, 89–91, 96; songs, 89, 90, 92–93
Whitman, Walt: *Leaves of Grass,* 219
Whittall, Arnold, 166
Wild, Earl, 167, 171–72
Wilde, David, 152
Wilde, Oscar, 5, 13, 55, 58, 60, 64, 69, 83, 99n.55, 164, 165, 211n.11, 226, 227, 254, 287; *Salome,* 95; trials of, 4, 55, 69, 179, 220, 221, 225
Winckelmann, Johann Joachim, 179
Winterbottom, Frank: Symphony Concerts (Plymouth), 88
Women: as composers, 81–82, 91, 95, 196; and creativity, 80, 82, 88; and music profession, 3, 81, 82, 92, 196, 212n.20, 293–94; and songwriting, 92; stereotypical ideal of, 81, 82, 293. *See also* Music: women's education in; New Woman
Women's movement. *See* Feminism
Wood, Elizabeth, 5–6, 11, 91, 94
Woodhouse, Violet Gordon, 83
Working-class men, desire for, 182, 218, 255
Worthington, Julia, 228, 236

Yingling, Thomas, 5
Yturri, Gabriel, 58, 59

Zellars, Parker, 130n.1
Zimmermann, Agnes, 79, 80, 81, 96
Zola, Émile, 195, 205, 208

The University of Illinois Press
is a founding member of the
Association of American University Presses

———————————————————

Composed in 10.5/13 Minion
with Jute and Gill Sans display
by Jim Proefrock
at the University of Illinois Press
Designed by Dennis Roberts
Manufactured by Thomson-Shore, Inc

University of Illinois Press
1325 South Oak Street
Champaign, IL 61820-6903
www.press.uillinois.edu